SAHARAN FRONTIERS

Public Cultures of the Middle East and North Africa

Paul A. Silverstein, Susan Slyomovics,
and Ted Swedenburg
EDITORS

SAHARAN FRONTIERS

Space and Mobility in Northwest Africa

EDITED BY
James McDougall and Judith Scheele

Indiana University Press
Bloomington and Indianapolis

This book is a publication of

Indiana University Press
601 North Morton Street
Bloomington, Indiana 47404-3797 USA

iupress.indiana.edu

Telephone orders 800-842-6796
Fax orders 812-855-7931

∞ The paper used in this publication meets the minimum requirements of the American National Standard for Information Sciences—Permanence of Paper for Printed Library Materials, ANSI Z39.48-1992.

Manufactured in the United States of America

Library of Congress Cataloging-in-Publication Data
Saharan frontiers : space and mobility in Northwest Africa /
edited by James McDougall and Judith Scheele.
p. cm. — (Public cultures of the Middle East and North Africa)
Includes bibliographical references and index.
ISBN 978-0-253-00124-5 (cloth : alk. paper) — ISBN 978-0-253-00126-9 (pbk. : alk. paper) — ISBN 978-0-253-00131-3 (e-book) 1. Africans—Sahara—Migrations. 2. Sahara—Emigration and immigration. 3. Trade routes—Sahara. 4. Sahara—Ethnic relations. 5. Africa, North—Relations—Africa, West. 6. Africa, West—Relations—Africa, North. I. McDougall, James, [date] II. Scheele, Judith, [date]
DT333.S27 2012
304.8'20966—dc23 2011049611

1 2 3 4 5 17 16 15 14 13 12

CONTENTS

ACKNOWLEDGMENTS

This book developed from a series of conversations between the editors over several years, arising from a convergence of interests between our separate projects on the history and anthropology of northwest Africa, and more particularly from a three-day, international, multidisciplinary conference, "Navigating Northwest Africa: Towards an Analysis of Saharan Connectivity?," which was held at Magdalen College, Oxford, in September 2008. Most of the chapters in this volume originated as papers presented at that conference. The meeting was generously sponsored by a number of institutions without whose support this project would not have been possible, and we are very happy to be able to record our thanks to them: Magdalen College, Oxford; the International Migration Institute at the James Martin 21st Century School, University of Oxford; the Middle East Centre, St. Antony's College, Oxford; the African Studies Centre, University of Oxford; the Oxford Research Network on Government in Africa; the Khalid Abdallah Al Saud Chair for the Study of the Contemporary Arab World at the University of Oxford; the African Studies Association (UK); the Moroccan-British Society; and the Maison Française, Oxford.

We are grateful to Hein de Haas, Clive Holes, Michael Willis, and Benedetta Rossi, who as panel chairs and discussants not only facilitated discussion of the papers but also provided invaluable comments from their different areas of expertise. Our students at the School of Oriental and African Studies and Oxford (especially those in James McDougall's undergraduate class "The Saharan World: Society, Culture, and Politics in Northwest Africa" at SOAS in 2008–2009, and in our jointly taught graduate seminar "History and Anthropology in the Sahara" at Oxford in 2010–2011) have been thoughtful and constructive (if unwitting) audiences on whom many of the ideas in this book have been tried out.

Bringing the volume to completion has taken—of course—rather longer than we originally anticipated, and we would like to thank all the contributors for their patience as well as for their timeliness in responding to our queries and requests. Katia Schörle, Charles Grémont, Armelle Choplin, and most especially Julien Brachet deserve additional and heartfelt thanks for providing expertly drawn maps in unreasonably quick time. Apart from chapters 1–4 and 13, all of the contributions to this book were originally written in French, and were translated by the editors. Each chapter was subsequently revised by both editors in collaboration with each author. While the ideas and arguments of these chapters, as well as the original research on which they are based, are therefore entirely the property of their authors, any infelicities or errors in their expression are the responsibility of the editors.

NOTE ON SPELLING AND TRANSLITERATION

For the sake of clarity, words in Berber, Arabic, or other West African languages have been transliterated according to the simplest available method in each case. For Arabic, we have adopted a simplified transliteration showing long vowels with a macron (*awlād*) and indicating the ʿayn (*sharīʿa*), but we have not used diacritics to indicate emphatic consonants. Hamza is indicated when it occurs mid-word (*qāʾid*), in a phrase (*biʾsmi-llāh*), or at the end of a plural form (*shurafāʾ*). Place names and proper names are given in the most familiar form in use in the region, elsewhere in the English-language literature, and on the most widely available maps (especially Michelin map 741, "Africa North and West"). We depart from widespread conventions only in a few cases for precision of transliteration, e.g., *qsar* instead of ksar, *qsūr* instead of ksur/ksour, *shaykh* instead of sheikh/cheikh.

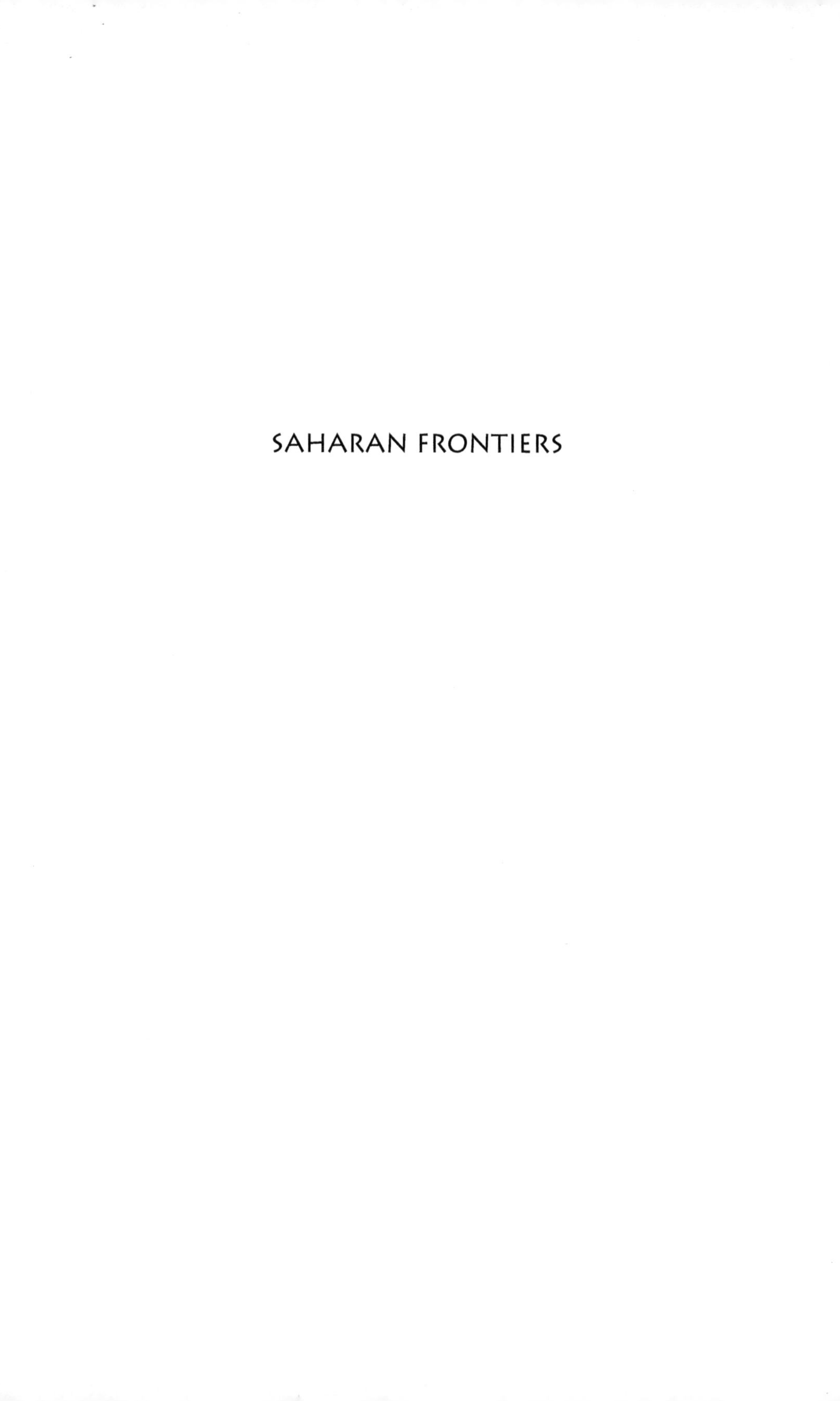

SAHARAN FRONTIERS

INTRODUCTION

Time and Space in the Sahara

Judith Scheele and James McDougall

And much I mus'd on legends quaint and old
Which whilome won the hearts of all on Earth
Toward their brightness, ev'n as flame draws air;
But had their being in the heart of Man
As air in th'life of flame: and thou wert then
A centr'd glory-circled Memory,
Divinest Atlantis, whom the waves
Have buried deep, and thou of later name
Imperial Eldorado roof'd with gold:
Shadows to which, despite all shocks of Change,
All on-set of capricious Accident,
Men clung with yearning Hope which would not die.

—Tennyson, "Timbuctoo" (1829)

In the early nineteenth century, when the young Tennyson submitted his poem "Timbuctoo" to a poetry competition launched by the chancellor of Cambridge University, attempts to reach the fabled city of gold in the heart of the Sahara had become a vivid expression of the rivalry between France and England, the two "great nations" that were then vying for commercial supremacy on the African continent (Heffernan 2001; Davoine 2003). The topic chosen by the chancellor clearly reflected political concerns and patriotic enthusiasm as well as a long-standing fascination with the Sahara. Tennyson had first composed the poem with the title "Armageddon," but found he hardly had to change its content once the title was amended. And indeed, from a European point of view in the Romantic age, the hill of Megiddo and the city of Timbuktu stood for much the same thing: they both mattered not so much for what they were, but for how they were imagined, as sites of timeless truth, objects of longing for deep antiquity and of melancholic reflection on its decadence. Even in the more ordinarily hardheaded calculations of European imperial policy, the Sahara was largely left to poetic license. Until the discovery of oil in the mid-1950s, the region figured more as a status symbol than as a physical region of human habitation, or—once the long-standing perception of northwest Africa's interior as a commercial El Dorado awaiting capture proved wholly mythical—even as an economic stake in the scramble for Africa.[1] For the French army, the vast and open spaces of the Sahara, conquered and unified under military rule, were a stage for the display of grandiose, transcontinental territorial power, gained and maintained by reckless courage and political skill in the face of the most unforgiving environment on earth. British statesmen, on the other hand, mocked the millions of acres of "light soil" which overly romantic French gullibility (and Britain's earlier-established trading position in the Niger delta and its hinterlands) had made into the unprofitable semblance of an empire.

Such images of the Sahara as an empty stage for European agency, courage, and imagination were, of course, much older than Tennyson's poem (Mollat de Jourdin 1984), and also outlived the Sahara's real inaccessibility. The fantasy of the Sahara as a pristine space untouched by time, inveterately hostile to all but the most dauntless, lived on long after the nineteenth-century reports of exploratory missions by Dixon Denham and Hugh Clapperton (1826), Heinrich Barth (1857–1858), and Gustav Nachtigal (1879–1889) had provided ample documentation of the existing realities of states and cities through which safe passage could be gained from Tripoli to Agadez, Sokoto, and Timbuktu, and of the functioning trade routes along which they traveled. In April 1881, a French newspaper reporting the loss of the Flatters mission described the Ahaggar massif, where Flatters and his soldiers met their end, as a land "absolutely desolate, sterile, and, so to speak, a desert in the full meaning of the word. . . . In these cursed regions, to which so many of our men of science and civilization have fallen victim, one must reckon with the ferocious passions of bloodthirsty populations."[2] Twenty years later, with the region firmly in French hands, André Gide could still find the "bliss" of savage authenticity and vitality among the streams and palm groves of Biskra, on the desert's northern edge.[3] In 1920, the first trans-Saharan automobile rally was organized by Citroën, and Saharan crossings by airplane were attempted; by the 1930s, these had become common, and trading missions were launched from southern Algeria toward the Niger bend. In the 1940s, regular trans-Saharan truck routes were established, linking French West Africa to Algeria (Guitart 1989). At the same time, the Sahara became a destination for curious tourists.[4] And although most "rebellious" Saharan tribes had been subdued, and the first desert crossings by automobile and airplane had literally laid the Sahara open to the European gaze by the 1920s, the aura of mystique and of real and imagined dangers found new and wider expression in literature and film. It was in the Sahara that the aviator Antoine de Saint-Exupéry encountered "the little prince" (1943). The American heroes of Paul Bowles's debut novel *The Sheltering Sky* (1949; filmed by Bernardo Bertolucci in 1990 with Debra Winger and John Malkovich) could still be confronted with their own psychological anguish and alienation when facing the "emptiness" of the desert years later. In his review of Bowles's novel, Tennessee Williams (1949) saw the empty desert as an allegory of "the Sahara of moral nihilism" in which he saw "the race of man . . . wandering blindly." Michael Ondaatje adapted the real-life geographer and writer Làszlo Almàsy as the wandering, adventurous, and passionate central character of his Booker Prize–winning 1992 novel, *The English Patient,* the 1996 film version of which won nine Oscars. The Gilf Kebir, on the borders of Egypt, Sudan, and Libya, considered one of the last remaining suitable locations for adventurous exploration in the romantic style when it was already being documented with cars and aircraft by Almàsy and others in the 1930s (Wingate 1934; Almàsy 1939), is still written up today as an exceptionally remote and romantic destination for European "adventure" tourists. It also remains a "lawless region" where those same tourists are liable to be held for ransom by unidentified bandits.[5] In the twenty-first century, in the age of satellite phones and affordable GPS, the Sahara of popular imagination remains both mysterious and empty, a place where, if we believe specialized tour operators, we are confronted with our own true being, where "the sun pulls us towards the imagined horizon of the unsubdued desert."[6] For Hollywood—thanks in part to the well-developed movie location industries of southern Morocco and Tunisia—the Sahara provides a ready-made backdrop for tales of adventure, anarchy, dictatorship, ruthlessness, and the unlikeliest of age-old relics, where (imported) madness and large-scale destruction find their natural home.[7] Even extraterrestrial fantasies seem at home here: the Tunisian Saharan town of Tatawin first gave its name to Luke Skywalker's home planet in *Star Wars* (1977) before becoming the supposed location of sinister alien disease experiments in the *X Files* movie (1998).

Hence the paradox of our (Euro-Americans') relationship with the Sahara: it is an overly familiar symbol of the unknown, an empty stage to display our own courage and fears, but one that remains threateningly beyond control; it is quintessentially the space of mystery, timelessness, and an eternal succession of catastrophes whose root causes and dynamic impetus must come from elsewhere. This is as apparent in contemporary news coverage and Hollywood flicks as it was in nineteenth-century poetry. Beyond travelers' fantasies, the contemporary Sahara is mainly known even to relatively well-informed European and North American audiences as a site of tragedy, inhabited by nameless (and usually numberless) victims of humanitarian catastrophes or natural disasters: insurgency in Algeria; uprising and civil war in Libya; genocide and slavery in Sudan; military putsches in Chad and Mauritania; Islamist bombings in Morocco; drought, famine, and rebellion in Niger and Mali. Behind these sometimes only dimly perceived states and their intractable problems lurk more familiar global threats: desertification, terrorism, "waves" of clandestine trans-Saharan migrants and "climate change refugees," all set against a more generally unpleasant background noise of extreme poverty. The Sahara covers parts of ten countries, four of which are counted among the poorest in the world, while at least three others are seen as more or less willing "havens" for "Islamist threats."[8] The Sahara is thus a place not only of fascination with purity, but also of obsession with danger, a place whose "emptiness" is all too readily filled with the nightmares of contemporary Western imaginations. Of course one cannot blame the media for favoring the spectacular—and of course, many parts of the Sahara have indeed been shaken by a series of political, social, and ecological crises.[9] Yet, clearly, this is not all that can be said about the region, with its almost 3.2 million square miles (a quarter of the African continent), several million inhabitants, and corresponding variety of languages, cultures, societies, and livelihoods; settlement patterns; human ecologies; sophisticated agriculture; complex transport systems; and striking capacity to innovate.

This book is about that other Sahara, not the empty waste of romantic imagination but the vast and highly differentiated space—a social and political as well as an ecologically challenging geographic space—in which Saharan peoples and, increasingly, incomers from other parts of Africa, live, work, and move. It is primarily about the contemporary Sahara, about key aspects of the ways of life of its inhabitants, and about how the changes of recent times have shaped or been resisted by them, with a focus on the ways in which Saharan peoples have moved through time and space, and on the limits, both long-established and recent, to those movements. It also places our understanding of today's Sahara in a longer historical context, for the northwest corner of Africa is no more empty of its own history than it is of people, culture, or resources.

Barrier, Bridge, or Borderland?

It has often been assumed that the Sahara has primarily acted as a barrier, dividing the Mediterranean world from "real" (i.e., *sub*-Saharan) Africa, isolating the countries of North Africa from their southern and eastern neighbors, and demarcating entirely distinct areas of study for scholars and students. The concentration of northwest Africa's major cities, political centers, and densest populations on or near its northern, western, and southern edges and the establishment of frontiers that created its contemporary states have tended to relegate the Sahara to a space of marginality. Academic categories, dividing fields of research and literature between Mediterranean, Middle Eastern, Arab/Islamic, and African studies, have often replicated the region's political divisions and reproduced this view of the relationship between North and West Africa, and of the Sahara as a void between them.

Another view suggests that the Sahara has never constituted a serious obstacle to cross-regional interaction but has instead furthered it: it has been less a barrier than a bridge in African history (Zartman 1963; Lydon 2005). Yet despite renewed interest in patterns of trans-Saharan trade and migration, now fueled by security concerns over clandestine migration and international terrorism, more far-reaching, conceptually innovative, and empirically detailed research on both the shared world of and the boundaries between North and West Africa has not been much pursued. Though scholars (e.g., E. A. McDougall 2005a) have noted the desirability of work that would examine the connections between North and West Africa, few studies (exceptions being Grégoire and Schmitz 2000; Marfaing and Wippel 2004; Lydon 2009; Austen 2010) have systematically pursued and enriched this agenda. Historically deep and enduringly vigorous aspects of life in the region, which arguably not only connect, but *create* the various, complementary, and interdependent spaces of northwest Africa, have attracted little attention. And such research as has been done has often privileged conceptual frameworks imposed from the outside, viewing the region, implicitly, from a synoptic or from a "coastal" viewpoint (from above or from the outside in), rather than studying movement, connection, and the creation of place and space from within the region itself, either socially from the bottom up or spatially from the inside out. Studies of the Sahara as a bridge have often ended up reiterating the older notion of the region as an empty interior, a gap that must simply be *crossed*. They have continued to focus, for example, on *trans*-Saharan rather than on *intra*-Saharan trade or migration, or, though to a lesser extent, on the translocal "spread of Islam" from Mediterranean Africa to West Africa rather than on the local logics of societies in between that have historically underpinned Islamization in the region, or on the region's own contributions to Islam.This approach, despite its intention to open up study of the region across an African divide, has tended to perpetuate isolatable ideas of place, space, race, and culture as belonging to distinct worlds of North and West Africa, leaving us without a way of grasping the subtler realities of regional interdependence.

The great French historian Fernand Braudel once wrote of the Sahara as "the second face of the Mediterranean" (1972 [1966]). Although Braudel's work was enormously influential in other areas, his perceptive suggestion about the

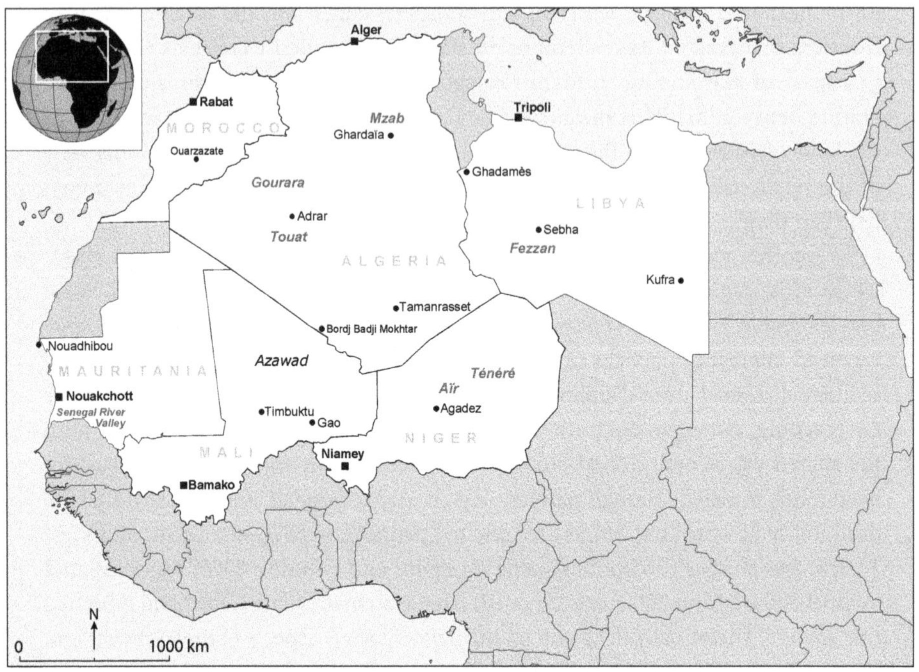

Map 0.1. Northwest Africa. J. Brachet 2010

Sahara has generally been ignored. One aim of this book is to explore the ways in which we might recast our understanding of the Sahara by seeing the desert and its margins as a region composed of densely interdependent networks not only crossing, but created by the desert and the relationship between its "islands" and "shores." Recent work on Mediterranean history (Horden and Purcell 2000) has located the dynamics of "connectivity" that created the sea's distinctive, long-term historical unity in the symbiosis of a managed scarcity of resources among precarious and intensely fragmented ecological "micro-regions" with the density and persistence of interactions between them (see also Horden this volume). This book investigates whether a similar set of conditions (ecological precariousness, productive specialization, and intensive resource management producing commercial interdependence; and the organized—often violent—mobility of people and commodities, ideas and practices) can be seen at work in the Sahara, thus recasting it as a dynamic space of human history and change over the long term and at the present time. Our focus on connection and commonality does not, however, mean "flattening out" hard surfaces of conflict and disparity, nor overlooking the very real barriers to free movement, whether social or physical, that are arguably increasingly important today in the region. The title of this book evokes both the openness and the friction of movement, the porosity but also the sharpness of frontiers in a region that has often been viewed merely as peripheral, but that is perhaps better thought of as a global borderland (J. McDougall this volume).

Contemporary Saharan Africa

The Sahara is perhaps the fastest changing, most dynamic, and wealthiest region of the African continent. Urbanization has been rapid since the 1970s, as has demographic growth, caused by in-migration rather than high birth rates.[10] Governments in the Maghreb have made considerable efforts to integrate their Saharan territories into the nation-state, an effort that in many cases has paid off. Southern Algeria, for instance, sports modern cities with urban facilities, relatively efficient transportation networks, numerous universities, almost nationwide internet and telephone coverage, strictly imposed national security, and rates of schooling comparable to many European countries (Côte 2005). Libya has revived Saharan agriculture through heavy investment in mechanized irrigation and deep wells, as a showcase of the victory of man over sand (Bisson 2003). This means that urban structures have changed: although a strong case can be made for the structural dependency of Saharan cities on the outside world (Bensaâd 2005a), the past variety of external sources of investment are now marginalized by the economic and political clout of Maghrebi states, whose oil-fueled financial resources have dwarfed any revenue that might be made from agriculture, causing people to abandon outlying oases in favor of administrative centers and their immediate surroundings. In the Sahel, ecological and political changes have led to new patterns of residence and economic exploitation, and even here, state revenues and development aid, alongside booming cross-border trade, have become key to local power struggles and livelihoods (Nijenhuis 2003; Giuffrida 2005; Grémont this volume). Yet part of the reason that Saharan cities are growing faster than many others on the continent has to be sought beyond the Sahara itself, as is shown by such cities' growing population diversity, including Chinese workers, Middle Eastern teachers, Malay migrants, Pakistani preachers, European tourists, Mauritanian traders, Malian tailors, Cameroonian builders, Nigerian fraudsters, and Ghanaian barbers, alongside national in-migrants from the north (Spiga 2002; Boesen and Marfaing 2007). While images of a uniquely Arabic- and Tamasheq-speaking Sahara of taciturn camel herders have little or no historic underpinning, they certainly falter when confronted with the observable multilingualism of contemporary Saharan cities and oases; their Sahelian restaurants, music, and tailors; and other ways of organizing urban space that indicate, to many "real" Saharans, their own growing marginality—but that also offer them lucrative economic prospects (Choplin, Brachet this volume).

Most of these developments are due in one way or another to the Sahara's main natural resource. Libya and Algeria possess some of the world's most important oil and gas reserves, much of which remains to be fully exploited. However, although this means that oil dominates economic policy, leading to an almost complete reliance on hydrocarbon exports[11] and internally to a growing dependency on state resources, the oil wells and concomitant investments in infrastructure have led to a diversification of local economic activities, especially in the service sector. While most of Algeria's nomadic population have settled, the raising of livestock remains profitable, and large herds are hurried across the desert in vehicles as soon as rain is reported to have fallen in any particular place, thus supplying the urban market in the Tell (the plateau region north of the Saharan Atlas mountains). Livestock imports from the Sahelian countries are similarly booming, thereby often reinventing older commercial patterns: Algerian traders with longstanding connections in northern Mali employ Tuareg drivers to smuggle herds north; in-migrants from the garrison town of Bechar near the Algerian border with Morocco make a fortune by trading in Malian camels destined for illegal export to Morocco; and Libyans have heavily invested in livestock kept by Arabic-speaking groups in northern Niger. Other kinds of extralegal trading activities are equally profitable: gasoline, foodstuffs, and building materials are exported south in great quantities, often accompanied by and complementing more traditional exchanges of dates and grains. Cigarettes and guns circulate on different routes, but with similar ease.[12] Kabyle and Sahelian restaurants have sprung up throughout the Algerian Sahara, alongside other specialized services catering to the local economy or to the aspirations of a growing middle class: mobile phones, computer equipment and repairs, garages, repair shops, satellite communication systems. New construction is booming in order to house state functionaries and the northerners keen to make a fortune or to invest in real estate; a posting to the Algerian border region, long considered a dreadful misfortune among Algerian civil servants, is now seen as a unique chance for upward social mobility and the accumulation of wealth.

Oil wealth, of course, like everything else, is unevenly distributed in the Sahara. Although some oil has been discovered in Niger and Mali, the main producer countries are those of the Maghreb, and the capacity of nation-states to convert subsoil resources into state revenue varies from country to country, generally declining as one moves south. This means that the Sahara is marked by a strong division of labor and much regional migration: building sites and gardens in southern Algeria and Libya tend to be worked by Sahelian migrants, while trade networks frequently reproduce regional inequalities and hierarchies which are now backed by national legal regimes. Alongside regional migrants, citizens of West and Central African nations attempt to make their way north, and often stay for considerable periods of time in the Sahara, where they are obliged to find their own position in local economies, sometimes with Sahelian migrants acting as intermediaries, and always with national security forces on their backs.[13] Migration, in particular when criminalized by North African states, has led to a diversification of transportation networks and local services (telecommunications, money transfer) that cater to migrants who are "stuck" en route, or that feed on their labor (Brachet 2005, and this volume). As Sahelian dress has become fashionable among middle-class northern Algerians living in the south, its availability relies on complex networks that bind Malian importers and dyers, Arab traders, Tuareg drivers, Ghanaian tailors, and complacent Algerian border police together in one common enterprise of mutual dependency and various degrees of exploitation. This increased diversity is more than purely economic: many West and Central African immigrants are Christian, unashamedly so, and have given Algerian churches an unexpected (and perhaps not always welcome) impetus. Meanwhile, growing access to outside sources of knowledge, via radio, the internet, and satellite television, has led to a profound rethinking of Islam and of Islamic hierarchies in the area, encouraged by the presence of preachers, in particular from Pakistan (Lecocq and Schrijver 2007). While this can easily be read as an Islamization or even as an "Islamist threat" by Western observers, it is perhaps more properly described as part of a wider restructuring of patterns of knowledge transmission and of notions of legitimacy, both religious and political, that have run through all Saharan societies for centuries (see, e.g., Choplin, Grémont, Oussedik this volume).

Histories from the Inside Out

Very few of these developments are visible in the existing academic literature, especially in the English-speaking world, where one image of the Sahara continues to dominate: a deserted place, where the permanent struggle of humanity against nature has deprived people of one of their most human characteristics, namely, the ability to change and to creatively influence the course of events. Where the Sahara is granted any kind of historicity at all, historical time has been telescoped into one overwhelming impression of permanence. Airborne geographical explorers in the early twentieth century still liked to evoke Herodotus as their guide, and it seems to be taken for granted even among more recent writers that histories of the Sahara ought to start in prehistoric or at least Roman times (see, e.g., Bovill 1968, and even Lydon 2009). This is not to say that such long-term perspectives are necessarily flawed, but rather that permanence cannot be taken for granted but needs to be, here as elsewhere, problematized and explained—and that, here as elsewhere, we are more likely to find continuities of structures and patterns than of things. Conceptually linked to this is the relative absence of Saharans themselves from historical—but also from economic and even ecological—studies of the region. A newcomer to much of the writing on the Sahara might well infer that date palms—which, after all, cannot properly reproduce without human intervention—have a mysterious tendency to plant themselves, or that the long-established technology of the elaborate irrigation systems that underpin all oasis life exists as a kind of timeless given, rather than being the result of a long historical process of human ingenuity and constantly renewed labor.

This is certainly not due to the absence of historical sources, nor to any local or regional disregard for history. The Sahara has long been at least semiliterate, and some areas have a long-standing reputation for scholarship. History, if mainly in the form of genealogies or hagiographies, is crucial to local worldviews. The Sahara is dotted with local archives containing standard libraries mostly of a religious kind, but also notarial documents, letters, title deeds, collections of fatwas (Islamic judicial opinions), contracts, and records of irrigation works and other matters of municipal administration, which have quite simply been ignored by most researchers.[14] Even the French colonial archives, which can be expected to yield much precious information about local economies and sociopolitical patterns of interaction, have not been properly explored. The reasons for this neglect therefore cannot merely be sought in the inaccessibility of such documentation, but rather in the conceptual frameworks employed, which leave little room for local studies—or rather, create a conceptual breach between local studies, which are often rooted in geography or anthropology and are concerned with "remote" and "illiterate" settled agriculturalists or nomadic pastoralists, paying little heed to regional connections or concerns, and historical studies that take a transregional approach, with a special emphasis on trade, but that often quite simply ignore local particularities. Hence, the long-standing emphasis on *trans*-Saharan trade implies a dearth of Saharan production, consumption, and agency. The current emphasis on *trans*-Saharan migration similarly assumes that the Sahara itself provides neither migrants nor their destination, despite the long-standing acknowledgment, for instance in the literature on slavery, that much "trans"-Saharan traffic has historically been directed *into* and not *across* the desert.[15] In the same way, studies on the "spread of Islam," the gradual "imposition" of *sharīʿa* (Islamic law), or "Islamist conversions" all conceive of their subjects of study as more or less uniform, one-way processes, in which the Sahara and its peoples are simply crossed over or acted upon from outside, rather than as a series of local negotiations with context-specific results and side effects, bounded by local interests and agency (see, e.g., Grandguillaume 1978; Layish 2005).[16] Such views are unsurprising, given that the Sahara is usually seen as lying on the empty outer edge, rather than at the intersection, of distinct, well-established areas of expertise: "Africa," meaning sub-Saharan Africa, and the Middle East or "the Arab world," of which North Africa is still commonly taken to be a mere (relatively unimportant) appendage.[17] This means that the Sahara falls through conceptual grids and lies outside of research projects, but it also means that as the regional specialists that all academic researchers are largely obliged to be, most scholars (and we include ourselves in this category) do not possess the necessary knowledge and skills to approach the Sahara on its own terms. How many Africanists think it necessary to study Arabic, for instance, and how many Arabists would seriously concentrate on any West African language? How many of either would get the time and funding to do so?

Yet Europeans and Americans by no means hold a monopoly over imagining the Sahara as an empty abode of "savages." The Sahara's own North and West African borderlands furnish such notions with equal insistence, forceful cultural implications, and added local color. Images of Saharan emptiness and inherent anarchy fed into colonial policies that were often continued by independent nation-states in the region. Although the Sahara straddles ten countries, it only contains one capital (that of Mauritania, Nouakchott). Despite its rapid demographic growth and increased in-migration, especially from the northern edge of the Sahara, only a small proportion of the residents of each nation would define themselves as Saharan, and those who do often feel marginalized as such. In Algeria, Saharans complain about the ongoing expropriation of "their" natural resources and have at times protested violently against their exclusion from national government and especially from oil revenues.[18] However, if these populations are presented to a national audience at all, it is as a faceless group of submissive and backward *beni oui-oui* (compliant yes-men) with no political education or will.[19] After all, most Algerian intellectuals (and *harraga*s, clandestine trans-Mediterranean migrants) are more familiar with Paris or Cairo than with Tamanrasset. The Moroccan dynasty traces its origin to the Sahara, but despite the symbolic political importance of the kingdom's "Saharan provinces" in the Seguia el Hamra and Rio de Oro (the disputed western Sahara), modern Morocco clearly exists mainly elsewhere, north of the mountains, and remains much more interested in its northern than in its southern neighbors (Rebbo 1990). Mauritania and Libya, despite their rhetoric of rootedness in desert life and strident appeals to African unity, are mainly preoccupied with protecting their own national territories and wealth from their southern neighbors (Choplin 2008; Lemarchand 1998). In Mali and Niger, northern areas have been treated with suspicion since independence, declared to be military security zones, and used as political prisons (Bourgeot 1995; Boilley 1999). Throughout the Sahel, cleavages between north and south have been marked and often violent since independence. Rebellions have been frequent and often quelled with violence more than with promises of development and integration. More generally, national culture, as defined in political and cultural centers of production and decision making remote from the desert and as presented to the national public, largely excludes northern languages, people, and forms of livelihood, or reduces them to sites of particular, folkloric interest for foreign tourists (Lecocq 2010).

Ecology, Connectivity, and the Frontiers of Mobility

An even stronger reliance on national historiography and social sciences, then, will not do; neither will a quantitative increase in the kind of research that is already being undertaken. Clearly, we need to look for inspiration elsewhere. Approaches rooted in human ecology—in the relationship between human populations and their physical environment—have yielded valuable results in the study of Saharan subregions and might suggest concepts for approaching the Sahara as a whole.[20] From such a perspective, the Sahara appears first and foremost as an area marked by particularly scarce resources. Such resources are never given but are, rather, shaped by human interaction and ingenuity, thereby creating various micro-regions of sometimes extreme specialization and ecological precariousness; niches, in other words, that are cultural, social, and linguistic as much as they are properly ecological. But how conducive to an overall analysis of such a vast region can this attention to high degrees of micro-level local diversity possibly be? There are two possible answers to this objection. On the one hand, we need to take into account local perceptions of regional connections, and analyze how these relate to local practices. On the other, we need to ask whether the "local" is not potentially as fictional as the "regional," or rather, whether one can exist without the other, especially in an area that is characterized by such a high degree of micro-regional specialization and hence large-scale, long-distance, and long-term patterns of connection and interdependence.

Just such an approach has been developed for the Mediterranean by Peregrine Horden and Nicholas Purcell (2000). In the Mediterranean, they argue, climatic and geographical conditions are such that small areas tend to specialize, and seasonal instability has to be taken for granted. Life depends on exchange or on "connectivity," a term they borrow from mathematics and geography to denote the ways in which ecological micro-regions coalesce internally and cohere with one another across distance (ibid.: 123). It makes no sense to think of places in isolation; rather, places (of production, habitation, and exchange) are made and maintained by regional interactions. In turn, "regions" are not given, but developed through sustained communication. Depending on the logics of such communication, then, regions can at times include places situated at considerable distances from each other while excluding neighboring areas. For the Sahara, we suggest, both the argument of regional specialization and that of intrinsic dependency on exchange hold true over the long term and at present, with perhaps even greater force than in the Mediterranean (but see Horden this volume). As a result, this "Sahara" as lived, experienced, and imagined by Saharans does not necessarily correspond to its conventional geographic boundaries. Braudel's Sahara, defined by the distribution of the palm grove (as his Mediterranean was defined by that of the olive), gives way to a more fluid and open space when viewed from the perspective of logics defined from within the region rather than from arbitrary or hydrological lines drawn around it from outside. Indeed, an argument could be made that Saharan regions that make sense both socially and ecologically tend to straddle various ecological zones, linking parts of the desert to lands beyond it.[21] The boundaries of our area of study cannot be taken for granted from the outset as defined by isohyets or soil composition, but need to be part and parcel of our investigation.

This is, then, the conceptual framework adopted in this book: hence the need for in-depth local studies as a necessary precondition of any further regional analysis (Moussaoui and Oussedik this volume); hence the importance of a historical perspective that alone can illustrate the particular rhythm at which human ecologies develop, change, or remain stable (Schörle, E. A. McDougall, J. McDougall this volume); hence also the necessary questioning of apparently self-evident boundaries, whether political, linguistic, ecological, or "ethnic" (Leservoisier this volume). Similarly, we need to trace carefully the local importance, regional connections, and actual routes taken by traders, with reference to larger social, political, and ecological patterns that are first and foremost Saharan.[22] Ann McDougall (2005a) has argued that most trade in the region was properly "Saharan" rather than *trans*-Saharan; research based on local archives (see, e.g., Pascon 1984) bears out her conclusion, as does ethnographic fieldwork in the Algerian south. To the extent that we can judge from the figures available to us, and in marked contrast to the obsession with high-value, low-bulk, long-distance commodities like gold dust or ostrich plumes in most of the trans-Saharan trade literature, up to 80 percent of all Saharan freight was composed of high-bulk staples, *intra*regional trade goods that made survival in the central Sahara possible (see also Gast 1989).

Similarly, contemporary trade first and foremost supplies local markets, and is indeed indispensable for their survival, much as patterns of regional and transregional trade impact the making of place throughout the area (see, e.g., Oudada, Scheele this volume).

In much the same way, regional logics of migration also need to be approached from a local point of view. Migration not only has an important impact on local economies (Marfaing, Choplin this volume), but it also follows and thereby transforms regional patterns of interaction and connectivity (Brachet this volume). More generally, the production of any kind of place in the Sahara is historically dependent on in-migration of some sort, voluntary or not. Beginning in the late twentieth century, many oases and towns in the border regions have experienced exponential demographic growth (Brachet, Badi this volume), at times creating new towns from scratch, and changing local transportation arrangements, trading routes, and political and economic structures, while regional capitals bear the visible and lasting traces of changing patterns of mobility (Choplin, Marfaing this volume). Conversely, notions of place and settlement also need to be investigated with reference to the different forms and functions of mobility past and present, including the significance of the freedom to move across space—or the unfreedom of being fixed in it—and the power relations that are thus expressed (Grémont this volume).

This last point indicates that "connectivity" in no way connotes unfettered freedom of movement, frictionless surfaces of instant communication, nor the egalitarian, happy-go-lucky free-for-all implied by much of the literature on globalization (e.g., Hannerz 1992; Appadurai 1996; Friedman 2005). On the contrary, where movement and exchange are essential for survival, the denial of the freedom to move is an important means of control and an expression of power. Many ethnographic and historical accounts of Saharan societies point to an intimate connection between the ability to move and local social hierarchies and ethnic boundaries (Cleaveland 2002; Rossi 2009). In the Sahara, as in much of Africa as a whole, people and their labor have often been historically the scarcest resource of all, with local constructions and symbolisms of power being linked to the control of people rather than land (Leservoisier 1994; Grémont, Leservoisier this volume). Slavery, the ability to protect travelers, and the great emphasis locally placed on the depth of genealogical time in constructions of ancestry are aspects of this historical connection between status and potential mobility.

More recently, the imposition of national borders, first by colonial regimes and then by independent nation-states (and their frontier wars or, conversely, their more or less abortive attempts at union), has had a powerful effect on Saharan life, less by interrupting regional networks of interdependence than by restructuring them, as the control of smuggling networks and semi-official trade has created new regional power structures that are dependent on borders—whether they are officially open or closed—and often rely on or feed back into regional states (Scheele, Oudada this volume).[23] People travel within and across the Sahara now as they always have done, but new forms of control, more or less closely related to national policies and international pressures exerted on Maghrebi and West African states, have led to a monopolization of the means of mobility, which are sold dearly to those who find themselves stuck at various stages of their intended journeys. Nationalism too has proved a powerful force, both socially and culturally, especially where it has been backed by oil money, and inhabitants of the Maghrebi states appear increasingly reluctant to recognize past relations with their southern neighbors. Indeed, from an Algerian perspective, for instance, too much connectivity of the wrong kind (with now-undesirable kin from farther south) might be positively embarrassing, and genealogical accounts are pruned accordingly, while contemporary migrants from Sahelian countries—yesteryear's cousins—are often treated with great suspicion (Bellil and Badi 1993).

The Sahara in Perspective

As well as offering a fuller, wider, and deeper perspective on Saharan Africa itself, such a framework allows us to see the logics at work in this region, which has too often been seen in isolation, in comparison, and in contact with regional histories produced elsewhere: in the Mediterranean, of course, but also in the worlds of the Atlantic and Indian oceans. Literature on the latter in particular has grown by leaps and bounds, pointing toward certain parallels with Saharan concerns: the importance of genealogical reckoning, for instance, and the "spread of Islam," which is often still badly understood (Ho 2002, 2006); short-range peddling, or cabotage, and the technicalities of shipping, winds, and currents (Parkin and Barnes 2002); the creation of port cities and independent mini-states that often governed trade from a scant territorial basis while developing less-than-straightforward regional relations, whose fate depended entirely on outside connections (Chaudhuri 1985, 1990; McPherson 1993); linguistic diversity and religio-legal pluralism, combining in successful interactions beyond the control of more canonically "world-central" state systems (Freitag and Clarence-Smith 1997; Markovits 2000); contemporary attempts to make sense of past connectivity and present transformations (Deutsch and Reinwald 2002); and notions of cosmopolitanism outside the "West" (Simpson and Kresse 2007).

This last point is perhaps the most interesting, as the notion of cosmopolitanism has received some coverage in the anthropological literature, often, it seems, as shorthand for "globalization." Yet material from the Indian Ocean and the Sahara shows clearly that local cosmopolitanisms are not, as is often assumed, based on equality and gradual homogenization, but on the contrary, they are intrinsically dependent on the recognition of differences rooted in hierarchy. Further, the emphasis on interdependence stresses that we are dealing here with two-way (or polycentric, multidirectional) systems that are essential to the making of place. This nuances the world system approaches that postulate primarily unidirectional economic influences and outside exploitation.[24] Saharan exchange is often unequal, has long been so (think of the slave trade), and has certainly become more so over the last century. However, it contains and gives rise to myriad power relations that we cannot take for granted but need to make the object of careful analysis; world historical regions do not necessarily have to have a core, let alone one situated outside themselves. Lastly, there is an argument to be made for treating much Saharan settlement as "colonial," to the extent that it requires initial and ongoing investments from without (the flipside of connectivity); models borrowed from studies of the "frontier" as a dynamic colonial venture rather than as the limit to mobility, both in sub-Saharan Africa (Kopytoff 1987; Iliffe 1995) and in the North American West, hence provide further potentially useful grounds for comparison (see also Leservoisier, J. McDougall this volume).

These reflections have two immediate practical implications for research. First, the only way in which we can fill the conceptual emptiness of the Sahara while avoiding long-standing stereotypes and misleading categorizations is by conducting research locally, with great attention to detail, and over time. Plainly, an argument that hinges on regional variation and particularity cannot proceed from generalization, but requires ongoing open-mindedness about how things observed locally might fit together over time and space. Further, any attention paid to conceptual units and local imaginations requires long-term acquaintance with the people involved; detailed attention to local archives and linguistic and cultural idiosyncrasies and connections; and a thorough familiarity with local economies, marriage patterns, and everyday struggles. Further, *ecology* implies interdisciplinarity: anthropological and geographic knowledge are both important here, but they cannot do without insights borrowed from sociology and economics. Second, in order to understand the Sahara as a historical region and recognize its inhabitants' historic agency, and in order fully to grasp changes and stability, we need a long-term historical approach drawing on related disciplines such as linguistics, archaeology, and Islamic studies. In an area such as the Sahara, where much local research needs to be done from scratch and where societies are marked by a high degree of linguistic and cultural variation (and indeed by the multilingualism inherent in long-standing cosmopolitanism), this can only be achieved through sustained collaborative and truly interdisciplinary endeavors. And in this regard, there is another level on which Saharan research tends to stumble over linguistic boundaries: while excellent local case studies have been conducted by primarily French-speaking researchers, these are little known to English-speaking readers. On the other hand, many of the conceptual advances discussed above have been made within English-speaking academia, and they have had little or no impact south of the Channel. As we will try to show throughout this book, the dynamics both of this region and of the scholarship that seeks to understand it are inherently interdependent. It is only if different approaches from different scholarly communities are combined, and their underlying conceptual assumptions confronted with one another, that we can hope to produce studies of the Sahara from a more satisfactory perspective.

This volume takes a step in that direction. Part 1, "Framing Saharan Africa," considers Saharan regional history over the long term, situating the subject theoretically and empirically with reference to a set of broader comparative questions. Peregrine Horden's chapter provides an overview of the new ecological history of the Mediterranean, of which he has been a pioneer, and considers the relevance of the connectivity identified there to the Sahara. In a broad survey of the field of Saharan studies and the major interventions in its literature to date, Ann McDougall draws on a series of key areas in the region's social, economic, and cultural history to illuminate the significance of Saharan-ness in local self-perceptions and in categorization by outsiders (scholarly or otherwise). Katia Schörle provides an account of the groundbreaking archaeological research on the Garamantian kingdom in the Fezzan that has cast new and important light on the ecology and economy of Saharan trade in classical antiquity. James McDougall examines the limitations and possibilities of a comparative history of borderlands and frontier zones for an understanding of long-term patterns and recent trends in Saharan history, situating the region both within and at the margins of African, Arab/Middle Eastern, Mediterranean, and Islamic histories and considering its significance in the context of world history. Together with this introduction, these chapters situate this book relative to the existing literature on the Sahara, and suggest a framework for thinking about Saharan Africa over the very long term, giving a background against which the more specialized thematic chapters can be considered.

Part 2, "Environment, Territory, and Community," revisits the notion of Saharan place and local notions of territoriality through fine-grained ethnographic and historical studies, proposing a consideration of place as fundamentally part of and synchronous with, rather than prior to, regional dynamics of resource management, social hierarchy, and group formation. These four chapters draw on fieldwork in the Sahel and the northern Sahara to illustrate how, in recent times, modes of social power in the region have been variously related to the control of territory and the ability to move through it, the control of people and their places of settlement, and the control of resources (both material and cultural) and their local and regional distribution. Rituals, studied in the Mzab by Fatma Oussedik and in the Gourara by Abderrahmane Moussaoui, have often served to confirm or momentarily subvert such power. These patterns changed over the course of the twentieth century, enabling some forms of movement and restricting others. Both social mobility and physical movement are also considered, in studies of northern Mali by Charles Grémont and of the Senegal-Mauritania border zone by Olivier Leservoisier, in relation to the ecological possibilities and constraints of particular environments, and the ways in which social space is constructed within or across geographic territory.

Part 3, "Strangers, Space, and Labor," pursues this question of the intimate connections between mobility, economic practice, and the making and transformation of place through analysis of various forms of contemporary Saharan and trans-Saharan urban settlement. By understanding the social mobility and physical movement of people toward new urban centers not as a recent threat or a sign of social instability, but as an integral part of the Saharan political and cultural economy, the chapters in this part suggest new ways of describing the rapidly growing cities of the Sahara as both inherently cosmopolitan and fractured, and as evolving their own particular means of incorporation and marginalization of "strangers." Armelle Choplin and Laurence Marfaing study the changing configuration of labor markets, residential patterns, and migration flows in Nouadhibou and Nouakchott, Mauritania, while Dida Badi looks at the relationship between migrant labor, residence, techniques of production, and commercialization in the southern Algerian town of Tamanrasset. These cases demonstrate that Saharan cities are not merely way stations for a migratory "flood" northward (despite persistent images in the media and the suppositions of European Union policy), but a fundamental factor in the development of regional economies with their own internal logics.

Part 4, "Economies of Movement," expands the question of migration, labor, and exchange to consider local and long-distance economic factors in the making of contemporary informal commercial and migration networks, which exist in the interstices of or traverse the formal political economies of regional states. Mohamed Oudada sketches the workings of the long-distance, parallel cross-border economy in southern Morocco, Judith Scheele investigates the making of a contemporary trade center on the Algerian-Malian border, and Julien Brachet tracks the movements of migrant workers and commodities through northern Niger and into Libya and Algeria. Exploring the connection between the local and the regional, these chapters show how distinct localities and social identities are shaped by often far-flung relations of exchange. Whether "legal" or "illegal," cross-border movements of goods and people here appear not as the result of helpless poverty nor as anarchic threats to regional security, but rather as fundamental elements of the region's economic reality, in which mobile wage labor, a (carefully managed and locally rule-bound, though sometimes morally suspect) informality of regional exchange, and the importance of such exchange over production are all central to local strategies of survival and accumulation.

Taken together, these studies suggest a new way of approaching the Sahara, beyond images of fearful disaster or unchanging emptiness. We hope that they will be a step toward understanding the Sahara and Saharans on their own terms, in the context of their own histories, in relation to the broader regional and global past of which those histories are a part, and in relation to the historical, political, social, and ecological complexities they are facing today.

NOTES

1. The first Portuguese voyages that began the Atlantic slave trade set out in the sixteenth century in an attempt to capture the Saharan gold trade (see Crone 1937); French visionaries in the early nineteenth century still imagined that vast wealth must lie untapped in the "commercial empire" of northwest Africa.

2. *Le Figaro* (Paris), 4 April 1881. Colonel Paul Flatters' expeditions in 1880 and 1881 into the Ahaggar, an important zone of independent Tuareg rule in the central Sahara, were meant to survey a possible route for the chimerical trans-Saharan railway. Flatters and his men were killed on 16 February 1881.

3. The Algerian Sahara was considered effectively subdued after the defeat of the Ahaggar Tuareg at Tit in May 1902, and permanently so after Kaosen's 1916–1918 rebellion was brutally put down (see, e.g., Claudot-Hawad 1996), although tribes based in Saqiya al-Hamra in the western Sahara resisted into the 1930s. Gide's *L'immoraliste* (1902) was partly set in Algeria; for a discussion of his relation to Algeria, see Gellner (1995).

4. See, e.g., Hall (1927), Morand (1928).

5. A group of eleven European tourists and their Egyptian guides were kidnapped and held for ransom in the region in September 2008.

6. www.saharatravel.co.uk, accessed 8 November 2009.

7. See, e.g., Breck Eisner (dir.), *Sahara* (Paramount, 2005).

8. The Sahara became a theater of the "war on terror" with the establishment of the U.S. special forces' Pan-Sahel Initiative in 2002, which developed into the Trans-Sahara Counterterrorism Initiative in 2005. The U.S. military's Africa Command (AFRICOM—albeit based in Stuttgart, Germany) was set up in October 2007. On this "second front" in the "war on terror," see, e.g., Keenan (2005, 2009), McGovern (2005), and Lecocq and Schrijver (2007).

9. Literature on these is too vast to be cited here in full. For the successive Sahel droughts, see Comité d'Information du Sahel (1975), Glantz (1976), and Spittler (1993); for

civil wars in northern Niger and Mali, see Maiga (1997), Grémont et al. (2004), Bourgeot (1996), and Crombé and Jézéquel (2008).

10. Figures are mainly available for Algeria (Côte 2005), where 80 percent of all Saharans now reside in cities or towns, and Libya (Pliez 2003; Bisson 2003).

11. Ninety-five percent of all exports from Algeria and Libya are crude oil or gas, accounting for 30 percent and 60 percent of GDP, respectively.

12. The literature on Saharan smuggling networks is still limited, but see Grégoire (1999), Boubekri (2000), Bordes and Labrousse (2004), and Scheele (2009) for case studies of Saharan and related Maghrebi cases; and Houafani (1986) for a popular literary treatment. See also Brachet, Oudada, and Scheele this volume.

13. The literature on sub-Saharan migrants in North Africa is growing fast; for a few examples, see Bensaâd (2002, 2005b, 2009), relevant chapters in Marfaing and Wippel (2004), Ba and Choplin (2005), Bredeloup and Pliez (2005), Pliez (2006), Brachet (2009a), Choplin (2009), and Choplin, Marfaing, and Brachet this volume.

14. Notable exceptions are Haarmann (1998) and Lydon (2008, 2009). On manuscript libraries in the Sahara and their often difficult preservation, see Gaudio (2002), Bouterfa (2005), and Krätli and Lydon (2010).

15. For a fuller discussion of the problematic overemphasis on trans-Saharan trade and its consequences, see E. A. McDougall (2005a); for classic examples of studies of trans-Saharan trade, see Newbury (1966), Bovill (1968), Miège (1981), and Savage (1992a); for other work in a similar vein, see Austen (1990) and Lydon (2009). For a reflection on the implications of the emphasis on trans-Saharan (as opposed to intraregional) migration, see de Haas (2007).

16. Mauritania and northwestern Mali are the exception here. For well-informed accounts of the local development of Islamic scholarship and its interplay with local social hierarchies, see Stewart (1973), Norris (1968, 1975, 1990), Saad (1983), Osswald (1986, 1993), Batran (2001), Cleaveland (2002), Nouhi (2009), and Hall (2011). But most of these works are purely historical, and there moreover remains a real gap in the literature where the Central Sahara is concerned, with the notable exception of Hunwick (1985).

17. For a critique of this latter view, see Burke (2000: 17–19); for correctives, see J. McDougall (2011) and Clancy-Smith et al. (forthcoming).

18. The typical expression of this since the early 2000s has been endemic rioting in southern towns, routinely reported in the Algerian press: "Khenchela, Ouargla, Adrar, Bordj Bou Arreridj, Djelfa: Le cycle des émeutes reprend," *El Watan,* 16 May 2004; "Les émeutes se propagent dans le M'zab," *Liberté,* 25 October 2004; and "Violentes émeutes à Laghouat," *El Watan,* 14 November 2005.

19. This was especially evident in northern criticisms of Algerian president Abd al-Aziz Bouteflika's "tribal" and "maraboutic" constituency-building prior to his reelection in 2004. See, for example "Les tribus du Tidikelt soutiennent Bouteflika," *Le Quotidien d'Oran,* 16 February 2004.

20. Such an ecological approach has been adopted very successfully in the Sahel belt by Baier and Lovejoy (1975), Bourgeot (1995), and, less subtly perhaps, J. L. A. Webb (1995); and in the Sahara by Gast (1989); see also Brooks (1993).

21. See, e.g., Geoffroy (1887), Baier (1980), and Spittler (1993). Kopytoff's (1987) concept of the "African frontier" as a broad and dynamic zone of contact might be useful here; see J. McDougall (this volume) and, for a much earlier period, Trousset (1984).

22. For examples of such an approach, see E. A. McDougall (1986, 1990) and Bonte (1998, 2000).

23. On the establishment of borders between North and West African colonies, see Bouguetaia (1981); and see Boilley (1999) for the Algerian case. For reflections on the links between states and transnational smuggling networks, see Bayart (2004).

24. Wallerstein (1974–1989). For an attempt to apply this approach to Sahelian material, see Kea (2004).

PART 1

FRAMING SAHARAN AFRICA

1 SITUATIONS BOTH ALIKE?

Connectivity, the Mediterranean, the Sahara

Peregrine Horden

> I tell you, captain, if you look in the maps of the 'orld, I warrant you sall find, in the comparisons, between Macedon and Monmouth, that the situations, look you, is both alike. There is a river in Macedon, and there is also moreover a river at Monmouth: it is called Wye at Monmouth; but it is out of my prains what is the name of the other river; but 'tis all one, 'tis so like as my fingers is to my fingers, and there is salmons in both. —Shakespeare, *Henry V*

Fluellen showed the way. With ingenious selectivity, almost anything—certainly any piece of geography—can be made to seem similar enough to anything else to be classified under the same broad heading. Comparison of the two then becomes a plausible exercise.[1]

The attraction of comparing the Mediterranean and the Sahara derives of course not only from the applicability of nautical similes (camels as ships of the desert, oases as islands) but from the proximity of the two regions. Along with Northern Europe, the Middle East, and, from early modern times onward, the Atlantic, the Sahara is one of the big adjacent geographical expressions with which the Mediterranean historian must engage, at least since the long third millennium BCE, possibly since 120,000 years ago.[2]

No one saw this more clearly than Braudel. He placed the Sahara first in the third chapter of his opening section on the role of the environment. The chapter was entitled "Boundaries: The Greater Mediterranean." The Mediterranean of the geologist and geographer was much too small. The historical (or human) Mediterranean extended well beyond the sea's shores and their hinterlands, like a magnetic field radiating outward and slowly losing strength with distance rather than giving out at any precise, frontier-like moment. Beside his "greater Mediterranean," a field of influence that was potentially global, Braudel in effect set a "greater Sahara": "the entire range of warm deserts as far as Iran and Arabia," south of the northern limits of the palm grove (1972 [1966]: 171). In a few characteristically vivid pages he conjured up the life of the camel drivers, the mountain nomads moving within a small area, and, crucially for Mediterranean history, the longer-range nomads whose movements "from steppe to coast, then from the sea back to the desert, inevitably acted as one of the pressures on Mediterranean history" (177). The other, less invasive pressure was from the gold and spice caravans, "long distance voyages from one side of the desert to the other, linking the Mediterranean . . . to the *Bled es Soudan* and Black Africa." Thus Braudel came to the trans-Saharan trade that has so attracted historians before and since for its sheer scale and, perhaps, its exoticism: "a luxury, an adventure, a complicated operation" (181).

Historians and ethnographers of the Sahara still reasonably enough complain that their area is viewed not as a "thing in itself" but as a transparent medium for trans-Saharan trade, above all linking sub-Saharan economies and those of the Middle East, the Mediterranean, and Europe (E. A. McDougall 2005a): what might be caricatured, but only slightly, as an obsession with gold, slaves, and ostrich feathers (Austen 2010: 27–35). Historians of the "greater Mediterranean" have naturally also privileged long-distance exchange (while of course registering the shifting North African frontiers created by the advance and retreat of nomadism). Especially if their purview is the sea itself, movements across it, and only a thin strip of coastline, they are far less likely to be interested in local environmental questions than in those to do with the long-haul transport of goods. Their conception of the relationship between Mediterranean and Saharan history will correspondingly emphasize exchange between the two, with the Maghreb as a pivotal area;[3] and the Sahara will resemble the Mediterranean in being simply the setting for the transport required (Abulafia 2003; Matvejević 1999; Horden 2005). Thus David Abulafia, the foremost representative of this school of thought:

> A network of contacts enabled Jewish merchants to make payments in Sijilmasa [today in southern Morocco] for purchases as far away as Walata [in southern Mauritania], and Walata, deep in the interior, was a transit post in a great sandy sea with a similar entrepôt function to, say, Majorca. . . . These were critical stages, islands if you like, along the caravan trade routes that brought gold northwards and salt and textiles southwards. (2005: 75)

Not only is it all long distance, it is also essentially north-south, linking the Mediterranean and sub-Saharan territories. The Sahara itself is a blank, ready to be washed by cultural "tides" from elsewhere. Again Abulafia: "The Sahara was a true Mediterranean in the sense that it brought very different cultures into contact, and across the open spaces they brought not merely articles of trade but ideas, notably religious ones" (75).

Connectivity

It therefore marks a novel twist to the story of the interplay between sea and desert, and particularly of related conceptions of the two areas, that a term used to characterize and thus delimit the whole Mediterranean environment, by land as well as sea (and not just a thin coastal strip), should be taken over by desert specialists as a way of capturing Saharan space. The tool by which this space is rescued from the condescension implied in the emphasis on trans-Saharan trade is "connectivity." Its use raises questions about the extent to which Mediterranean-style movements and communications have reached beyond the region and even continued it, the extent to which the Sahara contributes to a "greater Mediterranean."

"Routes et villes, villes et routes." Such was Lucien Febvre's response on first reading Braudel's chapter on the Mediterranean as a human unit, and Braudel planned to return the compliment by making those words the chapter title. "The Mediterranean," he wrote, "has no unity but that created by the movements of men. . . . the whole Mediterranean consists of movement in space" (1972 [1966]: 276–277). That was movement above all along fairly well-defined routes linking ports, towns, and cities—points and lines on the map.

By contrast, within Mediterranean studies "connectivity" has become a way of characterizing the ease of communications between one place and another in a much broader sense. As a term of art in the field, it seems to have been given wide currency by Horden and Purcell in *The Corrupting Sea* (2000). Some reviewers of that book (e.g., Squatriti 2002) pointed to the political overtones that the word had gained during the 1990s when *The Corrupting Sea* was being written, and a range of other meanings have since been adduced, not least in information technology and neuroscience. Yet Horden and Purcell, oblivious in their ivory tower, borrowed the term from locational analysis in human geography (Haggett, Cliff, and Frey 1977), inspired by the way it had already been taken up by some archaeologists (e.g., Sanders and Whitbread 1990). The term had originated (by around 1960) in mathematical graph theory. Its initial geographical application was apparently to the analysis of regional road networks, with the measure of connectivity being the ratio between the number of edges (lines) and the number of vertices (nodes) in the network. Thus any space that can be modeled by one line joining two nodes is—trivially—connective. The degree zero of connectivity would be an utter singularity.

Horden and Purcell used connectivity, however, in a way that involved much more than joining up the dots; and (at least so it seems in retrospect) they tended to treat it as shorthand for quite intense connectivity, well above that absolute zero. Connectivity became a crucial ingredient in their summary of the Mediterranean environment and the way humanity has interacted with it. As they saw it, the Mediterranean is overall a zone of intense topographical fragmentation, overlaid by a kaleidoscope of human micro-ecologies, which are in turn densely interconnected. Connectivity describes the way micro-regions cohere, both internally and with one another. Throughout much of Mediterranean history, this coherence has been more than a matter of fixed routes, whether laid down by planners in defiance of nature (as with Roman roads) or prompted by geography. Indeed, the point of bringing a then relatively unusual term into the discussion of the Mediterranean past was, in the first place, to get away from the idea that communications are, like graph theory, a matter of nodes and straight lines, or that they are, in some deterministic way, the product of geography or climate. Routes there of course have been, over water and land. But roads, tracks, mountain paths, shipping lanes, and river channels should all, according to *The Corrupting Sea,* be envisaged as particular instances of a much broader phenomenon—the *potentially* all-round, sometimes nearly frictionless communication between Mediterranean micro-regions. Thus sea travel was not, in premodern times, as constrained by wind, current, and season as has often been made out—nor was it as uniformly fearful and hazardous. There was much confident *hors piste* sailing—and in winter too. Nor should the difficulties of overland transport be exaggerated, even over mountain ranges in severe weather. Indeed, an additional advantage of thinking in terms of connectivity may be to help us avoid (unthinkingly) privileging certain forms of communication. To put it another way, the determining capacity of the environment has been weak. The choice of lines or corridors of communication cannot, in the majority of cases, simply be predicted by studying a physical map.

Mediterranean micro-regions connect in many ways. They connect in the movements of peoples and goods and information. Some of these movements have involved well-trodden tracks and their nautical equivalents. Others have been more variable; hence the poor predictive power of maps. But micro-ecologies connect by mutual visibility and audibility as well. So we must reckon with lines of sight and lines of sound as well as shifting terrestrial or maritime networks. Connectivities may thus be genuinely all-round.

They may also be far-reaching. Thanks to seaborne contacts—not to be emphasized unduly but still of course vital to Mediterranean peoples—a given micro-region may be more intensely connected to another one a hundred miles away than to its geographical neighbor. The high levels of connectivity characteristic of much of the region's history help define the Mediterranean. If we could only plot all the connections, we would find that the Mediterranean region possesses unity and distinctiveness, partly in virtue of being an area of net introversion. That is, connectivity between micro-regions has generally been more intense around and across the sea's coastlands than between those coastlands and their continental neighbors. The first development of such intense connectivity in prehistory thus marks the beginning of Mediterranean history, just as the very different configurations of connectivity across Europe, the Mediterranean, and the Middle East in the twentieth and twenty-first centuries may in that sense mark its end (Broodbank forthcoming).

Saharan Routes

Has the Sahara been at all similar? A case of a limited kind could be made for its ecological diversity: mountains, foothills, plateaus, steppes, stony plains, various types of dune, sand fields, inter-dunal depressions (Lydon 2009: 8). But the more productive question to pursue is: has the Sahara been an extra-Mediterranean zone of Mediterranean-type communications? Take first the premodern world, the world defined, as far as Saharan transport and communications are concerned, by the camel, which dominated from about the first century CE, if not earlier (Lydon 2009: 54, 209; Austen 2010: 17).

The first comparative point to make is that there is no Mediterranean equivalent to this dominance of transport, and indeed of human mobility in general, over such a long period, by one species—a species that is almost always, for obvious reasons of safety, moved about in groups.

The relative fluidity, or mutability, of lines of communication is harder to judge. Where could the direction of travel be potentially more all-round than in the central Sahara, in which open ground may stretch in all directions, as far as the eye can see? Certainly there were no fixed routes in the Sahara, and in their absence there was always some choice of itinerary for caravans, some flexibility. Indeed, caravans could hardly take the same route twice in quick succession, since they relied on the availability of pasture on the way—pasture that varied from year to year, or even month to month, and that needed time to recuperate after a major caravan had departed. Smaller groups of camels, or occasional solitary travelers, were even more flexible; they depended primarily on the availability of water, but they also had to rely on networks of protection that changed over time and that hence curtailed their freedom of movement in unpredictable ways. Access to wells was more often than not a political matter, rather than one of infrastructure. Wells remained under the protection of those who had dug them (if they happened still to be around).[4] More important, they were easily filled in by those with less desire to facilitate travel. The danger of raiders was always very real and the time it took to haul the water required to refresh a major caravan—often several days—made travelers vulnerable to attack.[5] Freedom of movement was thus curtailed, but less by the environment than by those who lived in it. Regular patterns of movement along well-defined routes—as imagined by colonial geographers—were by definition impossible.[6]

Moreover, camels are really not ships. Although strikingly resistant to the hardships of climate and able to carry heavy loads for several days without requiring fodder or water, they remain most efficient for distances that can be covered in no more than a month.[7] But camels have provided a basis for Saharan livelihoods beyond their function as beasts of burden: ships cannot be milked for daily sustenance, nor do they breed. The means of transportation lay mostly in the hands of the camel owners, whose primary aim was to keep them alive as long as possible. Consideration of the camels' seasonal dietary needs and ability to recuperate hence often outweighed the imperatives of swift and flexible travel. Further, the type of camel used determined to a great extent the kind of terrain that could be traversed and the distance that could be covered. Camels bred in and for the mountainous terrain of the Ahaggar, for instance, were badly adapted to sand dunes, and the converse applied (Nicolaisen 1963: 54–57). Hence, although travel was theoretically unrestricted and omnidirectional, to be sustainable it had to form part of larger socioecological patterns. These did not determine its exact course, but they did set limits to individual freedom of movement.

All this seems closer to the Mediterranean as presented by Braudel than to that of Horden and Purcell. To say that is not to pronounce on the final outcome of any comparison of the Sahara with the Mediterranean. It is simply to suggest that the regime of connectivity as sketched for the Mediterranean in *The Corrupting Sea* has to be significantly modified to fit the Sahara.

Once we move up to the level of long-distance exchange, however, the resemblance of sea to desert world may be closer. In the Mediterranean region, the landscape can be dominated by long straight roads, preeminently Roman ones—the assertion of power over terrain symbolizing as well as facilitating military dominance. And there can be fairly straight crossings over the open sea, to a lesser extent in defiance of nature, that is, wind and current, but facilitated in navigational terms by the relatively small areas of the sea from which no coastline is visible. More commonly, though (*The Corrupting Sea* argued, following Braudel), there has been coastal cabotage by sea and comparable short-haul transport over land. In the Sahara the regional level of movement is reflected in the geography of oases. But it is also constrained by the desirability of not pushing camels beyond their limit and beyond areas known to transporters and considered to be safe. So the map of regional movements is much simpler and more predictable than that which could be envisaged for the Mediterranean. Even so, it is far from the simple north-south corridor implicit in many scholarly accounts. According to Liverani's (2000) plausible reconstruction, the caravan itinerary implied by Herodotus for ca. 500 BCE connects Egypt and the Niger bend.[8] The annual pilgrimage from the western Sahara to Mecca was an occasion for trade and travel as much as a religious obligation.[9] Even the major north-south exchanges involved broadly regional east-west connections.[10] Conversely, in some cases recorded in local archives in Ghadamès (Haarmann 1998), trans-Saharan goods moving roughly east-west crossed the Sahara twice in a broadly south-north direction before reaching their final destination. They did so by traversing what can be envisaged cartographically as a series of loop-shaped regional networks. Walata, mentioned by Abulafia in the passage quoted above, may have been "a transit post in a great sandy sea" on the long route north to Sijilmassa, but its role has to be understood first in terms of its centrality to far more local livestock breeding (Cleaveland 2002).

How large, here, is a region? Camels can move within a radius of several hundred miles as part of their seasonal migrations. Knowledge of good pastures and easy passages spreads quickly in the Sahara, and camel owners arrange their movements accordingly, mostly within this given radius. These areas of frequent travel and exchange can be combined to form a chain. Very long-distance, trans-Saharan movement necessarily depended on such chains, with trans-shipment from one set of camels to another at the oases where these areas overlap.[11] That is reminiscent of Mediterranean trans-shipment and especially of the way the journey of a *caboteur* may, overall, involve several complete changes of cargo. But as far as premodern times are concerned, it is different from the open-sea voyages and their equivalents in road building that have additionally been possible in the Mediterranean, possibly for as long as 130,000 years (Strasser et al. 2010). Indeed, in the Sahara, attempts by regional states to override regional patterns and to cross the area in a straight line—exemplified by the Moroccan conquest of Timbuktu in 1591 or, much later, by French colonial attempts to subdue the desert—have notoriously failed. The Moroccan army took the city of Timbuktu, but never went back to Morocco, and Moroccan rule over the area remained formal at best.[12] The French caused camel hecatombs in failed supply journeys and were unable to control the Sahara effectively—or even to staff military outposts properly—until they could rely on motorized transportation and airplanes.[13]

The caravan is indeed everything in the unmotorized Sahara. Communications can be no more rapid than the best-paced camel courier. In general, of course, the occasional use of carrier pigeons apart, the movement of information and ideas in premodern times (i.e., before the telegraph) must be epiphenomenal to the movement of people. Still, it is worth recalling the ties of mutual visibility and audibility by which some quite distant Mediterranean places are linked. There seems to be no equivalent history of signaling for the Sahara. More generally, routes and travel have not been defined by landmarks. So the really deserted deserts, places of death and demonic power broken only by the occasional salt mine (which were perhaps known as early as the twelfth century), are not to be compared with the deeps of the sea, out of sight of land, despite the desert simile that Braudel applied to them: "Great stretches of the sea were as empty as the Sahara" (1972 [1966]: 103): true, alas for him, of neither sea nor desert.

Modern Routes

Today, the Mediterranean of Horden and Purcell has more or less disappeared, as the net introversion observed in historic times has been reversed through the power and infrastructure established by the nation-states that now govern the Mediterranean coast. Most of the contributions in this volume describe the contemporary Sahara. If the notion of connectivity can be of some use for the historical Sahara, if only to bring out important contrasts, what then about Saharan modernity? In the Sahara, modernity meant first of all the occasional quasi-Roman attempts at domination of the landscape, including projects for trans-Saharan railways from the 1880s that filled France with dreams of profitable empire, feeding on comparisons with the American West and Siberia, which had both been "opened up" by the construction of apparently "impossible" railway lines.[14] These projects failed, at times spectacularly, and added further to the myth of Saharan inaccessibility and "anarchy."[15] The great change came much later, with the introduction of motorized transportation from the 1920s onward. This finally broke the long-standing dependence on camels—and hence on camel owners, herders, and transporters (Guitart 1989). Once more, however, the impetus for infrastructural change was not merely technical, but political too. Fearful of an Allied blockade, the Vichy government established in Algeria from 1940 to 1942 finally constructed a trans-Saharan road network that linked Algeria to French West Africa overland. It also established a regular truck service. Although they initially relied on supplies of gasoline that were, ironically, mostly carried by camels (Clauzel 1960b), trucks became popular because during World War II they enabled large profits to be made from trading on the black market. While the new roads clearly reduced the variability of movement patterns, the need for some degree of secrecy in conveying black market goods promoted a contrary reversion to *hors piste* routes in all their variety.

Since World War II various social considerations have promoted stability in the patterns of communication. As most transborder exchange remains illegal (see Brachet, Oudada, and Scheele this volume), people continue to trade within areas where they can enjoy the protection of scattered family members—their in-laws. For obvious reasons of convenience, as well as of security, they favor routes, areas, and stopping places that they know. Such comfort zones have taken time to create, and they continue to function in the interstices of state endeavors to control the area (again indicating the relative predominance of social and political over environmental and technical factors). Nonetheless, investment in trucks is increasingly concentrated in the hands of the wealthy few, and camels remain primarily prestige objects. Whereas in the past, traders could not own their means of transport, doing so has now become a major form of capital investment—and in this sense trucks are more like ships than camels ever were. Thanks to modern road infrastructure, the transition from the camel to the wheel has brought about some hardening of arteries: a reduction in the variety of routes as trucks dominate. But because of social pressures, the reduction has been less than might have been predicted from the technological history alone. More recently, the Sahara has increasingly been drawn into transregional illegal trade, such as international cocaine smuggling, that consciously attempts to destroy long-standing regional connections and networks (Scheele 2009) and that will perhaps play a role analogous to that of Mediterranean nation-states in reconfiguring the entire region—if, that is, the trade lasts long enough.

It is hard to say how far this constrained modernizing resembles the twentieth-century history of communications in the Mediterranean. Steamships, trains, telegraph, telephone, the internet—each was an empire of movement and communication superimposed on an already immense variety of patterns without by any means effacing them or altering their potential for nearly limitless choice of routes and nearly frictionless movement. It is surely a different story, and a far more complicated one. The history of camels and trucks sums up a far greater proportion of Saharan movement (so limited is internet access, for example, and so expensive are satellite phones) than any pairing of Mediterranean vehicles, any simple "from X to Y" type of heading ever could.

Nodes

This comparison of movement has so far omitted a crucial component: the nodes in the network. In *The Corrupting Sea*, Horden and Purcell outlined a vision of Mediterranean places as special instances of the essentially mutable and overlapping micro-ecologies into which they conceptually divided Mediterranean geography. Towns and cities dissolved into a broader category of "the larger settlement," which was *in principle* as amenable to the same sort of analysis of its shifting and scattered hinterlands, and its diverse entangled networks of movement, as any other part of the landscape. Places were made—and remade—by the movements intrinsic to human ecology. Locality had always to be interpreted, whether in political, cultural, or ecological terms, with reference to wider, sometimes quite distant, horizons.

How does this compare with Saharan nodes? Water supply is again, and very obviously, crucial. There are some areas where the variability of annual rainfall approaches that of the Mediterranean, especially the mountainous regions (in the pre-Saharan Atlas, northern Mali, the Aïr in Niger, or the Ahaggar mountains in southern Algeria: areas crucial for local pastoralists). But on the whole, of course, desert aridity is wholly different in character from most circum-Mediterranean environments—with the exception of the eastern end of Braudel's "greater Sahara"—and it is pastoral economies rather than agriculture that are most affected by seasonal variations. By digging deeply enough, water can be found in many parts of the Sahara (Bisson 2003). But it is often salty, and because of the labor and cost involved, investment in digging wells makes sense only if they can be protected against both the vagaries of the environment and human interference. So, since antiquity it seems, all major oases have been artificial creations, built by slave or servile labor and fed by sophisticated irrigation systems, relying on investment, foresight, and considerable technical skill.[16] In the sense that "here" is inevitably defined by "elsewhere" (Pascon 1984), there is some limited resemblance to the dispersed or fractured hinterlands of Mediterranean settlements. But those settlements to the north depended on a much greater variety of water sources, both local and distant.

Whereas trade, security, and the requirements of pastoral nomadism have been the single biggest determinants of the geography of oases, at least since the seventeenth century, Mediterranean settlements have reflected in their distribution a larger range of pressures: cultural, political, and ecological. It seems to be a matter of Mediterranean polyculture as against Saharan monoculture: although oases produced some grains and vegetables in addition to dates, it was dates that allowed them to participate in the regional networks of exchange that were vital for their survival. In the Sahara a man might own land in five or more separate oases, livestock, stakes in salt mines, and goods kept elsewhere—to spread risk rather than simply because of Islamic inheritance laws (Scheele 2010a). But that is hardly analogous to the scattered and diverse holdings favored, where landlords permit, by Mediterranean producers as a buffer against the bad years in local environmental fluctuation. The preponderance of dates in oasis production makes these centers dependent on an enormous range of imports, while the dispersed hinterlands of larger settlements in the Mediterranean are not normally there to counteract any comparable hyper-concentration on a single product.

Ramifications

The comparison of the Mediterranean and the Sahara could be extended into subjects that do not strictly fall under the heading of connectivity.

There is the chronological dimension: first, the question of when premodern patterns of movement should be seen as developing—in the time of the caravan route described by Herodotus, or later, in early Islamic times.[17] Can there be a rounded prehistory of the Sahara in the process of becoming the Sahara as we know it, in terms of its connectivity, as there is of the Mediterranean (Holl 2004)? At the other end, how far does the declining economic centrality of the Sahara within Africa, after the European opening up of the Atlantic coast, match the slightly later decline attributed to the Mediterranean by historians from Braudel onward (E. A. McDougall 1998: 468; Tabak 2008)?

There is also the political dimension: how far can the rise and decline of polities and empires be explained in terms of the ambition to control the movement between oases as, *mutatis mutandis*, Horden and Purcell claimed that Mediterranean empires could? Such attempts were clearly made, both in pre-Islamic and Islamic times. Muhammad Bello, ruler of the Sokoto caliphate who drew a map of his domains in 1824 for a European explorer, and imaged them in terms of strategic bases along major trade routes, may exemplify a widely shared vision of the geography of power (Austen 2010: 67–68). Such a vision was not, however, easily translated into effective control (cf. Holl 2004: chs. 6–7). One of the most striking differences between the Mediterranean and the Sahara is perhaps the relative absence of state control over most Saharan territories for most of their history—although this has by no means precluded pronounced social hierarchies and local exploitation.

Yet another line of inquiry must concern religion. Local legends attach Islamic saints to oases and credit them, more than irrigators, with making the desert bloom. Through such legends, place names, and ritual practices—pilgrimage is especially important here (see Moussaoui and Oussedik this volume)—the Saharan landscape is profoundly Islamic and profoundly sacralized. There is some equivalent there to the way religions have sacralized Mediterranean landscapes even if, again, it is one predominant form of religious geography (centered of course on Mecca to the east) to set alongside Mediterranean diversity, in which almost every part of the region has at some time or another been polytheistic, Christian, and Islamic. In the Sahara, pre-Islamic traditions existed, of course, and have sometimes survived in rumor and folklore, but as far as we know, there is no historical evidence that would allow us to understand pre-Islamic religious diversity.

Two final points of comparison, both relating to frontiers. The historical Mediterranean has (it was suggested by Horden and Purcell) been a zone of overall introversion—movements and communications within, on balance, being more dense and significant than those with neighboring zones, across frontiers. These frontiers are not to be reduced to lines on a map. They are shifting zones. In the case of the Mediterranean, they will be areas in which the character of the ecologies and of the networks connecting them changes as one moves away from the sea. But these frontier areas are not particularly related to rainfall, or olives and vines, or any other traditional Mediterranean marker. The area of Mediterranean communications that they encircle overlaps with, but does not correspond to, the Mediterranean of the physical geographer. The question here is: how far do maps of the principal regions of movement in the Sahara delineate a macro-area that matches the Sahara of physical geography? Preliminary indications suggest that they do not match. There is overlap, but not correspondence.[18]

If that seems to put the Mediterranean and the Sahara on an equal level, it raises the question of how the two areas, identified by their respective connectivities, have related to one another and to a larger whole. The relationship, I have argued, is not simply to be described in terms of the "old" trans-Saharan south-north trade in luxuries. It will require closer study, archaeological as well as historical, of the small-scale regions that overlap in frontier zones. There is also the task of developing what may, not too grandiosely, be called a new historiographical vision, in which seas, oceans, and large terrestrial areas, rather than nation-states and empires, are the constituent parts of a global history. Horden and Purcell (2006) have argued that because of its scale (it is quite a small sea), its extreme ecological diversity, its cultural history, and its disputed status in modern philosophizing, the Mediterranean is different from all other such geographical-historical divisions of the world, despite its multifarious links with them.

In that sense the Sahara might, despite its relatively tiny population, and for all the efforts of a latter-day Fluellen, be better put in a category with the area of the Great Lakes, or the Philippines, than with its northern neighbor. But this is only a first, tentative statement on the matter: "it is not well done, mark you now, to take the tales out of my [Fluellen's] mouth, ere it is made and finished. I speak but in the figures and comparisons of it."

NOTES

1. This chapter derives in part from my continuing collaboration with Nicholas Purcell, who is, however, absolved from complicity in its failings. The contribution of Judith Scheele has been tantamount to co-authorship, although she too is not to be blamed for what I have made of the ideas and information generously supplied.

2. See Broodbank (2008) and, for possible trans-Saharan humid corridors for the migration of modern humans "out of Africa," Osborne et al. (2008).

3. Although for the Maghreb in Roman antiquity, see Shaw (2006).

4. On changing patterns of ownership and rights of access to resources, see Bonte (1987, 2001a), Leservoisier (1994), Bourgeot (1995), and Grémont (2005).

5. Raiding was part of most Saharan exchange economies and followed set patterns of conduct; see Claudot-Hawad (1996).

6. The classic colonial treatise here is Carette (1844, 1848). Colonial reports long attempted to record and regulate trade routes and patterns of seasonal migration, generally to no avail; see Bonète (1962) and Boukhobza (1976) for the reasons, and Geoffroy (1887) for an outline of the seasonal migration patterns of a nomadic family from central Algeria.

7. Certain caravan routes could take up to sixty days (such as the one linking the Touat to Timbuktu), but they were exceptional, undertaken only once a year, and attempted only after much preparation.

8. See also Schörle this volume, on the diffusion of bananas and other staple crops.

9. For a description of the northern route through the central Sahara via Cairo, see Aucapitaine (1861); for the more recent southern route, see Birks (1978).

10. For the example of the salt trade between the Ahaggar mountains and the Amadror to the east, see Museur (1977); for trade between the Touat and the salt mines of Tawdanni to the west, see Clauzel (1960a).

11. Trans-Saharan traders and merchants hardly ever owned their means of transportation, since camel husbandry required a lifestyle incompatible with that of centers of commerce (Holsinger 1980; Austen 1990; Lydon 2008). Saharan pastoral nomads might double as traders for short- to medium-range ventures, but larger merchants inevitably had to subcontract with them.

12. For historical background to the Moroccan military expedition and later developments, see Abitbol (1979) and Saad (1983); for contemporary accounts, see the Timbuktu chronicles *Ta'rīkh al-Sūdān* and *Ta'rīkh al-fattāsh,* translated and published by Hunwick (1999) and Houdas and Delafosse (1964 [1913]).

13. Hence, the 1916 revolt led by the Tuareg leader Kaosen could still challenge French garrisons in Djanet and lead to a general panic among French officers; see Salifou (1973), Triaud (1995), and Claudot-Hawad (1990).

14. The nineteenth-century literature on the trans-Saharan railway is vast, bearing witness to metropolitan *engouement.* For example, see Derrien (1879) and Leroy-Beaulieu (1904). The project, in the revised form of a motorway from Algeria through Niger to northern Nigeria, was revived by independent African governments in the 1970s, and even in 2010 was still occasionally the subject of ministerial-level meetings.

15. The most notorious of these failures was the Flatters mission, sent in 1881 to map a potential route for the trans-Saharan railway; most of its members were massacred by Tuareg from the Ahaggar (Derrécagaix 1882; see also Grévoz 1989).

16. On irrigation systems in the Sahara, see Cressey (1958), Eldblom (1968), Grandguillaume (1973), Bédoucha (1987), and Wilson (2006).

17. See Schörle this volume.

18. Most of these Saharan areas of communication still need to be mapped, but some work has been done on the southern shore of the Sahara in particular; see Baier and Lovejoy (1975), Baier (1980), S. Bernus (1981), and J. L. A. Webb (1995).

2 ON BEING SAHARAN

E. Ann McDougall

The introduction to this volume began with a brief rehearsal of Euro-American stereotypes about the Sahara, with a nod to their North and West African counterparts. My focus will be on notions of the Sahara that, albeit perhaps not any more "real" than those described and criticized there, are internal rather than external, and inform the way Saharans themselves think about the Sahara, both as a geographic space and as a marker of identity. This is a preliminary exploration and will ask more questions than it can answer. Nonetheless, I think it is central to the matter at hand: as scholars and academics, and especially as historians, it is all too easy to be seduced into a well-entrenched set of paradigms and perspectives such that even when we do seek out the "local" (be it oral, written, visual, or material), we often do not really hear, see, or understand its meaning.

This is perhaps best illustrated by two anecdotes that although very different in content, deliver, to my mind, a similar message. While I was conducting postdoctoral research in Nouakchott in the 1980s, I attended a local celebration of Mauritania and its culture organized by students.[1] I was struck by the fact that over and over, young Mauritanian men (women were not much in evidence at such events yet) talked about themselves as "Saharan," as "people of the desert," although I knew that most of them had never traveled much closer to the desert than the suburbs of Nouakchott, while a few might have attended a family holiday or date festival in one of the many—and mostly declining—oases of the region. At the same event, a presentation on the contemporary, eastern Mauritanian desert oasis of Walata not so subtly suggested that the inhabitants of Walata were not quite as Saharan as these students were themselves: that they were in fact "people of the Sudan."[2] By implication, neither were the Walatis "really" Mauritanian, if to be Mauritanian was to be associated with a particular understanding of "being Saharan." But what did this mean to the city-dwelling, modernizing youth of the 1980s? And who was included in this category, on what grounds, and in what particular context?

My second anecdote dates from some years later, from a workshop in Bellagio, Italy, on the trans-Saharan slave trade.[3] After several days of discussion, the well-known historian Ralph Austen finally lost patience with my nagging questions, all based on examples drawn from the Sahara and all challenging assumptions that, to his mind, represented the "larger picture." In frustration, he turned to me and said: "But Ann, the Sahara is not the center of the universe." Deeply embarrassed and blushing, I nonetheless managed to reply: "But it *is* if you happen to live in the middle of it!" This became for me one of those moments when I realized that in essence, what I was trying to do—and what I am still trying to do—was to understand what it might mean to "be Saharan," not to Euro-American scholars, but to those who live and lived *in* the desert and to those who considered themselves to be *of* the desert, whether residing in Nouakchott, Timbuktu, or Rabat. If there is more to this than just geography and climate, and if we agree on the absolute necessity of taking local perceptions seriously, the meaning of being Saharan can and will change over time, influenced by economic, political, and cultural factors. Most important, perhaps, the meaning can and will be contested by different societal groups, divided along lines of ethnicity, generation, gender, and other factors.

I will begin with an overview of ways in which the Sahara has been constructed in European scholarship since the 1970s, from Anthony Hopkins's *Economic History of West Africa* (1973) to Ralph Austen's *Trans-Saharan Africa in World History* (2010). This will situate the remainder of this chapter, in which I propose four lines of inquiry that I believe can be useful for understanding more about how Saharans reflect upon their own identities and worldview, and how the Sahara might be constructed from an internal perspective. These concerns intersect and overlap in many ways, and in spite of the different perspectives, methodologies, and paradigms one might employ to develop them, I see them as belonging to a single discourse. First, there is the Sahara that is created by the exploitation of resources: the networks that emerge to support intersecting systems of production, distribution, and consumption, and the politics that develop to manage and control them. Second, there is the Sahara that is developed by multilayered, versatile labor systems enabling economic exploitation; these go beyond the more easily recognizable groups of slaves and workers, incorporating them into a web of kin, religious, political, and social relations. While they are never totally disconnected from the infrastructure of resources referred to above, they acquire their own social and cultural identities that can, over time, claim power and direction independent of their material economic base and are therefore worthy of analysis in their own terms. Third, there is the negotiated Sahara, in which concepts of power held by major competitors for authority (such as religious *zawāyā* and military *hassān,* and more centralized polities to the north and south) are engaged in ongoing contests that can take many forms. Religion, in this case Islam, is a central but not, as is often thought, controlling factor. And finally, there is the Sahara as experienced and constructed by those officially denied a role in the public social and political structure: the slaves and freed slaves (*harāṭīn*). Although I have long instinctively refused to accept that slavery has been the essence of Saharan history, I have come to appreciate the central role played by such groups in relations that are both productive and reproductive, but that are often only badly captured by the externally derived categories used in much scholarship. Playing off Orlando Patterson's (1982) famous concept of "slavery as social death," I think exploring "slavery as social life" reveals much about the nature of the Sahara in time and space and much about the concept, historical and contemporary, of being Saharan. Overall, I hope to show that we are today in a position both to draw on aspects of these conceptual Saharas and to challenge them with new positioning, new questions, new tools, and new methodologies.

Concepts and Constructions

In the early 1960s, William Zartman's edited volume *Sahara: Bridge or Barrier* (1963) opened a door that invited Africanists to reconsider the role of the Sahara in the history of the continent. The invitation was not taken up until A. G. Hopkins's *An Economic History of West Africa* appeared a decade later (1973). Hopkins's book, although not a common citation in works by Saharanists, put forward several important ideas that brought the notion of the Sahara as a "bridge" rather than as a "barrier" into mainstream African history. Hopkins included a chapter on "external trades" (ibid.: 79–87), one of which was Saharan. The fact that he conceptualized as "external" a Saharan trade that clearly took place *within* the African continent would today be regarded as antithetical to any discussion of either North or West Africa. But this was the early 1970s, and his inclusion of Saharan-generated economic activity, external or not, in his conceptualization of West African history was new. Moreover, Hopkins made two crucial points: caravans moving across this desert were "like slow moving markets"; further, they were instrumental in generating a socially differentiated society within the Sahara.[4] Markets, slow moving or not, were serving customers—in other words, people living in the desert were consumers. And those who serviced these markets by providing transport animals and other services were also Saharans, of different social groups, acting as shepherds, merchants, butchers, cooks, laundry women, and prostitutes, thereby creating and maintaining internal differentiations and hierarchies. Moreover, Hopkins identified one central commodity produced *in* the Sahara—and that was therefore exported *from* it—that facilitated trade *with* the Sahara: salt.

Hopkins framed his discussion in the context of the then-popular Atlantic model, but in applying that model to the Sahara, he began to reveal a quite different entity. The emphasis on "production" and "social development" was explicit; unfortunately it was articulated in a very few pages. But it was enough to support Hopkins's argument that Saharan trade was essentially an extension of the economy of West Africa, and that it played a critical role in West Africa's nineteenth-century economic takeoff. Moreover, he argued that until railroads successfully turned most of West Africa toward the Atlantic, economically the region had mainly looked northward. Finally, borrowing innovatively from a notion key to analyses measuring the impact of the Atlantic trade on West Africa, he applied the model of an "enclave economy" to the Sahara. He argued that the nature of Saharan society, slave- and client-based as it was, meant that it could never grow into a "proper" consumer economy in spite of the Sahara's natural resources. As a result, after the French ending of slavery deprived the region of its main source of labor, the Sahara became marginalized with respect to the new dynamics of colonial West Africa (E. A. McDougall 2010c).

There is much to dispute here; there is also much to remember in terms of the existing state of research on the Sahara at the time Hopkins prepared *An Economic History*. My point in directing attention to this work now is that whether we agree or not with Hopkins's conceptualization, there is no doubt that he had one and, as such, that it deserves recognition. Hopkins's Sahara existed as a site of production, consumption, labor, and transport; social differentiation both supported and emerged as a consequence of economic growth over several centuries. Moreover, the Sahara that developed as a result played a crucial role in the economic growth experienced by West Africa to the south. We can also disagree with Hopkins's assumption of its fate under colonial rule—the railway was not as "powerful" or as "immediate" in its impact on northward-looking West African connections as he then thought (E. A. McDougall 2002a, 2007a). But he kept the Sahara and its economy (if not its people) integral to his analysis of early colonial rule. In the early 1970s, this was both innovative and important.

In the mid-1980s, a conceptually different understanding of the Sahara was explored by Harry T. Norris. Hopkins was a classically trained economic historian bringing the traditional tools of his trade to bear, but Norris was a folklorist and Arabist who applied the fieldwork methodologies and language skills of his training to see and hear a Sahara articulated from within. He had made Saharan writing, poetry, and oral tradition (especially in what is now Mauritania) accessible to non-Saharans in his earlier works (for instance, Norris 1968, 1972). In *Arab Conquest of the Western Sahara* (1986), Norris envisioned a geographic space both larger and more malleable than the title suggests. And his "conquest" was not a physical one of swords or guns, but an internalized one of language, literature, and culture. In fact, in many ways the title was misleading in terms of both space and process. *Arab Conquest* was really about Saharans and how their acceptance, rejection, or negotiation with "Arab" culture became part of their own self-definition. As a "conquest" that was about the adoption and spread of ideas and expression, it followed people's movements and integrated their interest in Arabic language and culture into their political, religious, and economic lives. This adoption moved quixotically through time and space on one level, and on another followed particular clan movements, power-building activities, and commercial developments. Most strikingly, Norris's conception of the Sahara, although it was uniquely rooted in the humanities, mapped in geographical terms almost exactly onto the economic area explored by Hopkins: the Sahara that focused on salt as a key source of wealth and development and on the people who controlled both. Its frontiers were for the most part delineated by the infrastructure set up by the major Saharan rock-salt trades: Tegaza and Tawdeni in the central region focused on Timbuktu (the most familiar site of the Saharan salt industries to Hopkins and other researchers in the late 1960s and early 1970s), but also Ijil in northwest Mauritania, known to Norris because of his earlier work on this region (especially Norris 1968). This system in turn involved the earth-salt sources of the Tishit-Walata escarpment in its larger distribution network, linking the area northward to Morocco.[5] The "overlapping mapping" of culture on economy presented by Norris's *Arab Conquest* was both striking and provocative. Unfortunately, Saharan scholarship did not, at the time, pursue its challenges.

Yet another decade later, a very different Sahara emerged from the pen of James L. A. Webb Jr. His Ph.D. thesis, "Shifting Sands," published in 1995 as *Desert Frontier: Ecological and Economic Change along the Western Sahel* was based on a materialistic analysis and connected human to climatic violence in imagining a Sahara and its peoples as a force aggressively launched upon the Sahel and Sudan in the eighteenth and nineteenth centuries.[6] It added considerable detail to our understanding of the economics underlying trans-Saharan trade, in particular with respect to the regional trade in slaves for horses, shown to be crucial to local economics and politics, and the interaction of regional transactions with the more widely recognized Atlantic slave trade.

Yet the central piece of Webb's innovative analysis lay elsewhere. He argued that the gradual climatic change toward drier conditions that took place in the seventeenth century shaped both the Sahara and its relations with the Sudan: as the desert became drier, people were forced south, where they took advantage of the situation to force more Sudanese Africans into slavery. As a consequence, Webb further argued, a race-based identity for Saharans developed: Saharans became "white" masters of slaves who were "black." Gradually, this last category was expanded to include all of the inhabitants of the Sudan, in a move crucial to the definition and affirmation of Saharan identity. But unlike Hopkins and Norris, whose Saharans encompassed a sense of north and south (albeit in different ways), Webb's Saharans looked only south, thereby implicitly dissociating the Maghreb from Saharan and sub-Saharan Africa. The Sahara that emerges from his analysis remains part of West Africa; indeed, it embellishes Hopkins's notion of a purely economic influence by arguing for a consideration of identity issues as an attendant catalyst. Nonetheless, *Desert Frontier* raises a critical question for Saharan studies: can one comfortably (or otherwise) subsume the image of "southward-moving waves of violence" and its explicitly conflictual racial implications, which is repeated to this day and remains of great symbolic force, into attempts to imagine the Sahara as an integral part of both its northern and southern shores?

Finally, two works of the early 2000s return us firmly to a Sahara built on a "trans-Saharan" model: Ghislaine Lydon's *On Trans-Saharan Trails* (2009) and Ralph Austen's *Trans-Saharan Africa in World History* (2010), although they rely on very different conceptual frameworks. Lydon returns to Hopkins's focus on trade and production, reflecting a wealth of knowledge about both Saharan traders and Saharan production and producers that simply was not available to scholars in the late 1960s and early 1970s. By relying heavily on internally generated texts, both written and oral, she is able to add local perspectives to our understanding of how production and trade occurred and of who was involved, why, and to what effect. Salt remains an important focus, but other agricultural and animal sectors of desert economies are also revealed. Despite the importance of her source materials, it is Lydon's definitions of the space and of the dynamics that shape production and trade that are most significant. She draws on the model of commercial and religious diaspora developed in the context of West Africa in the 1970s.[7] Lydon's diaspora has its heartland in southern Morocco, in the region claimed by the historically economically powerful Tekna tribe, who have long dominated trade throughout the westernmost part of the Sahara. Yet using "diaspora" as a conceptual framing device means that Lydon's "Sahara" is defined by the movements (primarily economic but also cultural and religious) of those who, according to her, considered themselves to be *strangers* to the region. Hopkins might well have had traders like the Tekna in mind when he spoke of the importance of trans-Saharan trade. But his argument that the movement of commercial profits into such "external" hands was financial "leakage" (and therefore part of the limitation of Saharan commerce to classical economic development) is quite a different one from Lydon's, for whom the Tekna are key catalysts for regional as well as international trade. Similarly, while Lydon, like Norris, considers the cultural and religious components involved in expansion into the Sahara, her understanding of the dynamics involved in a "Tekna diaspora" contrasts significantly with Norris's "Arab conquest." For Norris, what was central to the "Arabization" of the Sahara was the agency of local Saharans in drawing from the Arab world what they wanted, according to their own social, economic, and political goals; Lydon's diaspora framework suggests strongly an external agency to the dynamics she observes: the story is primarily one of how strangers integrate and hence about who is—and who is not—truly Saharan.

Lydon's book constitutes a major intervention in Saharan studies. Ralph Austen's *Trans-Saharan Africa* similarly promises to be a challenge for Saharanists, but for very different reasons. In this work, the Sahara's centrality derives from its effective nonexistence. Where Lydon creates a reality of being "trans-Saharan" in her Tekna diaspora, in a masterful historical overview of "the Sahara in history," Austen does the opposite. His goal in this work, the title notwithstanding, is to bring (sub-Saharan) West Africa into the world economy, *through the Sahara.* On the one hand, it is a complete reconceptualization of the Sahara as an intrinsic part of international commerce—certainly as bridge and not as barrier, building on the early historiographical challenges referred to above. But Austen does considerably more. He sees the actual management of trans-Saharan commerce in terms of a global economy, arguing that the former was as important (to that economy) as other commercial systems that we have come to recognize and understand. In short, although not directly referencing Hopkins, he too is using economic theory to "mainstream the marginal," albeit in different ways.[8] Austen is in effect responding to the challenge raised some twenty years ago in Bellagio: to start from the Sahara and to look outward. He treats the Sahara as the means by which West Africa became a full-fledged part of world economic history and as a central contributor to its development. This is hugely important. But this particular reconceptualization of "trans-Saharan" Africa effectively erases the Sahara from view, subsuming its production, its consumption, and its societies to the "larger picture" of global development. While it will certainly bring Africa back into global history (which is the aim of the book, reflecting the series of which it is a part), it will, I believe, further complicate Saharanists' efforts to bring the Sahara back into Africa.[9]

Saharan Salts and Other Resources

In the remainder of this chapter, I will suggest four different approaches to studying the Sahara from the inside out, building on my own work and on the authors discussed so far. First and foremost here is the question of resources and the social networks that develop in order to exploit, control, and distribute them.

When studying sub-Saharan Africa, economic historians usually have little problem creating economic regions, defined by interacting networks generated by the production of marketable (or exchangeable) commodities. In West Africa specifically, it has long been recognized that one of these key commodities is salt—hence my decision to focus my (1976) master's research on one of these regions defined by a combination of sea salts (produced by evaporation), vegetable salts (produced by a combination of burning, boiling, filtering, and drying), and desert salts (produced both underground in exploitable seams and on the surface) (for further discussion, see E. A. McDougall 1990). I realized that the largest trade and, seemingly, the largest profit were generated not by sub-Saharan sea or vegetable salts but by salt mined in the Sahara. Consequently, I moved my doctoral research into the Sahara, specifically to the Ijil salt mine whose functioning I explored from medieval to modern times (E. A. McDougall 1980).

Much to the dismay of my supervisor, Anthony Hopkins, this world of Saharan salts was not determined solely by supply and demand, nor could its workforce be classified easily as slave or wage labor. Nor was it easy to see how the profits from owning or even transporting salt were realized, or how economic profit was necessarily transformed into "power"—another assumption underlying classical economic thought. Instead, I found that salt-trading networks tended to delineate zones in which people's involvement with salt in some way created ties that went beyond the economic. These ties cut across society, establishing client relations between what the French called *fractions de tribus* (tribal fractions). Within these networks, power was negotiated in various ways over time and space; the framework went well beyond the classically assumed opposition between "warriors," "clerics," and "dependents." Relations were at times cemented by religious ties, at others by political or military connections; they were constantly in flux depending on various factors, but their essential focus remained the salt industry. Some workers involved were miners, others raised transport animals (and the animals needed varied, depending on where markets developed), while yet others worked in or with the households of major merchants. Moreover, it was often profits derived from salt that provided the capital for associated developments in the Sahara: various forms of animal husbandry, oasis agriculture, commodity exchanges (involving for instance artisanal crafts and special foodstuffs), investment in the Sahel, and at times even a permanent move south—implicating clients, animals, agriculture, and commerce. Salt, then, played a key role in something much larger and more complex than its immediate regional industry.

Extrapolating from the example of the Ijil salt industry, the exploitation of Saharan resources, whatever they may have been, has tended to involve local, regional, interregional, and what we think of as international trade. It not only generated long-distance commercial caravan routes, but established and maintained vital networks that permeated all aspects of Saharan society. Conversely, to understand fully how Saharan economies functioned, we need to pay attention to the intersection of these networks at any given moment in time. I have argued elsewhere that the long-standing focus on trans-Saharan trade in historical scholarship has blinded us to the interregional trade and local networks that used to be—and in some instances remain—the basis of the economy (E. A. McDougall 2005a). Put another way, transregional trade, with either Europe or Mediterranean North Africa, always had to tie back into regional patterns and connections in order to be sustainable. And these regions, while certainly responsive to outside influences, were Saharan in structure: their modes of production, their credit facilities, their Islamic cultural character, their morality and value systems, and their vital needs.

This, however, does not mean that they were geographically limited to the Sahara. Indeed, most of them linked Saharans to places beyond the desert (as defined in climatic or environmental terms), thereby extending the frontiers of the Sahara into neighboring areas and pulling them, in turn, into the Sahara's economy. This is clearly revealed in the seventeenth-century collection of *nawāzil* (legal cases; sing. *nāzila*) attributed to Muhammad ibn al-Mukhtār ibn La'mish of Shinqit.[10] In these cases, not only is the centrality of salt to commerce made abundantly clear, but the overwhelmingly regional and interregional emphasis of the ostensibly local exchange economy is revealed. Questions are asked by merchants from a geographic area stretching from southwestern Morocco via the Tafilalt near what is now the Moroccan border with Algeria, to Timbuktu and farther east. This documentation suggests that in addition to looking at caravan routes and market networks, there may be another way to conceptualize economic regions in the Saharan context—namely, as areas delineated by the collective recognition among merchants of a particular religious authority with respect to "proper," ethical commercial practices (E. A. McDougall 2006b).

Another key factor, one that is often overlooked, is the form of transport involved. It was always difficult for one string of camels to traverse the often extremely different terrains that together make up what we all too frequently tend to imagine as a unified Saharan ecosystem. Regional variations played their part in determining routes and trans-shipment points where new animals were of necessity taken on: camels with different abilities (to handle dunes, rocks, and changing forage situations), or even different animals altogether (e.g., oxen or donkeys, to move into regions inappropriate for camel use). As a result, gaining access to suitable animals, water, and pasture during and between the various stages of long-distance exchange became key negotiating issues—key "costs," if we borrow a term favored by economic historians. Such processes drew in "politicians" (those with the power to demand payments), "soldiers" (those with the ability to enforce agreements), and "workers" (those who could provide or withhold transport): a whole economic subsystem, key to shaping local communities and economies but often overlooked in the broader analyses of trans-Saharan commerce discussed above (e.g., E. A. McDougall 1980; J. L. A. Webb 1995; Lydon 2009). In contemporary times, similar reflections apply to the availability of trucks, repair stations, spare parts, and gasoline, and to the ability to provide safe passage and deal with the security forces or other local organizations keen to "tax"—officially or unofficially—contemporary Saharan trade (see also the relevant articles in E. A. McDougall, ed., 2007; and Brachet, Oudada, and Scheele this volume).

My final points in this section derive from an analysis of commercial registers produced by trading families in southern Morocco, in particular the Bayruk family. While Lydon's work on these documents is more extensive than my own, I analyzed many of the same commercial registers.[11] Lydon used her research to draw the trading diaspora model into and across the Sahara. I, on the other hand, would argue that the Bayruk did not consider the family to constitute a diaspora but rather thought of itself as an inherently open, family-based network—with "family" used in the broadest possible sense, including many not directly related by blood. Ultimately, it was the goods traded, whether they were produced locally or not, rather than the people involved, that determined where the Bayruk "set up house." In other words: "the market" determined where they acquired wives, left sisters, and installed *harātīn* to support the network.[12] Wherever that was, their relatives and *harātīn* rooted their presence and ultimately their identity. In this way, they could easily extend or contract the space in which they operated—not only along the more commonly observed north-south trajectory, but also in one reaching farther east and south, at times as far as Niger and Mali—without ever experiencing a radical discontinuity. To my mind, the Bayruk did not see themselves as strangers to the Sahara.

After examining in some detail the contents of these commercial registers, I concluded that when we look at them as entities, as actual books, and when we consider the range of issues regarded by their owners as significant enough to be recorded, we can discern a much broader and more diversified notion of what constitutes "commerce" than has been suggested by our habitual focus on routes, goods, prices, profits, and losses. These registers show the degree to which the Bayruk family was involved in local affairs; the intermingling of social, kin, and commercial enterprises; and the absence of distinction between commercial and political issues. In the registers, all these matters are recorded together—and in much the same way. Similarly, there is an obvious lack of distinction between trans-Saharan matters and those that pertain to "home," the oasis town of Goulimine in southern Morocco. This suggests a much closer integration of economic activities than perhaps we have been willing to allow. Moreover, the registers show that capital and profit moved between what we would normally regard as completely separate economic spheres (local, regional, international) in a very efficient way: quite simply, from the perspective of the Bayruk, they were neither "separate" nor "spheres" at all. Last, while not all entries indicated where they were written or where goods given on credit were meant to be sold, many did. People's names often incorporated a reference to their town of origin; even a tribal signifier was an indication of regional affiliation. This allows us to map the region within which the Bayruk were active, showing that their commerce did not operate only to the north (Goulimine) and the south (Timbuktu) of the Sahara, but also *within* it. Some activity was centered on the Timbuktu region and supports our more traditional understanding of trans-Saharan commerce; however, looked at as a whole, the collection of registers suggests a much more diversified concept of trading *in* the Sahara, with intraregional and transregional activities closely interdependent and interlinked. Hence, in their nature and vision, these registers are "Saharan," or rather, the reflection of a particular way of living the Sahara, as experienced and recorded by one major commercial family in the nineteenth century (E. A. McDougall 2005a; see also Lydon 2005).

Labor Systems

It can certainly be argued that labor systems are a simple outcome of economic activity and that hence seeking a different perspective on local conceptions of being Saharan through their analysis is redundant. Yet I think that they provide their own way into the questions of identity that interest us here because they cannot be fully understood in economic terms. In a sense, this pulls us back to the debate, ripe in the mid-1970s, between economic historians and economic anthropologists, between Hopkins's (1973) "economic man" and Polanyi's (1944) "embedded economy."[13] Saharans have drawn on a range of signifiers to identify social groups and then used them in a variety of ways at different moments in time to accomplish what we would recognize as economic goals. "Ethnicity," which could be determined by origin, by occupation, by color, by religion, and probably by many other criteria, in turn has been exploited to assign (or, alternatively, to claim) rights to particular work. So, too, age and gender. For a long time scholars assumed that these groups had emerged definitively in the seventeenth century, with neatly divided tasks and responsibilities, organized according to a stable hierarchy, with slaves, freed people, tribute-paying "vassals," "nobles," and specialized castes of metalworkers and *griots,* or "bards" (E. A. McDougall 2007b; see also J. L. A. Webb 1995). There is a fascinating chart in Charles Stewart's seminal *Islam and Social Order in Mauritania* (1973) in which he presents such a schema of social hierarchy—a pyramid divided vertically into *hassān* and *zawāyā* ("warrior" and "religious" specialists, respectively), then horizontally into the various hierarchical social categories. But he adds a wavy line which confuses this neat schema totally because it suggests that in one place a *hartāni* might be socially superior to a slave, in another, the reverse.

A Moroccan colleague to this day can make no sense of the diagram, so ingrained is the notion of a stable social organization that is fixed in the labor it provides to society that it shapes even very attuned scholarly thought. Yet as Stewart rightly indicates, any system that we—or local power-holders—might represent as immutable is specific to time and place, fluid in its delineations, and inherently context-bound. Today, Stewart's diagram is seldom discussed, yet the more I think about it, the more I am convinced that it highlights a key concern of being Saharan. The issue of the *harātīn* is perhaps most revealing in this sense. During the colonial era, *harātīn* were seen by both Saharans and the French as key to economic development. The French portrayed them as a social class with slave origins (some recent, some ancient), destined to become "the new working class"; Saharan masters, on the other hand, understood them to be extensions of their own families, wealth, and influence: *harātīn* had always done most of the work, especially as agricultural laborers. Consequently, when the French started to educate them and to pay them wages, from Saharan families' point of view, this was a way of increasing the value of their own patrimony. Where colonial authorities thought of educated, salaried *harātīn* as "revolutionary," masters saw them strengthening traditional Saharan social structures and values. If somebody had to become French, let it be the *harātīn*—as long as they continued to work (E. A. McDougall 2007b).[14]

Alongside imaginings of social order, Stewart's *Islam and Social Order* was very much about the evolution of a labor system rooted in, justified by, and built upon evolving eighteenth- and nineteenth-century understandings of the role of the *zawāyā,* in the double meaning of the word: both as clerical clans and communities and as the physical places in which Islam was taught, studied, and implemented by scholars and students. Whereas Stewart was uniquely concerned with southwestern Mauritania in the nineteenth century, I applied his ideas to an earlier period and a larger geographic area, extending from the Mauritanian Adrar across the Tagant to the Malian Azawad. I argued for a similar evolution in the practice of religion that simultaneously created new labor systems (e.g., E. A. McDougall 1985, 1986). Contemporaneous research carried out elsewhere in the Sahara by

Glen McLaughlin (1997), David Gutelius (2001, 2002), and James L. A. Webb Jr. (1995) revealed similar dynamics. The study of Saharan labor systems cannot be separated from that of changing perceptions and practices of religion. Otherwise put, the evolution of these systems cannot be explained in economic terms only, however tempting such an explanation may be. Long-standing scholarly disagreements about the labor used to exploit Saharan salts can stand as an example here. For Paul Lovejoy (1986), the Saharan salt industry was always synonymous with slave labor. Knut Vikør (1982, 1999), on the other hand, found a more complex social formation underlying the mining of salt in Kawar, as did I at Ijil and Tishit (E. A. McDougall 1980, 1990, 2004). These different perspectives are perhaps best explained by asking questions about the broader social systems that supplied labor to such key resources. These would move us beyond strict dichotomies of slave-versus-wage labor and the common teleology of the inevitable evolution of one to the other (in turn, harking back to Hopkins's "logical" assumption that a lack of slaves led to the decline of Saharan industry). This approach might also help us understand the adaptability of Saharan labor systems to the changing realities of the twentieth and twenty-first centuries, including their ability to expand and contract in places beyond the boundaries of the (geographical) Sahara itself.

The Negotiated Sahara

As seen above, there are many negotiated Saharas. To cite but one example, some years ago, in collaboration with Mohamed Lahbib Nouhi, I built on the economic data presented in my earlier work to look at how religious groups like the Kunta were using material wealth/resources—or access to it—to negotiate "real" power with their *hassān* (warrior) and Tuareg neighbors (E. A. McDougall and Nouhi 1996). I had for some time been suspicious of the stylized image of a Saharan "segmentary society."[15] We further explored this idea of negotiating power, looking at how the Sahara as a whole was shaped through changing *zawāyā* definitions of power and authority. Nouhi's subsequent doctoral research asked how one such group, the Kunta, was drawing on traditional Islamic rhetoric to redefine the concept of "sainthood" and ultimately creating an authority comparable to the political power claimed by its secular warrior neighbors (Nouhi 2009). Raymond Taylor, in his earlier work on southwestern, Senegal-bordering Mauritania (1995, 1996), asked similar questions. He showed how the powerful *zawāyā* of Boutilimit, themselves once "students" of the very Kunta family Nouhi discusses, drew on the same tradition of Islamic rhetoric to redefine their identity. In this instance, the *zawāyā* were successful in challenging local *hassān* as well as the European competitors whose commercial and political presence was becoming increasingly threatening.

A similar, more flexible approach can also illuminate the relationship between various Saharan groups and their more powerful northern neighbor, the sultanate of Morocco. With some legitimacy, the Moroccan-Saharan relationship is usually characterized principally in terms of conflict—slave raiding and of course the infamous conquest of Timbuktu in 1591 that led to the demise of the Songhay empire. However, both before and after the conquest, alternative vantage points reveal ongoing negotiations between the sultan and various Saharan groups. If instead of seeing the conquest as a purely political attempt to destroy a competitive empire and gain control of lucrative trans-Saharan trade routes, we replace it with a vision of a larger chronological and geographic framework, the "conquest" becomes both more and less of a historical catalyst. Histories, both written and oral, indicate ongoing Moroccan involvement in the Sahara. In the century preceding 1591, successive Moroccan sultans made several attempts to increase their influence in the Sahara, which was regarded as an important region of the empire. Numerous efforts were made to benefit from not only the Tegaza salt mine north of Timbuktu, but also from Ijil, situated much farther to the west (E. A. McDougall 1994–1995). Late seventeenth-century letters from the sultan to his son spelled out clearly the father's awareness of the value of the Saharan people and resources, in particular the salt of Tegaza, to the empire as a whole. In these letters, the sultan mentioned his reliance on Saharan allies, and chastised his son for failing to collect salt taxes. By the mid- to late eighteenth century, it is clear that the sultan's interests in the region remained strong; moreover, his authority was recognized as legitimate by at least some important Saharans. In correspondence with him, the famous Kunta *shaykh* Sidi al-Mukhtar al-Kunti claimed that the Kunta should be exempt from paying salt taxes not because the sultan had no right to levy them in the first place, but because as a respected family of venerated saints, the Kunta should answer to no secular authority, such as Moroccan representatives, or *qā'id*s. During this same historical moment (purportedly ca. 1766–1767), a western branch of the Kunta family claimed ownership of the Ijil mine—but, reportedly, only after seeking approval from the Moroccan sultan (E. A. McDougall 2006b).

Moroccan interests in the Sahara were twofold: the sultan gazed possessively toward Ijil and its commercial center of Shinqit, on the one hand, and toward Tegaza (and later Tawdeni) and Timbuktu, on the other. The mines were geographically distant, but the regions to which they gave economic shape were an integrated part of the Moroccan empire. In the eighteenth century, this situation was accentuated politically when the Kunta emerged in each area as leading power holders. But the debate between Sidi al-Mukhtar and the sultan was conducted on a different plane. It was not only Sidi al-Mukhtar who argued on the basis of his saintly prerogatives. The sultan's claims to Saharan resources only partially rested on his ability to back them up with military might. Rather, his essential argument was that he was the rightful Islamic ruler of the area, in whose name prayers were to be said, and whose spiritual legitimacy ought to be recognized by all Saharans. In other words, he claimed both a moral and a military right to the Sahara. In a sense, then, this negotiation over who would control Saharan Islamic culture (not to mention Saharan material resources) was not really one between different political entities, but a struggle over who would *define* Saharan identity, most especially its spiritual identity (E. A. McDougall 2006b).

There are other vantage points to develop here, including looking toward the Sahel and the kinds of alliances that were formed in the particularly dynamic nineteenth century. This perspective of course opens the door to incorporating the role of Europeans, in terms of competing political economies that were in large part negotiated by Saharan clerics and warriors (Taylor was essentially making this point in his 1996 doctoral thesis). But as a final point in this section, I would like to suggest that exploring the roles of evolving *tarīqas*, or religious brotherhoods, which are often isolated and treated solely as part of the study of Islam rather than as part of a broader socioeconomic and historical approach, would be fruitful. Much of this work has already been done for the Qadiriyya, the Nasiriyya, the Tijaniyya, and various sub-branches of each.[16] However, to date, there has been no comparative study, nor one that gives a comprehensive overview of their emergence and development from the eighteenth to the twenty-first centuries. Such a study would allow us to understand the emergence of yet another Sahara, shaped by the specific spiritual and socioeconomic allegiances they represented.[17]

Slavery as Social Life

Finally, let me turn to what may seem an overly specific topic to usefully qualify as a conduit to understanding Saharans and the Sahara: slavery, or, put another way, categories of people not normally included in the list of "noble" Saharans. Although the study of slavery in Africa and of something sometimes called "Islamic slavery" overlap in the Sahara, this perspective on Saharan identity is remarkably underdeveloped. While we find Saharan chapters here and there in various collections on slavery, they are supposed to be read through the paradigm established for the study as a whole (e.g., E. A. McDougall 1989, 2006a). It is indeed to be celebrated that the Sahara is making such contributions, but what is missing is the effort to see in what ways Saharan studies might challenge or reshape some of the extant paradigms themselves, in the same way that slavery as an institution has shaped Saharan society as a whole (E. A. McDougall 2002b). To give but one example, the fattening of women (*gavage*, as the French termed it) is a cultural practice that cuts across the divide between Arabic- and Tamasheq-speakers (see especially Popenoe 2004 for a comparative scenario among Kunta Arabs in northern Niger). As a result, at least in the past, slave concubines played a critical role in physically reproducing society, giving birth both to slave and free children, depending on the father's status. Moreover, slave women, being more physically fit and healthy than their obese mistresses, were often wet nurses for the whole family and their friends and neighbors. Hence, relations of milk kinship—construed to be almost analogous to those of blood relations—in turn not only knitted non-blood communities together, but also created irreversible links across class and race lines, creating something specifically "Saharan" (E. A. McDougall 1989, 2010b). My initial impression of the Saharan society in which I researched was that the *harāṭīn* were more significant both historically and in contemporary developments than "slaves" per se. Since then, I have realized that gender is a key factor here, and that to underestimate the various roles played by female slaves in both physical and cultural reproduction would be a mistake. Indeed, this was made abundantly clear by Mauritanian masters during the colonial era, when they agreed to free male slaves but fought long and hard to retain access to female slaves because the women were capable of producing children, both slave and free (E. A. McDougall 1989).

Yet the *harāṭīn* are equally central to understanding Saharan identity. Although all freed slaves in the Sahara are *harāṭīn,* not all *harāṭīn* are necessarily freed slaves. This differentiation at first appeared to be regional: *harāṭīn* in the desert-edge region of Morocco often said that they descended from indigenous sedentary cultivators, whereas Mauritanians almost universally claimed freed-slave status. But this situation seems to be changing now. At least in Mauritania, *harāṭīn* are beginning to draw on genealogies that ultimately refer to "indigenous cultivators," while simultaneously trying to embrace slaves and freed slaves for a very real political purpose (E. A. McDougall 2010a).[18] This raises some interesting questions about the role this process will play in the ongoing democratization of different parts of the Sahara (see also Leservoisier this volume). That said, perhaps the most important period in the history of the *harāṭīn* (and, to some extent, slaves as well) was the colonial era. My research on an extended *harāṭīnī* family suggests that the Saharan system of encouraging slave reproduction, which in turn allowed for growth in both slave and free populations, ultimately allowed Saharan society to expand so that it was able to benefit from various changes and developments introduced by the colonial economy. Slavery, narrowly defined, produced workers and child-bearers; in comparison, the *harāṭīn* system was much more complicated. It created freed slaves, as distinct from free persons, who remained in various kinds of relationships with former masters; freeing male slaves was thus a way of expanding "normal" families—hence the masters' relatively easy agreement to colonial regulations. Male *harātīn* preferred *hartāniyyāt,* or so I was told, but it seems that they often married slave women from the immediate family of their former master—or from a relation or an ally. This meant in theory that their children still belonged to the master, but as that master was also their former master and now like kin, this was less of a problem than one might think. And, according to my case study, the female slaves were often freed at some point following their marriages. Furthermore, slaves who became *harātīn* could and did purchase slaves themselves. Hence, they could become masters and then former masters as they freed their own slaves. As a result, over time and especially in the colonial period, *harātīn* became a large and increasingly significant component of Saharan society. Their development as a social, economic, and increasingly political class is key to understanding the evolution of Saharan society more generally (E. A. McDougall 2005b).

On Being "Saharan": Pathways to Understanding

Much as I was intrigued by the use of the term "Saharan" in the Nouakchott of the 1980s, in the years following the Bellagio conference, it gradually became clear to me that as a historian, I needed to understand what this term might have meant to a nineteenth-century trader living in Shinqit, an early twentieth-century merchant living in Atar, or a mid-twentieth-century former slave, male or female, living in a Mauritanian household. And I needed to see how this reality of "being Saharan" had evolved, dynamically, over time. Indeed, in reappraising my earlier works, I realized that this question had perhaps always been the driving force behind my interests. I thus undertook more research that overtly tried to understand how Saharans saw themselves and their world, and that relied on interviews to give perspective and direction to my reading of written texts and to raise the fundamental questions I needed to be asking. Many years later, I am not sure that I am any closer to answers. But I am convinced that to study the Sahara is to study a dynamic historical construct—it is as much a study in identity creation as that of any given people or group. Put another way, I think the Sahara of our "Saharan studies" can only be defined properly by focusing on the people who give meaning to "being Saharan." And that meaning will never be stable, never free from challenge, and never purely internal or external in construction because, as the Sahara has always been, it remains today very much part of an international, if not global, nexus. Saharans define themselves in terms of various understandings of both their immediate and the more distant worlds brought to them by TV, the internet, and air travel. And "we" of such distant worlds, like our predecessors, continue to interact with their immediate lives by writing about them, by influencing policy decisions, and sometimes by changing the material profile of the Sahara itself such that it has an impact on how people can relate to it and even live in it. In this sense, I wonder how different we really are from the early travelers whose observations often informed European opinion and actions vis-à-vis the African continent. Or from the colonial administrators who interpreted Saharans for European policy makers—their social customs, their religions, and their politics. Or, indeed, from the contemporary development workers whose "Saharans" are viewed through the prism of input-output, production figures, and "success stories." Willingly or not, Saharans have taken these ideas, images, and policies and have digested, distorted, and appropriated them into their own experiences and identity definitions, to the point where no history of the Sahara could possibly ignore this intimate relation between the internal and the external. This process will continue, with and through our own work. If there is to be a difference in the outcome, perhaps it will lie in our increased ability to listen, to give greater currency to the issues thought to be important by Saharans themselves, to give greater leeway in establishing the parameters of scholarly discourse such that there is genuine room for Saharan voices and experiences, to accept greater responsibility for the role we play in people's lives as we seek to study them, and to adjust our academic expectations and paradigms accordingly.

NOTES

1. The event was sponsored by the Centre Culturel Français; all the students were francophone.

2. For a masterful treatment of questions of identity in Walata, see Cleaveland (1998, 2002).

3. The Bellagio workshop resulted in a collection edited by Elizabeth Savage (1992a).

4. On slow-moving markets, the role of salt, and Hopkins's contribution to Saharan history, see the more detailed discussion in E. A. McDougall (2010c).

5. It was this same Ijil network that had attracted my earlier thesis research (1976–1980) and continued to shape my work in the early 1980s.

6. For a fuller discussion of this work in the context of Saharan studies at the time, see E. A. McDougall (1998).

7. For the pioneers in this approach, see Cohen (1971), Meillassoux (1971), Curtin (1975), Sanneh (1979), and Lovejoy (1980).

8. While the book, essentially a textbook, does not use footnotes, it is still surprising that there is not even a nod to Hopkins.

9. I thank Ralph Austen for making available to me a penultimate manuscript; whatever the work's goal with respect to world history, there is no question that Austen has been concerned with Saharan economic and cultural realities for many years. His contributions to this field are seminal.

10. I am grateful to Mohamed Lahbib Nouhi for acquiring the microfilm, translating the relevant sections, and working through a final translation and analysis of them with me.

11. I wish to acknowledge the generous support of the University of Alberta, in the form of several travel, research, and conference grants, and especially the support of the Social Sciences and Humanities Research Council of Canada, whose standard research grant (1993–1996) made this particular research possible.

12. Furthermore, they invariably married locally, if possible almost immediately after establishing themselves; this allowed them to establish local credentials and the right to purchase land and other forms of property. The frequency of the practice reinforces my contention that they saw themselves—and were seen by others—as linked by a common identity to their host populations, an identity that we may perhaps gloss as "Saharan."

13. It was spurred by the publication of Hopkins's *An Economic History* (1973). See especially George Dalton's (1976) review and Hopkins's (1976) reply.

14. *Harātīn* also became masters—purchasing, exploiting, and eventually even freeing their own slaves (see E. A. McDougall 1989).

15. This was thanks in large part to correspondence with Charles Stewart who, in the early stages of my doctoral research, suggested that I not follow his use of this model. Since then, the idea has been largely rejected (see, for example, Cleaveland 1998).

16. See, for instance, Batran (2001), Gutelius (2001), and Triaud and Robinson (2000), respectively.

17. Nouhi's (2009) doctoral thesis takes this approach for the eighteenth and nineteenth centuries; Stewart (1973) pioneered the concept for a more limited region (the Gebla) in the nineteenth century. My work overall treads an in-between line as an economic historian with an appreciation for Islamic studies, attempting to point future work in an exciting and useful direction but lacking the Islamic and Arabic skills necessary to undertake it myself.

18. The question of *harātīn* identity, including historical perspectives and contemporary political significance, forms the core of a current research project I am carrying out with Abdel Wedoud Ould Cheikh. It involves comparing *harātīn* in Saharan Mauritania and in the southern, desert-edge region of Morocco and is engaging local scholars in each region as much as possible. We are grateful to the Social Sciences and Humanities Research Council of Canada, standard grants (interdisciplinary studies) division, for funding this four-year endeavor.

SAHARAN TRADE IN CLASSICAL ANTIQUITY

Katia Schörle

In classical antiquity, the Sahara (whether called *deserta* or *solitudines Africae* in Latin, or *eremoi* in Greek; Desanges 1999a: 239) was constructed by Greek and Roman writers alike as a place of distinctive otherness. Exotic, empty, wild, or peopled by bizarre creatures, it served to represent the antithesis of the known civilized world (Liverani 2000a: 498; J. McDougall this volume). Yet, much like the classical Mediterranean as described by Horden and Purcell in *The Corrupting Sea* (2000), the Sahara is perhaps best imagined as constituted by shifting interactions, related microcosms, and overlapping networks than by rigid patterns: a network of hubs, central nodes around which activities revolved and which were involved in multidirectional exchange (Wilson 2009). Settled at the edges of the Sahara or in oases—islands in the Saharan sea—Saharan populations relied and throve on interactions with their neighbors (Crawley Quinn 2009). This chapter's main emphasis is on the Libyan Sahara between the sixth century BC and the sixth century AD, a period that corresponds to the rise and fall of the Garamantian civilization and roughly to the classical Greek and Roman period in the Mediterranean.[1] The Garamantian kingdom (ca. 500 BC–AD 650), whose territories were centered on the oasis belts in the Fezzan region in southwestern Libya, communicated with both North Africa and sub-Saharan regions. The Fezzan is one of the few areas in the Sahara to have received much archaeological attention, and findings strongly suggest that it constituted a powerful center of trading activity within the Sahara (Mattingly 2003, 2007, 2010). Although there has been some past debate over the exact nature of these long-distance trading networks (see, for instance, Law 1967; Swanson 1975), more recent archaeological work in the Fezzan by both Italian and British teams dispels any doubt about their existence (Mattingly 2003, 2007, 2010; Liverani 2005). Goods from the Mediterranean or (to a lesser extent) from sub-Saharan Africa are found in burial sites associated with Garamantian settlements. These trading activities across various parts of the Sahara varied over time and

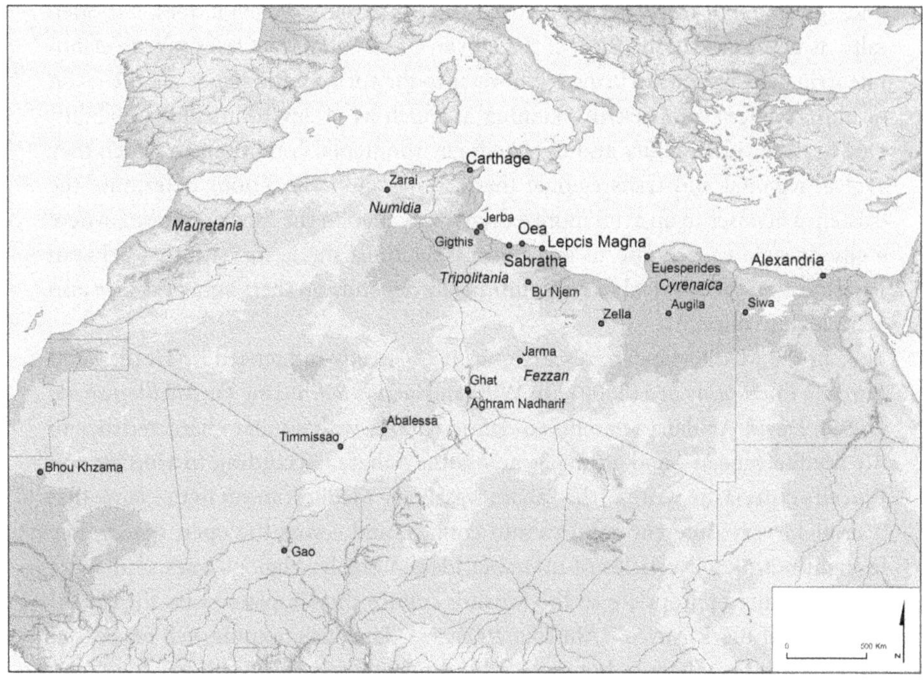

Map 3.1. The Sahara in classical antiquity. K. Schörle 2010

space, both in the intensity of exchange and in the routes taken, showing a pattern that is much more varied and flexible than we might expect.

Rethinking the Sahara

Like the Mediterranean, the Sahara is best approached as an area of broad geographical connectivity. Such a framework makes it possible to understand far-reaching phenomena which previous historical frameworks have been unable to explain: the archaeological find of *Musa* genus banana phytoliths (microscopic silica plant bodies) in West Africa dating to the sixth century BC (Mbida et al. 2005) only makes sense within a wider context of complex trading relations that linked Africa to the Indian Ocean (Mitchell 2005: 106–108). Multidisciplinary and long-term historical approaches therefore allow us to affirm that, on the African continent as elsewhere, individual localities were connected on a large scale, most often via the intermediary of prominent trading nodes.[2] In the Sahara, these networks and hubs are remarkable for their fragility and artificiality. Water is abundant underground, but rarely occurs naturally on the surface.[3] When it does, it is often salty, as in the case of the lakes of the Libyan Great Sand Sea. Oases rely on elaborate irrigation systems to bring fresh water to the surface, and hence are the result of human intent and careful planning as much as of environmental suitability. Due to their vulnerability and the harsh environmental conditions in which they evolve, regional and transregional interactions and connections determine the existence of oases in an even more extreme way than in the Mediterranean, where a city or state can choose to enter into isolationist mode in ways that Saharan oases cannot: the survival of oases ultimately depends on their networks (see also Scheele this volume).

In the Mediterranean, research has been greatly influenced by Horden and Purcell's *Corrupting Sea* (2000).[4] In William Harris's *Rethinking the Mediterranean* (2005), David Abulafia attempts to define regions with similar characteristics to the Mediterranean—and stumbles across the Sahara. According to Horden and Purcell's criteria, he writes, "the Sahara was a true Mediterranean in the sense that it brought very different cultures into contact, and across the open spaces they brought not merely articles of trade but ideas, notably religious ones, and styles of architecture appropriate to the Muslim culture they implanted on the northern edges of Black Africa" (Abulafia 2005: 75). Abulafia's point is well made (but see Horden this volume), but despite his tendency (also shared by Lydon 2009) to ascribe trans-Saharan connections to Islamic endeavors, commercial connectivity in the Sahara clearly predates the Islamic period; this bias must partially be attributed to a lingering reluctance to engage with, or lack of awareness of, the transregional patterns that emerged earlier.[5] Since 2000, the research led by David Mattingly and published in three volumes as *The Archaeology of Fazzān* (2003, 2007, 2010) has provided a groundbreaking and thorough overview of the Fezzan and of the Garamantes. The current Desert Migration Project continues to investigate the Garamantian civilization through the analysis of burial contents, which include items such as Roman ceramics (fineware, coarseware, cooking pots), amphorae (mainly used for liquids such as wine, oil, and *garum*, or fish sauce, but which could also contain dried or salted goods), and beads or glass from the Roman Mediterranean (such as vessels, fruit bowls, drinking cups) (Mattingly, Lahr, and Wilson 2009).

Most of the Garamantian traffic passing through North Africa toward the Mediterranean and Rome was funneled toward the western coast of Libya and the southern tip of Tunisia to places such as Gigthis, Sabratha, Oea (modern Tripoli), and Lepcis Magna.[6] The island of Djerba, which in the first century AD was connected by a bridge to the mainland, became another strategic terminus of the long-distance overland routes (Frachetti 2009: 57). The importance of these routes is confirmed by the presence of North African amphorae in burial sites in the Fezzan. The majority of these are from Tripolitania; some unusual ones, such as the late Roman Keay 62, are particularly big.[7] The fact that the late Roman Keay 62 amphora is found both in burials and in settlements in the Fezzan (Mattingly et al. 2010: 122) suggests that the long-distance trade with Roman North Africa continued to flourish into the fifth and sixth centuries, despite a contraction from the mid-Roman period on (second–fourth centuries AD). Of those coastal termini, Sabratha and Lepcis are the only cities that have received considerable archaeological attention. Oea, which received support from the Garamantes—perhaps because of trading ties—during a conflict with Lepcis Magna over territorial boundaries in AD 68–69,[8] is overlain by modern Tripoli, and has so far been understudied. A review of the available inscriptions of Roman Tripolitania gives a sense of the paucity of information we have concerning Oea: there are only 36 inscriptions, compared to 609 recorded for Lepcis and 230 for Sabratha. Moreover, some of these are now lost, and others are from funerary contexts located outside Oea itself. This issue of investigating the terminal cities of the Saharan trade is further complicated since, as suggested by Fentress (2007), we ought to be investigating archaeologically the large empty spaces (such as the one suggested for Gigthis) *outside* North African towns for the periodic marketplaces where trans-Saharan goods would have been bought and sold.

A few major issues still affect our understanding of Saharan trade in antiquity, including gaps in areas covered by archaeological work, and geographic specialization combined with scarce communications between specialists working on either side of the Sahara. Above all, international archaeological research in Algeria, in other Saharan regions, and along the North African coastline is much needed. The Zaraï tariff, for example, which was found some fifty kilometers southeast of Sétif in Algeria, within the confines of "two large bioclimatic entities of complementary economies" (Trousset 2005: 355), namely the Tell and the pre-desert, gives us an idea of the kind of trade that occurred in this area in Roman times. This list of internal custom duties from the early third century AD details the various goods passing through this point, such as sponges; *garum* and wine carried in amphorae; hides and textiles; figs, nuts, and other goods. It also gives the prices of animals. Although a local rather than a frontier taxation document (see Trousset 2005), it indicates to some extent the movement of trade in the pre-desert zone: foodstuffs such as Roman wine or *garum* were probably going southward into the Sahara; and hides and textiles were probably traveling north.[9]

While the tariff remains a key epigraphic document concerning taxes in the Roman world and the movement of goods, the archaeological evidence to substantiate trade via Algeria in antiquity is still lacking. To date, two pieces of archaeological evidence imply the potential for Saharan trading connections: the presence of underground canals (*fagāgīr,* sing. *faggāra,* elsewhere known as *qanāt*) in the greater Touat in southwestern Algeria, and imported goods found in the tomb of Tin Hinan in the Ahaggar mountains, in Algeria's extreme south near contemporary Tamanrasset. *Fagāgīr,* based on technology that was clearly imported into the region from farther east, channel water from higher-lying underground water tables to lower-lying settlements. Along with the *fagāgīr* in the Garamantian heartland of the Fezzan, the oases of the Touat, Gourara, and Tidikelt in the Algerian Sahara contain the highest concentration of *fagāgīr* in North Africa (Wilson 2006: 213). The suggestion that *faggāra* technologies spread in the early to middle years of the first millennium AD from the Fezzan to the Algerian oases is potentially interesting, yet so far these areas remain to be archaeologically explored and fully documented, and the hope is that urban expansion has not yet fully obscured or destroyed the evidence (Wilson and Mattingly 2003: 42). Nonetheless, if similar in date to the Garamantian ones, the sheer quantity of *fagāgīr* in the Algerian Sahara points to the existence of another major Saharan hub capable of maintaining a substantial population and affording yet another crucial stop for any long-distance commerce toward the Niger bend or the gold-producing areas of the western tip of Africa, while the commerce bound for Lake Chad presumably proceeded southward via the Ghat oases in contemporary Libya. The striking continuity of weights and measures remains an argument for trans-Saharan trade along these routes: it has been suggested that the *mithqāl,* the Arabic gold weight used in Saharan commerce, may have been based on the Roman standard, thereby indicating continuity with the late Roman gold trade with sub-Saharan Africa (Garrard 1982).

The tomb of Tin Hinan at Abalessa in the Ahaggar, at a distance of more than 1,500 kilometers from the Mediterranean coast, is another indicator of trade and contact but is so far not well contextualized within the wider patterns of connections and trading in this particular section of the Sahara; this will not change until further archaeological research is carried out in southern Algeria. This tomb, found together with twelve lesser surrounding tumuli (burial mounds) containing thirty individuals altogether, held the remains of a woman whose rich burial eventually associated her with a putative queen called Tin Hinan from the Tafilalet, according to local traditions.[10] The burial site has a *terminus post quem* of AD 308–324, provided by a coin imprint on gold leaf, and contained various Roman goods, gold and silver bracelets, a Roman oil lamp, and fragments of glassware (Baistrocchi 1989: 94), pointing to long-distance trading connections with the Roman world and to the penetration of goods far into what is now southern Algeria. Several hypotheses have been proposed concerning the origins of the inhumed person and the nature of the tomb, including that it was part of a Roman outpost fort (which it was not), or the tomb of a traveler from northern areas who was marginal to the Roman empire (for a summary of these arguments, ibid.: 94, 98). However, the deceased woman was wearing a red leather garment, as well as one or several bead necklaces (ibid.: 92), which would rather point to an origin from outside the Roman empire. Her dress is also strikingly close to Garamantian traditional wear, as is her taste for red ochre (Mattingly 2003: 227), while the funerary assemblage, though richer in precious metals than most Garamantian tombs, shows some cultural affinities with tombs in the Fezzan.[11] Hence, the evidence so far may suggest another node of Saharan connections situated in the Ahaggar mountains. At Timmissao, which is 220 kilometers southwest of Abalessa, the presence of Roman coins (Mauny 1956) and a Latin inscription mentioning a water point (*lacus*) further advances the hypothesis that a route to the Adrar des Iforas and Gao was perhaps known in classical antiquity (Rebuffat 2004: 243, 253–257).

Fragile Environments and Adaptive Ecologies

In *The Corrupting Sea* (2000), Horden and Purcell describe ecological instability and frequent crises as key drivers to the creation of networks of exchange, the only way in which some degree of security could be achieved. A similar ecological instability has characterized the Sahara ever since it assumed its current state and climatic conditions, more or less 5,000 years ago. On the basis of research in the Wadi Tanezzuft, south of the Fezzan, on cypress (*Cupressus dupreziana*) tree rings, which serve as indicators of annual rainfall, Cremaschi, Pelfini, and Santili (2006) identify pronounced wetter periods with short dry phases from ca. 1570 BC on, and a final onset of hyper-arid conditions only occurring in ca. AD 450. If this evidence can be extrapolated more widely to the Fezzan, then we can expect it to have affected the Garamantes: the onset of hyper-arid conditions in particular coincides with the collapse of their civilization (Liverani 2003; Cremaschi, Pelfini, and Santili 2006). Whether the landscape farther north was similarly affected is debatable: the use and abandonment of farms in the Libyan pre-desert, as identified by the UNESCO Libyan Valleys Survey, cannot be simply attributed to climatic changes,[12] just as the final collapse of the Garamantian center may have reasons beyond climatic determinism.[13] The solution probably has to be sought in the complex ecological interplay of climate and wider historical trends. All life in the Sahara is subject to the availability of fresh water: the Fezzan, for example, receives less than ten millimeters of annual rainfall (Mattingly 1995: 9), and the Garamantes could not have sustained such a large center of civilization without irrigation and hence *fagāgīr*. Although centers of power and directions of trade shifted from one network to another, in the long run, the feasibility, construction, and maintenance of water points dictated the survival of centers of trade, trade routes, and travel in the desert. Thus the control of Saharan trade can be put in terms of who controls access to water: Pliny the Elder, writing in the first century AD, noted the ease with which water could be obtained if one knew where to look for it, but he also explained that trade routes through the Sahara were in part controlled by the Garamantes, who filled in the wells along the way to prevent their use by others, and thus prohibited any travel in the Sahara independent of their oversight.[14] The tight control that the Garamantes had over the trading routes and their reluctance to allow the Romans any access to it at that time could not be more explicit. The Garamantes controlled and regulated one of the major Saharan routes between sub-Saharan Africa and the Libyan coast from the sixth century BC to the fifth century AD (Crawley Quinn 2009). The success of the Garamantes lay not only in their control of a strategic geographic area, but also in their ingenious management of available resources, whether new irrigation technologies or new crops. These probably enabled a Garamantian population boom: the estimate is some 50,000–100,000 inhabitants at its peak (Mattingly and Wilson 2003: 37). Their control and management of resources also helped them establish a center of food and water resources with sufficient surplus to allow trade. Aerial photographs showing lines of spoil rings placed at regular intervals over the stretch of the Wadi al-Ajal also emphasize the extensive use of canal systems bringing water from aquifers to various sites in the Fezzan during the Garamantian period. The more than 600 known *fagāgīr* surveyed so far in the Fezzan were used not only to supply the Garamantes' settlements with water for agriculture and drinking (Wilson and Mattingly 2003), but also to generate the surplus necessary to enable trade and the periodic stay of men and animals involved in long-distance commerce. If different breeds of camels, which are adapted to variations in climate, terrain, and food resources, were used for different sections of journeys through the Sahara in antiquity as they are today (Mikesell 1955: 234; E. A. McDougall this volume), we might expect that the necessary stopovers for trans-shipment were facilitated by the presence of a powerful center such as the Garamantian kingdom. The fragility of trans-Saharan trade meant striking a balance in the use of water points and trading centers, managing food resources for humans and animals, and communicating with traders and populations from throughout the Sahara.

Coping with Vulnerability

Several major events in the agricultural history of the northern Saharan oases had a long-lasting impact on their development in antiquity, and clearly point to established patterns of connectivity within the Saharan system, as well as to an ongoing search for ways of coping with the Saharan environment. The first change in cereal agriculture in the Fezzan consisted of a shift from hulled to free-threshing wheat crops in the late first millennium BC, a similar date to the change in Egypt (Pelling 2008: 57), while a comparable change occurred in the early first millennium BC in the Mediterranean. The shift to free-threshing wheat, as the name implies, would have significantly lowered the labor requirements associated with the harvest. This might reflect an early strong connection to Egypt. Second, the appearance of pearl millet (*Pennisetum glaucum*) and sorghum (*Sorghum bicolor*) in the archaeological record in the last centuries of the first millennium BC at Jarma in the Fezzan directly testifies to trading networks reaching the south of the Sahara, where these plants originate.[15] The evidence of pearl millet and sorghum at Jarma is the earliest attestation of these crops in the northern Sahara, a fact that precludes it from coming from elsewhere: they are not found in the western oases of Egypt and only appear later, during the Roman period, at Qasr Ibrim in Nubia (Pelling 2008). The introduction of pearl millet and sorghum, which are summer crops, allowed for a biannual harvest, which in turn might have permitted an increase in trade, if we assume that more resources meant the ability to cope with more traders.

Barley, one of the most salt-tolerant species, and sorghum, which is also salt-tolerant, would have helped the Garamantes overcome some of the challenges posed by their salt-rich soil.[16] While barley has the further potential to produce two annual harvests, sorghum has a lower water requirement, therefore making it a good supplement as feed and fodder. The introduction of pearl millet, which has even lower water requirements than either sorghum or barley, might have marked a period of agricultural expansion, and the grain could have been used to make marginal lands more productive. The discovery of small but constant quantities of cotton seeds (*Gossypium* sp.), showing signs of its harvest at Jarma by the third or fourth century AD at the latest (Pelling 2008: 58–59), is surprising as, unlike these food crops, cotton cultivation requires relatively substantial quantities of water and was thus only feasible through the use of *faggāra* technologies. It also hints at specialization in a crop cultivated on the basis of its high commercial value rather than for subsistence. Cotton, which probably originated in India or the Indian Ocean, possibly came through the Egyptian corridor, as it was found in the Dakhla and Kharga oases in Roman times (ibid.: 59; Van der Veen 2011: 89).

Equally, the poppy (*Papaver somniferum*) found in the Fezzan (Pelling 2008: 49) may have spread from the Mediterranean: originally a western Mediterranean domesticate, it may have been used as a condiment or as a narcotic/soporific, although too few samples have been found to confirm this. The presence of chickens in Mali by AD 500 (MacDonald and Edwards 1993) could indicate North African or Egyptian imports potentially via the Fezzan, where they are found in the Garamantian period (Grant 2006: 181). Similarly, the continuous presence of pigs in the Fezzan in the Garamantian period and from at least 700 BC–400 BC (Van der Veen 2006: 173; Grant 2006: 181) is potentially another indication of transregional trade, given that the pig is not native to this part of the world (Albarella, Dobney, and Rowley-Conwy 2006). The first- or second-century AD terracotta figurine in the Ashmolean Museum (Oxford) of a camel carrying two live pigs, although from Syria, reminds us that live animals too could be carried over long distances in desert areas, although no traces of this traffic might remain in the archaeological record.

One of the more stifling concepts in the classical scholarship on Saharan trade has been the notion that trade was unidirectional (as noted by Liverani 2000b: 20). The presence of *fagāgīr* in the Fezzan can serve as evidence for trade via the oases systems to the east, probably the western Egyptian oases, where similar technology was used as early as the fifth and fourth centuries BC (Wilson 2006: 211). The claim that trade routes linked these areas to Egypt in the second half of the first millennium BC is therefore entirely plausible (Liverani 2000a). It is interesting to note the appearance both of new crop species and of irrigation technologies within a roughly similar time period in both areas, suggesting crop diversification and optimization, a search for competitive strains, or crops that were primarily cultivated for exchange (if we suppose that cotton was not only for local consumption). It is equally interesting to note a continued transregional interest in agricultural improvements, leading to the introduction of new sub-Saharan crops along with a shift to free-threshing wheat in alignment with changes in Egypt and the transfer of irrigation technologies. While we do have good archaeological data for crop species, the *fagāgīr* are still in the process of being more accurately dated: they were certainly present in the Fezzan by the classical Garamantian period, certainly between the first and fourth centuries AD, if not closer to the second century BC–second century AD date suggested by the Taglilt *fagāgīr* (Wilson 2006: 209–210). The connection from the Garamantian kingdom to places farther west remains difficult to assess. The problem of the current scarcity of research undertaken in Algeria has already been mentioned, and the argument for the spread of *fagāgīr* to Algeria (and perhaps Morocco) via the Fezzan remains key to identifying connections within the northern Saharan regions.

Transport Hubs, Commercial Emporia, and the Garamantian Kingdom

We ought to consider movement within the Sahara not only as more fragmented than is often assumed, involving various Saharan players such as the

Garamantes (Wilson 2009), but also as multidirectional within the possibilities afforded by regional networks. In that sense the oases are "quite similar to 'islands' in a huge archipelago, which maintains strict unity disregarding its physical spread" (Liverani 2000b: 20). The desert hub is characterized by its insularity and its connections to the wider networks of trading. On an island, trade and goods can in theory come from any direction. Similarly, Saharan hubs can receive trade items from anywhere within the networks they are drawing on. This does not preclude preferential trade connections and hence general trends at one historic period or another, but we must be able to consider both the long-term preferential pattern and the short-term ability to trade with all.

In the Sahara, where the next stage of the journey might require weeks of traveling, trips are often fragmented, and undertaken step by step. Herodotus's account from the fifth century BC of a trans-Saharan journey provides us with the earliest description. In a reevaluation (Liverani 2000a), it has been convincingly argued that his narrative represents the various stops and stages of a caravan route leading from the lower Nile to the Niger bend. As depicted by Herodotus, the concept is clear: the point of focus is always the next stop, rather than the end of the journey, just as time and space beyond that point become marginal concepts. Trade connections, and therefore knowledge, beyond the next stage may therefore not have been of interest from a local point of view: while Herodotus, as a historian, sought to explain the entire Saharan journey, from a trading perspective this may not have been relevant for those who held the monopoly over one particular section of the journey (see also E. A. McDougall this volume). Instead, it may be more useful to understand trading patterns from a local point of view (such as that of the Garamantes, for instance) and at the same time envisage different types, ranges, and lengths of focus of trading routes, of short-, medium-, and long-distance ranges (Wilson 2009). While some goods may have moved *across* the Sahara from one side to the other, the majority probably remained in the Fezzan.

Whereas the intensity of trade between the Garamantes and the Roman empire via North Africa is well attested through the abundance of Roman goods in both burials and surveyed settlements, evidence of sustained trading contact with sub-Saharan regions is less readily forthcoming. The amount of Roman material reaching Africa south of the Sahara seems to have been limited, and most Roman trading goods were probably used and consumed in the Garamantian heartland. Contact with the south, less apparent in the archaeological record, is better sought in different types of evidence, such as traces of agricultural changes and technology transfer across the Sahara and in the Garamantian corridor (crop imports, iron technology, or the need for a larger workforce for innovations in irrigation techniques). It is also hinted at by occasional finds of sub-Saharan goods, such as a hematite lip plug found in a burial in the Fezzan, probably implying the sub-Saharan origin of the deceased person (Mattingly, Lahr, and Wilson 2009: 119). Slaves, ivory, animals such as rhinoceroses, and gold may have crossed the breadth of the Sahara from south to north, while goods such as wine and oil remained in the Garamantian territory, as attested by the material found in funerary contexts (Mattingly and Edwards 2003: 227–229). If we believe Herodotus, the Garamantes acted mainly as suppliers of slaves, probably taken from the southern areas of Lake Chad and the Niger bend. Fentress (2011) argues that the increase in the number of black slaves in the ancient world may be gathered from their representation in small bronzes and ceramic figures: the gradual shift from Africans' quite regal appearance on Attic pottery, to often grotesque and sometimes malnourished and maltreated children in later representations may be associated with increased African slave populations.[17]

Meanwhile, the Garamantes themselves must have needed a large number of slaves for digging the hundreds of kilometers of underground water canals on which the Garamantian kingdom relied (Wilson 2006: 210). We can begin to see the interplay of the various systems of trade: while adult male slaves were kept for digging *fagāgīr* in the Garamantian heartland, the slave children that Fentress identifies were sold to the Mediterranean markets.[18] This minimized the risk associated with transport and maximized profit, since children fetched very high prices, as *deliciae* or *delicati* (luxury boys), but also due to their longer anticipated life spans, and their greater malleability and hence adaptive potential to the Roman world. Trade in slaves might reflect the realities of short- and long-distance trade in the Sahara more generally and the role played by the Garamantian trading platform. Although textual evidence is scant, a derogatory poem from Hadrumetum (modern Sousse, Tunisia) points to the presence of "Garamantian" slaves in North Africa though, as noted by Desanges (1999b: 236), the comment on the Garamantian slave's pitch-black color could have referred either to a Garamant, or to a slave from sub-Saharan Africa traded via the Garamantes.

Another indication of such multilateral networks is the possible spread of metallurgy from the Mediterranean to sub-Saharan Africa. At Bou Khzama (Tichitt, Mauritania), ironworking appears as early as the mid-first millennium BC, that is, roughly at the time of Herodotus's account of a trans-Saharan journey, but also at the time for which evidence of metal production is extant for Zinchecra in the Fezzan.[19] One suggestion is that the technology at Tichitt was brought into sub-Saharan Africa from the north by Berbers (MacDonald et al. 2009). Another possibility would be through maritime or coastal routes. But given the evidence for metal production in the Fezzan in the early period, this raises a number of issues.

Were iron technologies brought along or exchanged via established slave routes? If so, could the Fezzan, where much ironworking was needed in order to produce tools to dig *fagāgīr*, also be one of the potential areas of dissemination? One could indeed imagine the possibility that the Garamantes could have eventually found ways of negotiating alliances and hence had more sustained contact with tribes farther south: research south of Ghat identified another Garamantian fortified site at Aghram Nadharif, which controlled routes southward (Liverani 2005). These could have operated as part of the slave trade, thereby allowing the Garamantes to avoid risk taking and to unburden themselves of the logistical problems of the slave raiding which Herodotus ascribes to them.[20]

From the imperial period on, Rome showed a clear desire to engage in trade with or even to control the northern part of the Sahara. The growing influence of the Mediterranean world is clearly reflected in the archaeological evidence in the Fezzan. Cornelius Balbus's campaigns against the Garamantes in 20 or 19 BC, during which he seized various places and tribes on the way to the Fezzan, mark an important initial phase of contact with the Garamantian kingdom and toward control of the edges of the desert. In the third century, the names of several localities were recorded in *ostraca* at the Roman fort of Bu Njem, located 200 kilometers due south of Cape Misurata and on the Roman frontier: *ostracon* 64 mentions the name Bubeius, one of the places conquered by Balbus on his way to the Fezzan (Pliny 5, 5, 37); *ostracon* 80 mentions a *filius Fezinis* (son of Fezin).[21] The importance of Balbus's success[22] goes some way toward explaining the triumph he was granted in the city of Rome, a remarkable honor both because of his non-Italian origins (from Cadiz, Spain, he was the first non-Italian to be allowed a triumph in the capital) and because he was the last private citizen ever to be granted one. The Saharan campaigns were intended as punitive expeditions aiming at territorial control over the pre-desert and border consolidation under the emperor Augustus (27 BC–AD 14), but may well have gone hand in hand with a search for luxury goods from the margins of the empire, such as ivory or exotic animals from Africa, gems or marbles from the edges of the Eastern Desert, or Indian goods, which flowed in from the Red Sea.[23] Balbus's success in the Garamantian territory, however, did not imply control or long-term pacification of the area, and, according to the archaeological record, trade with the Garamantes mainly intensified later, in the second half of the first century AD (Mattingly and Wilson 2010). From this moment on and well into the sixth century AD, goods such as *sigillata* ceramic ware from Italy or Tripolitanian wine amphorae are commonly found in graves (Fontana 1995), indicating continuous and sustained contact with Roman North Africa. The *ostraca* from the third-century AD Roman fort at Bu Njem also show that the appearance of Garamantes with trading goods was part of the daily routine (Marichal 1992: 104n72).

The evidence from the Sahara of classical antiquity suggests that networks of contacts were established early on, if only to cope with the instability of the Saharan environment. Exchange occurred on different scales, and varied according to needs and preferential routes determined by trading alliances as much as by geography. The botanical record provides evidence of long-standing trade with sub-Saharan as well as northern Africa. Crops traveling through the Sahara led to agricultural changes that improved local living conditions, via the introduction of better adapted or less labor-intensive crops, and those planted essentially for trade, such as cotton. New technologies developed alongside agriculture, perhaps responding in part to commercial needs. The Garamantian kingdom provided a formidable point of contact in the Sahara, and its wealth is well attested in the abundance of goods, in particular those of Roman origin, found in burials and settlements. Garamantes routinely imported Mediterranean foodstuffs, such as oil and wine, as attested by the numerous finds of Roman amphorae in burials. Their presence in the majority of burial contexts excludes the hypothesis that imported goods were used by the elite only (Mattingly and Wilson 2010). Other imports included ceramic wares, cooking wares, and glass items, brought down directly from the Syrtes, the Roman world, and later from Egypt. It seems that, for reasons of infrastructure, goods destined for the Sahara had to transit via the Garamantian hub. Conversely, the Garamantes used sub-Saharan resources, such as manpower for digging *fagāgīr* or new drought-resistant crops, to produce a surplus for trading with the Roman world on a scale large enough that Roman goods are found in most of the burials in the Fezzan oases. Animals were probably traded as well.

Continued research in the Fezzan has gradually shown the extensive role played by the Garamantian community as a hub allowing access to places throughout the Sahara. The abundance of Roman goods found in the Fezzan certainly testifies to a strong link with the coastal areas of North Africa, but also implies the presence of less archaeologically visible trading items from the south. While archaeological and historical gaps remain to be filled, we can nonetheless say that the Sahara in classical antiquity was a space of vibrant interaction extending in all possible directions.

NOTES

1. I am grateful to Andrew Wilson and Josephine Crawley Quinn for reading various drafts of this chapter, and for discussions with Judith Scheele, in particular about camel changeover locations in the Sahara. I am equally indebted to Dorian Fuller, who kindly agreed to read and comment on the botanical section. Any mistakes, of course, remain my own.

2. For examples from the wider Indian Ocean corridor, see the SEALINKS project (http://www.homepages.ucl.ac.uk/~tcrndfu/sealinks/sealink1.htm), and Boivin and Fuller (2009).

3. Three of the world's largest aquifer systems (water-bearing layers) are located underneath its surface; the Northwestern Sahara Aquifer System alone covers over a million square kilometers, and has an estimated reserve of thirty billion cubic meters of fresh water.

4. See, for instance, Harris (2005), and Malkin, Constantakopoulou, and Panagopoulou (2009).

5. Lydon's (2009: 52–54) rather pessimistic perception of the early Saharan trade seems to be due to her reliance on a somewhat limited bibliography on the Sahara in antiquity, which does not include archaeological research undertaken since the 1990s by David Mattingly and others.

6. See Fentress (2007: 132) for the suggestion that Gigthis may be second to Lepcis in terms of trade with the Garamantes.

7. A camel charged with a normal load (150–200 kg) would probably only have been able to carry two of these, especially over long distances.

8. Tacitus, *Hist.* 4.50.

9. See Baratta (2008) and Trousset (2005: 364, 363) for goods possibly traded via the Garamantes (slaves, and alum from Ghat, Kaouar, or Nefzaoua). While both suggestions are likely, they do not exclude other proveniences, alum and slaves being available from other areas. Alum may have come from the island of Lipari, for example, via the ports of the Lesser Syrtes, along with other coastal goods, such as sponges.

10. It is more likely that Tin Hinan was a *sharīfa* (descendant of the Prophet Muhammad) from the Tafilalt who came to the Ahaggar in the seventeenth century, and whose story was superimposed onto that of the much earlier tomb (Baistrocchi 1989: 91).

11. Although gold has been almost absent from finds in the Garamantian tombs, probably due to the extensive robbing of wealthy burial sites, Mattingly has suggested on the grounds of similarities between the tomb of Tin Hinan (whose gold bracelets alone weigh 1.7 kg) and the Garamantian burials that the Garamantes may have had similar access to gold wealth in the Fezzan (Mattingly 2003: 229).

12. Gilbertson (1996).

13. Other factors, such as the over-extraction of available water resources, or the economic downturn and turmoil in North Africa starting as early as the mid-third century AD, are probably equally important.

14. Pliny, *NH* 5.5.38: "Hitherto it has been impossible to open up the road to the Garamantes country, because brigands of that race fill up the wells with sand—these do not need to be dug very deep if you are aided by the knowledge of the localities" (Loeb transl.).

15. Pelling (2008: 58). This introduction must have happened sometime in the mid- to late first millennium BC; these crops were not found at the earlier Garamantian site at Zinchecra (10th–5th century BC), while accelerated mass spectrometry dates them to 370–350 cal. BC (millet) and 390–110 BC (sorghum).

16. Herodotus, *Hist.* IV.183: "Men dwell there called Garamantes, an exceeding great nation, who sow in earth which they have laid on the salt" (Loeb transl.). This clearly refers to the salt-related issue in the agriculture of the Fezzan.

17. One *ostracon* (inscribed pottery fragment; pl. *ostraca*) at Bu Njem also records Garamantes and Egyptians bringing letters and a fugitive slave (Marichal 1992: n. 71).

18. On Djerba, for example, one of the possible outlets for Saharan trade, an *ostracon* mentions a *mango,* or slave trader, probably operating there (Fentress, Drine, and Holod 2009: 338). St. Augustine, writing at the turn of the fifth century, also comments on slave raiding (though on a more local basis) and slave shipments from the North African port of Hippo Regius (today's Annaba, Algeria) (*Epistulae* 10*).

19. On the Bou Khzama smelting furnace, see MacDonald et al. (2009). For Zinchecra, see Schrüfer-Kolb (2007: 457).

20. Herodotus, *Hist.* IV.183.

21. In Roman times, however, the area thus designated comprised districts much farther north than the region to which the term now refers (Marichal 1992). Adams (1994) has shown that the Latin extant at Bu Njem is that of Punic-speakers who have not fully mastered the Latin language.

22. Balbus's reconstruction of the harbor at Cadiz shows an understanding of the need to develop infrastructures to develop long-distance trade, and perhaps an anticipation of profits of some sort.

23. Virgil, *Aeneid* 6.791–796: "Augustus Caesar, son of a god, who will again establish a golden age in Latium amid fields once ruled by Saturn; he will advance his empire beyond the Garamants and Indians" (Loeb transl.)

4 FRONTIERS, BORDERLANDS, AND SAHARAN/WORLD HISTORY

James McDougall

> Places which yield only the bare necessities of men's lives must be inhabited by barbarous peoples, since no political society is possible. . . . The least populous countries are thus the most fitted to tyranny; wild beasts reign only in deserts.
>
> —Rousseau, *The Social Contract*

It would not be much of an exaggeration, and may even be a commonplace, to say that the question of how best to assess northwest Africa's place within the wider world and its history has engaged travelers, writers, and scholars since Herodotus. For the great Greek compiler of eyewitness veracity and astounding tales alike, the imaginable world (centered, of course, on the Mediterranean) was bounded to the south by what he believed to be the curve of the Nile, cutting east and north through the desert, and to the north by the Danube, meandering symmetrically east and south from the land of the Celts. Beyond both were unimaginable barbarian lands without comprehensible language or civilization.[1] The Sahara's credentials as a limit, an edge of the world, are thus well anchored in the European history of ideas about the world and its inhabitants, and the extent to which they might be known; unlike the deep forests of Central Europe, of course, the great desert maintained this ancient mystique well into modern times. Even from the much closer perspective of medieval Arabic writers, the *bilād al-sūdān* functioned in historical and geographical literature as a limit to what (and whom) could be known and included in the recognizable world, and what could be left to the imagination. Somewhere out across the desert there was a modicum of law, religion, manners, and settled life, and contacts between Sijilmassa and Awdaghust or between Ouargla and Tadmekka/Essouk were so regular that Ibadi texts could use them as the setting for morality tales (Levtzion and Hopkins 1981: 90–91). But there were also single-breasted women and kings riding horned beasts. From the dimly perceived states and potentates of the medieval era (like those depicted on the famous Catalan Atlas of 1356, showing the fourteenth-century Malian king Mansa Musa holding an apple-sized nugget of gold) through to much more recent images of the region, the Sahara's vast attraction as an unknowable frontier, alternately empty of anything or full of fears, has been inversely proportional to the extent to which it has been understood. This continues to be a barrier to broader understanding of the region in the wider world, and to some degree a potential danger for the region's peoples today (E. A. McDougall, ed., 2007).

Fernand Braudel, also looking at the world from the Mediterranean, nonetheless enabled a very different angle of view when, in the English translation of his monumental and massively influential *The Mediterranean and the Mediterranean World in the Age of Philip II,* he turned the map of the world upside down to illustrate the world-historical location of the middle sea, and the Sahara as its "second face" (1972 [1966]: 169, 171). Startlingly, on Braudel's map, the Sahara is suddenly the center of the world, or at least the center of a large part of the eastern hemisphere. For Braudel, who had taught at a secondary school in Algiers before World War II and was influenced there by a formidable tradition of French colonial geography and orientalism, the Sahara constituted a vast, connected zone unified by and enabling the unity of the classical Islamic world, just as the Mediterranean was unified by and had enabled the unity of classical Greco-Roman civilization and the Europe thought to have sprung from it. Still, and despite his own insistence to the contrary, Braudel's "Turkish" (i.e., Ottoman, Islamic) world lay beyond the frontier of the world he was most interested in knowing. The Islamic zone, stretching from the western Sahara through Cyrenaica and Egypt, through the successive deserts of the Sinai and north Arabia, to Iraq and the Iranian plateau, was an *anoikoumené* (ibid.: 174), an "un-environment" defined by its aridity and oases more than by the dynamic, long-term rhythms of interaction between environment and society that he so brilliantly traced in the temperate zone immediately adjacent to it.[2]

More recent scholarship, especially from West Africanists, has of course greatly improved on this older state of affairs, and as Ann McDougall's chapter in this volume explores, Saharan studies can now claim several decades of very distinguished existence. But, for reasons partly explored both in that chapter and in the introduction to this book, the location of the Sahara itself in much of even the best work continues to pose something of a problem. Austen (2010) calls his subject "trans-Saharan Africa," which—the importance of his book's contribution notwithstanding—is ultimately a way of writing the Saharan commercial economy into world history while writing the Sahara itself out of it. Austen's overarching narrative is of a delimited period (albeit a millennium long, from around the eighth century to the late nineteenth/early twentieth) in which the Sahara is open as a corridor of the world economy, connecting the producers of West Africa with consumers of their gold and slaves in the Mediterranean and Middle East. When this period closes, with the appearance of the colonial railway, the Sahara returns to what it seems to have been in the Roman and Phoenician age before the advent of the unifying bonds of Islam: an area marginal to the currents of world trade and a backwater of world history, dividing Africa "proper" to its south from the Arab world to its north and east, belonging properly to neither and unable to assert a singularity of its own.

In its broad traits, of course, this long-term history of northwest Africa is perfectly lucid, especially as a general account within a concise approach to major geographic regions of world history. But there is, inevitably, a good deal that is thereby left out of the picture, and in some respects it may be that the overall picture itself should be considerably altered. As archaeological research proceeds apace in the Fezzan and around the Niger bend, we may now need to revise the long-held, cautious view of the absence or extreme tenuousness of pre-Islamic commerce across the Sahara (Wilson 2009; Fentress 2009; Schörle this volume). And just as the caravel is no longer assumed to have displaced the caravan when European Atlantic shipping began to tap Saharan trade from West African seaports, it may be that patterns of intra-Saharan and cross-Saharan exchange have rebounded since the calamities of the colonial period, such that the "closure" of the desert corridor as a route of world trade in the early twentieth century might now look more like a brief parenthesis in a longer, continuous history than like a final and defining death knell.[3] Of course, the mobilities and connections of the later twentieth and early twenty-first centuries obey rather different logics and play out over very different patterns of possibility and constraint than did those of the preceding two millennia. And having long maintained a certain internal sovereignty over the spaces they inhabited and over the internally managed connections and exchanges that made these spaces habitable, the region's peoples have certainly found themselves more recently facing a world turned increasingly outward. But looking at the region in the very long run, there seem to be good reasons for directing attention not simply at the routes *across* the Sahara that have made it a global corridor, but at the "spaces in between" that have made it, and make it today, a "world crossroads" (Choplin 2009). More broadly, a recalibration not so much of *time frame* as of our *level of analysis* helps to put the Sahara back into focus as an intelligible region in its own right, one that certainly connects its contiguous—and very different—worlds of Mediterranean Africa to the north and highland-and-forest West Africa to the south, the Atlantic coast to the west with the Nile valley to the east, but that also has a distinct significance of its own. There is, in other words, a properly Saharan history within world history, which might repay comparative attention by giving visibility to a global region whose interest (as other chapters in this volume argue in more detail) lies at least as much in what constitutes the region from within as what moves across it from outside. One way of thinking usefully about this from a historical perspective is to return to the question of northwest Africa's location in a wider world, as a set of overlapping, interdependent places in between, and thus to resituate the Sahara within the recent comparative history of the frontier and the closely associated study of borderlands.

Saharan, African, and World History: Frontiers, Borderlands, and Spaces in Between

Beyond the ancient notion of the "edge of the unknown" with which we began, the concept of the frontier and models of historical development articulated around it have been very productive for scholarship in a variety of world-historical regions since the mid-twentieth century. While they have been applied to cases as far removed from each other as Latin America and China, the problematic of the frontier has remained for many tied to the Turner thesis and its successors in North American history.[4] This has been a fruitful comparative angle: the inversions and inflections experienced by Turner's progressive, pioneering, expanding U.S. frontier when transplanted to Africa or Latin America have enabled new perspectives on the social, cultural, and political histories of a variety of distinct but comparable world regions. From the original, triumphalist frontier, "the hither edge of free land," as Turner defined it (no doubt as much a poetic expression of a particular late nineteenth-century American sensibility as an analytical construct), to more recent concerns with the "edgy" intercultural margins, the shared and contested "middle grounds" of imperial expansion and indigenous survival struggle (White 1991; Silver 2008), the frontier concept within North American history has continued to stimulate debate and illuminate the complexities of early American history well beyond the significance of the east-to-west driving force of nineteenth-century "progress." On a larger scale, one of Turner's students, Walter Prescott Webb (1952), already anticipated more recent trends in the "Anglo world" literature that has emerged from the new (British) imperial history when he wrote of a "world frontier" comprising Australia, New Zealand, and southern Africa as well as South and North America: a vast horizon of European expansion, settlement, and capitalist enterprise. Elsewhere, other definitions of the frontier have brought other historical patterns to light. In the 1980s and early 1990s, the focus in frontier history shifted from the purely territorial line of demarcation at the edge of "progress" to the often-fraught and always fuzzy lines of contact between cultures: the frontier became "a territory or zone of interpenetration between two previously distinct societies" (Lamar and Thompson 1981: 7), "geographic zones of interaction between two or more distinctive cultures . . . , places where cultures contend with one another and with their physical environment to produce a dynamic that is unique to time and place"; in this latter sense, the frontier became "both place and process, linked inextricably" (Weber and Rausch 1994: xiv). The places and processes that emerged from these analyses were often considerably darker than the (deceptively) bright open sky of Turner's West; in Latin America the frontier seemed "a brutal place where the weak are devoured by the strong," characterized, when written about by city-bound nineteenth-century Latin American intellectuals, by "ignorance and primitivism" (ibid.: xvii). In southern Africa, the "opening frontier" of white settlement and black servitude in the eastern and northern Cape, Griqualand, and Transvaal produced unstable gun- and slave-running economies, endemic regional warfare, and, in the 1857 Xhosa cattle killing, catastrophic and suicidal millennialism.[5]

In African history, the major point of reference in this literature remains Igor Kopytoff's edited volume *The African Frontier: The Reproduction of Traditional African Societies* (1987), which combined the frontier as space at the leading edge of settlement with the frontier as cultural process. In Kopytoff's long introductory essay, the "internal African frontier," a perennially renewed space of social reproduction "lying at the fringes of the numerous established African societies," provides a continuous, cyclical incubator for the "perpetuation of a pan-African political culture" (3, 25–26). The sociocultural patterns that Kopytoff saw as being generated on the frontiers of existing societies, as new groups constantly broke away from established ones, "stood Turner's thesis on its head" in that Kopytoff's African frontier, instead of being a force for dynamic, progressive cultural transformation, instead serves as "a force for culture-historical [*sic*] continuity and conservatism" (3). This vision was important (and positively reviewed) in particular for its critique of what Kopytoff called the "tribal model" of progressively aggregated African polities emerging in "evolutionary" fashion from wandering bands of proto-historical hunters or herders, placing the emphasis instead on the dynamics of settlement and the "spinning-off" of new waves of population movement at the edges of societies as they "mature[d]." For historians of central and southern

Africa, in particular, this was an attractive approach to ethnogenesis and polity formation, and in a sense it chimes in well with John Iliffe's later characterization, within a largely demographically oriented history of the continent, of Africans as "the frontiersmen of mankind" whose history is structured by the progressive settlement and colonization (in the general sense) of an especially rich but also especially challenging set of productive environments (Iliffe 1995; see also, for example, Schoenbrun 1998).

None of the studies in Kopytoff's volume concerned northwest Africa, which figured in his deep history of ethnogenesis only as an almost mythical, "ancestral 'hearth'" where, sometime before 2500 BCE, "the 'incubation' of the ancestral pan-African culture patterns took place, often under frontier conditions and in contact with the kindred patterns of the pre-Islamic Near-East" (1987: 9). The recourse to a posited "cradle of ancestral culture," especially one so vaguely formulated, was perhaps unnecessary for Kopytoff's argument. But in this, as in the overarching conception of a single, ancestrally defined "pan-African political culture," despite both its conceptual originality and its detailed empirical observation, Kopytoff's account simply replaced the old essentialism of "tribal" origins with a more sophisticated but still essentialist theory of African history as "closed," cyclical, and self-replicating. In this sense, Kopytoff's frontier shared with other frontier histories a paradoxical tendency to reproduce the boundedness of the histories of the areas thus studied, reproducing their particularism, exceptionalism, and *enclavement* rather than opening them up beyond their various essentialisms to comparison and connection. The search for a more properly comparative frontier history that might enable the histories of different world regions to have something to say to each other remains here, as in much of the older American frontier literature, unresolved.

One possible way around this difficulty might be sought in a field that has developed in tandem with the frontier literature since the 1970s, and which again derives mainly from work on America, this time the southwestern United States: the study of borderlands. Together with the tradition of writing on the Spanish frontier in the Americas (a rather different, northward rather than westward and "inclusive" *mestizo* rather than exclusive binary-racialized boundary), and the newer history of early settlement and coexistence in areas such as the American Great Lakes (White 1991), the focus on borderlands has stressed the importance of more fluid, open, transitional zones than is often envisaged by the frontier as a demarcation of settlement. Borderlands can usefully be seen, for example, as spaces in which "autonomous peoples of different cultures are bound together by a greater, multi-imperial context" (Haefeli 1999: 1224). At the same time, such zones are set necessarily within the sphere of interstate competition for territorial sovereignty, access to resources, and jurisdiction over people, i.e., within struggles to create, maintain, and enforce the recognition of *borders.*[6] Here again, the possibility of engaging a more properly comparative history on the basis of the relationship between frontier/boundary and borderland, however productive the analysis in each particular case, has been questioned. North America's frontiers, for example, are said to have been "remarkable for their instability and fluidity" relative to the frontiers of other regions and societies, in "deserts, deep forests and vast steppe lands" which "tended to form along ecological boundaries and last for centuries" (ibid.).

This, though, is perhaps to overstate the case for the stability of frontiers in the "old" world. In northwest Africa, ecological boundaries themselves have moved, sometimes quite rapidly; they have been less fixed features of the landscape than they have been expressions of the frequently shifting balance between the environment, its resources, and human populations. (And as stated elsewhere in this volume, it is worth remembering that resources are not always simply given by environmental conditions—like salt—but, like date palms and irrigated gardens, are produced by human action in the environment. Even salt must be exposed, dug out or evaporated, and water tables must be tapped and channeled.) At the shortest end of the scale, the availability of pasture and water in parts of the Sahara and Sahel can be vanishingly brief, exploited at the moment of their seasonal appearance and almost immediately exhausted. Changing practices of settlement and land or animal husbandry can effect dramatic shifts in ecology over a few decades, as in the case of the water meadows (*bourgoutières*) of the Niger bend (Grémont this volume). At the other extreme, the *longue durée* environmental history of desertification since the seventeenth century, punctuated (notably, in the twentieth century, in the 1910s and recurrently since the 1970s) by dramatic shorter-term episodes of drought, might be seen as an inexorable, secular march of the arid frontier into the West African savanna. In between, the shorter-term spread of *bayoud,* the "whitening" disease of date palms caused by the fungus *Fusarium oxysporum albedinis,* from Morocco eastward through the Algerian oases over the course of the past century can be regarded as a pathogenic advance forcing (or at least threatening) the retreat of cultivation. Such shifts in the short, medium, and long term suggest that caution be exercised before we pronounce on the plasticity of new world political frontiers relative to the permanence of old world ecological ones. Perhaps, again, the level of analysis as well as the time frame need to be adjusted if we are to gain a more satisfactory grasp on the uses of frontiers and their borderlands for a comparative world history.

Edges, Empires, and Borderlands: A Politico-Ecological History of the Sahara?

Comparative history necessarily seeks to determine what is distinctive and particular to a specific case through examining how the distinctiveness and particularity of one time and place can be related to others, how setting one time and space in relief against other times, across wider or different spaces, enables us to trace the lineaments of commonalities and differences, and (if possible) identify or at least posit their causal factors. Some of the distinguishing features of Saharan history are clear enough in themselves, and doubly so when compared to other regions that have provided the focus for frontier or borderland history. Its vast geographic size and minuscule, exceedingly sparsely distributed (but also locally concentrated) population; the cultural centrality over most of the recorded past of a single religio-legal system, Islam, to both social practice and the inhabited landscape (Moussaoui this volume); the long-established patterns of settlement but the extreme precariousness as well as the dynamism of "towns" (Scheele this volume); the key importance of a very few commodities to local and long-distance production and exchange—all set off Saharan Africa from other parts of the continent (central or southern Africa) as well as from the Mediterranean, western China, Southeast Asia, the American West, the interior of Canada, or Latin America. What does Saharan Africa, understood through the lens of frontier/borderland dynamics, have to say to the very different histories of such regions? What does the understanding of such a Saharan history have to contribute to the broader comparative world history within which I have suggested it should be located?

If the problem of location has been particularly acute for the Sahara, perhaps the most "peripheral" region of Africa and of African studies, African history more generally has also long been preoccupied with the location of the continent relative to the wider world. Africa's long isolation from Eurasian connections, then its incorporated-and-marginalized position as a periphery of world systems centered elsewhere, the internal dynamics of the continent that have turned on dispersed and separate centers with only occasionally contiguous edges and frequently conflictual contact zones—all are recurrent themes in the literature. (They are also, to a degree, mirrored in the conditions of the production of Africanist scholarship itself: think of the extent to which, in academic departments, teaching programs, literatures, and fields of research, the various subregions of the continent—West, East, Central, and South—remain relatively distinct from each other, a fact surely not sufficiently accounted for by the undoubted difficulty of any single scholar working with any great expertise on more than a very small part of the continent.

The centers of interest and lines of demarcation also, of course, vary if one is looking at, say, American, British, or French fields of African studies, let alone Africana or African American studies in the U.S. academy.)

To a degree, the regionally oriented world history that has aimed to escape from the straitjacket of continental units of analysis and has given us instead studies of the Atlantic and Indian Ocean worlds has—despite the major role reserved for Africa and Africans in both—tended to reproduce the same patterns. The African shores of the Indian Ocean or the Arabian seas have become arenas of greater India or greater Arabia (or greater Hadramawt), albeit sometimes veneered with a poetically polished sense of cosmopolitanism smoother than is entirely tenable.[7] The Africa of the black Atlantic is above all one side of the slave triangle, and its Africans are primarily visible—through the records of slave shipping—once they enter the diaspora. Of course, one major stimulus for the internal history of northwest Africa, and a real strength of the literature in Saharan studies, has been precisely the concern to investigate the obverse of the Atlantic trade: the expanding internal slave markets of the nineteenth century and the longer-term desert-side and trans-Saharan economy in which they played so important a part.[8]

But the larger problematic of Africa's location in global histories, and the problem of the Sahara as a void within Africa, remain and are perhaps also linked. Indeed, many of the classic controversies in African history, especially (but not only) in the history of West Africa, arise *as* problems because of the way that Mediterranean Africa (as part of the Mediterranean, or Arab, and hence non-African world) has often been excised from conceptions of the continent "proper" and the way that the Sahara has correspondingly been seen—or, rather, unseen—as an *empty* space in between. The major concerns of establishing a properly autonomous African history, reliant on Africa's own internal historical dynamics rather than on putative external stimuli, were entirely comprehensible and even necessary in the wake of colonialism, the conceits of a supposedly "civilizing mission," and the racial fabrications of the Hamitic hypothesis.[9] In West Africa, the historiographical struggle to locate the beginnings of trade and state-building in the internal dynamics of the Sudanic zone independently of what was once assumed to be the necessary "stimulus" of cross-desert contact from the Islamic Maghreb happily revealed important local and regional patterns of change (Levtzion 1973). But the concern to locate the sources of historical "advancement," whether in ironworking, commerce, or state formation, axiomatically within Africa proper, i.e., to the south of the Sahara, has perhaps been founded on a category error, one that sets up a false opposition only because the Sahara is posited as a *limit*. Similarly, writing, religion, and legal practice transmitted from the north have been seen, like the Arab influence on the Swahili coast, as stemming from outside Africa, rather than being themselves fundamentally African.[10] In this sense, Kopytoff's proto-Sahara as an "ancestral hearth" of African traditions at least had the merit of bringing the region back into the *longue durée* of Africa proper, if only as a symbolic point of origin—and only up until the third millennium BCE. The otherness of the desert (or the sea) and the lands beyond is, of course, a local perception as well as a scholarly one: in the Sahel as in the Maghreb and Zanzibar, local claims to *external* genealogical origins have played a role in hierarchies of status for as long as there has been a perceived "outside" from which one's ancestors might credibly have come. But the fact that such perceptions of distinction are taken seriously within Africa does not oblige us to tailor our own analytical conception of Africa to their model. Relocating the Sahara as an intelligible, rather than as an empty, space means first of all reintegrating it into Africa. We need no longer fear that evidence for much older regional and cross-regional connections between Mediterranean, Saharan, and Sahelian Africa (Schörle this volume; MacDonald et al. 2009; Mattingly 2003, 2007, 2010), regions whose distinctiveness and diversity are simply part of the greater diversity of the continent, somehow denies "Africa" its proper history.

Saharan Africa in the sense this volume gives it, then, is not simply coterminous with the desert; it is not defined as a bioclimatic zone whose borders are drawn along lines of minimal rainfall and humidity, or even as loosely as the space between the Atlantic, the Senegal and Niger rivers, Lake Chad and Darfur, the Atlas, the Gulf of Syrte, and the Nile. It is rather a set of shifting and interdependent ecologies—relationships between people and environment—held together by a shared (though not necessarily unifying) set of characteristics and enduring over time. Geographically, the great desert connects these patterns of habitation and defines the marked challenges the region's peoples face. To make sense of the Sahara as an intelligible region within continental Africa, and within a wider global history, we must turn to histories and contemporary analyses of the environment and its inhabitants, to demography and ecology, the changing relations of people to space, and of both to political societies, states, and the borders they impose. It is in the relationship of ecological to political history that the concepts of frontier and borderland can be productively applied to this part of the world, so as to enable a distinctively Saharan African pattern of history to come into view.

The introduction to this volume has suggested that the notion of connectivity, borrowed from the newer ecological history of the Mediterranean (Horden and Purcell 2000), might, with suitable adjustments, have considerable explanatory force in capturing the ecological dynamics of the Sahara as a region. The Mediterranean, for Horden and Purcell, with its landscape intensely fragmented across short, easily navigable (or indeed audible or visible) distances, was characterized by an especially intense connectivity, producing "net introversion," at least until the twentieth century (Horden this volume). The Sahara's connectivity, with its very different configuration of topography and distance, might be seen to be determined by especially intense resource scarcity; the precariousness of ecological niches even more vulnerable (especially to annual variations in rainfall or the level of the water table) than those of the Mediterranean; and hyper-specialization in a small number of products (salt, dates), producing absolute reliance on outside inputs and connections to markets for exchange and the acquisition of labor. In these circumstances, inhabited areas have stimulated connectivity with other inhabited areas *simply by the fact of existing,* since existence in isolation has by definition been impossible. This has been true whether the inhabitants of such spaces were "nomadic" or "sedentary," and of course many groups have always moved between both lifestyles at different times of the year, or at least have made certain—like the Tuareg nobles (*imajeghen*) for whom mobility is bound up with status and laboring on the land defines its loss—of access to the products of both animal husbandry and cereal culture, metalwork and textiles, whenever necessary. Such connectivity is not the almost frictionless movement across easily navigable, short distances that is seen in the Mediterranean, but rather a combination of relatively intense patterns of interdependence (on kin, religious specialists, vassals, or slaves) within clusters that are short distances apart—the chains of oases that lie strung out along irrigation channels—with the arcing connections between such clusters and others across very long distances, distances which are often difficult and time-consuming to traverse.[11] And unlike the net introversion that defined the Mediterranean, it seems clear that Saharan ecologies, though fundamentally created in the dynamics of production and exchange within the region's highly interdependent networks of habitation and market, produced a connectivity of net extraversion, both over the long run and increasingly in the present. This can be seen in every respect, from its human inhabitants constantly renewed from beyond the fringes of the desert to its resources in grain and livestock that depended on relations with contiguous zones of savanna (to the south) or mountain pasture and tell (to the north). But crucially, while the Saharan economy—unlike the rest of Africa before the colonial period—might *always* have been thus turned out from the inside, making the Sahara always a borderland in the sense of a zone constituted by its multiple interactions with neighboring worlds without which it would be unable to survive, Saharans themselves until relatively recently retained control over the terms of access, the terms of trade, and the terms of alliance that regulated their precarious relationships across and beyond the spaces they inhabited. Until, that is, imperial competition and state formation undermined them.

A defining aspect of the history of the Sahara since the late twentieth century, as of Africa and the global South more generally, has been the stress laid by regional governments, under pressure and with (albeit financially modest) technical assistance from Europe and the United States, to engage in "border strengthening." Once looked to hopefully for the betterment of local livelihoods and opportunities, "trans-border cooperation as a cornerstone for effective subregional and regional integration" (Asiwaju 1996: 253) is nowadays more likely to mean securitization and anti-terrorist, anti-migration control (see Choplin this volume). But while the more recent history of "bordering"—the imposition of political boundaries as policed, bureaucratic barriers—in the region has undoubtedly had considerable and damaging effects, it also remains the case, as it long has been, that boundary marking "sets up a zone of interaction" (a borderland) "rather than representing a genuine partition" (Nugent and Asiwaju 1996: 2). And in this sense, again as has often been the case in Africa and elsewhere, borders have not simply been imposed out of nowhere by entirely arbitrary functionaries on high (and equally arbitrary soldiers and police officers on the ground), but rather, as Paul Nugent has argued for the Ghana-Togo frontier, are "reinforced on a daily basis by the peoples who live along [them]" (Nugent 1996: 36).

If we extend our concept of the frontier in this sense (as border, boundary) beyond the geopolitical and into the ecological field, it is easy enough to see the extent to which frontiers in the Sahara have always existed as lines of demarcation controlling access to resources, from water wells, salt deposits, and pasture, to uranium mines, gas fields, and oil exploration blocks. From the fluid and consensual (e.g., access to salt mines "owned by no one" and worked by all comers) to the heavily encoded and stratified (e.g., access to animal husbandry, from low-status goats to high-status camels; rights to mobility, water, or pasture; slave ownership; marriageability), such demarcations have long existed both as impositions from those with power and as systems of reciprocal rights and observances reproducible in daily life and livelihood, well before they began to be dictated by any form of state. If the absence of the state is a distinguishing feature for much of Saharan history, however, political society in the sense of established systems for the exercise and recognition of coercive power must be seen to have been a mainstay of existence in the desert over the very *longue durée.* Certainly the long-distance slave trade could not have existed without it, but nor could the much more intensively intraregional forced mobility of unfree labor required to irrigate and cultivate oases. Again, unlike the Mediterranean, movement in the Sahara, whether physical or social, is anything but friction free; the frictions of distance and social hierarchy are, on the contrary, extreme. As lines of demarcation shaping the distribution of resources, Saharan frontiers are drawn across both geographic and social space; and as the availability of resources (whether the means of subsistence or the mobility needed to procure them) expands or contracts in time and space, so the frontier moves, relaxes, or tightens, such that the internal "borderland" zones around or astride such frontiers similarly expand or contract, intensifying or restricting the degree of connectivity—the intensity or absence of exchange—between them and altering the overall shape of the region; the location, extent, and prosperity of its inhabited spaces; and the acuity of its dependence on the outside. The emergence or disappearance of access to resources, of course, is not simply an external stimulus to which people merely respond, but is also influenced by regional people's own agency as they move into new employment niches (Sahelian migrants heading to booming Mauritanian towns or young Tuareg *ishumar* to the labor markets of Libya; Choplin, Marfaing, Brachet this volume), abandon old ties of servility, or accept (however reluctantly) new relationships with the state or international development and aid organizations. The Saharan frontier, then, never simply opens or closes, and does not move in a straight line; it expands or contracts, advances or retreats relative to the numbers and movements of the population and their access to exploitable resources. This flexible, internally regulated frontier, however, has also been overlaid in modern times—broadly speaking, since the sixteenth century—with contests over the control of ecological boundaries which empires, and national states after them, have endeavored to turn into, or subordinate to, political borders.

The crucial historical shift, then, is perhaps to be located not so much in the *appearance* of borders *tout court* with the colonial and then the national state, but in the gradual loss by the region's peoples themselves of the ability to define, defend, and reproduce the borders that have been most salient to the management of their ecological livelihoods and the organization of their social lives. In their reassessment of the frontier and borderland history of North America, Jeremy Adelman and Stephen Aron (1999) discussed the various ways in which, caught between competing (British, French, Spanish) imperial powers in what were initially open, borderless lands, the indigenous American and inventively coexisting *mestizo* populations of "the spaces in between" were initially able to exercise control over their territories and exchanges, retaining a certain sovereignty over the terms of trade and alliance with rival outsiders. Gradually, though, as the relatively open frontier gave way to borderlands as areas of contested boundaries, and then to increasingly fixed, hierarchical, and nonporous borders (crystallized in the shift from imperial competition to the emergence of nation-states, especially the United States itself), the middle ground vanished, and indigenous control not only over the terms of trade with the outside, but even over the terms of their own habitation of space, was abolished. Similarly, although over a rather longer period of time, imperial competition succeeded by national boundary marking might be seen to have radically shifted the level of autonomy enjoyed by Saharans over the regulation of their own frontiers and the shape of the borderlands they inhabit.

In Saharan Africa, imperial competition first became really significant in the 1500s, with the emergence of rivalry between the Ottoman regencies of Tripoli, Tunis, and Algiers, on one hand, and Morocco, on the other, just as both Moroccans and Ottomans were themselves facing increased imperial competition from the Portuguese and Spanish. The injection of imperial rivalry into the Saharan borderlands came with the Moroccan expedition in 1591 to seize Timbuktu and the salt and gold trade of the Niger bend; in the relations between the Ottomans and the state of Bornu, west of Lake Chad, and those of Morocco with the Moorish *hassan* (military) emirates of the western Sahara north of the Senegal River. At first, and in some respects against the older narrative of regional collapse (Kaba 1981), the penetration of the region by outside imperial polities and the disintegration of the Songhay state increased the margin of maneuver for regional groups.[12] The late sixteenth through the late eighteenth centuries in the southern Sahara and Sahel can be seen as a dynamic period of both fragmentation and recomposition, with the appearance of new power centers controlled by emerging social groups and a proliferation of new states: Bagirmi and Wadai to the east of Lake Chad, Segu upstream of the Niger bend, the Songhay successor states downstream of Gao, as well as the—perhaps overemphasized—*arma* viceroyalty of Timbuktu and Jenné and the emergent Tuareg confederations that pressed upon it from the north. In the central and northern desert regions, recognition and correspondence as well as trade with one or another of the northern powers—the association of ultimate, however theoretical, authority in Shinqit or Tidikelt with "the sultan of Morocco" or recourse in the Gourara to the protection of the regency of Algiers—marked the presence but also the limits of imperial penetration in the region. The intensity of imperial rivalry in the Sahara was certainly far less than that between the French and British in the American Great Lakes (especially once Morocco succumbed to civil war upon the death of Ahmad al-Mansur in 1603), but the distribution of opportunities for regional initiative and the level of regional autonomy after the initial effects of regional disintegration were thereby correspondingly greater. Undoubtedly, the emergence of locally competing states out of the areas and populations previously federated by Songhay implied the generalization of warfare and the accompanying region-wide increase in the importance and volume of enslavement and the slave economy. Climatic change made its impact felt as well (J. L. A. Webb 1995). But the dynamics were internally generated, and when Europeans began to arrive on the scene, they were more drawn into these African dynamics than they were simply acting upon them from on high and afar; indeed this pattern would continue well into the more conventionally colonial period in the nineteenth century, in the northern Sahara as in West Africa (Clancy-Smith 1994; Brower 2009; Searing 2002).

At some point, however—or rather, at a variety of points along the relatively long and uneven chronology of colonial state formation, from the 1880s through the 1930s—the ability of Saharans themselves to exercise autonomy over the regulation of their political and ecological frontiers, the social and economic borderlands drawn around them, and the larger zone of connectivity encompassing them, was significantly decreased. Intensified regional interstate competition—first, the series of Sahelian jihads of the 1670s through the 1860s, then the expansion of more assertive and coercive French control into and beyond the Niger bend and southward across the desert from Algeria and Morocco, culminating in the establishment of the region's independent nation-states—segmented and bordered the intensively interdependent spaces of the Sahara as never before. It was not simply that, on a global scale, the railway turned trade and people away from the inward-facing shores of the desert to the outward-oriented world market and the "gatekeeper" states that controlled access to it (Austen 2010; Cooper 2002). Habitation, movement, and exchange within and across the desert hardly ceased; indeed, with the advent of motorized transportation they were able to expand in ways previously unimagined. The Sahara had always been extraverted within its own relations of connectivity, but now, instead of being turned outward from the inside, it was newly subordinated from the outside, its people relegated to frontier outbacks and no longer able to dictate the terms of exchange, of mobility, or of alliance with—now, recast as incorporation into—polities centered elsewhere. The Sahara would remain a global borderland, a crossroads region of transcontinental traffic and transition (Marfaing, Brachet this volume). But, with their own internal frontiers now overlaid by and (however unevenly) subject to limitation by the political boundary making of external agencies, its people would not recover the autonomy they had long held over access, movement, and exchange within their own distinctively delimited world (Oussedik this volume).

Toward an Opening: African Frontiers and the Frontiers of Africa

This loss of autonomy, of course, has played out differently for different people within the intensely hierarchical and often literally confining social relations governed by the older forms of politico-ecological regulation. *Harātīn* who leave the oasis on a truck and go find work in the expanding city cannot be aligned with *imajeghen* who abandon their unsustainable herds and settle by the river. But we ought not, perhaps, to idealize the "freeing" of individuals from older social systems any more than we should romanticize the "authentically" indigenous "freedom of the nomad" (and his relative benevolence to his slaves); the point is rather that the outcomes of the process described above have been intensely polarizing and frequently paradoxical. The normative status of the political frontier carries aspirations to freedom and self-determination for Sahrawis just as it presently confines them in the refugee camps of Tindouf. Tuareg may find themselves stripped of much that once denoted their status and autonomy; indeed their very culture may be becoming something alienated from them as it is commodified for the world market and the tourist trade, but in those processes young *ishumar* and impoverished *imajeghen,* artisans and world music performers can make their own niches in the transregional and global division of labor (Davis 1999).

In place of Kopytoff's frontier, replicating coherent cultural wholes, then, the history of Africa's Saharan borderlands since the sixteenth century at least is one of constant fragmentation and the reinvention of new norms—from jihad states to national self-determination to indigenous rights—through which, under pressure from the outside on which the region has always depended, Saharans have tried to retain control over the terms of their own existence. Conquest and incorporation here have usually meant subordination, exclusion, and the intensification of an extraversion that was always unavoidable, but could once be less unequally managed. Attempts to reassert a degree of control now, of course, must rely on the normative languages of a wider world, whether lobbying for the western Sahara or asserting Tuareg cultural autonomy and land rights over mineral resources. The "unbroken" history of the Sahara is visible in the degree to which, rather than being simply a corridor opened to the outside and then closed again, the region remains today a nexus as well as a contested border of exchange and migration. As elsewhere, such continuity is traced over a pattern of significant change and dislocation. The Sahara of the twenty-first century is part of wider connected networks of commodities—cigarettes, guns, labor, livestock, narcotics, hydrocarbons—and of culture, both produced and consumed: Arabic satellite TV beamed into the region and poetry, music, and artisanal manufactures coming out of it. The region's long-standing net extraversion has radically increased, concomitant with an internal loss of control over the terms of exchange and even of mobility and access (Grémont, Oussedik this volume). But there also remain, again as elsewhere in the global South, avenues of ingenuity and opportunity through which people retain their ability to manipulate and exploit the frontiers imposed upon them (Cordell 1985; Scheele this volume). While new boundaries and new solidarities are created to preserve or limit access to new opportunities in the state or the city (Marfaing, Choplin this volume) and to enhance regional states' and outside agencies' capacity for control, Saharans are no strangers to inventing the means of mobility to circumvent, or at least to optimize, the limitations of their environment.

NOTES

1. Herodotus, *Hist.* II.32; V.11.

2. Although Braudel professed himself convinced that "the Turkish Mediterranean lived and breathed with the same rhythms as the Christian," he also acknowledged the limits of his own sources, through which he could "glimpse the Turkish world from the outside only" (1972 [1966]: 13–14).

3. For the endurance and expansion of Saharan trade after the sixteenth century, see Newbury (1966), E. A. McDougall (1990, 2007a), and J. L. A. Webb (1995). Austen notes that global economic integration from the fifteenth century on "marginalised trans-Saharan commerce in global terms but stimulated its accelerated local growth" (2010: xi). For a similar argument in relation to the continent's economic history as a whole, see Austen (1987). For the persistence or resumption of exchange (and migration) in the Sahara, see Choplin, Brachet, Scheele, and Oudada this volume.

4. Although in 1960 it was possible to pinpoint "a neglect of comparative research" (Mikesell 1960: 64) as "the principal failing" of Frederick Jackson Turner and those who followed or critiqued him within U.S. history, subsequent years have seen considerable attempts to make good. From a vast literature, see especially Turner (2008 [1894]), Lattimore (1940), W. P. Webb (1952), Lamar and Thompson (1981), Kopytoff (1987), Weber and Rausch (1994), Faragher (1998), and Adelman and Aron (1999).

5. In 1857, in a deep societal crisis provoked by continuous and brutal frontier war, the Xhosa of the eastern Cape responded to a prophetic vision of salvation that demanded they slaughter their cattle and destroy their grain. The ensuing mass starvation may have killed up to two-thirds of the population.

6. See Baud and Van Schendel (1997) for a European perspective; Adelman and Aron (1999) for an American one.

7. See Barendse (2002) and Bose (2006). Hadramawt is a region of southern Arabia contiguous with the Indian Ocean coastline, from which generations of traders and Islamic scholars, often claiming prophetic descent as *sayyids*, engaged in trade and the spread of learning and religion throughout South and Southeast Asia. On cosmopolitanism, see Scheele and J. McDougall this volume.

8. The literature is now extensive, though John Hunwick (in Savage 1992a: 5) could still refer to the Mediterranean and Islamic slave trades as having "to date . . . stimulated little interest" relative to the larger literatures on the African diaspora in the Americas. See Manning (1990), Lovejoy (2000 [1983], 2004), Wright (2007), and Rossi (2009).

9. On the Hamitic hypothesis (attributing the origin of "advanced" peoples in East and Central Africa to in-migration from the north), see Collins (1968).

10. It is striking that the Africanization of religion (Islam and, later, Christianity) remains so central a term of analysis to scholarship, as if it were possible that such massive sociocultural change could happen *without* codes originating elsewhere becoming constitutively part of what it means to be "African," and being themselves adapted in the process.

In the case of Islam, the explanation can only lie in the persistent discomfort with "externality" combined with a persistent tendency to assume "Islam" as transhistorically and cross-culturally monolithic, whence the need to demonstrate how different it is in Africa. (But of course, "it" is both different *everywhere,* and everywhere defined by recognizable commonalities.)

11. On the relationship between locality, intraregional interdependence, and the "outside," see Scheele (2010a: 2–3).

12. The catastrophe thesis of the Moroccan invasion in Songhay history begins with, and is usually adduced from, the Timbuktu chronicles of al-Sa'di (*Ta'rīkh al-Sūdān*) and Ka'ti/Ibn al-Mukhtār (*Ta'rīkh al-fattāsh*) (Houdas and Delafosse 1964 [1913]; Houdas 1898, 1900; Hunwick 1999). Paolo de Moraes Farias's compelling argument for these texts as "an exercise in catastrophe management" by careful and accomplished "text craftsmen and ideological agents" (2003: lxx–lxxii) might be applied, at least to some extent, to their narrative of catastrophe itself as well as to the means they employ to cope with it; such visions of disaster are after all not uncommon elsewhere too, and frequently overlook other dimensions of the changes taking place.

PART 2

ENVIRONMENT, TERRITORY, AND COMMUNITY

5

THE RITES OF BABA MERZUG

Diaspora, Ibadism, and Social Status in the Valley of the Mzab

Fatma Oussedik

It is well known that for centuries, often intense patterns of exchange—of goods, ideas, architectural forms, beliefs—have developed in and across the Sahara. People and goods have moved through trade, but also through the dynamics of conquest, pilgrimage, and religious education. Like the Mediterranean world, the Sahara has experienced cycles of flourishing and reduced prosperity as these forces have ebbed and flowed across the *longue durée* and into the present. The end of the centuries-long caravan trade in the late nineteenth and early twentieth centuries marginalized or ruined the oasis cities whose lifeblood it had been; the recrudescence of movement and exchange within and across the desert today is having other effects on the populations that have for centuries inhabited these spaces. The inhabitants of the valley of the Mzab, situated in a rocky plateau whose altitude varies between 300 and 800 meters above sea level, 600 kilometers south of Algiers at the edge of the northern Sahara, have always depended on commercial activity for their survival. Ever since their arrival in the eleventh century CE, the Berber-speaking Zenata Muslims of the Ibadi rite who settled in the arid valley and built their cities here have been engaged in commerce.[1] Successfully adapting to changing economic circumstances over many centuries, the Ibadis of the Mzab were considered by the French sociologist Pierre Bourdieu (1958) as classic exemplars of the combination of "puritanism" and capital: commercial and financial entrepreneurs adhering strictly to a particularly rigorous form of Islamic doctrine.[2] For the people of the Mzab, a community whose social and political life was determined by their particular interpretation of Islam, Ibadism was a determining factor in relations with other social groups. It has therefore played a major role in the history of their exchanges with other populations, mandating a certain distinctiveness relative to other Muslim groups, requiring particular social and educational practices for the survival of the community, but also regulating the integration into the community of other ethnic groups, particularly those emerging from slavery within the Mzab itself.

This is a region with a long history of population mobility of various types. The Mzab, unable to live from the limited agriculture (mainly date palm cultivation) practicable in the valley itself, was a node in the Saharan slave trade, an area dependent for its own irrigation works on servile labor imported from across the desert to the south, and a financial and commercial point of origin for north-south caravan trade, but also the source of an important commercial diaspora of its own, with its men being sent north to trade in the Mediterranean cities of North Africa and remit their profits to their families in the valley. Enterprising, well-educated, and mobile, Mzabis have a long tradition of migration and today are found not only as elements of their old diaspora in other regions of North Africa, but as participants in the global economy of professional mobility. In addition to their skills at commerce, the Bani Mzab have also long been known for the independence of their municipal institutions, controlling life within the Mzab and also its inhabitants' movements to and from the valley. Today, however, the valley is thoroughly integrated into the Algerian state, its residents' customary independence of organization subordinated to rulings from the national administration in the north, and their local demographic predominance and long-standing patterns of social life submerged by increasing numbers of migrants from both north and south: the Ibadis have become a minority even within their own valley. It is against this background of a loss of relative autonomy and distinction that a local ritual, one particular to the black African Ibadi population of the valley, has been revived in the early 2000s. This ritual indicates not only the long historical trajectory of Islamization in Africa but also the local tensions of social organization, status, and hierarchy in the Mzab. It is an echo of a long history of slavery, and a trace of the tension within Mzabi society between the doctrinal principle, crucial to Ibadism throughout its history, of the fundamental equality of all Muslims, and the facts of local social hierarchy. As practiced today, however, it equally indicates the long-term durability and contemporary vulnerability of local processes of social and religious integration, long available to the community in its Ibadi doctrine, but today undermined by the minoritization within the Mzab of the Ibadis themselves and of their long-standing forms of social regulation.

Baba Merzug and the "Music of the Ancestors"

The ritual referred to as that "of Baba Merzug" is said to be an old practice, but was revived in the first decade of the twenty-first century.[3] It appears to be one expression (among several) of the tensions born locally of the recent influx of new migrants to the region.[4] The practice of commemoration illustrates the need for a group—here, black Ibadis of presumed slave or mixed ancestry—to situate themselves relative to others, and the means by which they do so. The singular relation to "origins" claimed by the celebrants of the rite of Baba Merzug sets them apart from the "white," Berber Ibadis, who were traditionally the locally dominant (property- and labor-owning) group; but in doing so it also serves to underline the importance of their (albeit ambivalent) belonging to the locally dominant doctrine. Conversion to Ibadism and insertion into local forms of social organization served over previous centuries as mechanisms for the integration of the descendants of slaves into Mzabi society. Today, the local forms of social integration as well as of social control seem to be undergoing a crisis, making the narration of origins and the practice of particular rituals of belonging newly important.

In the local social categorization of the Mzab, those considered to be descendants of slaves are referred to as forming two groups, *khumriyya* ("brown" people, said to be descended from male Mzabi slave owners and black African women) and *ousfan* ("blacks"). Both groups are Ibadi Muslims, but are thought to be less "reserved" or restrained by social prestige than are "white" Mzabis.[5] Today, these groups have several *majālis* (assemblies for the regulation of community affairs; sing. *majlis*), mainly run by younger men under the age of forty. The ritual of Baba Merzug is practiced exclusively by these groups. The event lasts a whole day and is organized under the auspices of a woman referred to as "Mama," who is said to have inherited the tradition from her father's family.[6] The family is of modest social status. Mama's father was a driver for a state-owned enterprise, her mother provided food for festivals and parties. Mama, now in her fifties, lives alone with her son, her husband having emigrated for work some years ago. The family has the reputation of "knowing the history" of their social group; she is a "woman who knows." "When I was a little girl," she tells us, "I used to hear my mother and grandmother talking about these rituals. For about ten years I wasn't interested in them, but now I've begun [to take an interest] again. . . . I feel my ancestors. My ancestors defended themselves, and that gives me courage. Perhaps for those ten years I didn't need them." Mama, we are told, revived the practice of the ritual in 2006. My principal interlocutor among the group is a young woman in her late twenties, whose family, it is said, was brought to the valley by the slave trade more than a century ago. Thanks to the aid of white members of the *'ashīra* (tribal fraction) to which they belong, the family now owns a house in the town of Beni Isguen (the mother's property) and a share in the palm groves there (the father's property). The purpose of the ceremony is explained as enabling the participants "to have a history, to have ancestors."

The ritual, as always in the Mzab, consists of two distinct phases, one reserved exclusively for men and the other for women. (I was able to participate only in the second.) The women's ceremony took place near Wadi Ntissa,[7] above the palm groves of Beni Isguen and about five kilometers out of town. People from the five major *qsūr* of the Mzab—El-Atteuf, Bounoura, Mélika, Beni Isguen, and Ghardaïa—gather for the celebration. In earlier times, according to the accounts we were given, women participating in the ritual would go in procession to the sound of music, from each town to the place where the celebration was to occur. The *dendoun* (tambourine) and *ghaïta* (flute) would be played: "This is the music of the ancestors; we play their music for them." Today, the women travel to the site by car or in hired buses, which are paid for by a collection taken up in advance. Various other preparations have been arranged by Mama, including the rental of a water truck, to provide water for the gathering throughout the day, and the purchase of a sheep for sacrifice (although attendees also bring additional portions of meat to add to the ritual meal). Some seventy women gather under an improvised tent, most of them wearing the *hawli,* the distinctive white linen veil of the Ibadi community in the Mzab, which wraps the head and body, leaving only one eye visible. Others wear the *hijāb* (headscarf), more commonly worn by women throughout Algeria. At Baba Merzug, a man comes to slaughter the sheep; he then departs, and the women, assisted by the children present, build a fire. Food is prepared: couscous, mutton, tea. The women eat together, and any leftover food, considered especially beneficial, will be taken home. In addition to food, they bring candles, *bkhor* (incense), and henna, which are used to invoke blessings for marriage on young single women; the henna and *bkhor* are passed in a circle seven times around a girl's head, while everyone prays that God grant her marriage. Each girl then throws the henna into a hole where candles have been placed and burns the incense in the wood fire. After tea has been drunk, music is played and some of the women enter into trance states, explained as indicating possession by *jnūn* (spirits; sing. *jinn*).[8] The women around me cover up my black pullover with a wrap, so as not to anger the *jnūn,* which are thought to be sensitive to certain colors (black and red in particular). I am told that the same music and the same mystic rituals occur in the men's meeting.

What is the significance of this spot and the ritual that takes place here? Local legend has it that the site is the burial place of seven black Ibadi men. Sometime in the nineteenth century, and acting on the principle of equality according to which, in Ibadi Islam, all believers of whatever origin are equal (and, in the original seventh-century controversy from which Ibadism sprang, equally fit to be elected caliph), these seven men asked the leader of the (white) community for wives. Unable to refuse them openly, the Mzabi notables instead took the seven men into the desert and killed them there, burying them according to Ibadi custom, in white tombs without any inscription. "Those who participate in the ritual are only *khumriyya* and *koriyya* [another word for *ousfan*]," we are told, "because those who were killed were *khumriyya* and *koriyya*." Other rituals, with similar practices, are also celebrated by the same community,[9] but according to the same informant, "Sidi Merzug is the best of the rituals, because it has not changed." And she concludes: "There is always music and dancing. Ibadis usually refuse to allow music, but we can play the *dendoun* because it's a reminder of our ancestors. I believe we mostly come from the *bilād al-sūdān* [sub-Saharan West Africa], from Niger, from Africa. I don't know how long my family has been here." On the subject of the seven men who were killed because they wished to marry white Mzabi women, the same interlocutor emphasizes that today, there are marriages between *khumriyya, koriyya,* and whites, and members of each group are to be found in each *ʿashīra*. "I belong to the *ʿashīra* of [O.]," she says, "and my father regularly attends its meetings." On the heights of the old city of Beni Isguen, near the old mosque, the *ʿargūb* quarter has "always" been home to *khumriyya, koriyya,* and white families, although with a recognized (if now disappearing) customary delimitation of space between them.[10] To this carefully graduated claim of inclusion in traditional Mzabi society is contrasted a distinct demarcation from more recent sub-Saharan migrants. "One of them works for us in the palm grove," I am told. "He comes from Mali, and we give him food during Ramadan; he comes to us for his food, or my brother takes it to him." Would she ever marry a Malian? "We don't give them women; the people from Mali, even if they're Muslims, even if they've got proper papers [i.e., are not 'illegal' immigrants], they're foreigners."[11] What about Tunisians, for instance, are they similarly foreigners? "The real question," she replies, "is Ibadism. They're not Ibadis."

Belonging to Ibadism, then, and to the traditionally dominant form of social organization in the Mzab, the *ʿashīra* and its council, distinguishes the nonwhite population from "foreigners," whether black African or Arab, and masks distinctions within the local community. The *ʿashīra*, a term possibly derived from the Arabic *ʿashara* (ten), indicating an original "senatorial" assembly of ten male heads of families, has long been identified as the building block of Mzabi society and its "city," in the sense of both the built urban space and the political society it contains. "Every Mzabi belongs to an *ʿashīra* by birth, and remains a member of it for life, unless he leaves the town where he was born and settles in another city in the Mzab. In this case, he must be integrated into another *ʿashīra*. The *ʿashīra* is therefore a local group" (Földessy 1994: 79). At the same time, it also connotes a community of (real or fictive) descent, uniting several families thought to be descended from a single ancestor (Merghoub 1972: 27). A woman belongs to the *ʿashīra* of her father for life; her children will belong to that of her husband. As a unit of social organization, the *ʿashīra* therefore combines descent and locality to assign a place to every inhabitant of the Mzabi *cité*, with incomers being absorbed through fictive kinship. As such, it is also a primary unit of social regulation and welfare provision: it "has a customary 'legal personality,' and so can hold property. It is concerned with the family's problems and particularly with those of the less well off. It holds meetings in the *hajba* (Arabic, '[place of] seclusion'), also called *tadert an ta'chirt* (Berber, 'house of the *'ashīra*'), discusses the problems of the group or the city and takes democratic decisions," decisions being "democratic" insofar as every family, of whatever socioeconomic status, that forms part of the "lineage" group is represented (Benyoucef 1986: 52). Today, the *'ashīra* is identified by the Mzabis' own cultural preservation movement as a key element of local patrimony as well as a functional institution, likened to both the clan in Scotland and the canton in Switzerland. According to the Association for the Promotion of the Arts and Traditions of Beni Isguen, while the state is "oversized," inefficient, and ill adapted to dealing with local realities and immediate relatives within the family lacking in resources, the *'ashīra* is the "optimal" social structure, allowing for individual development and a proper balance of rights and obligations. It has, in other words, become a local idiom for "civil society."

At the same time, *khumriyya* and *koriyya/ousfan*, in their self-identification as in their participation in rituals like that of Baba Merzug, its music, and the historical origin attributed to it, distinguish themselves from the old, white, notable families of the Mzab. Historically, the existence of a slave market in the Mzab and the practice, as elsewhere in North Africa, of at least nominally converting slaves to Islam, are well attested.[12] We also have, in the Ibadi "conventions," or *ittifāqāt* (agreements by which the community's scholar-leaders regulated all aspects of its life), references to the trade in slaves and their social position. A text from 1108 AH (1697 CE), for example, specifies that "a slave who has stolen must be sold by his master. But if he was born in the family [of his master], or if he is an Arab of the country, he is to be exiled for four years and he must be obliged to go to live by the sea. A free man who has stolen is to be punished by exile for two years." Thus the position of a slave varies: a slave who has been bought may be disposed of, but a slave born to a family has half the rights (or twice the punishment) of free men. As in the Muslim Mediterranean, in the Mzab gradual incorporation into the family structure, leading to manumission and the attenuation of a purely servile relation into one of dependence, seems to have been the norm historically.[13] Thus today, descendants of those originally brought to the area as slaves bear the name of an *'ashīra,* presumably originally that of their ancestors' masters, and they are at least sometimes, possibly always, eligible to attend its meetings, as suggested by an *ittifāq* text of 1197 AH (1782 CE), retranscribed in 1322 AH (1904 CE): "At this meeting [of the assembly of the *'ashīra*] were present a great number of inhabitants of the country, free men, slaves, and Arabs, and representative of all the *qsūr* who were thereby informed of the decision taken."[14] Within local society, nonetheless, *khumriyya* and *ousfan* have clearly held specific statuses, followed certain professions, and, while marrying among themselves, have rarely been allied by marriage with white Mzabi families. Indistinguishable from the property-owning notable families by religion or language, since they were all Ibadis and Berber-speakers, slaves' descendants lived in the same districts of the same towns as their former masters (though at least originally they were buried in separate cemeteries), but worked as porters, soldiers, messengers, butchers, shoemakers, or market criers. At weddings they would be expected to carry the dishes of couscous; they would refer to their patrons as *baba* (father). Above all, although they may identify themselves as Ibadis and have been fully integrated into the *'ashīra,* there are no known cases of *khumriyya* or *ousfan* having become members of the *halqa* of the *'azzāba,* the governing "circle," or council, of Ibadi religious scholars.

The *'Azzāba*, Ibadism, and Trade in the Sahara

Since the medieval period, the *'azzāba* have been relied upon as those qualified to practice *ijtihād* (the interpretation of the sources of Islamic law). Literally "those who distance themselves" from the mundane world to devote themselves to God and the study of Islam, the *'azzāba* historically played a crucial role in the government of the community. It was the *'azzāba* of the council of the mosque that long ago ruled that while men might travel outside the Mzab to engage in commerce, all the community's women must remain in the valley; the same assembly modified these restrictions when Algeria became independent from France in 1962. The council of scholars still determines whether innovations in the life of the community—for example, in the 1920s, the introduction of the telephone, more recently, the use of satellite dishes—are licit or not.[15] Along with the "lay" members of the assemblies of the *'ashīra*s and the different *qsūr,* their role has been to establish the "consensual opinion" (*ra'y ijmā'ī*) by which, in Ibadi doctrine, rulings of Islamic law are determined. The designation of the imam (leader of the community) is also a prerogative of the *halqa* of the *'azzāba.* The imam is chosen from among the leading scholars and presides at public prayer. He also has significant powers of sanction: "He can 'excommunicate' anyone who smokes, does not observe prayer, drinks fermented liquor, gambles, steals, does ill to his neighbour or is guilty of various other infractions" (Delheure 1986: 25). More junior scholars fall into two categories: *irwan* who have learned the Qur'an by heart and are eligible to become leading scholars and jurisconsults, and *imsurda,* "beginners" who are students of the Qur'an and the religious sciences.

In addition to the particular powers of the imam, the *ʿazzāba* collectively exercised a crucial veto over community life, though not by imposing punitive sanctions on lawbreakers; instead, the scholars would threaten to "withdraw" to the mosque in the event that their rulings were not followed. In their absence, the everyday flow of social life would be suddenly interrupted: legal decisions could not be taken, no circumcisions or marriages could be celebrated, the dead could not be buried. This "strike action" by the religious leaders of the community could be threatened in response to even apparently minor disturbances, as indicated by an *ittifāq* text of 1160 AH (1747 CE): "Following a dispute that occurred during the night on the *ʿargoub,* the playing of the flute there is prohibited. If this ruling is not observed, the scholars will shut themselves in the mosque and refuse to come out." Today, the regulatory role of the *ʿazzāba* is certainly reduced, but the vocation of religious scholar continues to attract young men who can be seen in public wearing the distinctive dress of the *irwan. Khumriyya* and *ousfan,* however, do not have access to this particular status within the community, an exclusion that, on the one hand, provides a space in which they enjoy a certain legitimate and public ritual creativity—including the playing of music—outside the limits of strict Ibadi orthodoxy. On the other, it marks the limits of their incorporation into the locally dominant society.

This restriction seems to derive historically from the association of the *khumriyya* and *ousfan* with slavery. Slavery was indeed an important part of both the long-distance trade and the local ecology that allowed the Mzab to function as a particularly precarious settlement in a deliberately isolated and arid zone beyond the reach of hostile neighbors. The particularism of the Mzab as an Ibadi society can be traced back to the origins of the settlement as a refuge for part of the Ibadi "diaspora" originating in northern Algeria. An Ibadi leader of Persian origin, ʿAbd al-Rahman ibn Rustum, founded the region's first Ibadi state (indeed the first independent Islamic state in North Africa), the Rustamid emirate of Tahert (near modern Tiaret), in the eighth century CE. After the destruction of Tahert in 908, the survivors of the Ibadi community fled south, arriving first at Sedrata, near today's Ouargla. Archaeological investigations at Sedrata have found the remains of a group of settlements buried in the sand, with a system of irrigation channels and examples of fine sculpture. The site seems to have been prosperous in the tenth and eleventh centuries, before it was in turn destroyed, perhaps in 1274 (Van Berchem 1953, 1954, 1960). The Ibadis, however, had already founded another settlement in a yet more remote location, the valley of the Mzab, protected by the rocky desert of the *shebka* ("net," the ravine-cut rocky plateau through which the valley winds). It was to the Mzab, as well as the successor city of Ouargla, that the survivors of Sedrata came, and from Ouargla and the Mzab that the community began to organize and finance part of the Saharan caravan trade.

Naturally enough, Ibadi merchants left traces of their doctrine along the roads they traveled. According to the leading historian Tadeusz Lewicki, Ibadism was known across the region for several centuries. It may have been carried by the expansion of the West African Soninké and Manding trading diasporas that were known to medieval Arab writers as Wangara and that are today referred to as Dioula (Dyula or Juula). Dioula Islam, as codified in the sixteenth century by el-Hajj Salim Suwari, explicitly refers to the Maliki school of jurisprudence that had by then become hegemonic in northwest Africa, but it may nonetheless contain traces of an Ibadi heritage.[16] In the fourteenth century, Ibn Battuta, on his travels in West Africa, found "white men who follow the sect of the Ibadis," living among "black merchants called Wanjarata": he referred to these Ibadis as Saghanughu, possibly to be identified with the Saganogo scholars whose influence among the Dioula lasted into the nineteenth century.[17] The great commercial road running northeast from the medieval Sahelian trade center of Tadmekka (or Essouk, northeast of Kidal in what is now northeastern Mali), to Ghadamès, the Libyan trading town on the way to Tripoli and Cairo, and Qayrawan in southern Tunisia, passed through Ouargla, the successor to Sedrata, and Touggourt, where Ibadi influence may have remained present up to or beyond the eleventh century. It may even be that the famous judgment of the Maliki jurist Ibn Abi Zayd al-Qayrawani (922/923–996) that "trading to the land of enmity and the *bilād al-sūdān* is disapproved," making the profits of trade across the desert illicit, expressed less a reservation about trade between Maghrebi Muslims and West African unbelievers than the opposition of a Maliki jurist to involvement in transactions involving the "heretical" Ibadis whose cities were along the road between the Sunni cities of the Mediterranean and the *bilād al-sūdān* itself.[18]

Part of this trade, which preexisted the Mzabis' own commercial diaspora and provided a major part of the area's commercial lifeblood for centuries, undoubtedly consisted of traffic in slaves. Converted to Islam, but remaining in their servile status, the slaves imported to work in irrigation, agriculture, and domestic service in the Mzab always constituted an anomaly in the community's self-designation as the persecuted followers of an especially egalitarian doctrinal school of "true" Islam, and a certain level of embarrassment can be discerned in accounting for their presence. Local accounts of Saharan trade emphasize the role of other groups—nomadic Arabs in particular—in the protection and actual management of the caravan routes that may have been financed by Mzabis but were often managed by others. In interviews with Ibadis, whether white or nonwhite, we were frequently told that black Africans were brought to the valley as slaves "by the Sha'anba," i.e., by the nomadic, Arabic-speaking, camel-herding entrepreneurs of the caravan trade rather than by (or for) the sedentary, Berber-speaking

Ibadis themselves.[19] The slave trade, in other words, was run by "others." Mzabis' own accounts of their commercial activities emphasize their status as "merchants," both in the caravan trade and in their own northward migration. No reference to the possibly violent practice of slave trading is admitted to, and the significance of slaves in the overall volume of Saharan commerce is downplayed. Indeed, it does seem likely that the smaller markets of the central Maghreb received proportionally fewer slaves over the long course of the "oriental" trade than did the larger urban centers of Morocco, Egypt, and the Ottoman empire, where the capacity to generate demand was correspondingly greater.

It is difficult to gain any clear picture of the size of the Mzab's slave population. We have, of course, no census by ethnic category preceding the colonial period, and the organization of population statistics by the French followed changing and disputed rules of classification. Even such early population figures as exist (for the 1840s and 1850s; Kateb 2001) of course excluded the Sahara, which was not as yet under French control but where most slaves were undoubtedly to be found: more than half the population of some settlements in areas like the Touat oases (in the west-central Algerian Sahara) were slaves or freed-slave laborers when the French arrived. Overall, the unreliability of the figures means that no satisfactory general evaluation can be made; what is certain is that servile labor remained well into the nineteenth century as the indispensable foundation of the ecological viability and economic success of areas such as the Mzab.

Slavery, of course, is not simply defined by racial classification but by different labor regimes. In the Mediterranean north, slaves were primarily domestics but some also worked in agriculture. In the Mzab, date palm cultivation provided the primary demand for servile labor in the past and remains today the main source of employment for new migrants from farther south. A certain complementarity can be seen to have developed, in the very particular case of the Mzab, between the deployment of servile labor in maintaining the palm groves and the self-imposed austerity of male migrants from the valley, whose lives in the north were regulated by a strict asceticism aimed at remitting a maximum of cash profits south to the community. While the inflow of commercial revenue was always essential to the maintenance of the settlement and the families left behind, the oases on which they were built were also created by human effort, their exploitation only possible because of a Saharan economy based on slave labor. On the other hand, the scale and rate of exploitation of servile labor were clearly limited by the restricted agricultural capacity of the valley, and this, like the adoption of former domestic servants into the family in the cities of the north, perhaps explains at least in part the relatively rapid social integration of former slaves into the *'ashīra*s of the Mzab.[20] Collective strategies of installation by families of slave descent within Mzabi society seem to be based on the existing norms of the Ibadi community, both in residential patterns and in genealogical claims (usually going back at least three generations). Within these groups, individuals considered to hold a certain degree of representative authority could emerge and take their place in relation to existing families within an adoptive *ʿashīra*. The success of this development explains easily enough the decision of slaves and formerly enslaved people to remain in the Mzab after the abolition of slavery, and the value placed by them on their integration into the *ʿashīra* and the Ibadi community.

A long-lived stance of resistance to abolition can nonetheless be traced in the community's internal self-regulation. The Mzab's autonomy and relative independence had been preserved even after the initial French incursions into the Sahara. In 1853, after the capture of Laghouat, the trading entrepôt on the rim of the Saharan Atlas to the north, the French commander, Marshal Randon, impressed by Mzabi municipal institutions, by their eloquence, and by their crucial importance for Saharan trade, agreed to a convention with the Mzabis according to which the people of the valley would pay an annual tribute (*lezma*, a term from the Ottoman period) in exchange for French non-interference in the internal administration of the area, provided order was maintained. This uneasy arrangement continued for three decades, until it was annulled with the extension of effective French military penetration of the Sahara in the later nineteenth century, among the justifications for which were the suppression of arms smuggling and the enforcement of the ban, declared in 1848, on trading in slaves in French-controlled territories.[21] The Mzab was administratively annexed to colonial Algeria in 1884—and slave trading continued until the early years of the twentieth century. French control over internal affairs, however, was at best patchy, and as late as 1929 we find reiterated attempts by the colonial authorities to impose their rulings over those of the *ʿazzāba* in matters such as those still being regulated by an *ittifāq* of 1830 (1245AH), which stated that in the case of inheritance from the estate of a slave, a woman might not inherit "because women inherit only from their own freedmen or from the freedmen of their freedmen." In the absence of a direct heir to a freed person's estate through the male line, his goods would revert to his patron or to the patron's male heirs, "exclusive of any women." As the reaffirmation of a tie of dependency still in use, this ruling was challenged by the colonial courts, which had stipulated in 1867 that "the estate of any person enslaved at the time of the publication of the decree [of abolition in 1848] cannot be attributed to his former masters, given that in Islamic as in French law, inheritance is regulated by the laws in effect at the time of the decease."[22] Evidently, neither the laws of the republic nor the egalitarian nature of Ibadi doctrine had overcome the hierarchies of a formerly slave-owning society eighty years after the formal abolition of slavery; nor had the qualified recognition of French dominance entailed an abandonment of the community's self-regulation by its own preexisting laws.

The End of Ibadi "Migration Control"

The press and public in Algeria, as elsewhere in North Africa, today regularly comment on the "illegal" or "clandestine" patterns of migration into North Africa from south of the Sahara. While official statistics are available for the number of regularly documented migrant workers in Algeria—some 20,000 from Mali and Niger in 1998, for example—no official estimates of the numbers of new "illegal" migrants entering Algeria exist, and unofficial figures vary (Khaled et al. 2007: 4n1). As has been abundantly illustrated in the literature on contemporary Saharan migration, while they are frequently depicted as absolutely impoverished, migrants are often well educated, having at some time held skilled or professional jobs in their countries of origin, and coming from middle-income, urban backgrounds. Sometimes fleeing violence or persecution, more commonly migrants move in response to the erosion of their income and living standards and the lack of opportunities for social mobility, issues that have characterized the continent since the structural adjustment of the 1990s. Finding their income insufficient to meet their families' needs, they travel, as migrants always have, in response to the perceived opportunities of labor markets elsewhere. In Algeria, most seem to work in the parallel economy, in the precarious but widespread informal commerce known as *trabendo.* Others might be shoemakers or tailors in small workshops, manual laborers in construction, or maids in domestic households. Prostitution is rarely mentioned in locally commissioned studies but certainly exists and might be supposed to involve some migrant women (Khaled et al. 2007: 18–24). Remittances from work obtained in Algeria can be sent home, and with the increased difficulty of moving on to Europe, Algeria like other North African states has become a destination rather than merely a transit zone. Among other towns in the northern Sahara, Ghardaïa in the Mzab has become a major way station on itineraries leading northward. Like Ouargla, according to a major study of irregular migration patterns across Algeria, Ghardaïa has become one of "the obligatory thoroughfares for almost any migrant wishing to reach the cities of the north" (ibid.: 21). In the *wilāya*s of Ouargla and Ghardaïa, a small minority of migrants (some 2,500–3,000 total in the two governorates) of all nationalities, but mainly from Mali, Cameroon, and Niger, have settled; some have now been living in these areas for years.

In addition to these migrations, whether "regular" or not, from the south, the Mzab has also seen an influx of people from the north. The population of Algeria has almost tripled since independence, now standing at almost 35 million; at the same time, the annual demographic growth rate has fallen from over 3 percent in the 1970s to around 1.8 percent in 2010, the fertility rate from some 7.4 children per woman in the 1970s to 3.8 at the beginning of the 1990s and 1.7 in 2010. The rising age of marriage, the improvement in education for girls, and the housing crisis have reduced rates of population growth considerably since the late 1980s, but Algeria's demographic bulge of the 1970s and '80s is very apparent in the median age of the population (twenty-seven years). National policy aims at relieving pressure on the overpopulated cities of the north by encouraging development and settlement in the south. At the same time, since independence the population of Algeria as a whole has become more homogeneous: the almost 150,000 Jews who had lived in the country before 1962 (including a significant population in the Mzab) left with the rest of the almost one million French citizens who departed at the end of the war. The proportion of foreigners living in the country has steadily decreased, leaving an Algeria almost entirely populated by people classified as Sunni Muslims.

In this context, the Ibadi community of the Mzab finds the long-standing autonomy of its local institutions facing a crisis. The rules of Ibadi institutions can hardly apply to the Arab and Sunni (Maliki) populations of Sha'anba or Metlili people now settled in the expanded towns of the valley.[23] The Ibadi community, long accustomed to exercising control over both entry into and—equally strictly controlled—departure from the cities of the valley through the *'azzāba* and the *majālis* of the *'ashīra*s, can no longer do so. Before the demographic and administrative changes of recent years, "nonwhite" communities in the valley were integrated by adherence to Ibadism and membership in the *'ashīra* while excluded from equality of status or alliances by marriage; in turn, they preserved their own distinctiveness within the Ibadi community as "having [other] ancestors," who could be remembered and celebrated against the dominant norms of Ibadi religious culture. Baba Merzug and the origin myth behind the rite can clearly be seen as an expression of this. Today, the new migrants from the south add to the numbers of those who have increasingly come from all over Algeria to settle in the valley, and the existing community has been unable to integrate any of them into its own frameworks. The new arrivals, from the south or from the cities of northern Algeria, are mostly Muslims, but none are Ibadis. The dissolution of forms of social control over entry into the city has also meant the end of long-established means of social integration. It has therefore had the effect of maintaining, indeed of sharpening, local hierarchies and the local valorization of belonging to Ibadism, an identity which the locally subordinate but integrated nonwhite population forcefully claims in order, it seems, to distinguish themselves from new black arrivals. To suggest a connection, or homology, between the new migrants from south of the Sahara and the men and women who gather to celebrate their ancestors at Baba Merzug is to remind the latter, whose family histories are now entirely tied into their respective *'ashīra*s, of their exogenous and servile origins. By renewing the rites of Baba Merzug they, on the contrary, underline their ancestral belonging to the valley, including its doctrinal particularism and their particular place within it. The distinctiveness of the ritual within the wider Ibadi community thus serves simultaneously to demarcate its celebrants from the dominant community and to associate them firmly with it. It therefore expresses, no less than does the loss of control over matters once regulated by the *'azzāba* to the new administrators of the state, the defensive posture of a minority no longer in control of its social and physical space.

The myth of the Mzab has long been, in the community's own terms, that of a *mujtama' mithālī*, a paradigmatic "model society": the earthly utopia of a truly virtuous republic under God. Here as elsewhere, however, even the egalitarian forms of social order have produced marked and persistent forms of social hierarchy. But this hierarchy has not undermined the group's institutions; on the contrary, it has inscribed itself within them, perpetuating the group's capacity to regulate entry and exit over the long term. The sociopolitical organization of the cities of the Mzab has had both a material and a symbolic reality, tying the people to the sacred and its interpretation. The *'ashīra* implies a solidarity within the city that can only with difficulty be compared to the tribe or family (*'arsh* or *ā'ila*) structures dominant in the rural world of much of Algeria. This urban(e) solidarity concerns every element of the group, including those who might be descendants of slaves. Indeed, despite its apparently genealogical expression, the *'ashīra* has less to do with connection to a mythical common ancestor than it does with the notion that free-born Zenata Berbers and the descendants of their slaves have shared and still share a common *destiny* as members of a distinct community of faith that today is a religious minority within Algerian Islam. This commonality is affirmed in the assemblies of the *'ashīra* but also by commemoration at anonymous tombs beside which are spaces for prayer. Within this single community, distinctions are maintained by limits on matrimonial exchange, by the impossibility of accession to the status of *'azzāba,* and by practices like those at Baba Merzug: music and a proximity to the world of the *jnūn*. It is this adherence to a distinctive position *within* the Ibadi community of faith that gives the locally established descendants of slaves the impetus and the means to distinguish themselves from newly arriving black Africans who are not (and will not become) Ibadis. It is not any right of birth, nor one of residence, but rather the long course of history that has successfully integrated the descendants of slaves into the society of the Mzab; but that society has itself become a minority, and the internal dynamic of the valley's history can no longer work the same way with those who arrive today.

NOTES

1. The five major towns of the Mzab are Ghardaïa—today the administrative center of the *wilāya* (governorate)—Beni Isguen, El-Ateuf, Mélika, and Bou Noura. Two other oases, Berriane and Guerrara, are situated a little farther north.

2. See also Holsinger (1980). Ibadis, adherents of one of the oldest schools of doctrine in the Islamic faith, constitute a very small minority of Muslims worldwide and are concentrated mainly in Oman, Zanzibar, and several peripheral areas of the Maghreb: the Mzab, the island of Jerba in Tunisia, and Jebel Nafusa in Libya (see Lewicki 1955, 1976; Bierschenk 1988; on Ibadis in Oman, see Wilkinson 1987). Although Ibadis were for many centuries a particularist community practicing "separation" from non-Ibadis (Sunnis or Shiis), since the early twentieth century a rapprochement with other Muslims has reduced the significance of doctrinal or ritual differences between them. On the relationship of Ibadism to Sunni Islamic reform *(islāh)* and nationalism in the twentieth century, see Ghazal (2010a, b).

3. The ritual is named after the site where it is celebrated, which in turn is named after an unknown figure: Baba Merzug. No other link has been established between this person and the ritual.

4. There have been a number of sometimes violent local disputes in the Mzab over land and property rights, generally opposing Mzabi Ibadis to Sha'anba (more recently settled, non-Ibadi Arab groups), which have been frequently reported in the Algerian press; see Bousquet (1986).

5. Color terms in the region refer, as elsewhere, to social coding and ought not to be understood as simple descriptions of skin tone. The terms "black" and "white," translating these local classifications, will henceforward be used without quotation marks.

6. The event described here took place on 20 May 2008.

7. A tributary of the Wadi Mzab; the river flows only once every three or more years.

8. *Jnūn* are mentioned in the Qur'an as creatures inhabiting a parallel (invisible) world to that of humans; in popular belief they are akin to spirits, which can be beneficent or malign. On spirit possession in Algeria more generally, see Andezian (2001); for similar spirit possession rituals in Muslim northwest Africa (e.g., *bori* and *hauka*), see Stoller (1995) and Hunwick (1994).

9. Notably, one in honor of Sidnā Blāl (Bilal ibn Rabah, the Prophet's black companion and Islam's first muezzin, here identified as "an ancestor who died in Tafilalt" in southeastern Morocco), which is celebrated outside the walls of Beni Isguen. On the incorporation of Bilal into local origin stories and religious practices in Tafilalt, see Becker (2002). Farther south, Bilal also figures as an original ancestor in the Mande Sundiata epic; see Niane (1965).

10. The old *qsūr* of the Mzab are all built up the steep slopes of hills above the valley, with the older districts clustered around the single, four-sided, unadorned, and tapering minaret of the principal Ibadi mosque.

11. Although Malian nationals do not need a visa to enter Algeria, they are often subsumed in a large and ill-defined category of "illegal immigrants" by the Algerian public, media, and police (Bensaâd 2009).

12. See, for instance, Duveyrier (1860), Amat (1885), and Brower (2009).

13. In Islamic law, manumission does not lead to the complete severance of ties between former master and slave; rather, they remain in a relationship of patron and client. The master retains some inheritance rights over his former slave's property, and often feels responsible for arranging his marriage. The manumission of female slaves was most commonly linked to the birth of a child fathered by their master (see also E. A. McDougall this volume).

14. On the *ittifāqāt*, see Oussedik (2007).

15. Initially resisted, satellite dishes were installed at Guerrara, for instance, only after one had been placed on the mosque (with certain channels blocked).

16. Lewicki (1960), Savage (1992b), and Wilks (2000). According to Joseph Schacht (1954), this Ibadi influence is clearly visible in mosque architecture throughout the region.

17. Hamdun and King (1975: 32), Wilks (2000: 101–102), and Reichmuth (2000: 426).

18. Ibn Abi Zayd remains a major source of Maliki doctrine in the Maghreb. On trade in this period and his fatwa, see Levtzion (2000), Wilks (2000), and Brett (1983).

19. This is confirmed by the archival evidence; see the many documents kept in Centre des Archives d'Outre Mer, Aix-en-Provence, France: Archives du gouvernement général de l'Algérie, 12H50; and Brower (2009). This, however, does not diminish the responsibility of the Bani Mzab, as leading financiers, for the slave trade.

20. On the development of dependence out of slavery in northern Algeria in the late Ottoman period, see Loualich (2003).

21. Cordell (1999). On the later history of slavery in French West Africa, see Klein (1998).

22. Decision of the Court of Appeal of Algiers, 30 December 1867.

23. The Sha'anba are one of the largest, formerly nomadic, Arab tribal groups in the area of the Mzab; Metlili is a town on the main road north from the Mzab, situated just north of Laghouat.

CELEBRATING *MAWLID* IN TIMIMOUN

Ritual as Words in Motion, Space as Time Stood Still

Abderrahmane Moussaoui

At Ouled Saïd, the whole oasis awaits the arrival of the procession. The standard of Sidi al-Hājj Bu M'hammad appears over the dunes just as the sun begins to set, enflaming the horizon red and ochre. Men, women, and children, scattered across the ridges of the dunes that border the oasis and its palm groves, stand up to meet it. Even the *tolbā,* the students of religion who just now were chanting verses from the Qur'an on the flank of the highest dune, and who seemed to be settled there forever, suddenly get to their feet. A group of men goes out to meet the procession that has now stopped at the foot of the last dune, beyond the limits of the oasis on its northern edge, and a large semicircle forms around three musicians playing the *tar,* a kind of drum. In a little valley between the dunes bordering the oasis, one of its inhabitants welcomes the group of visitors, presenting to them the members of the *jmāʿa,* the council, and the notables of the *qsar.*[1] The visitors and most of those who have awaited their arrival now form a large circle some fifty meters across, at the center of which stand six *tar* players and a dozen men carrying between them the green banner of Sidi al-Hājj Bu M'hammad. The drummers provide a backdrop to a chorus of voices in which the names of God and of his Prophet are profusely repeated. A *duʿa,* an invocation or prayer of salutation addressed to the Prophet, is raised in chorus by men and women together, in low voices, in devotion: *as-salāmu ʿalayka yā rasūl Allāh* (May peace be upon you, O messenger of God). One man, the *muqaddam* (guardian) of the *zāwiya,* is the focus of attention; he is everyone's host.[2] All the visitors seek to approach him, while the inhabitants of Ouled Saïd try to get close to the banner of Sidi Bu M'hammad. After about half an hour, everyone moves to the hollow of another little valley among the dunes. The circle is reformed, and the chorus begins again, as does the rhythm of the drums: *a rasūl Allāh* (O messenger of God). After a last prayer, the procession enters the *qsar* just as the sun sets. The Qur'an will be recited throughout the night—the *salka* (reading of the entire Qur'an at one sitting) will not be complete until the first light of dawn. Couscous is eaten, tea drunk, and rifles discharged into the air.

This ceremony at the little settlement of Ouled Saïd marks the first stop in an annual ritual marking *mawlid,* the birth of the Prophet, a ritual to which the town of Timimoun today largely owes its celebrity. The regional capital of the Gourara, Timimoun lies some 750 kilometers as the crow flies (or 1,300 kilometers by road) south of Algeria's Mediterranean coast, in an extremely arid zone very distant from any of the country's main urban centers. It remains, however, a place of annual gathering for an immense population of pilgrims who come from far away to celebrate the birth of the Prophet of Islam. *Muhibbīn,* "those who love [the Prophet],"[3] come from afar to join with the inhabitants of Timimoun and the surrounding *qsūr* in the intense experience of a festival in which, for seven days, the sacred and the secular are mixed. Circumscribed geographically within the local area, Timimoun's *mawlid* festival remained for many years an exclusively local celebration, and even at the end of the 1970s, it was largely unknown beyond the Algerian Sahara. In less than two decades, however, its reputation became international, and the *sbūʿ* (seven days' festival) of Timimoun has become an attraction for visitors from every region of the country and beyond.

More than any other event, the *mawlid* expresses the richness and subtlety of popular, collective belief. Beyond the aggregation of individual beliefs, which might add up to no more than a mystification, the plural discourse of such a widely shared festival becomes the expression of a community's collective memory, one that is more than the sum of the separate memories of isolated individuals. Rather than simply supposing that such collective memory necessarily exists for any social group, and that to study such a phenomenon it would be enough to listen to members of the group as they narrate it, the social process of festivals in general, and our example of the Timimoun *mawlid* in particular, can be seen as displaying the "raw material" from which social memory is constructed. A festival is the social high point in, and through, which the various normative structures (*montages normatifs*) elaborated by the community are deployed. At the same time, it is through such structures—rites, myths, beliefs, legends—enacted or displayed at such times and places, and through the particular symbols and insignia chosen by the group to distinguish itself from others, that the community affirms its existence. At such times, too, the physical as well as social space of the festival is recreated, meanings that are ordinarily hidden reemerge in the natural and the built environment. Through reading such events, then, we can also read the ways in which social groups are constituted and inscribed in a particular space. On these occasions, *place*—a space plus its history—is brought out of its everyday obscurity, lit up and made visible. A

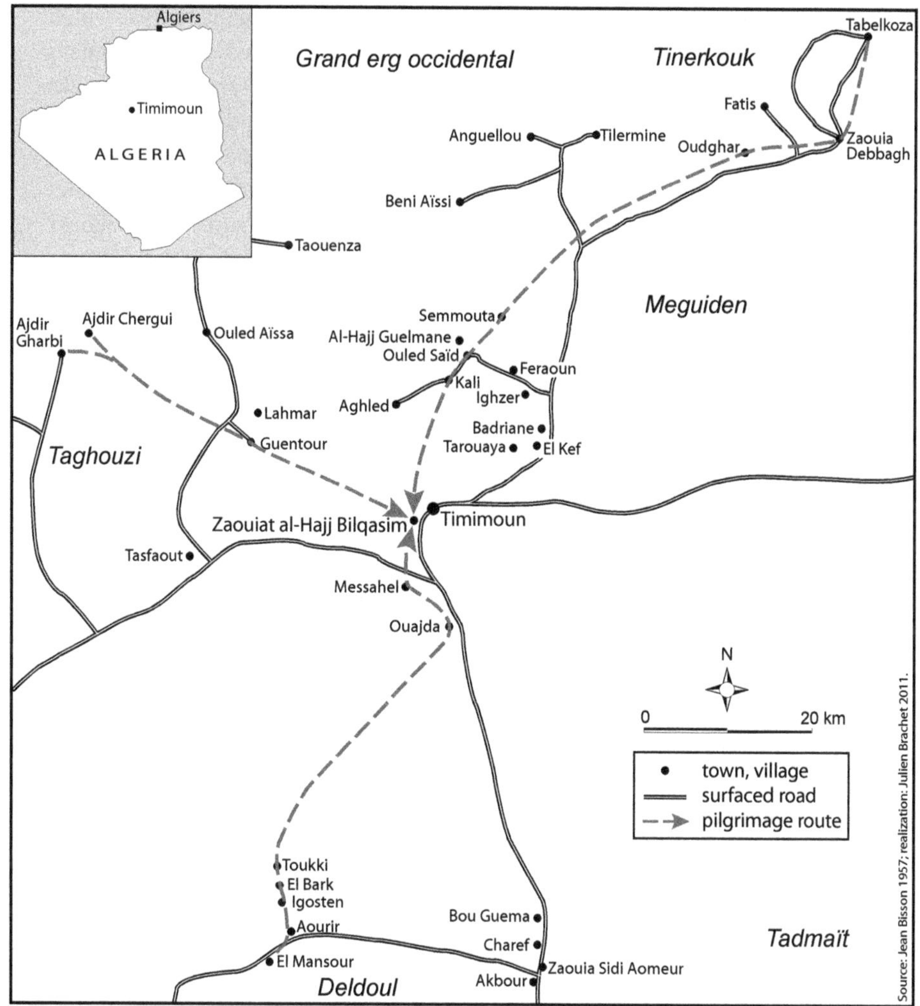

Map 6.1. The Gourara: *qsūr* and pilgrimage route. J. Brachet 2011

sanctuary, a square, becomes the object of particular attention, one often expressed by a reactualization of an etiological myth, a myth of origins.

The *Mawlid,* a Festival of Remembering Together

The word *sbūʿ,* meaning "week," refers to the seven days of uninterrupted celebration during which the Gourara celebrates *mawlid.* It also refers more particularly to the seventh day, the day of the ceremony closing the festival, which takes place in Timimoun itself. This ceremony of the seventh day (i.e., seven days after the date believed to commemorate the birth of the Prophet), which has become synonymous with the *mawlid,* is the most solemn and attracts pilgrims from surrounding *qsūr* and visitors from farther afield. It is, though, the end of a series of phases in the larger festival, the closing act of a cycle begun seven days earlier, some sixty kilometers to the north of Timimoun, in the oases of Tinerkouk.

On the day commemorating the Prophet's birth, the first of several processions of pilgrims sets out from Tinerkouk, on the edge of the Great Western Erg,[4] carrying the banner of the patron saint of the area. From there, it will travel southwest, passing through each of the principal *qsūr* of the Gourara—Sammouta, Ouled Saïd, Kali, Massine—before arriving at the *zāwiya* of Sidi al-Hājj Belqasim, in a small village of the same name just south of Timimoun, where the final celebrations will take place. Arriving at each *qsar,* the procession is received ceremonially and generously, as described at the opening of this chapter. When it leaves, the cortege will be a little larger, the inhabitants of the *qsar* just visited and people from nearby having joined it, bringing with them the banners of their own local saints. Pausing like this at each stop on the way, the pilgrimage will take seven days and seven nights, reaching its goal only at the end of the seventh day, the *sbūʿ,* when it arrives at the *zāwiya* of Sidi al-Hājj Belqasim with some thirty standards held aloft, banners that symbolize the saintly figures, memorable events, and sacred places of the region. In the course of the week, each group receives its neighbors before becoming the guests of another group, which in turn will welcome the pilgrims before joining the procession of banners through the chain of oases. At each point, members of the procession share among themselves generous offerings of couscous (*taʿm*) and celebrate together through the night in each *qsar* before the final ceremony.

"The procession from Tinerkouk to Ouled Saïd is as the son visiting his father," explains a local informant, and indeed, according to local tradition, it is Sidi Ahmad Bubakkar and Sidi Bubakkar, the father and grandfather of Sidi al-Hājj Bu M'hammad, the patron saint of Tinerkouk, who are interred at Ouled Saïd, making this the first major stopping point of the pilgrimage after Zāwiyat Debbagh in Tinerkouk.[5] As at each step of the way, the procession stops at the edge of the *qsar* and waits. The next day, after the night's celebrations and with its ranks swelled by the new pilgrims from Ouled Saïd and the smaller surrounding settlements, the procession moves on a little way southwest to Kali, where the *walī* Sidi Abd al-Hakam (locally called Sidi Haku) is buried. After a short visit to the *qubba* (mausoleum) of this *sharīf* (descendant of the Prophet), toward nightfall of the same day the pilgrims return to Ouled Saïd, where they will remain one more night before moving on across the desert southwest to Massine, the second important stopping point on their journey. In the afternoon, the procession, made up mainly of men, gets under way toward Massine, now carrying three banners: that of Tinerkouk, representing Sidi al-Hājj Bu M'hammad, and two from Ouled Saïd, representing the two local saints, Sidi Ahmad Bubakkar and Sidi Bubakkar. Massine is the most important stop before the last; it is here that the first reenactment of simulated combat and negotiation take place, commemorating the dispute and reconciliation that, according to local tradition, are the origin of the ritual.

In Massine, a *qsar* just northwest of Timimoun, the festival preparations are in full swing in anticipation of the pilgrims' arrival. By the afternoon, a large crowd has already gathered; people from all the neighboring *qsūr* are present, awaiting the arrival of the pilgrims and their banners. The day's rituals are to include whitewashing, with chalk, the *qubba* of Sidi Ahmad U Yusaf, the patron saint of Massine, and visiting the tomb of Sidi Sa'id adjoining the mosque, where prayers will be said in chorus. At the same time as the procession from Tinerkouk approaches from the north, a second group of pilgrims has formed at the *zāwiya* of Sidi al-Hājj Bilqasim. This group has formed from two separate processions, one from the *qsūr* of Lahmar, Ouled Aïssa and Ajdir in the *erg* to the northwest of Massine, the other from the oases of Messahel and Ouajda to the south. These groups converge on Timimoun, meeting there with the people of Massine in a carnival of celebratory rifle fire around the quarters of the town's old *qsar* two days before the *sbū'*. After this, the inhabitants of Massine return home to await the arrival of the pilgrims from the more distant northern *qsūr*, while the other groups leave Timimoun for the *zāwiya* of Sidi al-Hājj Bilqasim, whose mausoleum will be newly whitewashed in preparation for the great celebration the next day. They will remain there for three days after the *sbū'*.

The ceremony that now takes place, the chalking of the *qubba* of the saint, deserves some attention. The pilgrims from the various *qsūr* to the west and south, joined by those from Timimoun and nearby settlements, and accompanied by the disciples of Sidi al-Hājj Bilqasim, meet at the edge of town in a place known as *al-jbal*, "the hill" or "mountain." From here they move on to the *zāwiya* of the saint, where after the second afternoon prayer (the *'asr*), a group of notables and *tolbā* (students, disciples) begins a ceremony of invocations and communion. Among the prayers, one invokes God with the words *Bi'smi-llāh yā dhū 'l-fadā'il* (In the name of God, possessor of graces). The reference is to the local legend of Sidi al-Hājj Bilqasim, who, on coming to the site of Timimoun, is said to have heard voices in the desert glorifying God in these terms, thus causing him to stop there. When the prayers are over, the whitewashing begins. Everyone present contributes, dipping their hands in the chalky liquid, frequently covering themselves, too, in a coat of whitewash. When the work is over, the crowd disperses with the words *blāgh al-maqsūd, msallmīn sīdī* (The aim is achieved, greetings my lord). Everyone then heads to Massine, where a final night's celebration will take place before the *sbū'* begins the next day at the *zāwiya* of Sidi al-Hājj Bilqasim.

Those who have participated in the preparation of the mausoleum arrive at Massine toward nightfall. The ceremony begins with the sound of tambourines, played in a measured rhythm that announces the arrival of a group of men with the standard of Sidi al-Hājj Bilqasim. Men of all ages dressed in long, loose robes (*gandūras*) and turbans (*sheshs*)[6] process across the square where the ceremony will take place. Hundreds of pilgrims fill the labyrinthine alleyways of the *qsar* of Massine, heading for the tomb of Sidi Yusaf, in front of which a long prayer will be said by a *faqīh* (senior religious expert), echoed from time to time by a chorus of voices calling God's blessings on the Prophet. The text of this prayer, preserved in a small book and attributed to Sidi al-Hājj Bilqasim himself, consists of conventional prayers followed by a physical description of the beauty of the Prophet (evoking his "black eyes, arched brows, red cheeks, white teeth").[7] This ceremony lasts some twenty minutes, at the end of which the saint's banner that has been brought from Timimoun is rolled up and placed inside the mausoleum of Sidi Yusaf; it will not be taken out again until after the fifth and final prayer of the day (*al-'ishā*), when it will be returned to the tomb of Sidi al-Hājj Bilqasim in readiness for the *sbū'* the next day. The women of Massine, looking down on the ritual from the terraces of the surrounding houses, participate in the event with their *youyous* (ululations). Later that night, the banners from Ouled Saïd arrive. (In the ceremony observed in 1993, the group from Ouled Saïd did not arrive until around eleven o'clock at night, but even when these banners arrive at Massine earlier, their bearers wait outside the *qsar* until after the *'ishā* prayer.) First, only the shadows of the poles appear, then the cloth of the three long banners, and finally the pilgrims who carry and accompany them, advancing slowly toward the *qsar* and its open square. From the *qsar* itself, the banner of Sidi Yusaf is taken out to meet the visitors. This is a highly charged moment: the meeting of the two groups takes place in an energetic scramble, a kind of melee or disordered clash of ranks around the banners, in which everyone tries to touch the saintly emblems. The standard of Sidi Yusaf is snatched away and returned to the saint's *qubba*. This episode, in which mainly young men participate, lasts for some time. The crowd, leaping with their arms aloft, chants *rasūl Allāh* (messenger of God) for half an hour, at the end of which the *muqaddam* of the *zāwiya* of Massine, al-Hājj Muhammad al-Bashir Bawahhab (called al-Hājj Ahmad al-Qahira, or Ahmad "Cairo"), a descendant of Sidi Ahmad U Yusaf, the patron saint of Massine, climbs onto the roof of his house from where he leads the assembly in prayer: the *fātiha*, the opening chapter of the Qur'an, repeated three times, *qul huwwa Allāh* (say: He [alone] is God), the *muʿāwwidatayn* (the two final chapters of the Qur'an), and a final repetition of the *fātiha.*[8] All the banners are placed in the *qubba* of Sidi Yusaf, except that of Sidi al-Hājj Bilqasim, which is returned to its patron's *zāwiya* "to be ready to receive its visitors" the following day. This series of prayers, ending with the *fātiha,* marks the closing of one phase of the festival and the opening of another. It signals the beginning of a series of religious songs and dances that will last well into the night. These *hadra* (presence) ceremonies—Sufi practices of "remembrance," or "mindfulness," of God—are followed by the famous singers of the *ahallīl,* the local repertoire of sacred vocal music in Taznatit (the Berber dialect of the Gourara), which lasts almost until morning.[9]

With the final meeting of all the pilgrims at Massine, a ritual assembly has united the descendants of Sidi al-Hājj Bu M'hammad of Tinerkouk with those of Sidi al-Hājj Bilqasim. Local tradition relates that the saints of the region having opposed each other in an ancient quarrel, the Prophet himself intervened at the request of Sidi al-Hājj Bilqasim to reconcile them at a place called *al-hufra,* "the hollow," near the spot where the *zāwiya* of Sidi al-Hājj Bilqasim would later commemorate its founder. Like all origin myths, this one has several local variants. Sometimes it is the saints themselves, sometimes the region's tribes, who are said to have been parties to the dispute. But all the popular versions agree on drawing a direct line between the contemporary ritual and a past dissension resolved under the auspices of Sidi al-Hājj Bilqasim. Ever since then, it is said, the event is commemorated and the saint honored by a reenactment at the site of the reconciliation. The more "learned" version of the tradition considers the festival rather as the commemoration of a council of the region's religious scholars, called by Sidi al-Hājj Bilqasim to decide on the introduction of the celebration of the *mawlid* to the Gourara. This may be the more likely explanation of the origin of the site's importance, but local imagination remains persuaded of the veracity of its (simultaneously more saintly and more sociological) version.

On the seventh day, everyone assembles for the *sbūʿ* at the edge of the town of Timimoun, at the place locals call *al-jbal,* the "mountain," which, topographically, is only a slight elevation of the ground. While the pilgrims gather, continuous volleys of celebratory gunfire are loosed into the festive atmosphere. With the arrival of some thirty assembled saints' banners, the largest procession yet of men, women, and children, including the young and the elderly, begins to make its way, on foot and on donkey, by camel and by car, toward the final point of the pilgrimage trail, the *hufra* at the *zāwiya* of Sidi al-Hājj Bilqasim. The four banners collected together earlier at Massine have already arrived in the late morning; they will not enter the *qsar,* however, but remain outside, at the mausoleum of another saint, Sidi al-Hājj M'hammad, the grandson of Sidi Bilqasim, who is buried at the approach to the village, at a place known as *al-qasriya* (the little *qsar*). Before the arrival of the other banners from Timimoun, these four flags are taken down into the *hufra*, a depression near the *zāwiya* of the presiding saint, to begin a dance that will last more than an hour, until the arrival of the main procession.

The procession arrives, preceded by two men on horseback. These are said to be descendants of the Hammouzine, a family of notables whose eponymous ancestor, according to local tradition, offended Sidi al-Hājj Bilqasim, thus instituting the annual requital that has become part of the *mawlid*.[10] Another procession of banners, grouped behind that of Sidi al-Hājj Bilqasim, comes out from the *zāwiya*: those of Sidi 'Abbad, carried by the inhabitants of Ajdir and Ouled Aïssa; of Sidi Yadda, by those who have come from the *qsar* of Messahel; and of Sidi Brahim, by the people of Ouajda. A final group, the Ouled Ayyach from Tinerkouk, carrying the banner of the *walī* Sidi 'Abdallah, has arrived from the northeast via Anguellou, Tin Djellet, Feraoun, Ighzer, Badrian, El Kef, and Azekkour, a more direct route along the chain of oases down to Timimoun, without passing through Massine farther to the west. As soon as the processions meet one another, the scene is transformed into a busy spectacle mixing warm embraces with mock battles. The banner of Sidi al-Hājj Bilqasim is "stolen" before being placed, before the others, back in the *zāwiya*. Whoever joins in this part of the ceremony is sure to live out the year, it is said. At sunset, the ceremony is concluded with prayers. Handfuls of couscous are distributed with shreds of the cloth that, for the past year, has covered the saint's tomb and that has just been replaced. Some of the saints' banners are taken away at a run, as they arrived; others remain in place at the *zāwiya* of the presiding saint.[11] The *fātiha* is said in front of the mausoleum, and the *sbū'* officially ends. In fact, however, this marks the end of the solemn cycle of the festival and the opening of another phase of festivities, concerning the *zāwiya* of Sidi al-Hājj Bilqasim, where a *hadra* will take place the following day, and all the surrounding *qsūr*, especially that of Timimoun, which up until now has not been the center of attention.

It is particularly the events of the two nights *following* the seventh day that are remarkable at Timimoun. On the night of the seventh day, the night of the *manjūr*, a *barūd* (lit., gunpowder; a procession or assembly in which rifles are fired in celebration) crosses the *manjūr*, the principal road that traverses the town. Groups of men, every twenty meters or so, fire volleys one after another, after a sequence of chants and invocations. This slowly dancing procession sets off from Ouled Brahim, a district at the southern end of the *manjūr*, and ends at Suq Sidi Musa (the market of Sidi Musa), the largest open square of the *qsar*, near the great mosque of Sidi 'Uthman. It is here that, in former times, the slave market was located. The eighth night of the *mawlid* is the night of the *mishwar*. In a triangular open space before a large, tall building which was formerly the house of the *qā'id* (the local governor)—whence the name *mishwar* (palace; more literally "council house" or "place of consultation," which can also indicate the open space outside an official building)—another *barūd* takes place; it is as if, after the honor rendered to God and his saints, it is the turn of those in power here below to receive salutation. This is a *barūd* celebrated by the men of Aougrout (a separate chain of oases to the southeast) and Timimoun, in a competitive atmosphere that lasts all night. Dressed all in white, brandishing their rifles below a full moon (it is the nineteenth of the month of *rabī' al-awwal* in the lunar Islamic calendar), the crowd recites, rather than sings, invocations to God and the Prophet, weighing each syllable as they chant together. Two weeks previously, the people of Aougrout held their own night-long celebration in honor of their local saint, Sidi 'Awmar, in which they were joined by the folk of Timimoun; now, they are guests at Timimoun's festival. The small space in which the *barūd* takes place heightens the atmosphere. It ends only around six o'clock the next morning. Toward the conclusion of the event, all those present form a single large circle, occupying the whole space of the *mishwar*, and dance together. All at once, everyone sits and holds his rifle aloft, pointing to the sky; one after another, the rifles are discharged. Everyone stands and the circle is reformed; the discharged rifles are raised high and then brought together, such that the muzzles touch, forming a cone above the circle of white turbans. The rifles are made into a sort of protective roof, a kind of *qubba* (dome, usually that over a saint's tomb) whose vault is formed by rifle barrels and whose enclosure is formed by men. With this, the festival of the *mawlid* is over.

Consciousness of the Body and Care of the Self

What are the elements that structure such a series of ceremonies? Clearly, we can see basic paradigms in the use of words (supplications, singing, prayers, various exchanges) and in movement through space (processions, pilgrimages, sacred and secular visits), but there is also the importance of food, rifle play, and the presence of the saints' banners. These might be taken as the ritual materials which, with the body as their axis, provide the basis of the meaning of the celebration.

In the continuous movement of the pilgrimage, the physical effort of which implies not simply discomfort but rather a sort of desired suffering through mortification, the *mawlid* constitutes a place and a time of physical contact and exchange: a festival of encounters in which people touch one another when meeting, in dancing, and during and after prayer. Hands, shoulders, and heads are kissed. Men lean against the walls of *qubbas*, touch the tombs of saints and kiss the cloths that cover them, hang onto the flagpoles of the saints' banners; they embrace each other warmly, pray, sing, and dance side by side. During the *ahallīl*, participants stand shoulder to shoulder, the whole assembly forming one body. When the different processions meet, an immense jostling takes place as everyone tries to seize the saints' banners. From one point of view, then, the festival is a continuous celebration of the body. Indeed, the body seems to be the focus of particular attention, as if the festival were intended to satisfy the body's essential appetites. The couscous so abundantly served is the most revealing aspect of this; it is called not only *ta'm* (food) but also *'aysh* (life; elsewhere, the word also refers to bread), *m'ash* (that which gives life), and *nu'ma* (grace). The "care of the self," of course, to use Foucault's (1979) term, works not only through the satisfaction of the body but also through its mortification. A disciplining of the body might also be seen at the center of the process: praying means staying awake through the night, defying darkness and sleep in hope for the day, and maintaining painful physical postures, whether standing up or bowing down. As de Certeau puts it, "the worshipper prays 'out of his body,' *carried away* in supplication, *prostrate* in adoration, or *seized* by a sacred choreography" (1987: 16).

We have described the central place of the saints' standards in the unfolding of the ceremony. Each *qsar* possesses its own banner or banners, without which no procession can take place; each important moment of the festival is marked by a display of the banners. Arrivals, departures, prayers, dances—everything is articulated around these flags on their long poles, which stand, perhaps, as symbols of social cohesion. Each time the banners meet, the moment is ritually marked. Similarly, the care afforded each saint's resting place also emphasizes the sacred character of the site and provides today's community with the opportunity to participate in its annual refoundation. Walking through the *qsar*, one can easily identify the most important buildings by the quantity of chalk applied to their walls. In renewing the white covering of the saint's *qubba* and of other venerable sites, the people of the Gourara reaffirm their reverence for the region's saintly men and the places that sheltered them or that have become their resting places. The whitening of the *qubba* is also a physical process; those present mix the whitewash with their arms, then take hold of the stones that project from the walls of the mausoleum to climb up to the roof, from where the chalk mixture is spread. The middle of the participants' foreheads and their forearms are coated white. One might read this whitening as a regeneration of a surface saturated with passing time, like a blackboard cleaned to receive new writing. The medieval historian and anthropologist of religion Alphonse Dupront wrote of the graffiti that cover the walls of sanctuaries elsewhere: "the pilgrimage over and grace obtained, the believer's presence is affirmed by another, durable sign of the actions of grace, the *ex-voto*" (1987: 403). Here, on the other hand, the *ex-voto* (an inscription or offering honoring God, a saint, or, in Catholicism, the Virgin, for grace obtained) is an absence of traces, an absolutely clean surface. At the same time as it removes the marks and debris deposited by time and the elements, the whitewashing of the *qubba* constitutes a single, collective "trace" of the community's action and of its communion. The gestures of the individuals involved are not juxtaposed, but conjoined, to begin a new page. The marks of the past are rubbed out, providing a clean slate on which new events can be written. Thus, from one generation to another is transmitted the veneration of the site without which no "presence"—no maintenance of society and stability, or even of human habitation itself—can be imagined. And conversely, this fragile, reiterated marking of place, as a sign full of meaning, has allowed these tiny white structures, which could be lost in the immensity of the desert, to survive until today.

The pilgrim, then, writes with his body words that combine with space to produce texts. The body plays a key role throughout the process, as "the axis of the world" (de Certeau 1987: 14); standing, the worshipper makes his body the vector of a movement toward God, or sitting, returns introspectively toward himself. Hands placed together and cupped toward the sky evoke hope; put up to the face and kissed, they show gratitude. The closing of the eyes is a kind of interior movement toward the heart. As de Certeau puts it, "like voices, hands have different tonalities and meanings for speaking of God" (ibid.: 17). The physical postures of those at prayer, then, can be read too, as can the movements of dancers. The control of the individual body is the basis of the collective work of ritual that leads from the self to the community, the resulting work being offered to God in an act of communion. Pilgrimage stands as one of the major forms of such work; in it, space constitutes the canvas and the body the means of expression. It provides a means of apprehending and expressing meaning in line with a certain orientation toward the world. In this sense, pilgrimage is what the art historian and literary critic André Jolles called a "simple form," when in his analysis of literary genres he wrote of "these forms that are not encompassed by stylistics, rhetoric, poetics or even, perhaps, by 'writing,' which do not constitute 'works of art' although they are artful, nor poems, though they are poetic; in short, these forms that we commonly call legends, epics, myths, riddles, sayings, fables" (1972: 17).

Pilgrimage as Victory over Space; *Mawlid* as Words in Movement

"It is the test of space that makes the pilgrim," says Dupront (1987: 374). All the physical discomforts of such a journey make it a real and somewhat adventurous experience. However long-awaited and much hoped-for, the pilgrimage manifests differently each year. The number and type of pilgrims are never the same. Climatic, economic, and social conditions vary from one year to the next. A certain unpredictability hangs over each year's festival, which always manifests itself in a little fear: fear that the festival will not deliver its usual promise, but also a feeling of inadequacy in the face of a powerfully charged moment.

Once the moment arrives, the hazards of several days' journey must also be reckoned with: any comfort the pilgrims might enjoy is subject to many unpredictable circumstances. No one worries before setting out about shelter or lodging; these are guaranteed, at least to the extent possible in so harsh a physical environment and such precarious social conditions. The Gourara benefited little from post-independence Algeria's years of prosperity; salaries are very low and infrastructure is limited to a few state-owned enterprises essentially concerned with tourism.[12] Poverty is in some cases extreme. If the legendary hospitality and generosity of the region manage to overcome the rigors of deprivation, the hardships of the climate are more difficult to negotiate. Neither the proverbially cold winters nor the scorching heat of summer help matters in such an impoverished place. But rather than fearing them, the locals take such hardships as tests of their fortitude. During the *mawlid* of 1992, M. (a local informant) told me: "Myself, I look out for the times when the *mawlid* falls during the hottest part of the summer to see who the real pilgrims, our real friends, are."[13] Those who would achieve the merit of passing this test must win out not only over an unforgiving space, but also through a hard season.

This relationship to space as a testing ground is a theme found widely in Islamic cultures; going to the mosque on foot procures *hasanāt,* good graces, that are directly proportional to the number of paces taken on the road to prayer. Difficulty as well as distance qualifies the worshipper as meritorious: "clearly, in the collective consciousness . . . , the 'heroic' nature of the pilgrim's way derives not from its being a rite of initiation, but from its constituting a victory over the physical reality of space, over that which ordinarily limits all human movement, which itself is unlimited, hostile, vertiginous, crushing" (Dupront 1987: 374). The journey is a sacralizing process, in which the distance covered plays as important a role as the sites visited. To depart into the distance is to break with the familiar and tame the unknown. The *mawlid* of Timimoun bears out Dupront's remark that "in any culture, the basis and, as it were, the matter of pilgrimage is space" (ibid.).

At the same time, the festival of the *mawlid* is essentially composed of *words* in movement, sometimes in chorus, sometimes chaotic, punctuated by restorative pauses. Long prayers are followed by sung supplications in which God is worshipped and the saints venerated, often in a choreography that verges on the ecstatic; the speech, though, is sober and often reduced to the most fundamental, single words, *Allāh* (God), *al-latīf* ("the Kind," one of the names of God), *salām* (greeting/peace). Such words, repeated to breathlessness, illustrate that meaning in language is not always proportional to syntactic complexity or lexical sophistication. As de Certeau suggested:

> [I]n becoming more cerebral, oration may have higher pretensions, but does it therefore reach higher truths? It may believe itself more universal, but is it more "total"? It may think a greater number of things about God, but does it speak to him better? . . . Perhaps, at some times, words are "lacking" because they are inadequate to a situation; at other times, however, they lack because they have been exhausted, and the suppliant has no more, or only very simple ones, deprived of any arrogance. (1987: 17–18)

At such times, a simple, sober word is enough to express the intensity of a sentiment, but such frugality is not a lack (the beauty and degree of elaborateness of some prayers encountered in the ritual life of the Gourara leave no doubt as to the local availability and appreciation of words and the art of working with them) but simply another way of worshipping. What if this is a deliberate choice, to renounce words that have become too familiar through long use, and concentrate exclusively on a few, so as to regenerate their meanings? It also has the effect of enlarging the circle of communicants; the fewer the words, the greater the number who pray. The simpler the word, the better its meaning is felt and understood. The more it is repeated, the greater the intensity of the sentiment it expresses.

In Islam (as, in a somewhat different sense, in Christianity) the word carries a divinely creative power. In the Qur'an, God simply speaks to create beings and things: *subhānahu, idhā qāda amran fa-innamā yaqūlu lahu, kun fa-yakūn* (Glory to him, when he decides a thing, he has only to say to it, "be," and it is).[14] The word, then, is transcendent, the means of the constitution and constant remaking of the world; in order for something to exist, the word must be uttered. In popular belief, the *fāl*, the word of good omen, is paid particular attention. Tradition dictates that "one speaks while listening for the *fāl*" (*tkallam wa tsannat li'l-fāl*), an expression uttered whenever a word of good fortune has been spoken; if, in the midst of conversation, an inauspicious word is heard, the expression *sam'at l-'ard w bal'at* (the earth has heard and swallowed it) is used, evoking a chthonic world of subterranean spirits called upon by a simple expression to avert danger in the visible world. A slip of the tongue is often considered to be a sort of power carried in the word, expressing itself of its own volition, to speak absolute truths. The power inherent in speech is such that people in the region often avoid pronouncing certain words or evoking certain situations; the name of *jnūn* (pl. of *jinn*; see also Oussedik this volume), for example, is not spoken, the spirits being referred to instead as *dhūk al-nās*, "those ones," implicitly, those who must not be named.

A cry that forms a word, then, has a particular efficacy, but also expresses sacredness. A single cry is only that of an individual mind; speech expresses a collective consciousness, or community of meaning, and hence the sacred. One of the words most frequently repeated is *salāmu,* especially in the *ahallīl.* The local pronunciation of *salām,* greeting and peace, its centrality here seems to evoke the echo of the ancient regional rivalries whose settlement in peace under the aegis of the saints the festival commemorates. More than a simple salutation, the word conveys both the social and the transcendent peace for which the community prays. The whole festival, as we have seen, is placed under the sign of reconciliation; the reverence shown to Sidi al-Hājj Bilqasim is due at least as much to his role as pacifier as it is to his sanctity. He, according to the legend, established peace and put an end to discord; the historicity of the event is unimportant here, the important thing is that Gouraris today believe it. The *bi'smi-llāh* (In the name of God) and the *fātiha,* formulas for opening and beginning, words that act as rites of entry, are frequently repeated. Collectively uttered, they always express hope for harmony and unity, dispelling rivalry and dissension. The word becomes in a sense the offering, the oblatory matter of the ritual; like every "victim" in a sacrifice, it is beautified and adorned by the one making the sacrifice, to serve as something acceptable to be offered up. But the word here is offered not only to God but also to the men and women all around, who share and perceive it not only aurally but through the whole body. Prayer, invocation, song—all become whole-body auditory experiences. In this way the meaning of words is secondary to their effect on the receptive body; their force is not merely semantic, but resides in their consonance with the intense physicality of the voice, breathing, and movement.

Feeding, Symbolizing, and Celebrating the Social Body

The king of dishes in the Gourara, encountered in every ceremony whether public or private, is couscous. All over the Maghreb, from north to south, in cities and in villages, couscous is *the* regional festive food; a marriage or engagement without it is unimaginable. Locally, one of its synonyms, *ta'm,* has also become synonymous with "celebration." To "eat a couscous" in popular parlance means to attend a marriage. Since it is prepared almost exclusively by women, the central place of couscous in the festival might be considered as the gift of women to the event. The careful, collective preparation of the dish is a kind of qualifying test for the women of the community. Even a dish provided by a single household is a collective offering to which all the women of the family will have contributed, and through which they unite themselves in community with the male guests who will partake of it. In *Consuming Passions: The Anthropology of Eating,* Peter Farb and George Armelagos write of feasts, and their relation to redistribution and gift giving: "whatever the particular celebration, the foods that are eaten often have in common that they take time to prepare, are scarce, and are expensive" (1980: 176). The couscous at Timimoun is no exception; it is a dish that demands labor and attention. The semolina is ground, rolled, dried, and steamed two or three times before being buttered and served with sauce, which itself has demanded care to prepare and always, on these occasions, contains meat. Each of the pilgrims will "share salt," *shrak al-malh,* with the others, salt being the symbol of food fit for people, contrasted with the tasteless nourishment of *jnūn*. Salt here, as often, is a symbol of goodness and well-being (in Algerian Arabic, *mlīh,* lit., salt, also simply means something "good"). During the *mawlid,* houses are opened and enormous quantities of couscous eaten; the food is sacralizing in that it joins people together, creating the social fabric that at once reinforces and is reinforced by a sense of the sacred. Shared by all, in a circle larger than that of the domestic family, it becomes communal and an occasion for communion. Virtually unknown in the Arab Middle East, the consumption of couscous seems to have preceded the arrival of Islam in the Maghreb, making it a particular feature of Berber culinary culture. If not an indicator of the unity of origins of the Gourara's inhabitants, it nonetheless signifies a unity of the larger cultural area to which they belong.

An equally clear symbol of community cohesion is provided in the saints' banners (locally called *la'lamma,* from *'alam,* a sign or flag) to which all the pilgrims accord great deference and respect. And indeed, the banners are considered to be signs that refer to something else; when asked about the meanings of these flags, which are attached to long, decorated poles, local inhabitants answer by relating them to events or patron saints. At Ouled Saïd, one interlocutor connected the number of banners explicitly with the number of saints interred at each oasis: "We arrived at Ouled Saïd with only one, that of Bu M'hammad from Tinerkouk, and we leave with another two, those of the father and grandfather of Sidi Bu M'hammad, who are buried here at Ouled Saïd." To the banners representing particular saints are joined those that refer to particular moments or events, especially to pilgrimages to Mecca made by inhabitants of the different *zawāyā*. "Each time the *mrabtīn*[15] of the *zāwiya* of Sidi al-Hājj Bilqasim went to Mecca, a standard was brought back," says Sidi al-Hājj Muhammad, a descendant of Sidi al-Hājj Bilqasim and *muqaddam* of the *zāwiya*. "It's a gift [*hādiya*] that the pilgrims make to the saint each year," he explains, while lamenting the loss of such customs. It is worth noting this insistence on counting the number of pilgrimages made to Mecca, and relating them to the *mawlid* ceremonies. There is a clear desire to establish a parallel between the local pilgrimage and the *hajj* to

Mecca, which is its archetype; the local event takes place *under the sign* of the *hajj*, a *rukn* (pillar) of Islam, which is itself represented here by the symbol of the flag brought back from the holy places. In this way, the banners that signify particular, local saints and the events of local memory, signs that rally the community around its own specific symbols, also simultaneously point to the community's inclusion in the wider world of Islam.

The local saint and his place in local history are, of course, also key. The depositing of the banners in the *qubba* of Sidi al-Hājj Bilqasim is a way of giving the community into the care of the greatest of the region's saints after soliciting all the others in turn. In a sense the banner, as a symbol of the community and its place of habitation, is analogous to the modern keys to the city. Tinerkouk, from which the first procession sets out, was historically the domain of the Mharza, an incoming Arab tribe, and their local Zenata (Berber) allies. As noted earlier, the pilgrimage from Tinerkouk to the *zāwiya* of Sidi al-Hājj Bilqasim at Timimoun commemorates the peace, brokered by the latter, between the Mharza of Tinerkouk and their allies, on one side, and the Zenata *qsūr* of Timimoun, on the other. The great ceremony of the joining of the standards at the *hufra* of the *zāwiya* of Sidi al-Hājj Bilqasim reenacts, in local memory, the historic quarrel and its resolution; it is therefore a doubly commemorative event, recalling a founding drama (the clash of the two regional factions) and establishing the primacy of Sidi Bilqasim among the other saints of the region, marking him as above even Sidi Musa, the great saint of Tasfaout (a locale some distance west and south of Timimoun).[16] The region's saints, while each associated with a particular locale, are complementary rather than opposed to each other, but it is Sidi Bilqasim who occupies here the place of the *qutb*, the "pole," or axis, around which the others revolve. At the moment when the banners are united, Sidi al-Hājj Bilqasim is said to be seen in the company of the Prophet himself; everyone present falls on his back to see this collective vision, marking a kind of submissive reverence to the saint in an inversion of the face-down prostration reserved exclusively for God. The banners are also signs of the communities that carry them; those of different inherited social status, *'abīd* (descendants of slaves), *mrabtīn* (marabouts), and *shurfā* (descendants of the Prophet) are united under a single flag. Joining with others, under other banners, is a way of acknowledging that all such internal hierarchies are surpassed by a shared and universal spiritual affiliation.

Space as Time Stood Still

The Timimoun *mawlid* must also, in the end, be understood as a political event. Everything that is said about the event, the legends associated with it, and the explanations provided by the pilgrims refer to a political dimension of the celebration, whose origin is to be found in intertribal disputes.

At the time when the population structure of the Gourara, with its different ethnic groups as we see them today, became more or less stabilized, around the fifteenth century, the region fell under no unified, central political authority. The *qsūr* were organized as independent, autonomous municipalities, each administered by its own *jmāʿa* (assembly, council). Their atomization, however, was compensated by the existence of two overarching *sfūf* (federations, leagues), which allowed the formation of stable alliances in case of need. Among the many available definitions of the *saff*, the one suggested in the mid-nineteenth century by Renan—a "mutual aid society"—seems best suited to the way in which the inhabitants of the Gourara themselves understand the term.[17] Without its having any ambition to serve as a political or administrative form of organization, the *saff* has a political dimension in that it is always evoked in the context of conflict between neighboring groups. In the Gourara, one identifies either as Yahmad or as Sufyān, and these affiliations are held for life. These two *sfūf* are organized not only along ethnic lines, but also according to geography or by social position, and they are, in a much weaker sense, still pertinent today. Many inhabitants of Guentour (a Yahmad locality) will still avoid crossing the *manjur* of Timimoun, a Zenati, hence Sufyān, town (although today inhabited by many Arab families), even though past fears are no longer relevant. The Beni Mehlal, also Yahmad, never spend the night at Timimoun.

With the arrival of the saints (during the "maraboutic revolution" of the sixteenth century),[18] another structuring principle was introduced to local society. With the saints, or shortly after them, came the Sufi orders, or brotherhoods (*turuq*: Sufi "ways"; sing. *tarīqa*), especially the Tayibiyya order based in Ouezzane in northern Morocco, which became the most widespread order in the Gourara, encompassing most of the *qsūr* and leaving only a few footholds for other *turuq* such as the Shikhiyya. Cutting across the *sfūf* and other divisions, the Tayibiyya brings together both Sufyān and Yahmad. The Tayibiyya does, nonetheless, have rivals in the Qadiriyya order, to which the inhabitants of Tasfaout and some of the people of the *qsūr* of Timimoun, El-Haj Guelman, and Tabelkoza claim affiliation; and especially in the Shikhiyya (associated with the powerful maraboutic confederation, the Ouled Sidi Cheikh of the western Algerian Saharan Atlas mountains), to which some inhabitants of Tabelkoza and especially those of El-Haj Guelman and a few other *qsūr* belong. The *turuq* have succeeded in subsuming differences of ethnic groups, the spatial distribution of the population, and the ancient alliances of the *sfūf*.[19] The order that has done so most completely is undeniably the Tayibiyya, and it is this order that we see most prominently in the festival of the *mawlid*. The intersecting roles of the *sfūf* and the *turuq* in the festival suggest the *mawlid*'s role as a moment at which the region's historically antagonistic alliances are reformed, and simultaneously their peaceful coexistence under the auspices of the saints is reaffirmed. Thus the long historical (or memorial) past of the larger community is replayed in the present across the space in which it lives.

More generally, the pilgrimage, which lasts ritually seven days and nights but whose associated festivities carry on for much longer, expresses a tension between the transitory and the eternal. The slow processions, the prayers and invocations, the deliberate progress across the desert over several days—all create an intensity of experience such that the duration of the celebration seems drawn out almost endlessly. But at the same time, this desire to make time stand still reveals the elusive nature of the moment. At its simplest, the *mawlid* consists of a pilgrimage that leaves one place to reach another; in the terms of the chroniclers of the Crusades (wars that were also imagined as pilgrimages), it means leaving the "land of birth" for the "land of promise" (Dupront 1987: 373). Here, the land of birth is Tinerkouk, which does indeed seem to have been the first area of the Gourara settled by incoming Arab groups in the twelfth century (Echallier 1973: 355; Martin 1908: 67–68). If we accept the supposition that the establishment of the Arabic-speaking *qsūr* that exist today dates from the mid-twelfth century and that the *mawlid* festival must have arrived with the region's Arab population, who also introduced Islam to the area, then Tinerkouk is indeed historically the place of origin of the ritual. But the importance of the event for the whole community, Arabic- or Berber-speaking, is amply demonstrated by the multitude of sites at which the *mawlid* is celebrated. It is as if the intention of the celebration is to establish a synergy between the histories unfolding in different places, by bringing together the region's local histories—the different populations of the *qsūr* with their different social strata and their collective memories articulated around their individual saints—and uniting different times with different places. Place, after all, is in a sense simply time stood still, the crystallized and solidified experience of people over the centuries, matter into which history is condensed. The role of the saints in this materialization of social memory is both that of luminaries and that of transmitters. As luminaries, their biographies "light up" founding moments in local history that connect the region to the wider Muslim world; as transmitters, they enable the constitution of local memory over time by the accumulation of stories and legends that have grown up around them.

We can gain a clearer sense of the importance of this relation between local space and sacred history by looking again at the events that mark the *sbūʿ*, the seventh day that closes the festival. The pilgrims gather at the place called *al-jbal*, the "mountain," and proceed to the *zāwiya* of Sidi al-Hājj Bilqasim, or more exactly to the *hufra*, the "hollow" near it. Does the gathering of the pilgrims outside Timimoun recall the "standing" (*wuqūf*), a central ritual of the hajj, occurring as it does, like the crucial event of the greater pilgrimage to Mecca, at midday and finishing with sunset at the *hufra*? The procession from the *jbal* at Timimoun to the *hufra* of Zāwiyat al-Hājj Bilqasim perhaps also echoes the *ifādha*, the great procession of pilgrims from 'Arafat to Muzdalifa, with the ritual "dance of the sandals" at the *hufra* recalling both the *sa'y*, the ritual of passing at a run (for men) between the two hills of Safa and Marwah near Mecca, and the *ramy* (stoning of the devil) ritual at Mina. The pilgrim to Mecca walks around the Ka'ba (in *tawāf*, circumambulation), newly covered in a fresh black cloth cover (*kiswa*) and seeks to kiss or touch the black stone preserved in its wall; pilgrims arriving at the *zāwiya* visit the tomb of Sidi al-Hājj Bilqasim, newly covered in fresh white chalk.

The *hajj* provides a model for many local pilgrimages, and in this sense the Timimoun *mawlid* appears to be what Dupront refers to as a "substitute pilgrimage." Indeed, as in other regions, the *sbū'* in the Gourara is popularly held to be a replacement for the pilgrimage to Mecca, if it is accomplished in seven consecutive years; for the duration of the festival, Timimoun and its region are raised to the status of a "substitute" religious center. The Gourara is imagined and enacted, through the *mawlid*, not merely as an out-of-the-way part of the world of Islam, but as one of its high places, not a periphery but a center in its own right. And in placing the local veneration of Sidi al-Hājj Bilqasim, Sidi al-Hājj Bu M'hammad, and Sidi Yusaf under the sign and on the date of the birth of the Prophet, the social memory of the locality is tied to the broader, universal sacred history of Islam. The saints, whose virtue is to have approached in life the excellence of the Prophet's model beyond what is commonly attainable, are the actualization in this place of the Prophet's virtues and his message, and it is for this that they are honored today.

Metropoles of the Desert

The banners that are united in the course of the festival symbolize both these saints and the *qsūr* whose patrons the saints are. The villages and *qsūr* of the Gourara are like the fiefs of the saints, whose names they frequently bear: Zāwiyat Sidi al-Hājj Bilqasim, Beni Mehlal, Zāwiyat Sidi Aoumeur, Zāwiyat Sidi Abdallah, El-Haj Guelman. And any *qsar* whose name is not that of its saint nonetheless carries his legend in the memories of its inhabitants, who will willingly recount to outsiders the tales of the foundation of Tabelkoza in Tinerkouk by Sidi al-Hājj Bu M'hammad, of Tasfaout by Sidi Musa, of Ouled Aïssa by Sidi Abbad, of El-Ouajda by Sidi Brahim, and so on. A sort of umbilical connection between a place and its inhabitants, the legend is revivified annually by the local festival, the *ziyāra* (visit), in honor of its patron saint and of others, claimed as part of the local patrimony, who are interred in the *qsar* or nearby.

The hierarchy of the saints mirrors that of the settlements, which is remembered today for the duration of the festival, despite vastly changed circumstances of settlement patterns, road building and electrification, and the abandonment of many older *qsūr* in the region. Now quite eclipsed by the importance of Timimoun as a regional center, the little agglomerations of Massine and Zāwiyat al-Hājj Bilqasim reclaim for a few days the places of symbolic importance they once held. Timimoun, the administrative center of the oases in colonial times and the main regional town since independence, has monopolized power in the area for a century. Its ascent has not, however, eliminated from local memory either the importance of Tabelkoza, hidden in the dunes of Tinerkouk, or the past splendors of Ouled Saïd. Both places were once major spiritual centers, and they continue to recall that fact every year at *mawlid.* The festival reiterates that these *zāwiya* cities were metropoles of a kind, transcending the local and open to the outside world through both their mundane commercial activities and their production of spiritual belief. Linked to faraway markets, they were also affiliated with the far-flung networks of the Sufi brotherhoods. Each locality had its *zāwiya* and its association with a *tarīqa,* and was therefore tied to other locales: that of the "mother house" of its order, but also to all the other centers in which the order was represented. A disciple of the Tayibiyya, whether from Timimoun in the desert or Oran on the Mediterranean coast, would belong also to the original home of his order in Ouezzane, and wherever he traveled his first instinct would be to locate, in each town he passed through, the *zāwiya,* to which he equally belonged. Through the identification of its local saints with the wider brotherhoods, then, Timimoun and the whole region are linked to other cities, some of them very far away. Still today, the tiny *qsūr* of the Gourara are active parts of a vast urban network that crosses the frontiers of states. Every locality belongs to the very localized, spiritually and geographically limited, circle of the Gourara, perched as it is at the edge of the great sea of sand dunes, but each is also part of other circles whose centers are far away. The contemporary fragility of these cities, rather than suggesting their internal decline, illustrates the supersession of the economic and ecological logic on which they were long ago built; nonetheless, the festival returns annually, to recall the prosperity of yesteryear and the richness of a long-rooted, universal and local culture, as well as the constraints of present times.

NOTES

1. *Qsar,* pl. *qsūr*: here, an oasis settlement with residential buildings among or adjacent to gardens and palm groves fed by irrigation. Elsewhere, the term can denote a defensible, walled settlement, or a fortified granary or storehouse at the center of such a settlement.

2. *Zāwiya*, pl. *zawāyā*: a religious center, often combining the lodge of a brotherhood (*tarīqa*, a Sufi "way") and the shrine of a saint (*walī*, a "friend of God") in which the tomb of a venerated ancestor is maintained by his disciples or descendants, where pilgrims are welcomed and accommodated and (often) where Islamic instruction is given. Many Saharan *zawāyā*, like those elsewhere in the Islamic world, are important repositories of scriptural and legal learning, with significant libraries or manuscript collections, as well as of mystical, spiritual power (*baraka* associated with the founding saint). See Gellner (1969), Eickelman (1976), and Clancy-Smith (1994).

3. On popular Muslim veneration of the Prophet, see Schimmel (1985).

4. *Erg*, or *reg*: a region of high sand dunes. The Gourara sits on the southeastern edge of the Western Erg.

5. Although the procession has already stopped at Oudgha and Sammouta, two smaller *qsūr* on the way to Ouled Saïd.

6. A simple turban worn in the Sahara, formed from a single, long strip of white or colored cloth bound around and over the top of the head, and under the chin, as a protection against heat and dust.

7. At the 1994 *mawlid* that I attended, this text was read by two young celebrants because of the absence of the more usual elderly *faqīh*, who was ill at the time; the younger men found the text difficult to understand and stopped reading the prayer well before the end.

8. The *fātiha* is especially important in Muslim piety in general, and in mysticism in particular (see Corbin 1983: 192–193). Its utterance is an act of worship (*'ibāda*, a duty of the Muslim toward God) in which an intimate relationship is established between God and the believer. *Qul huwwa Allāh* is a formulaic celebration of God's divine unicity (oneness). *Al-mu'āwwidatayn*, "the two preservers," are the short closing *sūras* (chapters) of the Qur'an—Q.113, *sūrat al-falaq*, and Q.114, *sūrat al-nās*—both of which begin with the words *Qul a'ūdhu* . . . (say: I take refuge . . .), invoking God's protection from the devil and the temptations of the world.

9. On the *ahallīl*, see Mammeri (1984) and Bellil (1999–2000).

10. Having come to seek Sidi al-Hājj Bilqasim, the noble Hammouzine asked the first man he came across where the saint might be found; unimpressed and without raising his head from his basketwork, the man said, "I am he," at which Hammouzine, thinking himself mocked, slapped him. Realizing too late that the humble weaver was indeed the saint, the noble promised to make a *ziyāra* (devotional visit, pilgrimage) to him with the offering of a sheep once a year, a promise still honored by his descendants and that today has been incorporated into the larger ceremony.

11. The banner from Massine returns home the same day; the two that have come from Ouled Saïd will remain overnight. The standard of Sidi Bu M'hammad from Tinerkouk will remain for three days. Two more, from Ouled Aïssa, will not leave until after the noon prayer on the following Friday; this particularity is related to the legend of Sidi 'Abbad. From being an illiterate and marginal individual, he is said to have been raised by Sidi al-Hājj Bilqasim to the dignity of *khātib* (preacher at the mosque) because he read a *khutba* (sermon) on the saint's forehead. This *khutba* became justly famous, and it is recited at the first Friday prayer following the *mawlid*.

12. Such, at least, was the situation when I observed the ritual in the 1990s. The subsequent privatization of most state industries (not yet including the one principal hotel in Timimoun) has not noticeably improved matters.

13. Like other Islamic festivals, the date of the *mawlid* is fixed according to the lunar calendar; the date in the solar calendar, and in the season of the year, on which the celebration falls thus changes from one year to the next in a predictable cycle.

14. Q.19, 35 (*sūrat Maryam*).

15. *Mrabtīn*: marabouts; lit., those who are tied (to God); religious scholars and disciples, often here connected to or descended from a particular founding saint.

16. Another origin myth tells how Sidi Bilqasim, after many wanderings, desired to settle in Timimoun but before being allowed to do so, he was required to pass beneath the outstretched leg of Sidi Musa, who from Tasfaout exercised a great influence over the whole region. Sidi Bilqasim refused, and departed again. At the moment of his return, he found the people about to say prayers for Sidi Musa, who had just died; Sidi Bilqasim presided at the prayers. His future preeminence was thereby signified.

17. The *saff* (pl. *sfūf*) has been the subject of a large literature in the sociology of North Africa, much of it rooted in assumptions about "segmentary societies" that have often been unhelpful (see Eickelman 1985). Broadly speaking, it can be understood that tribes, which are often subdivided into smaller groups or fractions according to circumstances and resources, can also be agglomerated according to long-standing circumstantial relations of dependence and alliance into *sfūf*, for mutual protection against one another or against outsiders.

18. On the "maraboutic revolution" and sainthood in North Africa, see Eickelman (1976) and Cornell (1998).

19. Although it ought to be pointed out that this can work both ways; having come to supplant the *saff*, the *tarīqa* has sometimes followed in its footsteps. The brotherhood associated with Sidi Musa of Tasfaout was spread by his descendants (Sidi Brahim at El-Ouajda, for instance), essentially among those already identified as Sufyān.

7

VILLAGES AND CROSSROADS

Changing Territorialities among the Tuareg of Northern Mali

Charles Grémont

Let us begin with a historical observation: at the end of the nineteenth century, territorial control as exerted by the various dominant Tuareg groups in the area of what is today the north of the Republic of Mali was flexible, based on alliances with, and control over, people who were relatively mobile. Today, Tuareg livelihoods and political influence, like those of their neighbors, are increasingly defined with reference to geographical limits, while the control over specific locations and areas has become both the object of power struggles and a way of expressing them. My aim here is to show why local concepts of power have changed so drastically, under which circumstances this happened, and with what kinds of resistance these changes were met—resistances that bear witness to the profound impact of these transformations, but that also question the validity of the territorial model imposed by the colonial state and endorsed by the national state after independence.

At first sight, then, the case examined in this chapter appears to provide a counterexample to the central argument of this volume, which focuses on the interdependence between North Africa and the West African Sahel and aims to describe the Sahara as a "dynamic shared world." Indeed, most Tuareg in northern Mali are today much more rooted in the soil and more concerned with control over "their space"—from a social, economic, and political point of view—than they were three or four generations ago. Questions of outside origins and influence and of extensive networks, long put forward in historical accounts, are increasingly replaced by a rhetoric that gives priority to notions of territory and indigeneity. However, because of this dominant tendency toward fixity and closure, an important minority of the population has become even more mobile, by choice or by force, by protest or by bare necessity, thereby escaping exclusive forms of spatial organization. There seems to be a dialectical relation between the increasing rootedness in land of the majority of the population, in particular the dominant sectors, and the deterritorialization of a minority who are at odds with the established

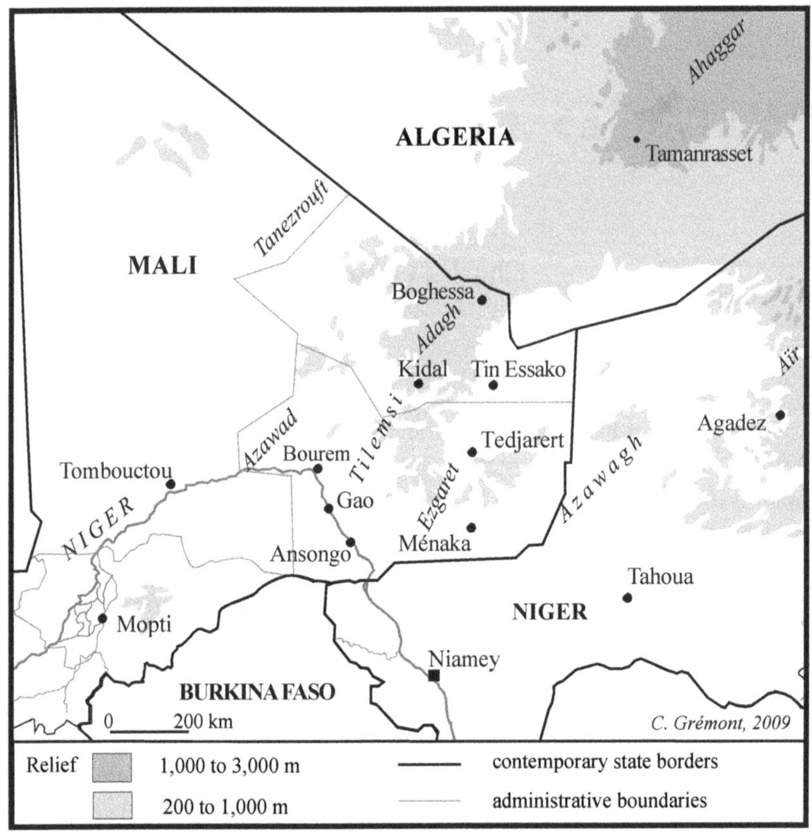

Map 7.1. Northern Mali: natural features and administrative boundaries.
C. Grémont 2009

order. Further, my research points toward a lasting correlation between spatial and social mobility, or at least between mobility and aspirations to social, political, and economic change.

"Territory" will be understood here from both a practical and a symbolic perspective: how natural resources are used, and how they are understood and imagined. These two levels can be distinguished for the sake of analysis, but they clearly cannot be dissociated in everyday life, where they constantly intrude on each other: "territory is both objectively organised and culturally constructed" (Bourgeot 1991: 704). I am thus using a minimal definition that, I think, can hardly be challenged. Yet we need to keep in mind that the mere use of the term territory implies a certain relation between land and political community: according to the *Petit Robert* French dictionary, for instance, a territory is "the surface area on which a human group, and especially a national political community, lives"; the *Oxford English Dictionary* has "the land or country belonging to or under the dominion of a ruler or state."[1] Such notions are remarkably absent from Tamasheq. Rather than trying to find, at all costs, the equivalent of a term imposed from the outside, I will retrace changing Tuareg concepts of power and their relation to spatial control, to access to natural resources, and to forms and representations of mobility. In other words, I will draw on elements of social, political, economic, and ecological history in order to understand the development of "territoriality" among the Tuareg of northern Mali. This chapter is based on long-term fieldwork in northern Mali and on extensive research in French colonial and military archives in Aix-en-Provence, Paris, and Bamako from 1993 on. The material on power relations in the eighteenth and nineteenth centuries is taken from my own research (Grémont 2010); more contemporary information is derived from work carried out in 2007 and 2008, as part of a collective research project conducted mostly in relatively recent settlement sites in the Gao region and among Tuareg from Kidal and Menaka.[2]

Shifting, Flexible, and Discontinuous Polities (Eighteenth and Nineteenth Centuries)

Again, the starting point for this reflection is a historical observation: in the eighteenth and nineteenth centuries, all political formations in the Niger bend were based on dynamic relations of dominance and alliance among people who were geographically relatively mobile. The territories that they produced were hence particularly unstable, flexible, and discontinuous—to the point where, when conducting research into the processes through which one of these polities, the Tuareg Iwellemedan, came into existence, I quickly had to abandon the question of geographic limits and borders altogether. Here and there, scholars had noted that among the political groupings in the Sahel (as in African polities more generally), power was based on control over people, which then indirectly determined control over land.[3] My reconstruction of the historical trajectory of the Iwellemedan, a powerful Tuareg confederation that emerged in the late seventeenth century north of the Niger bend and that led a final major rebellion against French rule in the area in 1916, clearly confirmed this. In the history of the Iwellemedan, strikingly little emphasis was placed on any kind of control over land, even where it was mediated through people.[4] From a Tuareg point of view, then, to "control space" seems to have had little meaning, and Tuareg of the eighteenth and nineteenth centuries rarely used this or similar concepts to express, construct, materialize, acknowledge, or defend political preeminence. In the pre-colonial period, among the western Iwellemedan in the northern Niger bend, any social group that needed access to natural resources, such as land, pasture, watering places, or salt pasture, had to negotiate with all other groups with similar intentions.[5] Access to resources was therefore essentially dependent on recognition by others, and land, pasture, and water were not appropriated in the sense in which we understand "property" today: a legal state justified by a title deed that authorizes exclusive occupation and alienation (see also Leroy 1998).

Therefore, the economic survival of a group, as well as its social and political standing, was essentially dependent on alliances with others, or on the ability to force them into compliance. In order to reproduce themselves in the best possible conditions, in order to conquer, extend, and maintain power, dominant groups needed to have "people with them." While land was abundant, men were scarce. Those in power thus had to act in such a way as to maintain control over others, knowing that the latter always had the option of emancipating themselves by quite simply moving away to settle elsewhere, or even by attempting to redefine the existing power relations to their advantage. In a region suffering from strong climatic variations, and at a time when pasture was abundant and political power little centralized and institutionalized, this meant that people were spatially very mobile. Accordingly, local historiography mainly consists in records of trajectories and long lists of temporary way stations, up until the colonial period. This is true of nomadic pastoralists (mainly Tuareg, Arabs, and Fulani) as well as of agriculturalists (Songhay, Arma, and Fulani) and fishermen (Bozo and Sorko), of dominant groups and of their dependents. It is beyond doubt that, since the Moroccan conquest and the end of the Songhay empire in 1591, political, military, religious, and commercial expansions—and attempts to elude and escape them—have led to never-ending delocalizations of people on all social levels.[6]

For most groups, these relocations play a central role in their historical lore. An ancestor's "outside" origins and the various stages traveled through before arriving at his final destination are status enhancing and, as such, hotly debated, both historically and socially. According to the stories collected, Karidenna, the first leader of the Iwellemedan at the end of the seventeenth century, was originally either from a warrior clan from what is today Mauritania or of Berber religious descent from the Tafilalt valley in southern Morocco, whence he traveled to the Timbuktu region where he founded the Iwellemedan. Their political and military expansion then carried them east to the valley of the Azawagh on the contemporary border between Mali and Niger, thus traveling more than 400 kilometers in the course of roughly one century. The oral tradition of most of the Tuareg groups who today live in the Timbuktu and Gao regions, in the Niger valley in Niger, and in Burkina Faso equally speak of a slow progress south from the Adagh of the Ifoghas near the contemporary Algerian border and the city of Essouk (medieval Tadmekka), the former commercial and spiritual center of the southern Sahara. These historical accounts indicate a clear link between social and spatial mobility: the Iwellemedan became important as and because they advanced east. On their way, they established new alliances and increased the number of their clients, while maintaining older relations. At the same time, client groups could escape their domination by settling elsewhere and claiming the protection of a new patron or, if they were able to do so, by becoming fully independent.

Such historic migrations existed alongside seasonal mobilities: Tuareg pastoralists regularly moved to the Niger in the dry season to water their herds and take advantage of underwater pastures (known as *bourgoutières*) uncovered by falling water levels.[7] They would stay two to three months, exchanging cereals and cloth for pastoral produce, and thereby establishing durable ties with local residents, sometimes based on unequal power relations, but often on mutual acquaintance and friendship. Hence, ecological and economic complementarity and flexible sociopolitical relations underpinned patterns of access to natural resources.[8] Access was never exclusive, but rather based on priority rights that depended on complicated networks of relations between the various groups involved.

The Invention of Territory (1894–1960)[9]

The French colonial army came to the Gao region from the west, along the Niger River. The French first attained control over the valley itself before attempting to conquer the vast pastoral regions of the Hausa and the Gourma, i.e., the left and the right banks of the Niger, respectively. While it was relatively easy to subdue the villages in the valley, Tuareg and Arab groups proved more formidable adversaries. The colonial authorities therefore developed two interrelated strategies: to deny access to the river to "rebellious" Tuareg and Arabs, and to sever the ties between different regional populations. In the first instance, the aim was quite simply to deprive nomadic pastoralists of vital resources, as was explicitly stated by the governor of the French Sudan in 1898:

> Considering that we will never succeed in making friends with these [Tuareg and Arab] tribes because of their religious and racial hatred towards us, and because we have deprived them of their only resource, namely plunder and theft, we have to eliminate them if we can. This is best done by starving them: the people by preventing them from buying the cereals that they need, and their beasts by keeping them away from the riverbanks. As a result, the tribes will either starve, or escape to other areas, or else they will feel powerless and will

> unconditionally surrender, and then we will be able to force them to adopt a way of life that will prevent them from doing any harm. . . . All we need to do is to establish several military posts on the banks of the river. These posts should contain stores of arms and ammunition to be used by the local [sedentary] population; villages should be fortified; if necessary, we could hand out muzzle-loading guns to local people. Furthermore, we should set up local militias and briefly train them together with our indigenous troops.[10]

The segregation of local populations was intended both as a short-term measure, to prevent nomads from reaching the river, and as a long-term strategy, to enhance the profitability of the conquered lands. These efforts were concentrated on a particular area, the "rich Niger valley," and on the only kind of activity that was seen to be truly productive: agriculture. From such a perspective, policies toward agriculturalists and pastoralists were treated as separate issues. For the French, this distinction seemed easy to apply as it dovetailed with another: that between "sedentary" and "nomadic" populations. These categories, which have no equivalent in either Songhay or Tamasheq, were used by the colonial government to index, separate, and divide local populations. Censuses, tax records, and other administrative paperwork systematically opposed the "sedentary" inhabitants of "villages" and "districts" with the "nomads" living in "fractions" and "tribes." These categories also justified the ascription of an exclusive space of reference to both sides: the river valley to the villagers, and the desert to the nomads. The power to name and classify thereby put the finishing touches to the military conquest:

> As our troops from Timbuktu fought the Tuareg of the Niger bend, the latter were gradually pushed into the interior. Every one of our victories diminished their prestige and deprived them of a stretch of land. These lands were given to villagers to be put under cultivation. . . . In the Gao region, as a general rule, nomads had to stay at a distance of twenty kilometres in the interior, without anybody worrying too much about where they might find pasture for their large herds.[11]

People reacted to the advance of the colonial army and to the subsequent establishment of territorial rule in various ways. During the military conquest (1894–1903), some Tuareg and Arab groups engaged in sporadic armed resistance, mainly raids on the colonial army, while others submitted without attempting to fight or flee. Yet others actively collaborated with the French and fought on their behalf. These different strategies were largely the result of local geopolitics (see also Grémont 2010: 407–430). For the present purpose, it is important to note that potential mobility was an important factor in such strategic choices. The Arma of Gao, who were less mobile than the Tuareg or the Arabs but who were without doubt equally opposed to the French conquest, felt compelled to submit:

> When the French arrived, they came from Hā [a village fifty kilometers from Gao]. Then they were received in Koyma [opposite Gao, on the right bank of the Niger]. All the Arma, from Hā to Bourem, came together to consult. They were divided into two camps: the first wanted to fight the white men, the second wanted to come to an agreement with them. After a week of discussions, the Gao Alkaydo [the head of the Gao Arma] opted for agreement. He justified his decision with an example. He said: You saw that the Surgey [Tuareg] left, and this is because they have camels and they took everybody with them. We, we only have horses, and nobody can take his wife and leave his children or take his family and leave his brothers. Thus we have to face up to the problem and receive the white men.[12]

The colonial principle of segregation between nomadic and sedentary populations, and the creation, on paper, of strict geographic limits between different groups of nomadic pastoralists from 1908–1910 on, of course did not change the preexisting patterns of social organization all at once. Relations of interdependence and political alliance between Tuareg and Songhay were maintained despite colonial repression and became clearly visible in the armed opposition to the military conquest and during later rebellions (especially in 1916). During the whole colonial period, Tuareg carried on taking their livestock to the river, as they had done for several generations. Similarly, pastoralists continued to cross administrative boundaries that had been established to control them, and this despite the warnings, fines, and deportations inflicted by local governors and their guards.

The establishment of stricter and more exclusive territorial forms proceeded in fits and starts, while practices and representations changed at their own rhythm, with at times violent periods of catching up. Reports by colonial administrators from the 1950s reveal how notions of territory imposed by the French started to creep into local conceptions, especially where leaders of tribes and fractions were concerned. In constant contact with minor French administrators, they had made their new prerogatives (to receive taxes, to judge in local matters) and the boundaries of their new administrative jurisdictions their own. The imposition of political authority and defined space, as recognized by the state, gradually started to make sense in local terms.

Crossroads; or, How to (Re)think and Construct Territory (1973–1990)

When Mali became independent in 1960, the new state broadly endorsed the administrative organization left behind by the French colonial state. All land was seen as belonging to the state and could not be privately owned. People were granted rights of use, acquired according to the principle that "the land belongs to those who cultivate it" (see Keïta 1998). State institutions clearly considered agriculture as the only real work, while raising stock was seen as a marginal and transitional activity, if not as an ecological threat and a potential source of conflict. Meanwhile, the high rate of demographic growth resulted in increased pressure on arable lands in the valley and on pastoral resources, while Songhay families started to invest in animal husbandry on their own account.[13] Tuareg and Arabs, who were already competing for access to pastoral resources, thus found that their former correspondents had become their competitors, competitors who had to be taken all the more seriously because state officials tended to ascribe rights to land to agriculturalists rather than to herders.

It was in this context that, in 1972–1974 and 1984–1985, two major droughts occurred in the Sahel.[14] This was certainly not the first time that the southern edge of the Sahara had been hit by an extreme scarcity of rain, but this time it had a particularly serious impact on the social organization of space. As the flood level of the Niger fell considerably, rice fields situated higher up but within the "normal" flood limit ceased to be inundated, and farmers decided to move them to the low-lying lands near the riverbed: to the areas that up until then had been the pasture of *bourgoutières*. Hence, pastoral resources, access to which had been managed collectively, were replaced by privately owned fields. Once under way, this transformation proved irreversible. It was difficult to take back land that had been granted on an individual basis, in particular as land shortages began to be felt in the villages; meanwhile, the Malian state was about to convert to the creed of private property.[15] The main consequence of this development was that Tuareg had lost all incentive to take their livestock to the banks of the river, and indeed, they now rarely do so. Hence, the droughts achieved what years of colonial policies had failed to accomplish: to keep the Tuareg away from the river. In a very short time, the multiple ties with the people and resources of the Niger valley that had long been fundamental to the history of the southern Tuareg were cut off.

All Tuareg pastoralists in northern Mali were badly affected by the droughts, but some suffered more than others. The inhabitants of the left (northern) bank had to face more difficult conditions than those on the right bank, and inhabitants of the region around Bourem, Kidal, and north of Gao were harder hit than those from Menaka. As a result, reactions to the droughts varied: some families decided to stay put in order to spare their people and animals further fatigue, while others traveled south toward the Niger valley or even as far as Burkina Faso. All decisions taken during the years of crisis reflected a rethinking of individual and collective attitudes toward land and mobility. The majority decided in favor of an increased attachment to land, while a minority started to look beyond their everyday horizons. These two opposing tendencies occurred within the same group, within the same fraction, and within the same family—and the same individual might endorse both at different times.

Arguments in favor of the first option are nicely summed up in the following statement, made by a member of the leading family of the Iwellemedan in 1997:

> In 1973, many families left. When we saw them leaving, we said to ourselves: if there is a second drought, we also will have to leave our country, and then, ten years on, we will have forgotten who we are. If we want to stay, without having to beg from those who, not long ago, lived under our protection, we have to change the way we live. We watched the villagers [to whom we used to leave the care of our animals], and saw how they managed to make a lot of money with our livestock. We saw how they were organized, and we said to ourselves: we need to start settling down, set up a small village, and diversify. It is better to lose part of your culture than all of it, and if you leave, this is what happens! Thus we all met to discuss these matters, first with people from our family, for two nights and two days. And then we decided to found this village called Anuzegren [eighty kilometers east of Menaka]. At that time, many people said that this would do no good, but we said that we would give it a try. In every section, we needed some people who could look after the storehouse, and who would also try to get help from NGOs and the Malian government. And we needed schools. We knew that settlement was the only way in which we could send our children to school. The first house in Anuzegren was built in October 1982, and several people came to live there. We became twinned with Saint-Agnant [a small rural commune in western France]. And then, in 1984, there was no rain! Many people came to live around Anuzegren, and our storehouses fed them and saved them from starvation.[16]

In the early 1980s, the first settlement sites, or Tuareg villages, were founded. Families camped near a permanent water source, generally a modern well or a borehole, where they constructed a granary, a few mud-brick houses, and at times even a school, a small health center, and a market, usually with the help of NGOs. The founders of these first villages tended to be from influential families who could muster the necessary support locally and who had access to outside agents and funding sources. Although these settlement projects are locally described as the only possible way of maintaining the necessary degree of autonomy to remain true to oneself, they imply a growing dependency on the outside. Without help from the state or NGOs, these villages could hardly be viable; and their number increased rapidly after the rebellion of 1990–1996 as considerable funds were deployed for regeneration and "inclusion" in the northern regions.[17] Obviously, political and social strategies also played an important part here. After the 1984 drought, and even more so after the rebellion, the settlement and exploitation of a permanent site became a sign of success: for some, it reaffirmed and consolidated preexisting power, and for others, the majority perhaps, it offered the possibility of becoming independent of dominant neighbors or relatives. In this local political game, recognition by the outside world, as represented by the establishment of a localized and clearly visible infrastructure, appears both as an indispensable resource and as an irrefutable proof of success.

Small-scale mobility provided a solution for others. Confronted with the loss of pasture, families moved to neighboring areas that had fared better. Pastoralists from Bourem, for instance, crossed the river toward the Gourma, where they had maintained relations with people who had settled there earlier, where natural resources could stretch to accommodate new arrivals, and where ongoing local power struggles made such a move feasible.[18] Nonetheless, tensions between earlier settlers, who had lived in this area since the second half of the nineteenth century, and the new arrivals soon arose and remain perceptible today. Although some of these conflicts have a long and complex history, they all now revolve around different concepts of territorial control: while the new arrivals from Bourem justify their presence by their greater force and with reference to their historic preeminence, earlier settlers invoke their superior administrative legitimacy and indigeneity. Hence, since the colonial conquest, two different and mutually exclusive concepts of political power and territorial organization have coexisted on the ground, and people draw on either according to circumstance.

Yet others chose to move on an individual basis, and over much longer distances. Many younger men from the three administrative regions of northern Mali (Timbuktu, Gao, and Kidal), most between fifteen and forty years of age and excluding the sons of notables, decided to take off for Algeria or Libya, where they worked in odd jobs to cover their daily expenses and intended to "wait and see."[19] Aware of the economic, social, and political dead end reached by their parents after the two major droughts, these younger men quickly adopted a very different position from the conservative stance held by their political representatives, local deputies, and members of the country's ruling party.[20] Impatient for change, and familiar with different social and cultural contexts, they openly challenged the Tuareg establishment by their dress—wearing a short turban wrapped as they pleased, or even none at all—by poems of resistance sung to guitar music, and, from the 1980s on, by secret projects of rebellion prepared in Libya.[21] I am not concerned here with the various steps that led to the Tuareg rebellion of the 1990s, but rather with the resentment against the Malian state that was shared by a fringe of Tuareg society. It is important to note that this was a resentment of the way in which state power was exercised, rather than a rejection of the concept of the state as such: the principle of a political community based on territorial unity was never questioned by the leaders of the rebellion. Instead, they demanded the independence of a territory that they called Azawad: in other words, a state to be.[22]

Territorial Exclusivity and Violence (1990–1998)

Such a demand was potentially contentious, to say the least. The Azawad is not just inhabited by Tuareg and Arabs, but also by Songhay, Arma, and Fulani—to name but the largest groups—who had chosen to play no part in the rebellion. At first, from June 1990 to January 1991, these peoples quietly observed (and sometimes helped) the rebels, who then claimed to be fighting in the name of "the people of the north" and only attacked government forces. From April 1991 on, and in particular in 1994, however, rebels started to resort to plunder and robbery, in the valley as well as in the pastoral areas of the Gourma and the Hausa. As a reaction, self-defense groups were set up almost everywhere. Fear, violence, and suspicion became widespread, increasingly understood through the framework of the trivial opposition between sedentary and nomadic populations, or even "blacks" and "whites" (or blacks and reds, according to local parlance). Separation became the order of the day: throughout 1994, the Songhay, Arma, and Fulani remained blocked in the valley and in the towns, while the Tuareg and Arabs avoided larger settlements, the main thoroughfares, and the vicinity of the river.

Although this is largely overlooked in the literature, issues of territory and land ownership were clearly at the heart of the conflict. The direct connection between the recurrent reference to the Azawad by Tuareg rebels and the name of the main Songhay self-defense movement—Ganda Koy, literally the "masters or owners of the land"—is obvious. The latter's official discourse is equally instructive: "For those who think that they live on conquered ground, we remind them that the fatherhood of the land cannot be taken away from those who have always and forever made it their only residence."[23]

The violence perpetrated in 1994 and especially the rhetoric that underpinned it and that is still drawn upon to justify it show the central role played by the appropriation of space in struggles for power. The territorial claims expressed are certainly of great symbolic importance, but they also indicate real changes on the ground. The division between sedentary and nomadic populations, institutionalized by the colonial state in the early twentieth century, has finally become reality. In the Gao region, the river valley is now exclusively reserved for agriculture—with only a few salt pastures and hardly any *bourgoutières* remaining. This area is densely populated, to the point where not all families in the villages have access to land. The Tuareg in the Gao region have thus lost their access to the river, as well as their former political dominance over the villagers. At the same time, the villagers' herds, constantly growing, are grazing in the interior, tens of kilometers away from the river, in an area that is still rather open and where priority access prevails over exclusive ownership. Yet in the new sociospatial layout, from the Tuareg point of view, these vast pastures have become "their territory," as, in the spirit of reciprocity, they attempt to monopolize those areas that since colonial times have been conventionally attributed to them. With political decentralization, such rivalries have grown even livelier. Since the first local elections in 1999, access to natural resources has been officially managed by locally elected representatives. Struggles over land are hence dealt with locally, where they dovetail with local political rivalries, thereby further strengthening the symbolic and practical importance of spatial control.

These conflicts, based on a new logic of spatial exclusivity, also pit neighboring Tuareg groups against each other. In 1998, as the boundaries of administrative districts were determined for the first time, people registered in the Kidal region but whose families had for several generations lived in the area of Tedjarert in the Menaka district wanted to establish an independent commune where they were living. Menaka representatives protested vehemently, claiming that such an attempt would amount to an "annexation of territory." People from other districts were welcome to live among them, they said, but only as long as their presence was not institutionally recognized. This matter caused quite a stir, made it all the way to the highest circles of power, and locally led to violent quarrels that caused at least five deaths. A more widespread conflict was only just avoided. After several meetings, an agreement was finally reached: the area of Tedjarert was divided into two independent districts, one for people registered in Kidal and the other for people from Menaka. Debates still continue, however, about where the administrative centers of the new districts should be located.

Once more, a historical perspective is illuminating. In this particular area, the colonial conquest in the early twentieth century profoundly changed, or even totally inverted, local power relations. In the second half of the nineteenth century, Kel Adagh Tuareg from Kidal were already in the habit of nomadizing in the area of Tedjarert, but they were then, at least symbolically, under the authority of the Iwellemedan, whose ruling families are today settled in Menaka. After the brutal suppression of the Iwellemedan rebellion in 1916, the Kel Adagh became independent of their formerly powerful neighbors. Throughout the colonial period, the Iwellemedan tried to contain the growing power of the Kel Adagh, but to little avail. They could only hope to do this through arguments that were acceptable and legitimate in the eyes of the French central authorities. In other words, they had to accept the administrative boundaries established by the French, and claim control over the territory indicated by French administrative diktat. (Today, these boundaries are totally internalized.) This meant that Kel Adagh grazing their livestock on Iwellemedan territory had no right to be there, and ought to be "turned back," as the French colonial terminology would have had it, to the other side of the fixed boundary, fifty kilometers north of Tedjarert. This tacit endorsement of colonial concepts of political authority goes a long way toward explaining the mounting tensions that led to violence in 1998.[24] It also indicates, perhaps, the emergence of a new kind of conflict among the Tuareg: conflicts that openly aim to establish sovereignty over a clearly defined and limited space.

The growing number of settlements established by Tuareg in northern Mali needs to be analyzed in depth in order to understand the changing forms of power and, more generally, the material and conceptual relations with space that underpin them. As Georg Simmel observed, the spatial aspect of social and political dynamics is "particularly visible to the outsider." In this sense, the growing number of settled villages is a tangible expression of aspirations to social mobility. Individuals or groups that aspire to autonomy increasingly attempt to set up their own villages, which in turn gives them a powerful claim to the land that surrounds them. They are thereby drawing on logics that have long governed the digging of wells. But wells—waterholes, more exactly, never deeper than fifteen or twenty meters—had to be redug each year, and not necessarily in the same place. The establishment of a village, on the other hand, implies a longer-term spatial investment. Initially, then, social mobility still requires physical movement, as people go and live elsewhere, by and for themselves. But in the end, it leads to an increased rootedness in the land, as the common recognition of claims to spatial control becomes the proof of emancipation and of social and political autonomy. Mostly, these developments occur at the lower levels of social organization, on the level of fractions, small pre-existing villages, lineages, or even families. Rebellion against the order imposed by the state and against its territorial model, whether openly expressed or implicit, is located on different levels of the social order and is based on other claims than the mere segmentary reproduction of the dominant system. A whole range of alternative responses also needs to be taken into account: the development of parallel and illegal trade; a new wave of migration to Algeria, Saudi Arabia, and especially Libya; adherence to religious movements that make no reference to, and do not recognize, spatial restrictions; and, of course, the reappearance in the early 2000s of armed rebellions in Mali and Niger, undertaken by groups that no longer refer to specific territories, but whose names rather proclaim more general aspirations of political recognition and justice.[25] These cross-cutting pathways, if they do not constitute the center of a system that we as outside observers have not been able to recognize sufficiently, nonetheless cannot be separated from the contexts that have created them: ecological constraints, local politics and the geopolitical environment, social developments, and the reemergence of colonial histories.

NOTES

1. In legal terminology, the term also indicates "the constituent element of the community or its limit of competence"; and an "area of a country governed by a specific authority or jurisdiction: the territory of a bishop, a judge" (according to the *Petit Robert*). Similarly, in German, *Herrschaft* refers both to power and to the territory over which this power is exercised.

2. This collaborative project was carried out by twelve researchers of various disciplinary and national backgrounds, under the title "La question du pouvoir dans les recompositions sociales et religieuses en Afrique du nord et de l'ouest" and directed by S. Caratini (CNRS, University of Tours).

3. In the second half of the nineteenth century, one of the founding fathers of social anthropology, Lewis Henry Morgan, established in his *Ancient Society* (1877) a distinction between societies "based on people and personal relations" and societies "based on territory and property." According to this classification, the populations who lived in the Niger bend in the nineteenth century would without doubt fall into the former category.

4. I here follow Georg Simmel's (1999: 600–601) approach: "Space is always but an activity of mind, the human habit of combining as coherent sensations that in themselves are unconnected. Despite this, we are justified in underlining the spatial aspect of things and events, because these often happen in a way that the formal condition, positive or negative, of their spatiality takes on a particular appearance for *the observer*. . . . Reciprocal action between people is felt as a filling of space—whatever else it might also be."

5. The notion of "pre-colonial" Africa is still commonplace, especially among authors writing on contemporary times, although, as Coquery-Vidrovitch (2004: 35) points out, "it is difficult to accept that the history of people should be defined with reference to what happened to their descendants: they are thus turned into objects of a history that is already inscribed into the order of things."

6. On the historical background of the region and the formation of the Iwellemedan, see Richer (1924), Willis (1974), Levtzion (1975), and Grémont (2010).

7. Such pastures are formed by *bourgou* (*Echinochloa stagnima*), a nutritious plant that grows in flood areas. Cattle are especially fond of it, and it is mostly consumed when water levels are low. More recently, it has been used as dry fodder, and marketed as such.

8. In the nineteenth century, Tuareg did not farm, and Songhay and Arma only rarely owned livestock (although nothing was stopping either from doing so). Yet these activities are necessarily complementary: pastoralists take advantage of straw after the harvest, while agriculturalists benefit from manure in grazed areas.

9. This subheading ("L'invention d'un territoire délimité en surface," in the original French) was inspired by an article by Denis Retaillé (1993), "Afrique: Le besoin de parler autrement qu'en surface" (Africa: The Need to Speak in Other than Superficial Terms). The author, a geographer, argues that "in Africa, in the late nineteenth century, what mattered was to take over geographical areas [*surfaces*] and to define their boundaries," and that "the arbitrariness of this does not lie in the random choice of borders—in any case, these were not 'chosen' but rather defined here for the first time—but in the very idea of the need for apportionment."

10. Aoudéoud, Governor of the French Sudan, to the Commander of Timbuktu, Kayes, 13 September 1898, Archives of the Service Historique de l'Armée de Terre, Vincennes (FR/SHAT), box Soudan 6.

11. Mangeot and Marty (1918: 457–458).

12. Halidu Arboncana Touré and Moussa T. Touré, interviewed in Gao, 16 September 1998. Similar statements collected among Tuareg confirm just how difficult it was for the inhabitants of the riverbanks to resist or to escape the advancing colonial army: "The French came by the river. Threatened by their guns, the Tuareg moved their tents and livestock. The Songhay could not do the same with their huts and their rice fields. They were obliged to submit, or at least to pretend they submitted. The French took foodstuffs from them, boats, porters, and later on soldiers" (Ag Youssouf 1999: 317).

13. From the 1940s on, Songhay began to travel to Ghana, mainly to trade in cloth. As they returned, they invested part of their profits in livestock, especially cattle.

14. For background information on these droughts, see Comité d'Information du Sahel (1975), Glantz (1976), and Spittler (1993) for a case study.

15. Keïta (1998: 375) notes: "if land at first could not be owned privately and absolutely, the state administration itself began to hand out large numbers of title deeds that were based on the notion of private property. By 1986, the government was thereby forced to legalise such practices, and did so with the ruling of August 1st that established private property in land."

16. Farok ag Hamatu, interviewed in Anuzegren, 25 March 1997.

17. On the Tuareg of Mali and the rebellion, see Klute (1995), Boilley (1996, 1999), and Lecocq (2010).

18. Judging from research undertaken in 1998 and 2000, new arrivals numbered roughly a thousand.

19. The Kidal region, even harder hit by the droughts and under military rule since the repression of the rebellion of 1963, undoubtedly registered the largest number of departures.

20. The Union Démocratique du Peuple Malien (Democratic Union of the Malian People), the single party until 1991.

21. These young men were called *ishumar,* a Tamasheq plural of the French *chômeur,* unemployed. For more background on this movement, see Ag Baye and Bellil (1986), Ag Ahar (1990), and Lecocq (2004).

22. Azawad refers to the vast plain north of the Niger, between Timbuktu and Bourem. The term has been expanded to include all of northern Mali, as claimed by the various rebellious parties. These included the Mouvement Populaire de l'Azawad (Popular Movement of the Azawad), the Front Populaire de Libération de l'Azawad (Popular Front for the Liberation of the Azawad), the Armée Révolutionnaire de Libération de l'Azawad (Popular Army for the Liberation of the Azawad), and the Front Islamique de l'Azawad (Islamic Front of the Azawad). The latter mainly attracted Arabic-speakers.

23. Cited by M. Dabo in "Ganda Koy: Que veut-on," *Nouvel Horizon* (Bamako) 97 (14 June 1994).

24. For further detail on territorial rivalries in the area of Tedjarert, see Grémont (2009).

25. Such as the Democratic Alliance for Change in Mali, and the National Movement for Justice in Niger.

8

ETHNICITY AND INTERDEPENDENCE

Moors and Haalpulaaren in the Senegal Valley

Olivier Leservoisier

The history of the relationship between Moorish and Haalpulaar[1] societies has mainly been described in terms of their opposition, understood especially through their competition over the control of resources in the Senegal valley. Adopting a different perspective, the aim of this chapter is to underline the numerous relations that link these societies by emphasizing their interdependence, which has often been neglected by researchers. Indeed, apart from the observations made by Paul Marty (1921), Shaykh Muusa Kamara (1998), O. Kané (1974), and I. Sal (1978), historical commentary has tended to focus on conflicts rather than alliances, thus perpetuating, at times unintentionally, the image of two antagonistic blocs composed, on the one hand, of Moors (*bīdān*),[2] who are Arabo-Berbers of a pastoral nomadic tradition, and, on the other hand, black African minorities (Haalpulaaren, Soninké, and Wolof), who are mainly agriculturalists living along the Senegal River.

This dualistic approach has become even more popular since the mid-1980s, in the wake of ecological and political upheavals in the Senegal valley, where most of Mauritania's agricultural and pastoral potential is concentrated.[3] Since the 1970s, severe drought, the development of irrigation through the construction of dams along the Senegal River,[4] and the promulgation of new land laws have increased the pressure on the land, leading to numerous conflicts often fought along "ethnic" lines. Many such ethnic struggles were caused by land redistribution policies applied by the Mauritanian government, which is mainly controlled by the Moorish majority and which favored Moorish property developers, and by land laws that systematically ignored the rights of people who lived on one side of the river but who lived off land on the other side. Such issues further played an important role in the outbreak of hostilities between Mauritania and Senegal in 1989, which led to the emigration and eviction of

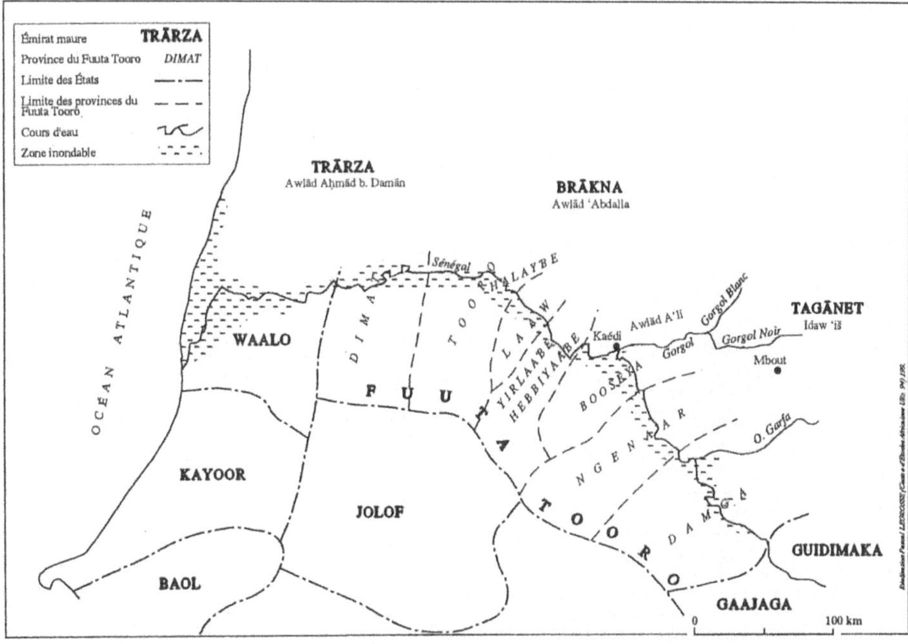

Map 8.1. The Moorish emirates and the Futa Toro (18th–19th century). P. Lecrosse 1992

several thousand people from both sides of the river (in particular Mauritanian Haalpulaar), while the border between the countries remained closed for three years (Leservoisier 1994).[5] They also contributed to the aggravation of struggles over Mauritanian national identity,[6] by favoring the development of an ethnic and racial rhetoric perpetuating the notion of a formal opposition between Moorish and black "worlds."

In addition to land conflicts in the Senegal valley, the issue of slavery tends to reinforce this image of social antagonism.[7] It is striking that international organizations and the media, as well as researchers, tend to approach this issue primarily with reference to Moorish society, thereby unwittingly reinforcing simplistic explanations of slavery as primarily the result of a presumed racial opposition between "Arabs" and "blacks." But forms of slavery have been equally present within the black African societies of the Senegal valley, and throughout the continent more generally (Meillassoux 1975; Miers and Kopytoff 1977; Lovejoy 2000 [1983]). It is also worth remembering that these populations, who themselves have at times been victims of slave raids, also actively participated in the trans-Saharan slave trade by supplying Moors with slaves (Curtin 1975; J. L. A. Webb 1995). Far from wanting to minimize the opposition between Moorish and Haalpulaar society, however, my intention here is to provide an alternative to interpretations that reduce all their relations to conflict without acknowledging their inherent interdependence. Through historical study of a particular region—Gorgol, on the border with Senegal in south-central Mauritania—from the eighteenth century to the present, this chapter describes the various interactions that were or still are possible on the local level between groups that, on the national level, are theoretically opposed to one another.

In order to do so, it is first of all necessary to discuss the notion of "territories" (*leydi*) in the valley. Such territories were once inherently political, and hence scattered and dispersed, so that historically the Senegal River appears as the center of one connected space, open to various populations, rather than as the current sharp dividing line between only two "national" states.

Between Right Bank and Left: The Political Construction of Haalpulaaren Territories (*Leydi*)

Far from being natural, the boundaries between *leydi* in the Senegal valley are the result of a turbulent history marked by shifting political alliances and oppositions, by a series of conquests and migrations, and by the hazards of climate.[8] These changes have been especially salient on the right bank, whose inhabitants were wont to move between the two sides of the river. We can identify three major migratory stages on the right bank of the central Senegal valley. The first dates back to the time of the Satigi Deniyankooße dynasty that ruled over the Futa Toro (the dominant regional political entity of the central Senegal valley) from the beginning of the sixteenth to the end of the eighteenth century (see map 8.1). During most of their reign, Haalpulaaren were settled on both sides of the river.[9] The second stage begins with the establishment of Moorish warrior states (Trarza, Brakna, and Tagant) in southern Mauritania, toward the end of the seventeenth century and the beginning of the eighteenth, which led to a gradual retreat of black African populations from the right to the left bank. After the maraboutic revolution of the *almaami*[10] put an end to the Satigi dynasty at the end of the eighteenth century, these movements intensified, as Abdul Kader Kan, the first *almaami* of the Futa Toro, organized a massive withdrawal to the left bank in a bid to avoid Moorish interference. For this purpose, he established fortified villages at all known fords (*juuwde*).[11] Finally, in the early twentieth century, French military conquest (originally started by the expansionist governor of Senegal, Louis

Faidherbe, in 1854 along the Senegal River) favored the (re)occupation of the right bank by black African populations.

This pendulum swing from one bank of the river to the other—a movement sadly repeated during the events of 1989—has clearly had an impact on the distribution of territories in the valley. Most notably, it favored the splitting of lineage groups, scattering them in various villages. This dispersal led to a division of land that necessarily changed the limits of the territories over time. The zone of influence of the "master" of a given territory (*jom leydi*), rather than being limited to one village, can stretch over various localities: it is hence preferable to speak of lineage rather than village territory. Thus, far from continuous territories, we are dealing here with overlapping and interlocking areas (Sautter and Pélissier 1964). Population movements from one bank to the other also resulted in the establishment of territories that spanned the river (Schmitz 1986), explaining the current presence of transborder residents throughout the valley.[12]

Judging by the distribution of *leydi* across the river, then, it is obvious that the Senegal has never acted as a closed border. Even at the end of the eighteenth century, when the *almaami* Abdul Kader organized a massive retreat of Haalpulaaren to the left bank, the lands on the right bank continued to act as an interstitial zone between the Moorish emirates and the provinces of the Futa Toro, offering some groups the option of occupying lands situated in the margins of the dominant political centers (Kopytoff 1987). The late twentieth-century establishment of a closed border, a political and military demarcation line between two states, thus appears to be in contradiction with the historical "African frontier," characteristically an open space between organized societies "that, in opposition to modern states, do not homogenise space, but polarise it around a central core, surrounded by a periphery that is linked to the central state in a much more flexible way" (Sautter 1982: 47). This explains why political entities were more often separated by a border *zone* than by a line.[13] These "frontier zones" (Kopytoff 1987), situated in the periphery of political centers, invited the settlement of newcomers who, by pledging allegiance to or by forging alliances with one of the political powers in the area, strengthened the latter's influence. This created a dynamic frontier, whose limits varied according to the strength or weakness of regional, powerful places. Far from defining itself with reference to linear boundaries, the spatial extension of power and the control of territories were above all determined by sociopolitical agreements and allegiances (Sautter 1982), as Charles Grémont (this volume) also shows for the Tuareg of northern Mali. This was the dominant model among the populations of southern Mauritania, allowing communities such as the Kaédi or the Moodi Nallankooɓe to settle on the peripheries both of the Moorish emirates and of the provinces of the Futa Toro.

Between Allies and Enemies: The Awlād A'li and the Haalpulaaren of Kaédi

Kaédi, situated at the confluence of the Gorgol and Senegal rivers, is one of the most ancient settlements in the central Senegal valley and is today the capital of the Gorgol region. It used to be the residence of Farmbaal, one of the Farba that dominated the valley before the arrival of the Haalpulaaren Koli Tenguella, founder of the dynasty of the Satigi Deniyankooɓe, in the sixteenth century. The Gorgol region, rich in agricultural and pastoral potential, became one of the most important economic and political centers under Satigi rule, and in the seventeenth century it became the seat of their capital, Gumel. Because of its fertility, the floodplain (*waalo,* called *raag* by the *bīdān*) was much fought over until, in the early eighteenth century, it was taken by the Litāma, a Moorish tribe from the Brakna emirate.[14] In the mid-eighteenth century, the Litāma were in turn expelled by the Awlād A'li,[15] with military support by Haalpulaaren from Kaédi.

Local oral traditions recount this alliance as follows. Hayba, the leader of the Awlād A'li, came to see Farmbaal and said to him: *Hettere tew e hettere heeñere kejjata e hunuko woto* (a piece of meat and a piece of liver cannot be put into the same mouth), indicating that the Litāma and the Awlād A'li could not both stay in the same area. Farmbaal, who had been forced to submit to the power of the Litāma in the Gorgol, granted his help to Hayba. After several years of fighting, the Awlād A'li drove out the Litāma, who broke up and went east to Damga province. Now masters of the Gorgol plain, the Awlād A'li maintained good relations with the inhabitants of Kaédi and the province of the Booseya more generally. This was particularly true at the time of Muhammad wull Hayba, one of Hayba's descendants who, in the second half of the nineteenth century, formed an alliance with Abdul Bokar Kan, leader of the Booseya.

One of the outward signs of the good relations between the Awlād A'li and Farmbaal was the division of land that occurred under the rule of Muhammad wull Hayba on the floodplain called Mbara.[16] Limits were marked with large stones brought by camel. In 1891, Lieutenant Benoit Duportail, commander of the military post of Kaédi, described these markers:

> As parts of the land, in particular the rack [*raag*], are still under water, I have not been able to visit them and to establish each and every one's property rights. On the side of the hills that border the river, however, the limits are shown by large boulders that act as boundary markers and that are linked by a series of small stones. These stretch from the river to a distance of more than a day's walk.[17]

To the northeast of this boundary, land was controlled by the Awlād A'li, and every shepherd who grazed his herds there had to pay one sheep to their leader. This zone was much sought after by pastoralists for the nutritional value of the grass (*mbiddi*) growing there. Lands situated in the Gorgol plain were also farmed by "religious" tribes (i.e., sedentary lineage groups specialized in religious learning and its transmission, distinct from "warrior" tribes), in particular the Lemtuna. As warriors, the Awlād A'li undertook to protect anyone living in their zone of influence. Marty (1921: 90) notes that the Lemtune Idegjmolla paid them a *ghafr* (protection fee), amounting to one *matar* (approx. eighty kilograms of millet) per harvest.

Yet the Kaédi communities that had kept their floodplain lands did not pay any dues to the head of the Awlād A'li. According to Duportail, "They recognise Abdul Boubakar as a king, but do not pay him any taxes. . . . Sidi Ahmet[18] is well received when he comes . . . they receive him as an important chief with whom they are friendly rather than as their own leader." The friendly relations between the Awlād A'li and the inhabitants of Kaédi were part of the general alliance between Muhammad wull Hayba and Abdul Bokar Kan, by which each granted the other assistance. The colonial conquest offered them one such occasion to fight together against the French. Faidherbe was well aware of their coalition:

> In the month of June 1864 the trade barges that had run aground near Saldé were attacked and plundered by the Ouled-Eyba Moors together with the Bosséiabé. Governor Faidherbe, having returned to the colony on 14 July 1863, sent a company in reprisal, commanded by colonel Despaillères. The villages of the Bosséa [Booseya] were burned, in particular those of Doualel and Kaédi. The Toucouleurs [Haalpulaaren] lost about a hundred men. Enormous booty was taken from the tribe of the Ouled-Eyba, who lost all their tents. (1889: 249)

During the last years of his life, the leader of the Booseya repeatedly sought refuge on the right bank to escape from the French army, while Sidi Ahmed wull Hayba remained close to the people of the Booseya.[19]

As we can see, far from a head-on opposition between two homogeneous blocs, Moors on one side and Haalpulaaren on the other, the history of Kaédi reveals the existence of many cross-cutting ties along the Senegal River, between individual Futa Toro provinces and Moorish emirates. Thus, as Paul Marty noted, local political and military coalitions were formed between some groups of Moors and Haalpulaaren to fight against structurally similar alliances of other groups:

> Thus it was common knowledge that the people of Lao and the Aleybé were allied to the Oulad Normach and Oulad Ahmed among the Hassan and to the Kunta, especially the Meterambrin; that the Toro were allied to the Oulad Siyyed, the Irlabé and the Ebyabé were allies of the Oulad Eli-Oulad Naceri; the

> Bosséa were allies of the Oulad Eli–Ahl Hiba. A war between Moorish tribes often led to the involvement of their Toucouleurs [Haalpulaaren] allies. The same is true of conflicts among Toucouleurs. (1921: 297)[20]

Similarly, the Moorish tribes that raided Kaédi, like the Awlād Swed for instance, were not those living in the vicinity, but rather came from farther inland, while the Awlād A'li supported the people of Kaédi in their counterattacks. Their last famous joint raid took place in 1903 at Wolde Bajar, near Lexeiba, against the Idegjmolla.

Between "Black" and "White": The Moodi Nallankooɓe

The Moodi Nallankooɓe, who today live in the villages of Dao and Dolol in the Gorgol region, are another example of a people who, because of links they had established with Moorish tribes (Litāma, Shorfa, and the Idaw 'Ish of the emirate of Tagant) managed to stay on the right bank throughout the nineteenth century. Religious ties were particularly important: thus, for instance, Hamme Juldo Kan, the most distant ancestor of the Dao and Dolol families, taught the Qur'an to the Idaw'li. As a general rule, the children of the Moodi Nallankooɓe, after first receiving a basic education at home, continued their studies with influential Moorish religious families. This situation inevitably favored marriage alliances. As Antonin, a colonial administrator and commander of the Gorgol *cercle,* noted in 1915: "A large number among them have studied with the Moors. Some got married there and stayed. A small fraction of the Ahel Sidi Mahmoud, the Ahel Tafsir who have their own camp, are descendents of the Ahel Moodi Nallah."[21] The Moodi Nallankooɓe's religious knowledge was recognized by religious and by warrior Moorish tribes. Links were especially close with the Litāma and the Twabir. Similarly, despite initial conflicts, relations with the Idaw 'Ish improved; oral sources (see, e.g., Kamara 1998) suggest that this was mainly because the Idaw 'Ish respected and feared the Moodi Nallankooɓe's mystical powers. Thus it was said of one of the leaders of the Moodi Nallankooɓe living in Daar al-Salaam:

> Nalla Umar had great charismatic powers and all his prayers were granted in extraordinary ways. [For instance], when Umar Nalla went to Gasambiri, the Idaw 'Ish attacked Daar al-Salaam and took all the belongings of the Nalla Moodi that had been left there. The latter wanted to pursue them, but Nalla Umar told them to stay [in Daar al-Salaam]. He then ordered them to dig a large trench from east to west. Then he asked them how far Daar al-Salaam was from the place where the Idaw 'Ish lived and they told him. The Idaw 'Ish lived at that time in a place called Nawa Mileyni in the Regeybaat. Nalla Umar asked two of his men who were brave to go to the Idaw 'Ish and to stay in the first tent offered to them. After they had left, Nalla Umar went into the trench, and called the leader of the Idaw 'Ish by his name, and the latter answered. People

> asked him: "Who called you?" "I heard the voice of a *sūdānī* who called me," he answered. He got up, took their hands, and died. Nalla Umar called the second man in the hierarchy [of the Idaw 'Ish], who also answered as had done the leader before him, and died straight after. Nalla Umar called the third and he also died the same day.[22] The Idaw 'Ish were afraid and said: "Two people from the Moodi Nalla have spent the night here. It must be they who caused these misfortunes. Let's give them their animals back!" They took all the herds back to Daar al-Salaam and asked Nalla Umar to brand their cattle with a special mark so that they would know to avoid it next time.[23] (Kamara 1998: 404–405)

The Moodi Nallankooɓe chose to brand their animals with the word *salām* (peace), a mark borne by their animals to this day.[24]

The Moodi Nallankooɓe also maintained close economic relations with the Moors. In addition to standard exchanges of agricultural for pastoral products, in colonial times they also acted as intermediaries in the gum trade. Because of their knowledge of Hassaniya (the Arabic dialect spoken by the Moors), they were able to act as interpreters in dealings with gum traders. According to Raffenel, their "trade consists in selling, to their own benefit, the gum with which they have been entrusted by the [Moorish] people of the Ouled-Elys" (1846: 55). These alliances with Moorish tribes also meant that they were frequently called upon to be mediators in conflicts between Moors and Haalpulaaren or Soninké. Shaykh Muusa Kamara (1998) gives us one such example, where the Moodi Nallankooɓe were able to return cattle stolen by Moors to the Raangaa Haalpulaaren.

The importance of these ties influenced the ways in which colonial administrators described the Moodi Nallankooɓe. In his monograph on the Gorgol *cercle*, Coup speaks of "a curious type of mixed Haalpulaaren and Moors."[25] Similarly, Vidal, in his *Report on Indigenous Land Rights in the Fuuta in the Senegal Valley* (1924), described them as "people of mixed Moorish race." Raffenel (1846), who was traveling on the river in 1844, was deceived into identifying them as Idaw 'Ish Moors. For the same reasons, other Haalpulaaren refer to the Moodi Nallankooɓe as *tooroɓɓe raneɓe* (white marabouts) rather than as *tooroɓɓe baleɓe* (black marabouts), or as *rewankooɓe,* people from the north.

Such names also indicate the Moodi Nallankooɓe's high degree of acculturation. The name of the ancestor of the Moodi Nallankooɓe, Hamme Juldo Kan, is significant in this respect: Hamme, short for Muhammad, is the generic Haalpulaar name for Moors. Further, the Moodi Nallankooɓe are generally referred to as the Ahl (Arabic for "people of") Moodi Nallankooɓe; the habit of referring to people by their putative ancestor's name is rare among Haalpulaaren, but common among Moors. Moodi Nallankooɓe women used to wear the long veils (*malhafa*) that are generally identified with Moorish women, as well as Moorish jewelry. They were also known for their skills in mat weaving, just like the Litāma women with whom they were closely connected as neighbors and often as in-laws. The Moodi Nallankooße's marriage customs are equally marked by Moorish influence: the wife remains with her family until the birth of her first child, whether her husband is a Moor or not, while among most Haalpulaaren, the wife resides with her husband from their wedding day on.

A final proof of the importance of relations with Moors is the large number of *harātīn* (people of slave descent) among the Moodi Nallankooße, especially in the village of Dolol. Many *harātīn* sought refuge among the Moodi Nallankooße, because the good relations they maintained with the Moors minimized the risk of the former masters insisting on their return. This movement of *harātīn* was by no means limited to the Moodi Nallankooße, however, but was common throughout the valley, where many descendants of Moorish slaves came to settle in black African villages and gradually adopted Haalpulaaren culture.

Between "Slave" and "Free": Identity Claims in Moorish and Haalpulaar Society

The situation of the descendants of Moorish slaves who sought refuge in Haalpulaar villages in the valley, where they were mostly assimilated into local servile groups, is of particular interest here, as it completes the observations made so far about the "aristocratic" elites and sheds light on the relations of interdependence between the Moorish and Haalpulaaren societies from a different perspective. The Saafaalße Hormankooße best illustrate my argument. Historically, the Saafaalße Hormankooße are said to be descendants of black Africans who were captured by raiding bands of Horman (warrior groups from present-day Morocco), settled in the Senegal valley in the early eighteenth century, and then fled their masters to seek refuge in the Futa Toro. Over time, however, this term has been extended to include all *harātīn* who have assimilated into Haalpulaar culture.

After the French colonial conquest, significant numbers of *harātīn* started to move toward the Senegal River, where they came into close contact with black Africans. Their reasons for moving were various: many captives took advantage of the French presence in the south of the country to escape their masters and to seek shelter near military and administrative posts in what came to be called "freedom quarters" or "liberty villages" (*villages de liberté*; see Bouche 1968).[26] Others, like the Moodi Nallankooße, preferred to apply for the direct protection of Haalpulaaren families. There was nothing new about this: well before the colonial conquest, several groups of *harātīn* living in the valley had distanced themselves from their former Moorish masters by seeking refuge with the Haalpulaaren. This was the case in the Brakna with the Zemarig who, as early as the eighteenth century, maintained close relations with the Haleyɓe, who granted them access to land in exchange for rents. According to Marty, "these Zemarig *sūdān,* much as those of other religious tribes, are dependents of the Toucouleurs who have given them shelter and land, rather than of their masters, with whom they have not been able to live" (1921: 338).

The colonial conquest intensified such movements in the wake of the (re) occupation of the right bank by black African groups. The gradual clearing of land by Haalpulaaren families who had recently settled on the "pacified" Mauritanian side was a decisive element in the arrival in the valley of *harātīn,* who were responding to Haalpulaaren demand for labor to cultivate the many plots of land that were at their disposal. These *harātīn* were mostly employed as sharecroppers and had to pay to their masters a *rempeccen* (lit., to farm and share), amounting to a third or half of the harvest.

Much as the extension of farmland on the right bank played a central role in the settlement of *harātīn* in the valley, it was also decisive for the development of seasonal migrations. *Harātīn* from the interior came to the valley to offer their services during the millet harvest, in March and April, and returned home for the rainy season in July. To these seasonal agricultural migrations were added labor migrations to the ports and villages by the river, where the *harātīn* were employed in different capacities (as laborers, woodcutters, domestics, shepherds, etc.). They also often filled places left empty by the departure of black Africans who had gone to cultivate peanuts in Senegal. Many of these migrants ended up settling among the Haalpulaaren.

So the reasons and the conditions of settlement of *harātīn* in the valley were diverse. Yet it would never have been quite so extensive had it not been strongly encouraged by the Haalpulaaren. As Marty noted: "The Toucouleurs are keener than ever to attract their black brothers, slaves or vassals of the Moors" (1921: 339). But their encouragement was not based on feelings of fraternal solidarity; the poaching of *harātīn* allowed Haalpulaaren landlords to count on a docile and taxable labor force. Thus, as they placed themselves under the protection of the Haalpulaaren, the *harātīn* most often fell into a new state of dependency. For those who had not totally severed their links with their former masters, the situation was even worse: they were doubly subjugated, paying rents to the Haalpulaaren and to their original tribe. But the encouragement of settlement of the *harātīn* by the Haalpulaaren was not merely a response to economic and agricultural imperatives. It also served political ends, providing them with additional military manpower as a protection against raids by Moors. This was the case in the area around the Bogué plain (Brakna region), where in the nineteenth century the Halayɓe Haalpulaaren encouraged the settlement of Jeyjuba *harātīn* by granting them land on the limits of their own floodplain. The Jeyjube thus set up a protective belt around the Bogué plain, whence they kept the Halayɓe informed about raids in the region (Jah 1986: 46).

Thus, although settlement in the Futa Toro provided in most cases opportunities to move away from former masters, potentially leading to a degree of emancipation, links with the inhabitants of the valley often led to new subordinations, as the Haalpulaaren tended to regard Moorish servile groups mainly as reservoirs of cheap labor. Nonetheless, most of these groups strongly assimilated to their Haalpulaar surroundings, to the point where today most of their descendants do not speak Hassaniya and have lost all memory of their former Moorish customs. They have thus become "Hormankooɓe" and taken new family names from the Haalpulaaren (Sy, Ba, Lih, and so on). In the Gorgol region, the *harātīn* who have maintained Arab traditions refer to the Hormankooɓe as *mitngeleb* (changelings).[27] Although it is impossible to distinguish them at first sight from other Haalpulaaren, these "changelings" are nonetheless discriminated against because of their origin. This is why certain Hormankooɓe say, in a somewhat resigned tone: *Ko leggal ɓoyi e diyam ko fof wattataa dum nooro* (However long a tree trunk stays in the water, it will never turn into a crocodile). They thus illustrate the limits of their integration into Haalpulaar society, where, much as among the Moors, origins and genealogies are a central element of status and social hierarchies. This is why most former *harātīn* are assimilated into the lowest social groups and remain deprived of political influence within the various Pulaar *leyyi* to which they are attached.[28] This is also why such "Pulaarized" male *harātīn* usually do not have much matrimonial choice beyond women of servile status. In fact, members of noble Haalpulaar groups hardly consider them different from *maccuɓe* ("real" slaves). Today, many Hormankooɓe, although they have only ever known Haalpulaar society, have decided to distance themselves from their host society, and more and more Saafaalɓe Hormankooɓe have claimed *harātīn* identity, showing their eagerness to break free of the Haalpulaar hierarchical order.

This assertion of a *harātīn* identity among Saafaalɓe Hormankooɓe seems to be motivated by two factors. First, the conflict that occurred in 1989 between Mauritania and Senegal included a series of violent confrontations that were, in Mauritania, mainly aimed at Haalpulaaren. In the face of such danger, numerous Hormankooɓe chose to redefine themselves as *harātīn,* thereby demonstrating the fragility of their integration among Haalpulaaren society and reasserting their place in indigenous, Moorish (Mauritanian) society—albeit at the bottom of its social scale.[29] Second, the democratic process launched in the early 1990s has nominally made it possible for subordinate groups to play a more active political role. Faced with their exclusion from all major electoral lists, such groups have increasingly attempted to organize themselves in order to make themselves heard. The Hormankooɓe of Kaédi were the first in the country to establish their own *leynol* in 1991 with explicit reference to their *harātīn* identity. This decision had much political and symbolic significance, as it meant that the Hormankooɓe were leaving the Haalpulaar lineages to which they had been attached. Their initiative was supported by Moorish politicians, who hoped to co-opt them. This rapprochement indicated, at a very early stage, the Hormankooɓe's desire to assert a new cultural identity and to rely on new political alliances that, in the long run, might help them obtain local positions of influence. In Kaédi, the Hormankooɓe's manifest desire to conform more closely to Moorish ways of life—which are, in fact, alien to most of them—also translates into a tendency to move from their existing homes into the *harātīn* quarter of Kaédi, inhabited mostly by Moorish families, and to prefer marriages with Arabic-speaking *hartāni* women. Similarly, when reciting their genealogies, many Hormankooɓe now insist on their *harātīn* ancestors, while those of Haalpulaar slave status are omitted or, at best, mentioned rather evasively.

The assertiveness of such claims to Moorish identity is stronger than their basis in fact, as most Hormankooɓe have hardly any practical knowledge of Moorish customs. What matters here is rather their desire to think of themselves as different, and to be publicly recognized as such. Thus it appears that in this case at least, it is indeed "the ethnic *boundary* that defines the group" rather than "the cultural stuff that it encloses" (F. Barth 1969: 15). Yet their objectives go beyond public recognition of their cultural distinctiveness, and include access to local political posts of influence. Here, their strategy has been crowned with success, as a few have succeeded in obtaining seats on municipal councils. Hormankooɓe identity politics thus seems to have paid off. The same can be said for similar choices made by other social groups, and this emphasis on identities seems to be one of the defining features of the democratic process in the region (Leservoisier 2009). As long as individuals only have a chance to be heard if they identify themselves and are identified by others in terms of certain social labels, political participation necessarily remains subordinate to group membership.

Identity claims among *harātīn* of Arab culture living in Moorish society provide a parallel case: many *harātīn* publicly assert their difference from the Moors, claiming that they are "Moors but black, black but Moors" and that "their culture will never destroy their race, nor will their race ever destroy their culture."[30] Hence, they use their black African origins as a prime marker of difference, which they see as closely related to qualities that are ascribed to them in Moorish society (hard work, strength, resilience) and to specific forms of cultural expression (dance, popular song, the use of certain musical instruments such as the flute, *zawzāya*, or the one-stringed lute, *gambra*). At times, they even proudly mention their reputation for witchcraft. Such claims to ethnocultural specificity allow *harātīn* to assert their difference from the Moors on grounds other than socioeconomic origin to revalorize their social identity as *harātīn*, now defined as an ethnic rather than a status group; and to increase the legitimacy of their political struggle. Yet if we take into account that in this case, ethnic boundaries tend to reinforce social distinctions (Poutignat and Streiff-Fénart 1995), the success of such strategies remains questionable. In any case, the "ethnicity" produced here is new, and can only be explained with reference to developments on the national level. Conflicts between *bīdān* and black Africans have been recurrent since independence, mainly sparked by Arabization policies and the implementation of new land laws. This explains why certain *harātīn* might see assertions of ethnic difference as the only possible way to make themselves heard on the national level. More generally, reference to ethnicity is an accepted way of achieving political recognition in the country, and thus of obtaining political and administrative posts.

The opposition between *harātīn* and *bīdān* as it is phrased today has developed to meet new political objectives, as debates over national identity have led *harātīn* to reformulate social relations according to ethnic, racial, or national criteria that held no such place in traditional *bīdān* society.[31] This can be seen in the ways in which the *harātīn* have succeeded, in the political arena, in redefining former relations of subordination to their own benefit. Notions of their special capacity for hard work and physical labor and of their resilience, formerly used to stigmatize them, are proudly taken up in their tracts. Further, *harātīn* now publicly claim to be *harātīn*, a term that in most other contexts would be seen as an insult. They are thereby putting old symbolic material to a new use, according to radically new concepts and logics: in Moorish tribal society, signs of status were never taken to symbolize culture or ethnic identity.

It thus becomes clear that the claims to "black" identity voiced by *harātīn* refer to an "invented tradition" in Hobsbawm's (1983) sense: its historical continuity is fictional, and it is turned toward new objectives that are alien to the tradition itself.[32] Anthropologists have to be particularly careful not to analyze the history of social groups by projecting onto them ethnic or racial identity categories that have emerged only recently.[33] Thus there is a need to resituate the history of societies in southern Mauritania in their longer-term context, in order to understand how they have evolved together to become what they are today.

The obvious parallels between claims made by certain Hormankooße who today refer to themselves as *harātīn* and those voiced by descendants of slaves owned by Moors who today claim black African origins illustrate particularly well the relations of interdependence between Moorish and Haalpulaar societies. Such claims to identity, while reaffirming distinctions between groups, also betray their closeness. Hence, such negotiations of identity are carried out with reference not to two, but rather to three categories: when emphasizing their black African origins, Moorish *harātīn* aim to situate themselves with reference to *bīdān* as well as to black African groups and traditions. Similarly, the Hormankooɓe who claim to be *harātīn* do this both with regard to the *bīdān* and in opposition to the Haalpulaaren. Hence, even though these various claims to identity can be read as part of a broader strategy to obtain social and political recognition on the national stage, they also indicate the close connections between Moorish and Haalpulaar societies, each existing as a definable social reality only in relation to the other, as well as the more general instability of ethnic boundaries in Mauritania. On closer analysis, the manifold relations of opposition and interdependence that exist between Moors and Haalpulaaren are essential for the self-definition of both societies: they need to be studied not separately, but with reference to and as a result of their interdependence.

NOTES

1. Meaning simply "Pulaar (Fulfulde)-speakers," Haalpulaaren (in French called "Peulhs" or "Toucouleurs") is the self-ascribed ethnonym for the mostly sedentary population in the central Senegal valley, whose origins are often identified with the regional state of Takrur (9th–13th centuries). "Moors" (French *maures*) is used here to denote the arabophone, Arabo-Berber population originally formed by the migrations of Znaga (Sanhaja) and Hassan peoples to the western Sahara in the eighth and thirteenth/fourteenth centuries.

2. In Moorish society, the term *bīdān* (lit., whites) refers to status and indicates free and noble people, in opposition to freed slaves (*harātīn*) and slaves (*'abīd*). Because of their black African origins, these latter people are also at times referred to as *sūdān* (blacks), a term that excludes non-Arabic-speakers. The non-arabophone black African populations of the Senegal valley are referred to as *kwār.*

3. There are two annual harvests in the Senegal valley: one fed by rain (*jeeri*) between July and September (millet), one by receding floods (*waalo*) between mid-October and April (sorghum).

4. These dams were built as part of the Organisation pour la Mise en Valeur de la Vallée du Sénégal (Senegal River Valley Development) scheme jointly established by Mauritania, Senegal, and Mali. They have provoked much debate, as they led to changes in water levels that threaten flood-irrigated agriculture, as well as to new administrative regulations in areas under irrigation.

5. The consequences of these events can still be felt in contemporary Mauritania. In June 2007, then Mauritanian president Sidi Ould Cheikh Abdallahi promised to repatriate refugees who had been in Senegal since 1989. Yet so far, it remains unclear who is going to cover the resulting administrative and legal costs, especially since the military coup on 3 August 2008.

6. Since Mauritanian independence in 1960, ethnic tensions have reflected the Arabization policies implemented by the Mauritanian government, which is largely controlled by Moors, and the difficulties encountered by black African candidates competing for political posts.

7. Migration to Mauritania by sub-Saharan Africans (see Choplin and Marfaing this volume) is another example that, by creating conflicts between indigenous and foreign populations, tends to maintain a division between Moorish and black on the level of national society.

8. "Agricultural" territories, moreover, remain open to fishermen and pastoralists. Thus, schematically at least, the relations between groups are organized around successive occupations of land. Fishermen are the first to occupy the flooded plain (*waalo*) when water levels are highest, in order to prepare the dams used to trap fish when the water recedes. As water levels fall, agriculturalists replace fishermen to prepare *waalo* fields. Once these fields have been harvested, pastoralists arrive to graze their herds (Schmitz 1986).

9. According to Bruë, who visited the Satigi Sire Sawa Laamu in 1696, the Satigi then lived on the right bank at Gumel, alongside the Gorgol tributary (Labat 1728).

10. One of a series of Islamic state-building movements in West Africa that continued until the nineteenth century, the Futa Toro imamate (*almaami* is a variant on Arabic imam) was established in the 1770s following the defeat of the earliest such movement in the region (known in English as the Shurr Bubba war), that of Nasir al-Din in the same area in the 1670s.

11. Such as the villages of Gaol, Dondou, Giuraye, Nguidilogne, and Sadel.

12. In the early 1980s, this raised the problem of nationals of one country working fields on the other side of the river, and thus violating the national border.

13. Fabio Viti (2000) notes that among the Baoulé in Ivory Coast, it was common practice to leave a stretch of no-man's land between two villages if their territories had to be demarcated. Similarly, in the Abron kingdom of Gyaman, as described by Terray (1995: 680), outside borders were constituted by uninhabited stretches of land that could be as wide as thirty or forty kilometers.

14. The Litāma descend from their name-giving ancestor al-Yatim, the brother of 'Abd Allah and 'Abd al-Jabbar, all sons of Kerroum. Having left the Brakna, the Litāma settled in Baqijmou, northeast of the Gorgol, before moving to the confluence of the White and the Black Gorgol, whence they controlled the *raag* plain between Lexeiba and Kaédi.

15. Also originally part of the Brakna emirate.

16. Friendly relations between the two parties encouraged some inhabitants of the left bank to start cultivating land on the right bank. At times, this led to conflicts over land rights. Muhammad wull Hayba could not evict these farmers, because of his friendship with the Kaédi Haalpulaaren. The delimitation of their respective zones of control was intended as a solution to this problem.

17. French National Archives, 200 MI 921.

18. The son of Muhammad wull Hayba, leader of the Awlād A'li in 1891.

19. He was married to Takko Arbi, the daughter of the head of the Hirnange Booseya.

20. The first-named groups in each of the alliances listed are Haalpulaaren, the second Moors.

21. Rapport Antonin, 1915, French National Archives, 9G42.

22. According to another version that I collected locally, the leader's child fell seriously ill because of a spell cast by the Moodi Nallankooße, who said they would cure him if their animals were returned to them.

23. This treaty was not always respected, but stolen animals were returned if they were claimed. The political report of the Bakel *cercle* of 1903 confirms this, noting how a theft of animals from the Moodi Nallankooße by the Abakāk was quickly resolved: "Lamine Mamadou [the village head of Boky Jammi] went to see Bakar to obtain the restitution of the herds that had been stolen by the Abakak last June. He was received by Bakar and Etman and his request was heeded because he was a *marabout*; thirty-five cows were returned" (privately held document kindly shared by Suleymaan Kan).

24. If the branding of cattle helped the Moodi Nallankooße to escape raids, another distinctive sign was used to protect their children: they shaved their heads, leaving only two tufts of hair on the sides, so that they could be recognized by allied Moorish tribes.

25. Archives Nationales (Paris), 1G331, administrative report entitled "Monographie du cercle du Gorgol," 1908.

26. Such were the settlements of Aleg, Bogué (or Boghé), Kaédi, M'bout, and Sélibaby (all on the right bank, which is today in Mauritania).

27. In the lower Senegal valley, *harātīn* settled among Wolof are called Bzouga.

28. Sing. *leynol.* In Haalpulaar society, *leyyi* are political units, more or less extensive, that each are led by a noble family which, through a history of settlement and political maneuvering, has incorporated various other families and social groups, including slaves.

29. The *harātīn* leaders of the El Horr movement (The Free, a pressure group founded in 1978 to press for the social and political advancement of lower-status Mauritanians) were well aware of such strategies: "The events of 1989 and 1990 revealed that many Haratines had 'assimilated' to Black African communities, especially Haalpulaaren. The violence which these communities were subjected to has forced these 'assimilated Haratines' to discover *their true identity* to escape massacre or eviction" ("Les Haratines . . . contribution à une compréhension juste de leur problématique," *El Horr,* 5 March 1993; emphasis added).

30. From the Constitutional Charter of El Horr, 5 March 1978, and the Manifesto of 5 March 1993, celebrating the fifteenth anniversary of the founding of El Horr, respectively.

31. For the sake of simplicity, this is here taken to refer to pre-colonial Moorish society at the end of the nineteenth century.

32. Thus, some *harātīn* like to refer to black populations who lived in the desert during the first millennium CE as their "ancestors," although the biological ancestors of many *harātīn* only arrived in what is now Mauritania in the nineteenth century, in particular after the jihads of al-Hajj 'Umar and Samory. Similarly, relatively few have kept any precise records of their diverse ethnic origins, or their genealogies.

33. The Ahl al-Gibla and the Ahl Gannar in southwestern Mauritania, as studied by Taylor (2000), are good examples. Before the French conquest, these groups were living on both sides of the Senegal River, on the margins of the two dominant political poles, the Trarza Moors and the Wolof of Waalo. Living in the middle, they could claim to belong to one or the other society, without having a well-defined status, until the arrival of the French forced them to choose sides. Some of these groups thus became clients of the Trarza, and ended up by being assimilated into the *harātīn.*

PART 3

STRANGERS, SPACE, AND LABOR

9

MAURITANIA AND THE NEW FRONTIER OF EUROPE

From Transit to Residence

Armelle Choplin

In September 2007, Mauritanians watched, not without surprise, as the first Moroccan semi-trailer trucks, brand new and loaded with perishable goods, came down the new road between Nouadhibou and Nouakchott. One month later, a local newspaper reported, "Mauritanian security forces have arrested fifty-one nationals of various sub-Saharan countries who were attempting to enter Nouadhibou illegally."[1] This implied that, for sub-Saharan Africans, to try to reach Nouadhibou, Mauritania's second largest city, had become a crime. These two events reveal many of the paradoxes that govern the western Sahara: although the liberalization of Mauritanian transport has led to an intensification of transborder exchange, the movements of people from neighboring countries, in particular Senegal and Mali, are increasingly restricted. This can only be understood with reference to the new dividing line between north and south, transplanted to the western Sahara by European policies.

During the winter of 2005–2006, it became commonplace for the European media to describe Mauritania as a hub for sub-Saharan migrants wanting to cross illegally into Europe. Nouadhibou in particular, located on the border with Morocco/Western Sahara, was presented as the main point of departure for small boats bound for the Canary Islands. In April 2006, however, such transit mostly came to a halt, after an intervention by the European Union: ever since, the EU has helped the Mauritanian government to monitor its territory, while "encouraging" it to establish a migration policy although it had never previously felt a need to do so. The European Union thereby delocalized its control mechanisms and thus its border, gradually letting it slide from the Mediterranean shores to the Sahara and its Atlantic coast. With this new dividing line between Europe and West Africa, Mauritania, whose borders had not long ago been rather porous, has become a barrier. As a result, migrants remain trapped, and as they cannot carry on farther north end up settling more permanently in Nouadhibou (120,000 inhabitants) or in the capital, Nouakchott (1 million inhabitants). There, they join other immigrants who have come to work in Mauritania. Indeed, although the media version of migration in Mauritania only ever considers transit migration, this vast and sparsely populated country (3 million inhabitants in 2007) is itself a sought-after destination for West African migrants (see Marfaing this volume). Its history is closely linked to immigration, and, with the discovery of oil, it has continued to attract sub-Saharan labor. Transit to Europe and this long tradition of immigration, although distinctive, are closely entangled.

This chapter will take a closer look at the consequences of the establishment of this new border by the European Union, from the perspective not of transit migration, but of the "post-transit" situation. In other words, what is at stake now are not Atlantic crossings, but rather the fate of those who are stuck and who are gradually transforming the cities that have, by default, become their places of residence. Because sub-Saharans are now more numerous in Mauritania, and thus more visible, the "problem" of migration frequently recurs in national public debate, in which migrants, immigrants, and "illegal" immigrants are often lumped together: in an already tense political and ethnic context, this is rather dangerous.[2]

The history of Mauritania has been marked by incessant controversies about the national identity of a country generally described as inhabited by "Arabo-Berbers" (Moors) and "Negro Mauritanians" (Haalpulaar, Soninké, and Wolof; see Leservoisier this volume).[3] Hence, even though these migrations lead to a renewal of exchanges and revitalize the region economically (Bredeloup and Pliez 2005), they also undermine its fragile social equilibrium. Beyond the various interlocking migratory movements, the question of the relation with the "other," especially the "black foreigner," is asked anew, despite the area's historically high degree of regional mobility. In a climate of socioeconomic uncertainty and increasingly exclusive notions of identity, such debates foster extremist rhetoric based on the rejection of all "outsiders."[4]

From Thoroughfare to Cul-de-Sac

Between August 2005 and May 2006, hundreds of black African migrants arrived in Nouadhibou and tried, aboard fishermen's dinghies, to sail along the coastline of the western Sahara and land on the Canary Islands—on Spanish and hence EU territory. This was but the latest stage of a long process. In the early 2000s, African migrants attempted to reach Europe via northern Morocco, on tiny fishing vessels across the fifteen kilometers of the Strait of Gibraltar. In 2002, increased controls in the Mediterranean forced them to change route. They first tried the ports of the Western Sahara, such as Laayoune, Dakhla, and especially Tarfaya, situated just opposite the Canary archipelago (see map 9.1). With the events of October 2005 in Ceuta and Melilla,[5] Moroccan border controls tightened, especially restricting travel to Morocco from the Western Sahara and Mauritania, and migrants attempting to reach the Canaries had to move their points of departure even farther south.

In this new situation, Mauritania, located 800 kilometers south of the Spanish islands, was for a time at the center of West African migration routes (Ba and Choplin 2005). For various reasons, in 2005 Nouadhibou became the place from which crossing appeared most feasible. First, the closure of the border with the Western Sahara—that was, besides, mined—made it impossible for migrants to reach Morocco. Second, tougher controls on fishing boats from Mauritania bound for the Canaries or Spain made it more difficult to disembark African crews taken on at Nouakchott or African migrants who had paid the captain for their sea passage. Finally, the completion of a paved road between Nouakchott and Nouadhibou in 2005 made travel to northern Mauritania easier for those wanting to make the crossing (Antil and Choplin 2003). Thus, in the late summer of 2005, the first fishing boats left Nouadhibou bound for the European islands, three days' sailing from the coast. Toward the end of autumn, four to five dinghies were putting to sea every night (Choplin and Lombard 2007).

Departures from Nouadhibou to Europe peaked in the winter of 2006—as did shipwrecks; although some Africans succeeded in landing on the Canaries, many others lost their lives at sea.[6] Forced by public pressure, the European Union started to intervene from April 2006 on, by setting up a system of surveillance as part of Frontex, the agency in charge of managing the EU's external borders: one helicopter and several surveillance craft were sent out, and 150 men from the Spanish Guardia Civil were dispatched to train Mauritanian police in border control. Four thousand people were arrested and "repatriated" to Nouadhibou, where, in the summer of 2006, a school was turned into a detention center. Migrants who were arrested spent two to three days in this detention center, nicknamed Guantanamito (Little Guantanamo), before being taken by bus to the Senegalese border, with €50 apiece in their pockets. This vast system of control on the Atlantic shores seems to have paid off: at the end of 2007, the Spanish government had registered only 17,000 arrivals on the Canary Islands, as compared to 40,000 in 2006. Meanwhile, the points of departure moved farther south, to Senegal and even Guinea-Bissau, resulting in ever more people sinking and drowning. In Nouadhibou, although stricter controls have not stopped departures altogether, they certainly act as a filter. Although some Mauritanians or foreigners boast that they know the route

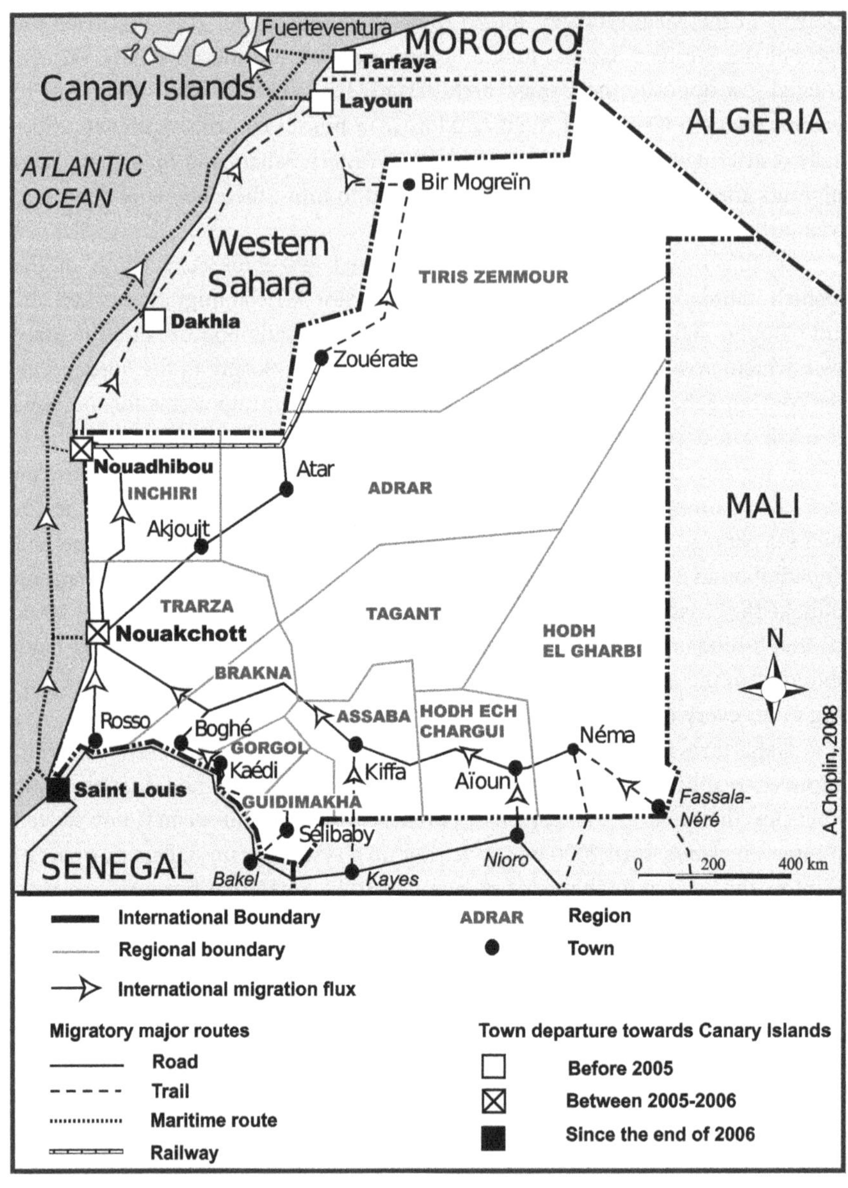

Map 9.1. Migration routes in Mauritania. A. CHOPLIN 2008

of the helicopter even before it takes off, and stress that nobody will ever be able to "barricade the sea," the number of departures has decreased. As an immediate result of these controls, a large number of migrants have found themselves stuck, and they eventually settle in Nouadhibou or Nouakchott, where they join the many other immigrants who have come to look for work in Mauritania. After all, the western Sahara has long been marked by regional and transregional exchange, and labor migration has a long history in the area.

International Migration, Regional Exchange, and Urban Networks

The focus of European cameras on clandestine migrants in small fishing boats has led to an overemphasis on illegal migration, neglecting the fact that foreigners have always constituted an important part of the Mauritanian population since independence was declared in 1960. To talk about transit only makes sense if we take into account the role played by Nouakchott and Nouadhibou in West African migration more generally. At independence, 70 percent of Mauritania's population were nomads, and the country desperately lacked skilled labor and clerks. Administrative posts were filled by workers from elsewhere—Senegal, Mali, Guinea, Benin—who also invested in construction projects or in electricity, plumbing, and laundry services. From 1957 on, the construction from scratch of the new capital, Nouakchott, had offered much employment. In the north of the country, the mining of iron ore, begun in 1952 with the establishment of the Mines de fer de Mauritanie (MIFERMA, Mauritanian Iron Mining),[7] and a renewed interest in fishing turned Nouadhibou into a center of attraction: the newly declared "economic capital" of the country, where fortunes could be made quickly.[8] At this time, few Moors showed any interest in the sea and its resources, which were mainly exploited by Senegalese fishermen who settled in the area (Diop and Thiam 1990; Marfaing 2005). Hence, before becoming points of transit, Nouakchott and Nouadhibou have long attracted migrants in their own right.

Among these, Senegalese and Malians were most strongly represented. The number of Senegalese living in Mauritania has greatly fluctuated since national independence; they numbered in the tens of thousands until they were expelled or fled during the events of 1989,[9] although many have since returned to Mauritania. Their number has increased in the twenty-first century since, alongside many other sub-Saharans, they hope to benefit from the economic upturn following the discovery of oil. Further, the democratic transition that started in 2005—interrupted in August 2008 by a military putsch led by General 'Abd al-'Aziz—led to hopes of a political opening, especially with the return of refugees from Senegal and Mali (Fresia 2009; Ciavolella 2010).[10] West African migrants have thus long been essential to Mauritania's economic dynamism, and the country is marked by a long tradition of regional interaction and exchange.

Among migrants hoping to reach Europe, only a few manage to get through as soon as they arrive in Nouadhibou. Many more stay for some time, because they need to look for an opportunity to leave, because they have to earn enough money to pay for their journey, or because of repeated failures. In all these cases, they rely on migrants who are already settled in the city to act as intermediaries with local society. Networks of solidarity—whose scope should not be overestimated—have developed among nationals of the same country (Streiff-Fénart and Poutignat 2006). Every national community has its own association, more or less well organized and active, led by a representative who is in charge of receiving and helping newcomers. He also acts as a mediator with the local authorities, if any problems arise with one of his co-nationals.[11] In addition to these "official" representatives, others act as *jatigi* (referees or guarantors), because they are known locally and play an important part in the local economy.[12] For instance, a Senegalese tailor who owns several ready-made clothing shops in Nouadhibou and Dakar works together with a Moor from an influential tribe who leases his shops and equipment in exchange for a share of the profits, and he welcomes, acts as a guide for, and sometimes employs young newly arrived Senegalese. Similarly, a young migrant from Casamance in southern Senegal, a painter and decorator who has lived in Nouadhibou since 2000, puts up migrants from his home region in unoccupied rooms in his compound, which he manages for the landlord, a Mauritanian Haalpulaar, in exchange for a reduction in his own rent. He often takes on young migrants as assistants.[13] Interactions between these foreign businessmen and migrants are frequent.

The example of the Senegalese tailor who is associated with a Moor and who employs young sub-Saharan migrants offers a useful framework for understanding the hierarchies based on work and employment. In the key sectors that attract large numbers of foreigners (fishing, transportation, construction), labor is mostly organized along similar lines: a Mauritanian contractor—frequently a Moor—dominates the sector and is backed up by local or foreign intermediaries (mostly Negro Mauritanians or Senegalese from the Senegal valley) who offer insecure and badly paid jobs to recently arrived migrants. The migrants are thereby made to fit into a society that is already strongly hierarchical and dominated by white Moors (*bīdān*), where they find themselves at the bottom of the pile, competing for jobs with *harātīn* (black Moors, descendants of former slaves). These examples show that some foreigners have become essential figures in the local economy because of their detailed knowledge of local constraints and their long presence in the

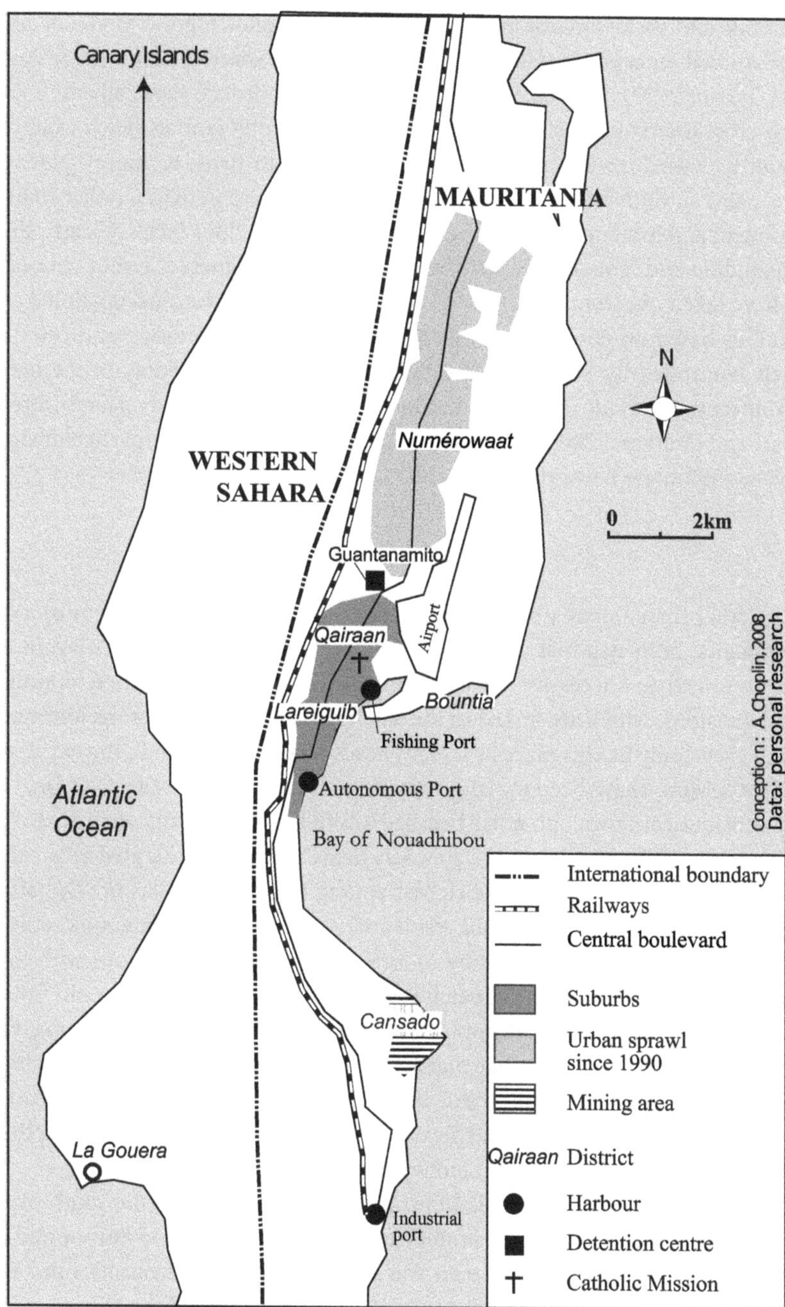

Map 9.2. Nouadhibou and its suburbs. A. Choplin 2008

economic and social environment of Nouadhibou. Following the model of small transnational enterprises (Glick Schiller, Basch, and Szanton Blanc 1995; Portes 1999; Tarrius 2002), they take advantage of national borders, especially their ability to cross them and thereby to benefit from price differentials. Such examples of success, based on the ability to claim to belong to two—or more—places at once, paint an unfamiliar image: migrants as active entrepreneurs, rather than as dependent and insecure wage laborers exploited by rapacious locals. Clearly, then, Nouadhibou and Nouakchott have been shaped by foreigners. Certain nationalities have taken over whole sectors, thereby almost turning into occupational corporations based on co-optation: this is the case for transportation and catering, largely controlled by Senegalese; for tailoring and leatherworking, in the hands of Guineans; and trade in dried and salted fish, dominated by Ghanaians (Streiff-Fénart and Poutignat 2006). Others have set up as traders: in one particular street in Nouadhibou, no fewer than forty shops are managed by foreigners.

City of Migrants

Rather than a mere point of transit, Nouadhibou is first and foremost a city of migrants, both national and international, and its history and its layout are directly linked to successive waves of migration. Spatial boundaries reproduce social divisions, which are linked to the date of arrival and the reasons for migration: if everybody has his place in society, he also has his position in the city. From the 1990s, Moors have been moving away from the center of the city, Qairaan, that they consider rundown and noisy because it is full of immigrants, in order to live in the north of the city, in a new, airy, less densely settled residential area called Numerouaat (the Numbers). The richest among them build villas in "Dubai" or "Baghdad," the most recently built residential quarters. Transit migrants settle in the center of the city, left vacant by Moors; in its various subsections with their rather eloquent names (Accra, Ghana-Town); and in the areas near the old fishing port (Lareiguib, SNIM City) (Choplin and Lombard 2008). Unlike the young, vulnerable men waiting for a passage that has by now become illusory, the majority of "old migrants" in Nouadhibou reside in the Numerouaat, especially in the earlier developments (Socogim, First and Second Water-Tap). Most of them are not there to travel north, but rather to earn money to send back home.

Nouadhibou is hence divided into three distinctive zones: the south of the city (Qairaan), full of young adventurers looking for a way to get to Europe and for temporary employment to fund their travels; the north (Numerouaat), inhabited by Mauritanians; and an intermediate zone (the older sections of the Numerouaat), home to migrants who have lived there for a while and who can draw on denser local social networks. Because Nouakchott is much larger, migrants are more spread out there, but freshly arrived migrants tend to settle in the old popular quarters (Médina and the Fifth and Sixth Districts).

The impact of transit migration, and its economic benefit to Moors, can also be seen in changes in housing. In the center of town, the few compounds still owned by old Moorish families have been redesigned in order to increase rents. The tent (*khayma*) that used to be pitched in the middle of the courtyard has been replaced by new rooms, housing four to five people each, reflecting the growing demand for rental accommodations caused by transit migration. In 2000, a rich Moorish businessman, a descendant of an influential local tribe, decided to build a "Senegalese housing estate" (*cité des Sénégalais*). After illegally appropriating a street between Qairaan and Lareiguib, he built on both sides a line of rooms of ten square meters each, rented on a daily or a monthly basis (for about 5,000 ouguiya).[14] As rents are high, migrants often share rooms. Malians and people from Casamance in Senegal have organized their own collective residences, bearing witness to the efficiency of community networks established by migrants abroad.

The different routes and rhythms of migration are transforming the appearance of the two principal Mauritanian cities. Sub-Saharan migrants, who bring their own ways and ideas about urban life, increasingly put their stamp on certain parts of Nouadhibou and Nouakchott. These now look rather different from the rest of each town, shaped as they are by the same type of housing, the same shops, and the same sociospatial practices as neighboring capitals. The names of the restaurants (the River, the Djolof) found in Qairaan, the center of Nouadhibou, and the business signs common in the Fifth District of Nouakchott (Mali Garage, Senegal Garage) evoke the presence of foreigners. Transit migrants and immigrants have produced their own urban spaces and points of reference. Today, through its migrant population, the center of Nouadhibou is directly linked to the Fifth District in Nouakchott, but also to Dakar, Saint-Louis, Bamako, and other Sahelian cities. These various transnational connections, established by repeated return travel and by the interplay of different migratory networks, situate Mauritania at the heart of a much larger region. Nouakchott has moved on from its image as the "capital of nomads" (implying "Arabic-speaking nomads") that the various governments have tried to create for it (Choplin 2009). The presence of migrants has made it possible to reforge the city's historic cultural links with the Senegal valley and to recall the Senegalese atmosphere that reigned here when it was first founded, an atmosphere that the Arabic-speaking governments have, since the 1980s, rather clumsily tried to hide. Similarly, Nouadhibou stands out as a "cosmopolitan" Saharan city (Brachet 2009a; Boesen and Marfaing 2007), clearly different from the otherwise rather austere towns of the Mauritanian desert. We are witnessing not merely exchanges between Saharans and sub-Saharan migrants, but rather the development of an original and locally specific kind of urbanity.

Since 2007 however, the almost complete stoppage of the crossings to the Canary Islands caused by stricter controls in Mauritanian waters and the high rate of expulsions have slowed down economic activities. Many shops in the center have closed down; Senegalese restaurants have reduced the daily quantity of rice prepared; rooms for rent by locals stay empty; young men have returned to their home countries. Although many Malians and Senegalese still arrive hoping to "make it," successful crossings have become rare, as the representative of the Senegalese in Nouadhibou, interviewed in September 2007, put it: "Those who were meant to make it have done so. For those who stayed behind, it is too late now." Migration to and through Nouadhibou seems to be running out of steam: even transit migration, which led to a revival of the city's economy in the early 2000s, appears to be in jeopardy. Nouadhibou no longer experiences urban and economic growth as it did in the 1980s. It is no longer the place where fortunes are made quickly, nor a bustling harbor on the way to Europe. The city is declining, as indicated by the decrease in employment offered and in fishing (Choplin and Lombard 2008). The situation is no longer one of transit, but rather one of post-transit; accordingly, the issue of migration is dealt with in new ways.

Ambiguous Management: EU Directives, the Lure of Statistics, and the Criminalization of Migrants

Although, unlike Libya (Pliez 2004a, b), Mauritania never openly encouraged sub-Saharan labor immigration, the country relies heavily on foreign laborers, who generally work for low wages and whose situation remains precarious. Their presence is also valuable because by showing a certain degree of tolerance toward these foreigners, without encouraging them to settle more permanently, the government puts itself in a strong position vis-à-vis outside powers that are thereby obliged to negotiate with it. In an interview on national television in October 2007, the then-president, Cheikh Abdallahi, put it rather bluntly: "Mauritania needs to cooperate with Europe, so that they can help us bear the costs of attempts to stop these migrants." He made clear that Mauritania was not a "sending" country, but rather, just like Europe itself, a "victim" of migration, and it was therefore ready to collaborate both in the protection of legal migrants and in the fight against illegal migration.

In late 2005, urged by the European Union to define a migration policy, the Mauritanian government created the Groupe d'Études des Flux Migratoires (Migration Study Group), which included the minister of the interior, the UNHCR,[15] the European Commission, the International Organization for Migration (IOM),[16] and two Mauritanian NGOs supposed to represent "civil society." Surprisingly perhaps, this group only met once; since the establishment of control mechanisms has reduced the number of migrants who finally reach Europe, the European Union has lost interest: the issue of migration is no longer on top of the political agenda. As of 2009, the IOM office in Nouakchott had reduced its personnel to three and now administratively depends on Dakar. As an employee of the UNHCR put it, "We have more important problems to deal with. We are no longer in 2006."[17] Nonetheless, he continued, "by now, we have 400,000 migrants!" Such a number is oddly incoherent: in late 2006, a report commissioned by the same UNHCR estimated that there were between 160,000 and 200,000 sub-Saharans in Mauritania[18]—figures that already seemed too large, judging by my own surveys. Even though the number of migrants probably increased immediately after controls tightened, two years later, fieldwork indicated a clear reduction in overall numbers.

Yet what matters is less which numbers are right or wrong, but rather, who produces them and for whom. It is striking that the Mauritanian state itself is very careful not to publish any figures. In 2007, a study commissioned by the Ministry of Employment, Integration and Professional Training set the number of foreign workers in Mauritania at a mere 65,000 (Marfaing 2008 and this volume). The Mauritanian state has much to gain by underestimating, or by reducing, the number of foreigners in order to avoid public resentment, while continuing to benefit from cheap foreign labor—much as it is in the country's interest to hide behind figures produced by international institutions without ever endorsing them officially. Conversely, the UNHCR and the European Union have much cause to overestimate the number of migrants, in order to justify their interference in Mauritanian internal affairs and the imposition of drastic border controls. These figures are manipulated easily because of the absence of reliable statistical evidence, and the virtual impossibility of distinguishing between permanently settled migrants and those who are in transit. Furthermore, the numbers vary throughout the year, depending on the agricultural and fishing seasons, for instance, while also responding to long-term changes sparked by the volatile political climate in West Africa. Hence, even the most absurd exaggerations become possible, while the distinction between "illegal migrants" and "sub-Saharan immigrants" is often blurred. In 2006, my research showed that there were around 120,000–150,000 migrants in Mauritania. In 2008, the number decreased to between 95,000 and 130,000. These figures have been obtained from representatives of foreign communities (originating in Senegal, Mali, Guinea, Nigeria, Gambia, Ivory Coast, Sierra Leone, Benin, and the two Congos), embassies, and NGOs. I also compared them to numbers published by the Directorate of National Security.

To this day, the Mauritanian government has no clearly defined policy on migration. Nonetheless, the repression of illegal migration has intensified, with immediate effects on the everyday life of sub-Saharans settled in Mauritania: whereas before, security forces only arrested illegal migrants caught in the act, as they were getting onto a boat, they now arrest them beforehand, at home, in the streets, or even while they are entering the city. In a 2008 report, Amnesty International denounced such arbitrary arrests of migrants, who are accused, apparently without any proof, of intending to travel illegally to Spain. Today, every black foreigner is potentially considered an illegal migrant, and can be taken in for questioning. Such arrests are themselves illegal: although Mauritania has, since 2000, withdrawn from ECOWAS (Economic Community of West African States) the concomitant agreements on free movement between its members remain in force. Nationals of the fifteen member states, especially Senegalese and Malians, continue, to various degrees regulated by bilateral agreements, to have privileged rights of access and residence. According to this legislation, actual "illegal" entries and departures from Mauritanian territory are rare: to travel around Mauritania is usually neither a crime nor an offense. Yet the numerous arrests of migrants and their long stays in the Guantanamito detention camp seem to indicate the opposite. And indeed, the government appears to be somewhat embarrassed by this center: transfers and expulsions are generally carried out at night, and out of sight of the Mauritanian public.

Closed Borders, Open for Business

It is striking that, at a time when borders are closing for migrants, thanks to the liberalization of transport in August 2005 they are conversely more open than ever for commercial transactions. Since then, private transportation companies have been allowed to travel freely on the few paved roads that cross the country. With this shift and the completion of a paved road between Nouakchott and Nouadhibou, also in 2005, the image of an economic cul-de-sac that has long clung to the two cities seems to have been shaken off.

While Mauritania's current stance on migration implies a certain degree of dependency on the EU, it has also turned Mauritania into a privileged ally of Europe, one that is in a position to bargain over financial agreements. The presence of migrants has become a way of procuring funds and of negotiating a partnership with Europe—and also with Morocco and Senegal, which are equally active partners in cross-border cooperation. Mauritania has cashed in on the presence of migrants on its territory, by pushing through new financial agreements with the European Union and by establishing more intense partnerships with certain countries of the Schengen Area, especially Spain. Commercial transactions between the two countries are booming within the EU and also as part of the 5+5 group, the Barcelona Process, and the Mediterranean Union.[19] This can be explained by the ratification in 2003 of an agreement that obliges Mauritania to readmit not only its own nationals, but also those of third countries caught in Spain after transiting via Mauritania. In exchange for this and for promises to set up a detention camp, Mauritania was recognized as a "priority applicant" for development aid. The plan for economic integration between the Canary Islands and West Africa, set up by the Canary Islands government with support from Spain and the EU, illustrates this: although the issue of migration is never openly mentioned, it clearly lurks in the background.[20] A meeting of the European Regional Development Fund, held in January 2009 in the Canary Islands under the title "Ultra-Peripheral Regions of Europe and Zones of Its Neighbourhood," points in the same direction. Mauritania, Morocco, Senegal, and the Cape Verde Islands were, as "close neighbours," invited to the Canaries, an—albeit peripheral—"outpost of Europe."[21] By encouraging the establishment of joint ventures, Spain compensated for its intrusion into the management of migration with financial favors.

This stance has become perfectly clear with the inauguration of a "center for guidance on migration" in Nouakchott. The declared aim of this center, organized jointly by the Mauritanian and the Spanish general trade unions, is to protect the rights of foreign workers in Mauritania. It is altogether possible (probable?) that it is also used to survey and study potential migrants. The center relies on active support by migrant associations that are generally well informed of developments within their national communities. The general secretary of the Malian association has even suggested a closer connection with the Migration Information and Management Centre in Bamako, inaugurated on 6 October 2008. This "center for guidance on migration" is but one aspect of the growing Spanish presence in Mauritania, reflected in the large numbers of Spanish nationals in the country and by cultural activities following the opening of a Canary Islands cultural center in 2006. At the same time, relations with Morocco have similarly multiplied. By the end of 2008, up to a thousand trucks were entering Mauritanian territory each month through the northern border (according to the Central Customs Office, Nouakchott, November 2008). Market stalls in Nouadhibou now display supplies of imported fresh produce. Several Moroccans from the Sous region have settled in Mauritania's two main cities, where they work as fruit and vegetable wholesalers.

Faced with the demand that it control the movement of people on its territory, the Mauritanian government finds itself in an ambiguous position. On the one hand, it has no choice but to obey European wishes for border controls, for fear of becoming a receiving country or even a nationwide detention camp. Hence, in exchange for economic cooperation, it tolerates a growing European interference in local politics. On the other hand, Mauritania cannot close its borders at a time when, with the discovery of oil and the beginning of its extraction, the country is continuing to attract foreign labor. Comprehensive border controls are difficult, since many people commute on a regular basis between the two banks of the Senegal River (Leservoisier this volume), and since Mauritania is trying to improve relations with Senegal and has negotiated a return of the 1989 refugees. Moreover, the president, General 'Abd al-'Aziz, cannot risk any further deterioration in international relations because the Mauritanian diaspora is large and influential. More than 250,000 Mauritanians live abroad—at least 10 percent of the total population—which is a larger overall number than that of foreigners residing in Mauritania. Fifty thousand Mauritanians live in Ivory Coast, 20,000 in Saudi Arabia, 20,000 in France, 20,000 in Gambia, 20,000 in Mali, 10,000 in Senegal, 4,000 in the United Arab Emirates, 2,500 in Congo, 2,000 in the Canary Islands, and others in Italy, Spain, Belgium, and the United States (Ould Ramdane 2007). Bad treatment of foreigners would put the Mauritanians living in neighboring countries at risk of reprisals, thereby further weakening the regime.

From Migrant to Foreigner: "Good" and "Bad" Migrants, Growing Tensions, and Tightened Identities

Post-transit—the term that best describes the contemporary situation in Mauritania—has led to a worsening of relations between Mauritanians and sub-Saharans. Following the heyday of successful boat crossings, several Mauritanians who have been swindled by migrants taking advantage of advance payments to pay for their trip, feel cheated and say that they have stopped trusting foreigners, "who don't even come to work any more, but who only want to travel on" (Nouadhibou, September 2007). Similarly, sub-Saharans settled in Mauritania, some of whom used to host migrants and sometimes even help them to cross into Europe, now prefer to distance themselves publicly from and even openly show their contempt for those whom they call "adventurers," whom they blame for their own growing exclusion. This resentment is often expressed in terms borrowed from European discourses of illegal migration. The general secretary of the Association of Malians in Mauritania in January 2009 said: "There are so many illegal migrants here: thousands of them, loads and loads of them!"—before quickly adding that he had been there for more than ten years, implying that length of stay is a guarantee of reliability. He had just set up an association called AIDES SIGUI, supplying "help and assistance for information about immigration and integration in economic and social development." According to its constitution, the aim of this association is to "assist our co-nationals, alas so numerous! who are victims of the consequences of illegal emigration." Both his rhetorical style and declared purpose of encouraging migrants to return home were clearly aimed at an international audience of potential funders. Similarly, in Nouadhibou, the newly founded OCEAN association (Organisation for Culture, Education, and the Future of Nations) aimed to "alert public opinion" about "illegal migration," and organized several conferences in Nouadhibou for this purpose.[22] These and similar associations indirectly maintain the myth of successful migration to Europe, even if that means overestimating the number of illegal migrants, who can be said to make up their "business capital." And yet, no international institution has so far provided them with funds—another sign that the heyday of transit has passed and that international interest in migrants has waned. Meanwhile, one employee of the European Commission complained about his inability to spend the €1.2 million earmarked for migration, as the question is, for now, "shelved."

By appropriating the rhetoric of illegal migration, the associations described above help to freeze the categories of "good" and "bad" migrants, thereby strongly condemning those who just travel through. The representatives of foreign national communities hold one meeting after another, to lobby for the recognition of their rights as "honest foreign workers" and against illegal migrants "who undercut salaries." Tensions continue to mount and are openly expressed. In September 2009, in front of the Nouakchott polyclinic, day laborers waiting to be hired were physically threatened by Mauritanians, mainly *harātīn,* who accused them of accepting employment for cut-throat wages. The unrest lasted until the relevant embassies interceded with the minister of the interior. Similarly, Mauritanian workers employed in the Tasiast mines have accused their employers of taking on too many Malians and Ivorians, to the detriment of Mauritanians. Backed by national labor regulations that favor nationals for all jobs, they successfully petitioned the government to protect them against foreign labor that is increasingly perceived as a threat. A law on "traditional fishing" enacted in June 2011 is a good example of the economic discrimination practiced against foreigners. Formally, the law forbids foreigners from boarding fishing boats. In reality, this is a legal trick to ban them from their traditional fishing activity. The Ministry of Fisheries officially advocates the "Mauritanization" of the sector as a strategy to reduce unemployment. This affects mainly Senegalese fishermen, who have played a predominant role in such small-scale fishing. The result has been a shortage of fish in the country: the local workforce is too small and too inexperienced to replace foreign-born fishermen.

Such examples show the anxiety of ordinary Mauritanians who, with bitterness, point to the noticeable decline in their living standards, despite promises of rapid oil wealth and its just redistribution through nascent democratic processes.

This might account for the growing success of extremist rhetoric, be it religious or political, that invariably draws on increasingly noticeable fears of "invasion" by "black Africa." Such fears, which are at least partly the result of the media's overemphasis on transit migration, explain why public opinion largely endorses the government's compliance with European expectations and backs stricter border controls. Arab nationalists, who had been forced off the political stage with the abortive democratization launched by former president Ould Taya in 1991, are once more gaining support by drawing on a language of "autochthony."[23] The following political tract, distributed in November 2007 in the Fifth District of Nouakchott, was based on a letter to the president of the republic drafted by nationalist military officers:

> Mauritania's return to ECOWAS would compromise the future of our country whose national unity is still very fragile. Our country's tremendous economic potential turns it into a popular destination for nationals of sub-Saharan countries where unemployment reaches record levels. To take them in would be a catastrophe for our country: for its cultural identity, its demographic balance, the health and education of its inhabitants. To evict them would be equally disastrous: Mauritania would be accused of racism and all evils that the "defender of human rights" can possibly imagine. . . . Mauritania is *Arab* before being African. (unpublished tract obtained in Nouakchott, November 2007)

Everything seems to combine to stigmatize sub-Saharans, who are accused as job thieves and criminals. Here, for instance, are some hasty generalizations lumping together the presence of foreigners and general insecurity that are commonly broadcast in the local and foreign press:

> "The presence of foreigners is a great threat to our citizens' security, if one considers the rather high levels of crime in Nouakchott and Nouadhibou," insists a traffic policeman, stationed not far from the areas where illegal migrants are housed. Well-informed sources indicate that most crimes—theft, rape, assault—as well as drug dealing, are committed by illegal migrants. The areas most affected are the Fifth and Sixth Districts, where many Senegalese, Malians and Gambians live, and where crime levels are above the national average.[24]

The hostile reception of sub-Saharans, then, reflects more general tensions in the internal political dynamics in Mauritania. The problem of the integration of foreigners is bound up with the problem, so far unresolved, of the "national question": debates over racial discrimination among Mauritanians, and over ways in which all the country's constituents can be encompassed by one shared notion of citizenship. "Black" foreigners are the main victims of xenophobic discourses, and no other group of foreigners is similarly targeted. North Africans, for instance, who settle in ever-growing numbers in Mauritania, do not seem to bother Moors unduly, although they compete for the same jobs as sub-Saharan Africans (such as construction work or catering) and although their presence is increasingly visible since a few of them have opened coffee shops with terraces bordering the main thoroughfares of the capital city. Debates over the place of sub-Saharans in Mauritania are also linked to promises made by the "democratic government" about the return from Senegal and Mali of the thousands of Mauritanian refugees. Confronted with unfulfilled hopes of oil wealth and widely shared riches, many Mauritanians wonder whether this is the right moment to repatriate refugees, and how the government will pay for their return.[25] Some fear abuse and think that nationals of Senegal, or even Ivory Coast or Liberia—"illegal migrants," in other words—will take advantage of the situation and pretend to be refugees. Current plans for repatriation and resettlement are thus a source of real tension, feeding into radical discourses that lump together Negro Mauritanians and sub-Saharan immigrants under the category of "black foreigners."

Developments in Mauritania are contradictory, to say the least. On the one hand, borders are opening up for all kinds of trade; on the other, the national territory is gradually becoming inaccessible to many people, following stricter border controls that have led to public assertions of exacerbated nationalism. This is a situation of post-transit rather than transit migration, marked by a decrease in transcontinental crossings and hence of new migrant arrivals, and by a clear loss of interest in the actual problems of migration by international organizations on the ground. At the same time, the latter continue to produce migration statistics, often exaggerating the number of migrants as a justification of their legal armature and control mechanisms. Foreigners from the south are increasingly criminalized, to the point that longer-established migrants endorse the image of the "good" legal worker to distinguish themselves from "bad" illegal migrants, while the number of foreigners from the north is on the increase. In exchange for a little money and a few financial partnerships, Mauritania has allowed foreign organizations to increase their control over the national territory and local politics. By outsourcing its frontiers on the Atlantic coast, and by concluding agreements with Morocco, Mauritania, Senegal, and then Gambia (always moving south),[26] the European Union has succeeded in restricting the movement of certain individuals judged undesirable before they even leave the African continent. Hence, in the very heart of the Sahara, in a region that has always been marked by the intense movement of people and goods, the European Union has the power to grant the right to move to some, and refuse it to many others: the issue of free movement in the Sahara can now only be understood with reference to European policies. However, while it is closing its southern borders, Mauritania is also furthering the establishment of a cross-border free trade zone with Mali and Senegal.[27] Finally, and this is perhaps the most striking aspect of all, Mauritanians themselves seem to accept, or even to demand, the closure of their national borders as a material reflection of their more general rejection of others. The post-transit situation is reflected in the tightened notions of identity and the open xenophobia toward migrants and more generally toward black Africans residing in the country. The borders of Europe have moved abroad, as easily and rapidly, it seems, as ideas about security and protection have spread among southern governments and their citizens.

NOTES

1. www.cridem.org, consulted in the spring of 2009.

2. For a discussion of the plural figure of the migrant, and especially the "adventurer," see Bredeloup (2008).

3. In employing the term "Negro Mauritanian," rather than "black Mauritanian" to talk about Mauritanians who are not Moors, I follow local usage. The same applies to "sub-Saharans," rather than "blacks."

4. This chapter is based on four research trips carried out in January 2007 and January 2009 with Jérôme Lombard (IRD) as part of a program financed by the FSP-MAE, "Migrations and Territorial Changes in West Africa and the Sahara." More generally, these reflections are based on research undertaken since 2003 in transit towns, as part of the LPED research group (IRD/Université de Provence) (Bredeloup and Pliez 2005). I have published various articles and a monograph based on this research; see, for instance, Ba and Choplin (2005), Choplin and Lombard (2007, 2008), and Choplin (2008, 2009).

5. In October 2005, sub-Saharan African migrants tried to cross the heavily guarded barriers and fences of Ceuta and Melilla, the Spanish enclaves on the Moroccan coast, in order to gain access to the EU. Seventeen migrants were killed by Spanish policemen.

6. About 20,000 people are said to have attempted to reach Europe from Nouadhibou in 2006. The Catholic mission in Nouadhibou and the Mauritanian Red Crescent, respectively, estimate the deaths en route at 20 percent and 30 percent (and up to 40 percent in the worst period, in February and March 2006).

7. MIFERMA was nationalized in 1974 and renamed SNIM (Société Nationale Industrielle et Minière).

8. As early as 1970, the population of Nouadhibou, estimated at 18,000 inhabitants, included 11,500 Mauritanians, 3,000 sub-Saharan Africans, 1,800 French, and 1,000 Spanish, mainly from the Canary Islands (Bonte 2001b).

9. The "events of 1989" is the term used by Senegalese and Mauritanians to refer to the struggles that took place along the Senegal River in April 1989 (see Leservoisier this volume). Fueled by the Mauritanian government, and initially pitting Moors against black African populations, the situation degenerated into open conflict between the two countries. Senegalese residents were driven out of Mauritania and, in retaliation, Mauritanians were evicted from Senegal.

10. During the events of 1989, "black" Mauritanians, especially Haalpulaaren, were stripped of their nationality and expelled to the other side of the Senegal River. According

to the UNHCR and numerous other sources (Fresia 2009; Ciavolella 2010), 20,000 are now refugees in Senegal, and 6,000 in Mali. In June 2007, the democratically elected Mauritanian president, Sidi Ould Cheikh Abdallahi, encouraged these refugees to return, as a step toward national reconciliation. The repatriation program ended in 2010.

11. In 2001, several associations of foreign nationals came together in the Union des Associations d'Étrangers à Nouadhibou (UAEN), allowing them to acquire a certain public visibility and local recognition. The UAEN ceased to exist in 2005 (Ba and Choplin 2005). In December 2010, the Fédération des Associations des Migrants de l'Afrique de l'Ouest en Mauritanie was created.

12. For a more detailed discussion of the role of the *jatigi* ("guarantor" in Pulaar, meaning both landlord and trader), see Bredeloup (2007).

13. Interviews, Nouadhibou, January and September 2007.

14. As of August 2011, the ouguiya was exchanged at 380 to the euro and 280 to the U.S. dollar.

15. The presence of the UNHCR might come as a surprise, as its primary duties certainly do not lie with international migration, let alone illegal migration. Today, however, the policy of the UNHCR oscillates rather paradoxically between the "protection of the stateless" and the "control of undesirables" (Agier 2006).

16. The IOM makes itself out to be the official institution in charge of helping the Mauritanian state to control its borders and to facilitate "voluntary" repatriations. In reality, it mainly trains members of the General Security service in the maintenance of "law and order" and in evictions that are hardly ever voluntary.

17. Interview, UNHCR office, Nouakchott, 21 January 2009.

18. See IOM, UNHCR, and the European Union, *Profil migratoire de la Mauritanie* (December 2006); FNUAP, *Transit Migrants in Mauritania* (October 2007); and *Transit Migration Survey in Mauritania* (2008). These reports emphasize the difficulty of distinguishing transit migrants from those long settled.

19. The Euro-Mediterranean Partnership, formerly known as the Barcelona Process, was relaunched in 2008 and renamed Union for the Mediterranean. The 5+5 group, which is part of the Euro-Mediterranean Partnership, includes five countries of the Arab Maghreb Union (Morocco, Algeria, Libya, Mauritania, and Tunisia) and five European countries (Spain, France, Italy, Malta, and Portugal).

20. As part of this project, representatives of thirty-three businesses from the Canaries traveled to Mauritania on 3 July 2007 to sign agreements in the sectors of building and engineering projects, water management, fishing, and tourism. This is not remarkable in itself, as the Canaries have always been an important economic partner for Mauritania. Canary Islanders have settled in Nouadhibou since the 1930s, the first to arrive being refugees from the Spanish Civil War. There were almost a thousand of them living there when, in 1975, the Western Sahara conflict broke out (Bonte 2001b). Today, they commonly invest in fishing. Members of the Moorish elite in Nouadhibou often speak Spanish and frequently travel to Las Palmas on business or holidays.

21. A European Commission report, *Les regions ultrapériphériques: Un atout pour l'Europe* (Brussels, 17 October 2008, available at http://europe.unsa.org/7ActuEurop/RegionsUltraperip17oct08.pdf), reminded Eurocrats that migration remains a key concern in the development of the EU's own offshore "ultraperiphery." Illegal migration is identified as a priority issue.

22. An initial awareness campaign was organized by the Catholic mission in November 2008 under the title "Illegal Immigration: What Duties for Africa and What Solutions for Europe?" In February 2009, the Catholic mission organized a three-day "Forum on Migration and Illegal Travel," to which all local institutions and leaders (consuls, Red Crescent, Médecins du Monde, UNHCR, EU, IOM, and so on) were invited.

23. The notion of autochthony in Mauritania has only recently come to the attention of researchers; see, e.g., Ciavolella (2010). In other African countries this notion has been discussed more widely; see especially Dozon (2000), Bayart, Geschiere, and Nyamnjoh (2001), Comaroff and Comaroff (2005), and Nyamnjoh (2006).

24. *Wal Fadjri* (Dakar), 6 September 2007.

25. Official resettlement policy requires granting refugees enough to live on for the first few months of their resettlement. Such processes have barely started, but official resettlements carried out between 1995 and 2006 mostly failed (Ciavolella 2010).

26. "La frontera sur baja hasta Gambia," *El País,* 10 March 2009.

27. "Frontières Mali-Mauritanie: Opération pilote dans le Bassin du Karakoro," *Club du Sahel,* 2008.

10 LIVING TOGETHER AND LIVING APART IN NOUAKCHOTT

Laurence Marfaing

As a result of long-standing habits of mobility throughout West Africa, but also, and especially since 2006, due to EU policies aiming to stop African migration to Europe, the number of West African migrants who live on a more or less temporary basis in Mauritania is currently estimated at 65,000, which is 2.5 percent of the total population of 2.7 million inhabitants.[1] A government survey carried out in 2007 shows that 60 percent of all foreign nationals in Mauritania have lived there since 2000, without, however, differentiating between their various migratory projects (République Islamique de Mauritanie [hereafter, RIM] 2007: 14). Most of these foreign residents are from neighboring countries, such as Senegal (60 percent) and Mali (30 percent). The remaining 10 percent are from other sub-Saharan countries, Asia, and the Maghreb (Marfaing 2009a). The majority live in cities: Nouakchott, the capital; Nouadhibou, an important harbor and industrial center; and Rosso, on the border between Senegal and Mauritania on the Senegal River. According to government statistics, the foreign residents account for 4.5 percent of the total population of these cities, and mostly live in districts primarily inhabited by black Mauritanians or nationals of neighboring countries, where they settle following community boundaries (RIM 2007: 11–12). Whole sections of these cities have become "intermediary spaces" both for migrants who ultimately aim to reach Europe and for those who are mainly looking for employment in Mauritania.[2] Moreover, for both categories, these areas of transit often turn into places of more permanent residence.

In this chapter, I will describe the situation in Mauritania that has led to this influx of foreigners, as well as their internal organization, the relation between long-term residents and more recent arrivals, their attempts to cope with the local labor market, and finally their ways of living together—or perhaps rather of coexisting—with others. This daily coexistence results in "social micro-innovations" (Tarrius 2007: 11), and migrants are factors of development, both in their host city and back home, due to remittances and the personal experience gained abroad. Among migrants themselves, the experience of migration and the proven ability to adapt to economic and social imperatives are seen as signs of social mobility. Migrants participate in larger movements of globalization, but their way of life is also part of the changes in their host cities. How, then, can we describe their daily experiences? Are we dealing with real sociocultural exchange and integration, or rather with people who live separately while maintaining a fragile balance between economic complementarity and mutual hostility? This chapter aims to show that an approach based on the notion of a particular kind of cosmopolitanism, a "cosmopolitanism from below" (Boesen and Marfaing 2007), can be helpful here.

Mauritania, Migrant Country

The modern nation-state of Mauritania is of recent creation. In the 1960s and 1970s, the majority of its population was still nomadic, while the newly constructed urban centers were mainly inhabited by more or less recent immigrants from rural Mauritania and neighboring countries. In the colonial period, the state administration and large businesses had heavily relied on foreign labor; when, at independence, French was chosen as the national language, this need for foreign labor and expertise continued. At the same time, the urban boom brought about by independence and subsequent state investment led to a great demand for foreign recruits, mainly from Mali and Senegal, whose presence became a normal part of everyday life. Even today, their knowledge and skills are much sought after in construction, mechanics, fishing, the service sector, and teaching. Moreover, Mauritania has long been a transit country for traders, pilgrims, and fishermen. The Senegal River never was a closed border between Senegal and Mauritania: "as far as neighboring countries were concerned, traders never worried much about borders, nationalities or commercial regulations."[3] According to another informant, a Mauritanian Haalpulaar: "the people from the river valley think of themselves as Mauritanian or Senegalese, but the idea of a border is incongruous."[4] All these elements have combined to turn Mauritania into an area of mobility that is both North and West African, with the Senegal River acting as much as a vector of exchange as a spatial boundary. The river is central to the wider region as a point of contact between the Arab and the African worlds, the Mediterranean and Africa "proper" (Ould Ahmed Salem 2005: 17).

Today, while most technical skills are acquired through apprenticeships in the informal sector of the economy, the Mauritanian state is attempting to remedy the lack of indigenous skilled labor. There are four technical high schools that can, put together, train 4,000 pupils a year, and in 2002, a national institute for professional training (INAP) offering three-year courses after high school or a BTS after middle school opened its gates; but technical training is socially looked down upon and few know about the range of courses that are offered and the careers they might open up.[5] Hence, despite gradual changes, Mauritania is still unable to function without foreign labor. The government is well aware of this, and in May 2008 the Ministry of Employment issued a decree facilitating the employment of foreign nationals in Mauritanian businesses.[6] They now merely need a work permit from the Ministry of Employment; these permits are easy to obtain and officially free of charge. The government further encourages local and foreign investment in order to create employment.[7] National business regulations are clear on this point: the freedom of enterprise is key, and the law treats foreigners in the same way as nationals (CNUCED/ICC 2004: 43). This generosity toward foreign nationals derives from an unspoken agreement of reciprocal non-interference with neighboring countries, where large numbers of Mauritanian nationals have long settled and seek to work and trade in peace.[8]

Foreign nationals come to Mauritania because they know of its need for labor. Since 2002, their number has been increased by migrants who are hoping to reach Europe, but who are stuck in Mauritania due to the impact of European migration policies in transit countries (Marfaing and Hein 2008; Choplin this volume). As a result, migrants in Mauritania have all kinds of different projects: they are international and regional migrants, migrants in transit, refugees, and especially seasonal and labor migrants. These classifications might make sense to European policy makers, but have little heuristic value on the ground. Any given person can have several of these statuses at once, or pass from one to the other, and they are perhaps best described as "circular migrants."[9] This concept problematizes the conventional classifications: if they are not actually redundant, they are at least more porous than is often assumed (Boyer 2005: 50). "Circular migration" seems to represent well the ways in which migrants think about their own mobility: rather than describing their projects in terms of linear migration, they tend to talk about repeated journeys, where places of destination and transit might overlap and easily become places of residence, and they always imply that they make regular trips back home. Women, who often remain absent from studies of migration although they account for almost half of all international migrants (UNFPA 2006), have always been particularly well represented in West African regional migrations (see Manchuelle 1997). In Mauritania, women are estimated to account for 44 percent of all foreign residents, 57 percent among the Senegalese (RIM 2007: 13). As commercial and religious relations between the two countries have always been intense, Senegalo-Mauritanian families are numerous, and thus parents and husbands feel that they can let women travel freely. Hence, most female migrants are from neighboring countries, are Muslim, and travel to join members of their family. But there are also many small tradeswomen and domestic servants, and the largest number of women are certainly those who are part of larger regional trade networks. For traders who want to expand internationally, Mauritania tends to be the first step toward wider horizons (Marfaing 2007: 165).

The Nouakchott Labor Market

Despite the depressed economic situation and the rudimentary organization of the national labor market, most foreign residents claim that "in Nouakchott, those who want work can find it."[10] In Mauritania, the majority of jobs are in the unofficial (informal) sector. Information about them is never complete, difficult to access, and badly organized. Nonetheless, a study of the labor market conducted among households and using official data (RIM 2007: 14) indicates that foreign nationals are more likely to be employed than are Mauritanians: 65 percent have a job, as compared to 46 percent of Mauritanians. For those who used to be employed in the official (formal) sector, only 19 percent are now out of work, as compared to 50 percent of Mauritanians.[11] Independent of the fact that the government is conscious of its need for foreign labor, popular opinion holds that foreign workers are more professional in certain fields (construction, fishing, and mechanics, for instance) and that they are more highly skilled; many Mauritanian companies rely on them to train young Mauritanians. They are further considered to be more "daring" than Mauritanians, who are often restrained by local social norms.[12] They are also said to be more "flexible," meaning that, as foreigners, they will undertake certain tasks that they would never do at home, but also that they can easily be exploited by local employers. This is true in all kinds of employment, formal and informal. For the slightest glitch or for any work that was allegedly badly carried out, foreign workers risk being made redundant, or being paid only a fraction of the salary initially agreed upon, or none at all. Aware of their vulnerability, most foreign workers dare not complain, convinced that they would never stand a chance against a Mauritanian defendant. Although they usually sign labor contracts, immigrant workers often feel cheated. Perhaps because they are foreign, often have problems with the language, and are less aware of the internal functioning of Mauritanian society, they may find it more difficult to evaluate risk and ask for the necessary guarantees when promises are made. Sometimes, conscious of their dependent position, they are quite simply afraid to ask for their due.[13]

Nonetheless, for skilled workers from neighboring countries where jobs are unstable, nonexistent, or badly paid, there is no doubt that migration to Mauritania is a route to social mobility, both for migrants themselves and for their families: socially because of their success abroad, and financially because of remittances sent home that in turn allow for local investment and further migration by other family members. Many complain about family pressure back home and hope to be able to save money abroad in order to set up a production unit or a larger business on their return. Moreover, salaries in Mauritania are higher than in most neighboring countries.

The Organization of Labor among Migrants

To gain a more detailed insight into migrant workers' experiences in Nouakchott, we conducted fifty-four interviews, thirty-one of them with migrants. Eighteen of these, including two women, are salaried employees: five, with only one woman among them, have no qualifications; eleven have been apprenticed; and two have been to university. Thirteen are self-employed: eleven, including four women, have their own businesses and employ others. Two own and manage a school, two others a regional transport company, one a construction company, and another a maintenance firm; two are hairdressers, two run their own restaurant, one owns a hardware shop. One self-employed skilled laborer and one taxi driver are working alone. These different levels of enterprise are often interdependent, for example small-scale skilled laborers are commonly indebted to local hardware shops that supply them on credit: they pay the shops after they have been paid by their customers.[14] The same system is used by small traders, often young migrants attempting to make a living while waiting for better opportunities, who receive goods on credit from local wholesalers and only pay for them once the goods have been sold.

Job-hunting strategies are often tied to informal professional networks or linked to groups of potential migrants, the first of whom acts as an intermediary in the host country. In Nouakchott, everybody knows that certain professions recruit by origin, and jobs are divided among twenty different nationalities according to a fixed pattern. There is no doubt that these arrangements are more important for the choice of profession than preexisting skills and competencies that would make one group more likely to adopt a certain trade than another. Senegalese and Malians are mainly stonemasons, fishermen, mechanics, and taxi drivers; Ghanaians and Nigerians specialize in refrigeration; women seasonal migrants work as maids; Lebanese, settled in the country since 1963, work in catering, the cloth trade, and hardware. Commercial success has allowed them to send their children to school in French-speaking countries, in particular Senegal, which means that the second generation of Lebanese work primarily in health care, as doctors and pharmacists, and in the liberal professions.[15] More generally, migrants tend to send their children to private schools, often hoping that they will then take over their parents' business or will find it easier to get on independently. The Lebanese are exceptional in having a second generation almost exclusively employed in the liberal professions, and this is certainly because sub-Saharan migrants rarely stay in Mauritania and prefer to send their children to school in their home country. Unskilled women, often servants, maids, or nannies, sometimes come on their own, but mostly they come to live with a friend; those who are from the upriver districts of the Senegal valley are in any case closer to home in Nouakchott than they would be in Dakar. Moreover, they can do their shopping in Mauritania, where food is cheaper than in Senegal.[16] When they come with a member of their family, they are quickly incorporated into the society of seasonal or international migrants, where they take charge of cooking, washing, and other everyday chores. They make some money on the side by selling cooked meals or homemade fruit juice in the neighborhood.

Female traders who travel between Senegal and Mauritania feel at home in both countries. They have a reputation for relying on particular organizational strategies, establishing networks that allow them to trade without large investments or capital, and for which their habitually slow rhythm of accumulation is largely sufficient.[17] The women organize into groups: Senegalese or Mauritanian, residing in either country. They can delegate members of their group to buy goods in Mauritania, or to take them there in bulk, thus saving money on travel and transport. Their bales of goods are brought back to Senegal by taxi or on freight trucks that otherwise would return empty to Senegal, or in the double walls of refrigerated trucks transporting fish. The time spent negotiating with customs officials in Rosso, or on the ferry that crosses the river, offers the opportunity to meet, make friends, find solutions to common problems, and plan future trips. Female traders living in Nouakchott order goods from Dakar and pay for them in Mauritanian currency, allowing Senegalese traders to pay in local currency in Nouakchott; others barter goods for goods.[18] Barter is especially popular for cloth: embroidered fabrics from Senegal are directly exchanged for Mauritanian veils. Moreover, certain imported goods are cheaper when they are unloaded in Nouakchott rather than Senegal, and therefore tend to enter Senegal by road. This latter kind of trade is mainly the domain of large-scale traders, who can draw on networks that stretch beyond the region and often include migrants residing in Europe, allowing them to order goods directly from Europe or Dubai.

Migrants who have not been able to find employment through their local communities look for piecework or jobs paid by the day. They spend their days in places where they know that those who might need them will come to look for them: behind the church in Nouakchott, for instance. Women offer help with domestic chores and washing, but they by no means hold the monopoly here: unskilled men also help in domestic tasks that are considered too hard for women. Otherwise, they are employed as warehousemen, porters, or in similar positions in the harbor and elsewhere. Those who have a trade wait at the main crossroads of the Capital district of Nouakchott, indicating their speciality by the tool they hold in their hands: a piece of pipe for plumbers, a light bulb for electricians, a trowel for builders. If employers are happy with their work, they come back daily to hire the same workers; after some time, they might offer them more stable employment.

Living Together in Nouakchott

Most foreign nationals in Nouakchott rent rooms in the Fifth and Sixth Districts of the city that today have mostly been abandoned by white Moors (Choplin this volume).[19] Some prefer to live in the older parts of town, the Capital district or the historic *qsar,* where the first migrants settled in the 1960s, either because they belong to these older families or because they prefer not to be marked as "foreigners": as we were told, "it is nice to live in the *qsar* because it is more mixed."[20] These districts are truly autonomous in relation to the wider urban setting that surrounds them (see Hayot 2002: 8; Ba and Choplin 2005: 34), and names of businesses, streets, and houses offering rental accommodations often loudly proclaim the origin of their inhabitants: Garage Mali or Garage Dar Mousty. Those who have the means to do so pool the resources of family members and "rent, or even buy, a house for everybody," as one interviewee said. "Today, life is much better for me, I have fewer problems. I now have a big house here with my brother who is a builder, my wife who is a maid, and my three nieces."[21] Migrants who own a house often act as a bridgehead for members of their extended family or people from their home village who are looking for work, hoping to settle abroad, or even wanting to migrate to Europe. "Of course, I am a bridgehead for my family; at the moment, there are about ten of us. [You never know,] you can't stop young people, one of them might just disappear one day [to go to Europe]. I know it's on their minds, even if they're in work here. But nobody ever talks about it. Girls, on the other hand, don't want to go to Europe; they work as maids or hairdressers."[22]

Foreign nationals organize themselves according to their place of origin, their profession, or their religious affiliation. These different forms of collective identity often intersect and complement each other; they are drawn on by migrants according to the problems they face, their needs, and their opportunities.

Social support groups, or *dā'iras*, organized abroad by Sufi brotherhoods, act as a rallying point, helping new arrivals to find their way around and allowing long-term residents to stay in touch with their religion and to socialize. Foreign nationals also set up more secular associations based on nationality, independent of any official diplomatic representation their country might have in Mauritania. These associations look after new arrivals, help them to find lodging, introduce them to potential employers, or put them in touch with resident families who can help them while they get on their feet in a new city: "When a Senegalese gets here, he asks for the *dā'ira* associated with his *shaykh* back home, or for the Senegalese [association]. They will look after him until he finds a job. That takes two months, usually, less if he has a profession: there is work to be had. But not longer than that."[23] These associations offer information on the host country and its inhabitants, and attempt to resolve the problems encountered by their co-nationals. For some time now, they have grouped together to defend the rights of foreign residents in Mauritania, many of whom fear that they will never be able to win a court case against their employer or the Mauritanian administration. As one interviewee told us: "I have studied law, I am a consultant and have started to deal with my own cases. I offer advice on setting up a business, on contracts between Senegalese and Mauritanians, and on dispute settlement: Senegalese who have lost their investments due to the dishonesty of their Mauritanian partners, but also Mauritanians who paid money to Senegalese who then made off with it."[24]

Although different national organizations at times share information and help each other, social and cultural boundaries between communities of different countries of origin are generally respected. Of course, sometimes "different foreign communities live together. We are each attached to our own culture and occupied with our own business; but if several communities live in the same house, there are no problems and we all live together."[25] People from neighboring countries know each other, and sometimes work for the same employer, but they rarely meet in their free time. "Everybody sticks to their own group, not because we don't get on, but we don't spend much time together. Not just because of religion; we just don't have the same education or upbringing."[26] If they get married in Mauritania, young migrants generally prefer their spouse to be from the same national community and of the same social status—much as they would back home. Mixed marriages, whether between foreigners of different nationalities, or between foreigners and white or black Mauritanians, are rare, and socially things can be difficult for the couple.[27] Projects to set up mixed businesses do exist, but they are few, and mostly involve Mauritanian rather than other West African partners. Foreign residents generally feel that by staying among themselves, they avoid problems and, hence, unnecessary involvement with the local authorities. Moreover, they worry that any quarrel with somebody from a different country might degenerate into a conflict between the two national communities.

Foreigners and Locals

Most foreign residents say that they have never had any problems with Mauritanians, whom they only meet at work. According to one Senegalese fisherman: "All relations with Mauritanians are work related. We respect each other but we never become friends, even after years of working together."[28] This is not new. Foreign nationals who used to live in Mauritania during the colonial period emphasize that outside the workplace, people kept to themselves. Various considerations were at play, including the French administration's desire to keep encounters to a minimum (Marfaing 2009b: 45). In the French colonial cities, black migrant workers generally lived separately. In Atar for instance, soldiers and civil servants tended to socialize with people from their own place of origin and rarely mixed with the local population outside their professional functions: "Soldiers did go out, sometimes, the Mossi and others—after all, the morale had to be kept up. But they only went to buy dates and peanuts, perhaps went for a walk, and then came back. My father, who was working as a driver, was more in touch with the local people."[29] The many foreign civil servants and white-collar workers, Europeans and Africans, formed their own little society apart (cf. Viollier 2003: 101). Today, nothing much has changed, and all insist that people do not mix. Reasons given for this include language barriers and the "weight of tradition: Mauritanians have a rather more austere way of life, compared to sub-Saharans."[30] "[Mauritanians] prohibit drinking and going out, but if you don't do either, you are fine."[31] Hence, everybody agrees that people should keep to themselves: "When you are abroad, you have to follow what other people do, you should never get involved in things you don't know, and if you do not meddle with other people's problems, they will leave you alone."[32] Or, to sum it all up: "In fact, we don't have the same culture! Mauritanians never introduce us to their families. We invite them, but they never invite us back."[33]

Interviews suggest that foreign residents avoid locals, for fear of being mixed up in problems with them and therefore having to confront the administration or the police, where they know that they will be treated badly and will lose a lot of money. Although work and residence permits for foreign nationals are theoretically free of charge, few foreign workers are aware of this. In Mauritania, as in West Africa generally, most employment is informal; legislation does little to capture local ways of doing things, and even less those of West African residents from south or east of the river: most migrants are just not in the habit of "officializing" their stay. Yet checks by authorities are common, and those who work without the necessary paperwork are penalized. In order to escape these controls, and ideally any contact with the Mauritanian administration altogether, some resort to illegal means of obtaining Mauritanian identification documents. Buying a Mauritanian passport is popular: "They buy them from Negro Mauritanian police officers for 200,000 to 300,000 UM. Or else they get married to Mauritanian women, black women [*harātīn* or Haalpulaaren from the river valley], and then they can work in peace."[34] There is in fact a separation of people in terms of color, even though such a distinction makes little sense in an area marked by a long history of mixing and the mutual subjugation of people of different origins (S. Kané 2005), and where "racial" differences rarely capture the subtlety of local hierarchies. Nonetheless, color terms are used as a reference point for identity, regardless of the actual skin color of the person concerned (Marfaing 2009b: 54; Leservoisier this volume), and they become of crucial importance in situations of conflict between foreign residents and the local population. Prejudices about "blacks" and "whites" are commonly expressed in songs and poems, local idioms, and stereotypes. Certain tasks remain associated with those of servile origin, especially fishing, mechanics, domestic service, and wet nursing. This association is often self-fulfilling, and in turn reinforces mutual prejudice: all is well as long as everybody remains in their place, and stays there.

Cosmopolitanism in Question

Foreign residents in Nouakchott have developed certain criteria of belonging through which they constantly redefine themselves according to the situation at hand, the person spoken to, and the general context. These criteria can be linked to a country or a place of origin, but also to religious affiliation or professional skill. Such group membership allows for solidarity among individuals; supplies an identity, or stability, within their mobility; and provides people with the support they need in precarious situations. In Mauritania, being a black foreigner necessarily implies vulnerability. Group solidarity also provides some social control and a way of retaining one's difference in relation to other foreign communities and locals. Mobility there is a means of success, the key to social recognition among one's peers abroad and back home, without ever totally erasing the prevalent social hierarchies. These groups are islands of security, outposts where foreigners can retire to live in their own world, a world that accompanies them, as "a place that travels" (Ben Arrous 2004), and offers protection in a foreign and often hostile environment. Intermediaries, mostly the representatives of community organizations, provide links between the individual and the group, but also between different groups of foreigners, on the one hand, and the local population, on the other.

In this way, members of the group can have one foot in their host country and one in their home society.

This art of living together while staying apart articulates a sedentary with a mobile way of life. Remaining faithful to one's home country and to solidarity networks with co-nationals, while interacting on a daily basis with other migrants and the local population, requires constant "social micro-innovations" (Tarrius 2007). These include credit facilities, information exchange, or ways of managing business that might lead to the development of new models. In the absence of technology transfers or favorable conditions for socioeconomic development, people dynamically adapt what they have, and respond to existing opportunities (see also Laperche 2008: 12). Foreign residents do not exclude each other, but independently develop their own economic vitality. In this context, the heterogeneity and complementarity of different groups create a way of living together, side by side, coexisting. Many studies have shown how transnational mobilities result in new economic and social norms and in the emergence of new spatialities and temporalities. But how are these best described? The notion of cosmopolitanism, especially when qualified as a "new cosmopolitanism" (Tarrius 2000) or as "cosmopolitanism from below" (in analogy with "globalization from below"; Portes 1999), emphasizes the agents' mobility, flexibility, and adaptability to new places and situations, as well as their ability to be "from here and from there all at once."[35] This new cosmopolitanism is the result of globalization, increased mobility, and a shared feeling of freedom, the freedom to move and the art of moving that is inherent in it. Freedom is here defined as the ability to cross boundaries, spatial and social, to live in the in-between, independently of states. Hence, the conventional question of "integration" or "exclusion" in host cities is redundant (*pace* Hily and Rinaudo 2003: 55). The "other" is only perceived and dealt with as part of the practical necessities of everyday life, at work or for business. Migrants use local structures, but do not attempt to transform them nor to integrate into them: rather, they retain their own social and cultural orders (Diouf 2000: 702; Evers Rosander 2005: 117).

In Nouakchott, the capital of a country created by migration, where unemployment is high and where the informal sector of the economy dominates the labor market, the migratory situation is complex. All kinds of scenarios coexist: transit migrants who attempt to reach Europe, those who have failed to do so, and those "drowned in the adventure" (Streiff-Fénart and Poutignat 2006: 8), frustrated and stigmatized by their peers, who, without money, having lost everything, "might turn to crime."[36] There are seasonal migrants and refugees, and then there are those who settle and become part of the city. International organizations such as ECOWAS

(Economic Community of West African States), UMA, and COMESSA provide a legal framework for free movement throughout the region, where in any case national borders are often of little account. Nouakchott can usefully be thought of as an intermediate space, crossed by flows and unstable dynamics, where new forms of meaningful social interaction are made up from scratch (Faget 2005). Certain districts are microcosms within the city where different lifestyles of various origins coexist with local ways of doing things, and sometimes stand out against them. On the one hand, the relationship between people in this area is complementary: they interact and adapt, like links in a flexible mesh. On the other hand, people say they do not know each other. In a context of general state failure or disinterest, it is necessary to invent new models of urban management, business opportunities, identity, and citizenship. In a context of widespread mobility, European migration policies are unhelpful; meanwhile, the national administration is necessarily welcoming to foreign nationals, and "for those who are in the loop, migration is not a social problem, quite the contrary."[37] These contradictory policies increasingly cause conflict when controls imposed to stop "illegal migrants" are undifferentiated and concern everybody who "looks foreign" (Choplin this volume). The image transmitted by the international and national media, which criminalizes all foreign nationals as "illegal migrants," fosters fear among locals who up until now were remarkably indifferent to their presence. Foreigners are blamed as the source of all evils: crime, disease, and unemployment.

The new socioeconomic configurations of Saharan cities call existing urban hierarchies into question, risking conflict in restricted and mostly badly equipped urban spaces, where hopes for the future meet past failures. They pose a challenge to urban and municipal administrators, but also to national policy makers, who already find it difficult to manage their own population, which is suffering from a lack of infrastructure and opportunities for work. National migration policies are central: on the ground, whether migrants have come to settle, or whether they are in constant danger of expulsion, has an impact on their integration. The state's attitude toward foreign nationals—whether it considers them to be migrants in transit or potential citizens—is crucially important. The perception of resident foreign nationals, even those who initially only intended to travel through, undoubtedly has an effect on their potential investment in the city and their relation to the state: many are no longer in transit, and do not nurture the thought of leaving "tomorrow," even though most continue to think that they will return "someday," like migrants all over the world. Some, mainly foreign businessmen, but also skilled laborers and seasonal migrants, consider their working conditions such that their migration has been "successful," and they have strong reasons to carry on working in Mauritania.

Taken together, our interviews question the assumption that foreign workers are external to the national community (Tripier 2008). Although the notion of integration clearly has to be revised, it is important to note the complementarity of foreign resident communities both among themselves and vis-à-vis the local population. Living in separate quarters does not exclude them from society, but rather allows them to develop their own social dynamics. Urban coexistence involves both local populations who have little interest in the presence of foreigners and migrants who remain attached to their place of origin and removed from local concerns and norms (Tarrius 2007: 12, 17), unless they can use them for their own advantage or need to be aware of them in order to carry on undisturbed with their own way of life. Hence, foreign residents have multiple identities (Diouf 2000; Werbner 2006) that they adapt to the local and global context. These migrants, regardless of the particular locale—from which they expect only an opportunity to reach their objectives—are an active part of the increased popular mobility that is inherent in globalization. They experience migration not as an act of desperation, but as a "developmental practice" (Adelkhah and Bayart 2007: 29). It is this fragile balance of coexistence in transit cities that is put under pressure by national or foreign state policies that lead to the undifferentiated stigmatization of all foreigners.

NOTES

1. Figures on West African and especially on Mauritanian migration are approximations, and vary considerably depending on the criteria employed (see also Choplin this volume). According to the World Bank (Worldbank Excel Database [December 2006], University of Sussex Development Research Centre: Bilateral Migration Matrix), there are 105,315 foreign nationals in Mauritania, of whom 30 percent are Euro-Americans and 65 percent from sub-Saharan Africa. Official documents mention 65,000 migrants, apparently concentrating exclusively on sub-Saharan migrants. The same text estimates the total population of Mauritania at 2.7 million, including 48,000 foreign nationals, or 1.7 percent of the total population (RIM 2007: 11–12). De Haas (2007) has 65,000 foreigners, or 2.49 percent of the total population. According to numbers put forward by the Office of National Security in 2002, foreign nationals account for 7 percent of the overall population. Finally, the Atlas on Regional Integration in West Africa, ECOWAS-SWA/OECD (August 2006: 10), estimates the percentage of migrants in Mauritania at 3 percent. The NGOs lobbying for the human rights of migrants, such as CIMADE, estimate the number of foreigners at 300,000, that is, roughly 10 percent of the overall population (http://www.Dailymotion.com/relevance/search/migrants%2BMauritanie/video/x56u5h_paroledemigrantsdemauritanie1_news, accessed 22 May 2008).

2. Roughly 15 percent of migrants traveling in West Africa aim to reach Europe illegally (Marfaing and Hein 2008: 4). The notion of intermediary spaces is borrowed from Jean Schmitz's use of the term in seminars held at the IISMM and the EHESS between 2001 and 2005.

3. According to interviews conducted in Nouakchott and Rosso, 16 August 2002.

4. Interview, Nouakchott, 3 November 2006.

5. Interview, INAP, 10 May 2008. The BTS (*brevet de technicien supérieur*) is a post-high school vocational qualification.

6. Interviews, Ministry of Employment, 20 April and 7 May 2008.

7. Interviews, Chamber of Commerce and General Delegation for the Promotion of Private Investment, 6 and 7 May 2008.

8. Interview, Ministry of Employment, 7 May 2008.

9. This term can be defined in various ways: until the 1990s, it was used to describe cases in which the eldest son of a family spent some time abroad to provide for his family, and was then, several years later, replaced by a younger sibling. This kind of migration ensured generational change abroad (see Pélissier 1966; Cordell, Gregory, and Piché 1996). Another possible use of the term is more concerned with the nonlinear way in which people's projects develop, in response to the various opportunities encountered along the way (Tall 2002: 551). Finally, European policy makers have adopted the term to refer to temporary migration that is "managed in such a way that it ensures an optimal balance between offer and demand on the labour market of the destination countries" (Synthèse CARIM, Florence, 28–29 January 2008).

10. Interview, Nouakchott, 14 December 2007. Since the coup d'état in August 2008 and the increased Mauritanization of employment, this has changed, especially in the fishing industry.

11. The distinctions between the official and the unofficial, or intermediary, sectors of the economy are too complex to be discussed here fully. As far as we are concerned, what matters is the status of the employee, whether he is officially registered, is insured, and has a right to a pension. According to the Ministry of Employment, all employees should be so registered. But in all of Mauritania, there are a mere twenty-eight labor inspectors, two at Nouakchott, to control businesses, while most labor contracts are concluded privately (interview, Ministry of Employment, 20 April 2008).

12. Interviews, INAP, 10 May 2008; and Nouakchott, 21 April and 10 December 2008.

13. Interview, 10 May 2008.

14. Interview, Nouakchott, 7 May 2008.

15. Interview, Nouakchott, 16 December 2007.

16. Interview, Nouakchott, 26 April 2008.

17. Such gradual accumulation relies on the rotation of capital: "you start with little and then when you have more, you go further" (interview, Dakar, 1 August 2002). This working capital generally amounts to around 500,000 CFA francs, or €760.

18. Interview, Nouakchott, 18 August 2002.

19. At the time of our survey (early and mid-2008), a room cost between 8,000 and 10,000 UM (compared to 5,000 UM in 2005), not counting water (an additional 7,000 UM per month) and electricity (5,000 UM). This meant that in many cases, "one salary is simply not enough to pay the rent and live" (interview, Nouakchott, 28 April 2008).

20. Interview, Nouakchott, 26 April 2008.

21. Interview, Nouakchott, 22 April 2008.

22. Interview, Nouakchott, 24 April 2008.

23. Interview, Nouakchott, 24 April 2008.

24. Interview, Nouakchott, 22 April 2008.

25. Interview, Nouakchott, 29 April 2008.

26. Interview, Nouakchott, 28 April 2008.

27. A notable exception here are marriages among either Haalpulaaren or Wolof from either side of the Senegal River, whose shared linguistic and cultural identity overrides national boundaries (Leservoisier this volume).

28. Interview, Nouakchott, 9 August 2004.

29. Interview, Nouakchott, 24 November 2006.

30. According to a report on Senegalese traders who sell handicrafts to tourists in the region of Atar, published in *Le Soleil,* 9 January 2002.

31. Interview, Nouakchott, 28 April 2008.

32. Interview, Nouakchott, 23 April 2008.

33. Interview, Nouadhibou, 3 August 2004.

34. Interview, Nouakchott, 12 December 2007.

35. We used the expression "cosmopolitanism from below" in Boesen and Marfaing (2007: 17) and also in Marfaing (2007: 180), as it seems to offer a different way of considering foreignness beyond Eurocentric perceptions, while still taking marginality into account. We further discussed the usefulness of this expression in a roundtable, "Cosmopolitanism Off the Beaten Track," held at the ZMO in Berlin on 9 July 2008 with Kai Kresse, Lars Amenda, Malte Fuhrmann, and Elisabeth Boesen.

36. Interviews with failed migrants, in *Victims of Our Riches* (2007), a film by M. Kal Touré.

37. Interview, Ministry of the Interior, 16 December 2007.

11

CULTURAL INTERACTION AND THE ARTISANAL ECONOMY IN TAMANRASSET

Dida Badi

This chapter investigates cultural interactions between the Sahara and its Sahelian borderlands, based on an analysis of skills and techniques shared by craftsmen who supply the markets of Tamanrasset and, to a lesser degree, Djanet and Illizi.[1] Since the 1970s, these towns, situated in the extreme south of the Algerian Sahara, have become privileged sites of interaction and exchange between local people and more or less temporary migrants. This has resulted in the revival of traditional sets of knowledge and skills that have long been shared by both, and that are today skillfully adapted to a changing social and economic context. In this analysis, I will use two key notions: "revivals" and "transformations." A "revival" indicates the use of traditional knowledge and skills in a modern context, while a "transformation" shows the dynamic nature of this use. Modern Sahelian industries found in southern Algeria today largely draw on a common cultural patrimony shared between the Sahara and the Sahel, one that, far from being immutable and outmoded, proves to be highly adaptable and to have an important part to play in local economic development and the regional integration of Tamanrasset.

Tamanrasset as a Site of Saharo-Sahelian Encounter

Originally, the location of what today has become the city of Tamanrasset was included in the traditional area of nomadization of the Dag Aghali, one of the groups that constituted the Tuareg federation of the Kel Ahaggar, and that owned a few gardens worked by sharecroppers on the banks of the dry riverbed (*wadi*) of the same name. This is where, after the colonial conquest, Charles de Foucauld built his hermitage. After the French military administration decided to transfer its headquarters from Taghawhawt, east of the Ahaggar mountains, to

Tamanrasset, and after Moussa ag Amastan, *amanukal* (head of the federation) of the Ahaggar Tuareg from 1904 to 1922, chose to follow suit by building a palace there, it became the administrative and political center of the Ahaggar, the mountainous massif in the central Sahara that today sits at the southern tip of Algeria. Ten years after Algerian independence in 1962, Tamanrasset was made the administrative capital of a *wilaya* (governorate) of the same name, and subsequently became one of the most important administrative and economic centers of the Algerian Sahara. The *wilaya* of Tamanrasset covers a quarter of the national territory, and shares borders with two Saharo-Sahelian states, Niger and Mali. Today, Tamanrasset has a dozen different *quartiers* (districts), the oldest of which are Tahaggart, Hofra/Hawanit, Ksar al-Fugani, Guet el-Oued, and Sersouf (see also Bellil and Badi 1995); its population continues to grow.

Tamanrasset is home to people of many different origins, who were mostly attracted to the city because of the economic opportunities it offers, or quite simply because it is an important way station between sub-Saharan Africa and the north. Superficially, these populations can be grouped as follows (although none of the following categories is ethnically or culturally homogeneous). The first group is composed of people from the Saharan oases who have long been in close contact with the Ahaggar Tuareg, due to the important role played by the latter in trade relations with the countries of the Sahel, especially when such trade still relied on camel caravans. Many of these are descendants of Sha'anba from Metlili or Ouargla, former French colonial soldiers who invested their wages and pensions in trade and who were the first to invest in truck transport to the cities of the Sahel. Also originally from Saharan oases, especially from Aoulef and In Salah in the Tidikelt, are the *harātīn* (of servile descent), who were brought to the Ahaggar in the middle of the nineteenth century as sharecroppers to cultivate the banks of the *wadi*, and the *mrabtīn* (Islamic religious figures) from the same region, who, due to their religious status, cultivated Tuareg land on more favorable terms. These were followed by *shurafā'* (descendants of the Prophet), who mainly came from Aoulef and Reggane in the Touat. Together, they set up the first urban center of Tamanrasset, which is today referred to as *al-hawānīt*, "the shops."

With the drought of the 1970s, many Tuareg families living in the vicinity of Tamanrasset and who had long used it as an administrative center and market started to settle in the suburbs. They tried to live with members of their own fraction or tribe, and as near as possible to their habitual pastoral grounds: those who used to graze their flocks in the east came to live in Ankof and Im Machawen, east of the city, while those who used to go south settled in Tahaggart. They often maintained a foothold in the desert, and still act as the prime link between the city and the surrounding areas. To these Saharans are added those who, in Tamanrasset, are generally referred to as "northerners." These are Algerians from the north, who are far from culturally homogeneous, as they include Berber- and Arabic-speakers, Kabyles, Shawiya, and people from Algiers and Oran, distinctions that are reflected in their residential patterns, which generally follow regional origins. Yet the category "northerner" is taken to encompass them all, bearing witness to the relative ignorance that southerners have of northern Algeria, an area that they only began to get to know after independence, and then mainly through the media. These northerners mainly arrived in the first decades after independence, and generally work in the national administration and construction, although they have started to invest in other economic activities, such as private clinics, restaurants, hotels, and shops.

Due to this strong northern presence, Tamanrasset would look like any other provincial Algerian city, were it not for the very visible presence of Saharo-Sahelians. These are mainly the nationals of neighboring countries: the majority are speakers of Hausa, Songhay, Tamasheq, and Hassaniya.[2] Although they are familiar with people from the Sahara, with whom they have long been in contact through transregional trade, they have little experience of northerners, whom they meet for the first time in Tamanrasset. The settlement of Sahelians, be they Arabs, Tuareg, Hausa, or Songhay, has been facilitated by the reactivation of older networks dating back to the time of caravan trade, which link the newcomers to former nomads who have become sedentary. Because of these long-standing ties, but also because of cultural affinities, such as the shared use of Hassaniya, Tamasheq, and Hausa, Saharo-Sahelians establish themselves easily in Tamanrasset, often renting private accommodations in the suburbs. These same houses then become gathering centers for their own relatives, and reception centers for black sub-Saharan migrants traveling through Tamanrasset.

Finally, there are black African migrants from West and Central Africa who, unlike the Saharo-Sahelians, only rarely intend to settle on a permanent basis or to become part of the local economy. Like the northerners, they are culturally different, sometimes speak English rather than French, and are from a region that is relatively unknown to Saharo-Sahelians, which means they are treated as a category apart. After a long and tiring journey through the desert, they spend some time in Tamanrasset to reorganize and replenish their supplies and equipment. They earn the money they need to continue their travels by working on public building sites or for private firms; sometimes, they receive money from their families through Western Union. Most of them buy food and rent a bed from Saharo-Sahelians, in rooms that the latter have set aside in the houses they themselves rent. The addresses of these lodging houses, called *tacha* in Hausa, are passed on by word of mouth through the networks that organize the transport of migrants from the border towns to Tamanrasset.

The African Market of Tamanrasset

Tamanrasset has no industry, and its economy rests almost exclusively on tourism and trade. Situated at the crossroads of northern Algeria and West Africa, it has become an important center of transborder exchange of all kinds. In the process, its commercial center has shifted from the central Hawanit district toward Guet el-Oued in the west of the city, away from the shops and the only market built by the colonial authorities toward the more recently opened *sūq al-suwādīn* (African market).[3] Following the development of trans-Saharan truck transportation from the 1950s on, the municipality of Tamanrasset organized an annual fair called Assihar, or "meeting point" in Tamasheq. Since the 1970s, once a year, the Algerian authorities have published a list of goods that are permitted to be exported or imported exclusively for the fair, where they are exchanged for another similarly defined set of commodities.[4] This trade is mainly in agricultural products, such as henna, onions, and peanuts, but also in local crafts, for instance sandals and camel saddles made in Agadez or indigo cloth from Kano. These products have long accounted for the majority of trade between the Ahaggar and the Sahel, and are much in demand among the settled population of Tamanrasset and among nomads living nearby. Exports include dried dates from the Saharan oases, salt, tobacco, and tea. The popularity of the fair among Saharo-Sahelian merchants indicates its importance for the local and regional economy.

Once the fair has officially closed, those traders who have not succeeded in selling all their stock move to an open space opposite the official market, where they continue to sell their goods. Since the 1980s, this area has come to be known as the *sūq al-suwādīn,* or the African market. Since 2000, the Assihar has been managed by a private entrepreneur who has turned it into a daily market dominated by West African produce and traders, adding a Sahelian flair to the city, reminiscent of Agadez and Gao. Next to it, the municipality has opened another covered market, called *sūq al-safsaf* (the market of trivia) or, more properly, the market of the eucalyptus trees, where private traders can lease individual stands. Over time, this market has absorbed all the available space and taken over the surrounding streets, outgrowing even the famous *sūq al-suwādīn.* In these markets, various examples of skills and techniques employed by Saharo-Sahelians living in Tamanrasset, and the goods they produce, can be observed. These can be divided into two principal sectors: service and industry.[5]

May Nama, Tires, and Inner Tubes; or, How to Make Something Out of Very Little

As an example of the many services offered and often also monopolized by Sahelians in Tamanrasset, I will focus on catering. In Tamanrasset, this involves two principal activities: first, barbeques, called *may nama* in Hausa, which are very popular among all inhabitants of the city, including northerners; and second, small, low-budget eating places offering home-cooked food in private lodgings in the evening or in the streets throughout the day. Here, I will concentrate on the latter, as they considerably add to the Sahelian appearance of Tamanrasset. Sahelian women, in particular Hausa-speakers, specialize in catering on all levels, from the sale of raw ingredients to serving cooked food. They can be recognized from afar by their colorful clothes with bright West African patterns, the same that they would wear back home. Most of their customers, whom they meet each day in places known to all, are black African migrants from countries beyond the Sahel. The owners set up their restaurants in the street, and their customers arrive one by one, or in small groups: first, before sunrise, are those who have a job, perhaps on one of the building sites in town; later, those without stable employment arrive. After breakfast, the latter wait on the bank of the dry *wadi* for potential employers to come and recruit them for the day. Breakfast consists of coffee, boiled eggs, rice, or millet porridge (*fuwra*). The dozens of customers sit in a circle around the owner of the restaurant, on empty gasoline cans, on large stones, or directly on the ground; others sit on the wall that borders the *wadi* next to the restaurant, which shelters from the sun in the shade of the only bridge that links the two banks of the *wadi*.

Another kind of open-air restaurant is exclusively run by men who, rather than carrying their merchandise on their heads as the women do, push wheelbarrows heavily loaded with all kinds of food. In this way, they can carry more food than the women and can range farther: while women mainly stay in their own neighborhoods, in Guet el-Oued and Tahaggart, men extend their business to all parts of Tamanrasset where they know they can find their primarily sub-Saharan customers. Women tend to cater to regular customers, as they work each day in the same place and start very early in the morning. Further, they are more popular because they benefit from the associations made, throughout northwest Africa, between women and food, and because they offer hot meals that they cook themselves (rice, *fuwra*), as opposed to the cold food sold by men, which has been bought in local shops or ordered from restaurants (such as hardboiled eggs, apples, sardines, and jam). Customers say that they prefer the women's restaurants because, in addition to the very affordable prices they charge, they remind them of their own homes. Hence, men have to travel far and wide in order to find customers on building sites or in streets throughout Tamanrasset, although some establish themselves near the women's restaurants, hoping to encroach on their clientele. Others can be seen on street corners with little tables, pushing their wheelbarrows, or, with a basket in their hands, crisscrossing the town, especially at the time when workers tend to break for lunch. By then, the women have moved their stands to the market, while their customers have scattered all over town looking for work. Most of the goods sold by women in the market are related to food, such as seasonings, spices, eggs, peanuts, millet porridge, and millet flour.

In the evening, women sell cooked food in their own homes. Hausa- or Bambara-speaking women, who usually live with their husbands and children, rent houses in Guet el-Oued and Tahaggart for approximately 5,000 DA (Algerian dinars) a month.[6] The family lives in one of the rooms of the house, while the other rooms are sublet to black African migrants for 200 DA per person per month, paid in advance. Each room can contain up to ten people. Houses usually have a courtyard and three rooms, two of which are rented out, while the courtyard is used as a kitchen to cook food for the tenants, who pay for their meals in cash. The landlady is thereby always sure of having customers, both for her rooms and for the food she prepares, and can make considerable profits because, in addition to the 4,000 DA paid for the rooms, she earns money on the food sold. A plate of rice with one piece of meat costs 50 DA at Fati's, which compares favorably to the 120 DA it would cost in town. If all her tenants dine in, Fati makes 1,000 DA of gross profits, plus the money earned from breakfast and from her various activities on the African market, where she sells food and seasonings. Fati thereby is able to pay the rent and support her three children, the oldest of whom is now twelve years old and sells fritters in the streets.[7]

Restaurateurs such as Fati clearly earn enough money to have no need to think about tempting fate elsewhere. But in contrast to the *may nama,* which attract a broad range of customers, Sahelian restaurants continue to be uniquely patronized by sub-Saharan migrants whose precarious circumstances force them to eat cheap food. Other restaurants in Tamanrasset, mainly run by northerners, have not successfully entered this important market, as they offer "traditional" Algerian food (chips, omelettes, kebabs, stews, couscous) that seem to have little appeal to black Africans, mainly because they are too expensive. In the same way, Sahelian restaurants have not been able to offer Algerian dishes, thus failing to attract northern Algerian customers, perhaps because neither group knows how to prepare the other's food. Further, northerners are little used to eating rice and millet, the basic staples of Sahelian cookery, but prefer wheat and barley; and transit migrants have little time to develop an interest in local food, and do not care particularly about the quality of the food they eat. Hence, we can observe a certain division of labor and relevant skills, although a few restaurants run by women at home have begun to attract customers among their Saharan neighbors, who are especially keen on dishes based on millet, such as the *fuwra,* or millet porridge. Millet is very popular among Saharans, who use it to make a drink called *ghajira,* traditionally prepared during the hot season and during Ramadan. Indeed, in the standard Tuareg diet in Tamanrasset, millet has only recently been replaced by semolina, which is cheaper and easier to prepare, although the availability of food processors has partly reversed this trend. Although in terms of food, the cultural gap between northerners and Sahelians appears at first enormous, the broadly shared popularity of the *may nama* and the intermediate position of local Saharans, customers to both, show that this gap might eventually be bridged.

In addition to such service activities, Tamenrasset's economy also incorporates various forms of "manufacturing" based on techniques of reclaiming and recycling materials. Sahelians started to use "traditional" techniques to repair tires in the 1980s, as a reaction to the double shortage of new inner tubes and of garages offering vulcanization. This method, used throughout the Sahel, consists of sewing patches onto holes in tires and inner tubes, and is reminiscent of techniques used by Tuareg leatherworkers to repair bags. This method is totally unknown elsewhere in Algeria, and although since its introduction many modern car repair shops have opened in Tamanrasset offering vulcanization, it remains very popular, in particular with Saharan truckers and drivers who claim that it adds another 30 percent to the life span of their tires. The price of this service depends on the size of the hole to be patched.

Another innovative Sahelian practice is to collect old inner tubes that are no longer of any use to truckers and to transform them into waterskins. These are then sold for 300 DA each in the market of Tamanrasset, mainly for use by the same long-distance truckers and by pastoral nomads. With its two handles and single opening, the inner-tube waterskin is modeled on traditional goatskin water bags. Like the original model, the inner-tube waterskin is strapped to the belly of a donkey or camel—or below a truck—using its two handles, while the opening serves as a spout to pour water: all that has changed is the material used. Saharo-Sahelians have adapted a traditional item to changes in transportation, thereby finding a solution to the shortage of goatskins by inventing a new type of waterskin that not only fulfills the same functions, but is better adapted to the new transportation systems. Their relatively low price—300 DA compared to 1,500 DA for a goatskin water bag—is justified by the bad taste of the water they contain.

The Smelters and Tanners of Tihagwen

The district of Tihagwen is situated in the far southwest of Tamanrasset. In the 1970s, it was a separate village, at a distance of eight kilometers from the center of town, inhabited by a few *harāṭīn* living from the produce of their gardens. The area between Tihagwen and Tamanrasset, today occupied by Guet el-Oued, the Assihar, and the *sūq al-suwādīn,* was open space until the construction there of a prison and municipal dump. This is where, in the early 1990s, in the shade of two tall acacias, Sahelian entrepreneurs set up what today has become a genuine industrial complex for the processing of recycled goods. There were several reasons for this choice of location: first, activities carried out in the vicinity of the municipal dump would not cause any worries about their effects on public health, hence reducing the risk of being closed down by the authorities. Second, the dump itself is the main source of the materials being recycled. Third, Tihagwen is right next to the *sūq al-suwādīn,* where most of its products are sold.

In the 1990s, this industrial complex started as a simple unit for the depilation of skins retrieved from local slaughterhouses. The skins were depilated using the extract of a local plant, called *timeknit* by the Tuareg, who have always used it in this way. The plant was picked, dried, and ground. The powder thus obtained was mixed with water, and the skins were then soaked in the mixture. In Tihagwen, gasoline cans were used for this purpose, since they can hold a larger number of skins than other readily available containers. Once depilated, the skins were dried in the sun, packed in bags, and sent on trucks to the cities of northern Niger, such as Tahoua and Agadez, where they were tanned and sold. A few tanned skins were then reimported to Tamanrasset or Djanet.

Due to the strong demand for leather and the high costs of transportation to Niger, a second unit of production was subsequently set up. Here, skins are treated on-site and turned into leather ready to use, to be sold directly in the local market. This is relatively easy because the raw material needed for tanning can be found locally, sold by nomadic Tuareg who collect it from *Acacia albida* trees. Dried, the pods of these trees are ground to a fine powder in a wooden mortar (*tendi*) with a wooden pestle, the same kind as those used in Tuareg camps and throughout the Sahel, which are sold in Tamanrasset by Tuareg craftsmen for 1,500 DA apiece. A finished skin is worth 220 DA in the market of Tamanrasset, where they are mostly sold to Tuareg who turn them into handicrafts for tourists. Like the utensils, all the techniques used, from the depilation to the drying to the tanning, are familiar to local Tuareg: they rely on skills shared throughout the Sahara and Sahel, and use naturally occurring materials that can be found in the region and that reflect a detailed knowledge of the natural environment based on experience accumulated over many generations. The same techniques can be observed in Sahelian towns such as Agadez, Tahoua, Zinder, and Arlit, as well as in Tamanrasset and Djanet. The fact that these skills have been revitalized by Sahelians residing in Tamanrasset in a quasi-industrial context bears witness to the people's economic dynamism and adaptability, and to their capacity to make an impact on the rapidly changing contemporary Sahara—making it more Sahelian than ever.

However, when the natural ingredients for tanning are scarce, Sahelian craftsmen in Tihagwen will use industrial products, such as lime for depilation and chromium salts for tanning. Leather created with such industrial processes is less sought after by Tuareg craftsmen, who say that these skins are hard and not flexible enough to produce goods for tourists, although they might serve to make soles for shoes and travel bags. Hence, Tuareg craftsmen have to tan these skins again, using organic materials. This indicates the degree to which Tuareg leatherworkers have become dependent on raw materials provided by others. It also poses several questions that reflect the global struggle between artisanal and industrial processes: will Sahelian producers totally give up using natural materials, even if this means risking the loss of their main customers, the Tuareg? Will Tuareg craftsmen take the easy option and start using industrially tanned leather instead, although this might imply a loss of the "authenticity" and originality of their products? Or will they reactivate their former knowledge, and reinvest in tanning themselves, in order to maintain the quality of their goods? Some nomadic Tuareg women have become involved in tanning and leatherwork, using traditional methods, a development that might in the long run indicate yet another solution. But will Tuareg women be able to satisfy the growing demand of local craftsmen, and thereby seriously compete with Sahelian products that are more easily found in the market?

The leather workshop at Tihagwen subsequently expanded to include a foundry that produces aluminum cooking pots for household use, copying the shape of old earthenware models. The raw material used in the foundry is collected from the municipal rubbish dump, in the form of old pots or cans. These used to be taken by truck to recycling plants located in Sahelian towns, for instance Agadez, before being reimported as finished products, such as cooking pots or other kitchen utensils. In order to cut transportation costs, a foundry was set up in Tamanrasset itself where the entire production process now takes place, with the necessary techniques and labor force imported from the Sahel.

The foundry functions according to very simple principles, identical to those used by Tuareg blacksmiths, employing earthenware crucibles and sand. The bellows used in Tihagwen, however, are different from those familiar to Tuareg craftsmen: they are entirely built out of pieces of metal, such as rims and chains, that are recycled from old bicycles, while Tuareg bellows are made out of goatskin, a wooden nozzle, and a metal pipe leading to a metal or earthenware nozzle that keeps the air pressure steady. Although the basic principles and the results obtained remain the same, the materials used are new, and well adapted to the new context. The fire of the foundry uses wood or charcoal rather than gas that, at 1,000 DA for an empty bottle and 200 DA for a refill, is considered too expensive. With constant fanning, a very small amount of wood or charcoal, picked up here and there, is sufficient to keep the fire at a constant temperature for most of the day.

The used beer and lemonade cans, old pots, and aluminum utensils that are used as raw material are retrieved from rubbish heaps by collectors, who are part of the production team. The aluminum is then melted down either according to the method used by Tuareg craftsmen, in open earthenware crucibles (*ebin*), or in steel pots. These are manipulated with the help of long tongs that are homemade and resemble those used by the Tuareg. The liquid aluminum is purged of all other materials that might attach to it, such as paint or other metals, which are removed with a long metal stick while the crucible is still on the fire. The crucible is then taken off the fire using tongs, and emptied into a mold made out of sand. About twelve empty cans make one small pot, which is sold in Tamanrasset for 600 DA. These pots are much appreciated in Saharan households; they are supposed to make food taste better, they are similar to traditional earthenware pots, and they last longer than ordinary metal pots. They can also be transformed into *couscoussières* (deep pots for steaming couscous) or, by covering them with a skin, turned into drums used in musical and poetic recitations (*ahal*).

Finally, the industrial complex at Tihagwen produces metal trunks. Such trunks have been used in the area for generations, but demand has risen as exchange with the towns of the Sahel has become more intense, following the opening of the Assihar in the 1970s and the subsequent establishment of the *sūq al-suwādīn*. These trunks, which are painted light blue, are available in two sizes, with white stenciled patterns that range from palm trees, flowers, and acacias to machine guns. They are spray-painted using a small hand pump, as is common among Saharo-Sahelian sheet-metal workers more generally. These trunks, instead of being imported from Sahelian towns, are now produced locally, taking advantage of the system of recycling established by Saharo-Sahelians. The development of this production unit followed the same steps as those described above: at first, metal trunks were imported from the Sahel, where the whole production process was located. Then, raw material was collected in Tamanrasset, where it was abundant and where a growing Saharo-Sahelian labor force made this feasible, and exported to Niger, whence the finished goods were reimported to Tamanrasset during the annual trans-Saharan fair. Now, production has shifted to Tamanrasset altogether, and only the labor and the necessary technical skills are still imported from the Sahel.

The workshop where these trunks are produced is located east of the two longer-established ones, and protected by makeshift shelters against the sun and the wind. The barrels or oil drums used to make these trunks are obtained for free from local companies, for which they are merely scrap, but they can also be bought from private traders for 1,000 DA per barrel. They are opened and flattened into metal sheets of the same kind that were used to construct the workshop itself. Two kinds of metal barrels are found on the Tamanrasset recycling market. Gasoline cans are considered to be the best, because they are easy to clean; being more valuable, they have become the object of an intermediary trade and have to be bought from private shops. On the other hand, barrels that have been used to transport bitumen or pitch need to be cleansed and reconditioned before they can be processed. This is done by heating them over a wood fire until the tar melts. Such barrels can be obtained free of charge. Barrels are opened, from the top to the bottom, with a short and rather coarse chisel that is hammered through the metal, and then the two metal plates that close both ends are taken off. The metal sheet is flattened on the ground using a hammer, while the two ends become small round plates that are put aside. If needed, they can be used to make locks for the trunks. Otherwise, they are thrown away, and the vast number of round plates that litter the ground around the workshop give an indication of the large quantity of trunks made. Two barrels are needed to make a large trunk, and one and a half for a small one. Large trunks are sold for 2,200 DA in Tamanrasset to private households and to local travel agencies that use them to carry food and kitchen equipment on tourist treks. All trans-Saharan truckers have at least one of these trunks with them, since they are especially suitable for desert travel.

Field research among Saharo-Sahelians in Tamanrasset has shown that many of the processes, techniques, and utensils employed in production, services, and recycling have long been in use throughout the area, and are familiar to both Saharan and Sahelian craftsmen. They draw on a common cultural repertoire shared by all those who live in the region, which has evolved over time in order to derive every possible advantage from the rare animal and plant resources available; at times, they are identical in the Sahara and the Sahel, at others, they are at least complementary. Saharo-Sahelian migrants to the area have been very successful in adapting these skills to contemporary circumstances, and have thereby become a vital part of the local economy, a considerable share of which they now control. In a similar way, the small everyday measures of food and staples that had long disappeared from the market of Tamanrasset after the introduction of metric measurement have been reintroduced by Sahelians, and this system remains readily comprehensible on either side of regional and national boundaries.

The popularity of Sahelian artisanal industries in Saharan towns such as Tamanrasset and Djanet is a clear example of the vitality of the skills they recycle, demonstrating their adaptability to the contemporary context, and proving that these simple, workmanlike, practical methods and techniques and the often improvised conditions in which they are employed clearly have a place in an increasingly globalized economy. It further shows that the towns of the Algerian Sahara are not only places of transit, but they also attract migrants in their own right, mostly from the countries of the Sahel that have long been in close contact with the Sahara and can draw on a shared fund of knowledge and skills to facilitate their insertion into the local economy. Meanwhile, the presence of northerners necessarily leads to cultural interactions, creating a privileged site of encounter between northern and sub-Saharan Africa, and continuing the long-standing tradition of transregional exchange.

NOTES

1. This study follows up on earlier research carried out among Saharo-Sahelians living in the Algerian Sahara; see Badi (2007).

2. Hausa-speaker here means everybody who defined themselves as such when asked, or else who spoke Hausa when asked about ethnic origin. The Songhay in Tamanrasset are mainly from Gao and Timbuktu on the Niger bend in Mali. Tamasheq-speakers include Tuareg from Mali and Niger in addition to local Kel Ahaggar, whose traditional pastoral migrations used to take them to northern Mali and Niger. Relations between them and Sahelian Tuareg thus have deep historic roots and are varied and complex. Hassaniya-speakers, the Moors of the historical and anthropological literature, have become active in transborder trade and control a considerable share. They have invested in new activities, such as trade in livestock, and have challenged the Shaʿanba monopoly in the truck trade with the Sahel. Beyond linguistic differences, their lifestyle is similar to that of the Tuareg.

3. *Suwādīn,* sing. *sūdānī*: blacks, the term commonly used to refer to all black African groups collectively. It echoes the historical term *bilād al-sūdān* (country of the blacks) used by medieval Islamic authors when referring to West Africa.

4. For the rest of the year, most cross-border trade is illegal; see Scheele this volume.

5. We are only looking here at those activities that seemed to be the most representative of the economic vitality of Sahelian communities in Tamanrasset. Other activities, such as handicrafts, construction, repairs of electrical goods, and so on, will be the object of further publications.

6. In 2009, 100 DA was worth about €1 on the black market.

7. Because they do not have the relevant papers that would legalize their stay in Algeria, none of her children go to school.

PART 4
ECONOMIES OF MOVEMENT

NOTES ON THE INFORMAL ECONOMY IN SOUTHERN MOROCCO

Mohamed Oudada

Contraband activity is a typical feature of frontier zones in developing countries as elsewhere but particularly where the frontier itself is relatively unstable. Where borders are closed, contraband networks provide the only means of organizing commercial exchange in response to local and regional requirements across the frontier zone; where borders are open, but policed by entry tariffs, contraband activity avoids customs and tariff controls and their limitations on "free" trade. Morocco's militarily controlled land borders provide two major points of exchange with neighboring states: the customs post on the Algerian border at Oujda, currently closed; and the post on the open frontier with Mauritania, at Fort Guergerrat south of Dakhla.[1] Southern Morocco and the western Saharan region therefore sit at the junction of two different frontiers: the Algerian border is illegally crossed by only the most valuable exchanges, while the Mauritanian border is open to trade in goods of all kinds.

Saharan Borders, Society, and the Economy of Informal Trade

The southern region of Morocco, from the foothills of the Anti-Atlas to the north of the Sahara, is an interface between the Mediterranean and tropical worlds. Historically a zone of transit via the trans-Saharan trade roads, which crossed from the Sahel and along which, over time, oases developed, it has also been a zone of settlement, with populations grouped around water sources. The economy of southern Morocco has tended historically to be oriented toward sub-Saharan Africa, maintaining especially close relations with Tindouf, a major regional trading center and the location of an annual market and gathering of the region's nomadic tribes. Nomadic pastoralism has long been the major way of life in this region, whose landscape across what is today the entire frontier zone between Algeria, Morocco, and Mauritania is predominantly characterized by continuous *hamada* (flat, arid, stony desert). While it is difficult to provide a precise account of the historical patterns of movement among nomadic groups in the region, it seems clear that a certain complementarity between nomadic and settled populations has defined the region's ecology. A long series of settlements founded at the northwestern edge of the Sahara is a marked feature of regional history: Tamdoult, built by the Idrissids (eighth–tenth centuries CE) and succeeded by Tizounine; Agadir Lhna, founded under the Saadian dynasty (sixteenth century), and Jbair at today's Tata; Agadir NTissint, Icht, Tamanart at Foum el-Hissen, and Assa; the Almoravid (eleventh century) foundation of Noul Lemta; Tagaoust (today's Laksabi); and Guelmim have all been centers of Saharan trade. The line of oases stretching south from these *qsūr* (fortified settlements) has constituted a transit and exchange corridor, a path of commerce and migration, over a long time span.

The region south of the Anti-Atlas mountains has long been, and is still today, divided between a number of major tribal confederations. The "far west" near the Atlantic coast is dominated by the Tekna and Kunta confederations, while the Aït Khabbach, Aït Rloan, Aït Sfoul, and Arib are the major groups inhabiting the eastern side of the region between Oued el-Dhahab (the former Spanish Rio de Oro) in the south and Errachidia in the north. A series of droughts in the area, but especially the relative insecurity of pastoral zones since the outbreak of the Western Sahara conflict in 1975,[2] has altered patterns of movement and relations between populations and territory, leading to the sedentarization of most formerly nomadic groups. Despite the recent history of political border disputes in the area, however, ethnic and sociocultural structures remain largely intact across contiguous territories, with long-standing relations uniting population groups across the divisions of political boundaries. The Sahara, after all, is a crossroads region of flourishing culture, languages and dialects, customs and traditions. Socially and culturally, two subregions can be discerned in this larger area: one to the east and another to the south. The zoning of the Sahara by political geography has not erased cross-border sociocultural relations. On the other hand, political frontiers *have* modified the nature of commercial relations between these same populations, leaving a major role for contraband smugglers whose social support system is found in existing tribal structures.

After the Green March of 1975[3] and the declaration of a duty-free zone in part of the region—creating an area of tax-free commerce uniting the southern Moroccan region of Guelmim and Essemara with the former Spanish Saharan provinces of Seguia el Hamra and Rio de Oro (Laayoune and Oued el-Dhahab)—an informal economy developed locally between the untaxed zone and nearby Saharan towns, creating a new dynamic in the regional economy. This informal trade, which has persisted up to the present, concerns only foodstuffs and necessary staples (oil, milk, sugar). With the deployment of the MINURSO (United Nations Mission for the Referendum in Western Sahara) peacekeeping operation in 1991 as part of the peace plan for the Western Sahara and the subsequent stabilization of the region, informal commercial networks also began to operate across the Algerian and Mauritanian borders. In neither case does the flat, open terrain pose an obstacle to such activities. Until 2001, four-wheel-drive vehicles and motorcycles were the primary means of transportation, but the reinforcement of border controls has subsequently obliged traffickers to develop other—and older—techniques. Camels have again become the most favored means of transport, because they can penetrate the tighter chain of frontier posts silently and by night, and also because they are able to cover short distances unaccompanied, thus reducing the risk of capture for the smugglers themselves.

From Algeria, goods moving into Morocco are dispersed along two major axes. From the east, a channel from Errachidia to the lower Draa valley, with a southern spur along the southern branch of the N9 highway through the oases of Zagora, Tagounite, and M'hamid, directs a variety of products—notably cigarettes and gasoline—northward, especially toward Casablanca. The Draa and Ziz valleys descend the southern flank of the High Atlas near Errachidia and Ouarzazate, respectively, before turning southwesterly and in the case of the lower Draa running south of the Anti-Atlas, along the Algerian border and toward Tan-Tan. Goods are carried through the valleys toward the Saharan Atlantic coast, with livestock for human consumption as the main commodity. From Mali, camels and goats transit via Algeria before entering Moroccan territory and traveling by truck to livestock markets, especially in Guelmim. The inhabitants of the northwestern Sahara are major consumers of livestock, especially camels brought into the area from elsewhere. This trade in livestock from the south and southeast has been a feature of the region at least since the early 1980s, but during the mid-1990s–2000s the reserve stocks of herding groups in southeastern Morocco, the Aït Atta and Aït Khabbach, have been exhausted. Intermediaries in the regional livestock trade, who themselves often belong to these nomadic groups, have therefore begun to seek out other sources of supply from across the border. Some livestock smugglers have met their needs more than satisfactorily by importing camels from Niger and Mali whose value doubles at the market in Guelmim. In 2006–2007, according to livestock wholesalers in Guelmim,[4] an estimated 3,600 camels were brought to market there through the lower Draa valley. The practice and organization of this trafficking are enabled and sustained by local group networks and the neighborly intergroup relations between inhabitants of the frontier zone.

The range of contraband products entering Morocco from Mauritania is considerably wider, mirroring the diversity of commodities that can legally be traded across the border. Consumer goods and basic commodities are brought to market, often via the same routes as are followed by migrants (see Brachet this volume). Although the volume of goods circulating as contraband is necessarily difficult to quantify, cigarettes clearly are in first place as the most-traded commodity in the informal economy. The organization of cigarette traffic begins on the Saharan Atlantic coast, with consignments entering Laayoune or Essemara moved north to Casablanca through a series of local markets, which are supplied along the way. A second route, from the Mauritanian border northeast, leads along the ridge of Jebel Ouarkziz, which skirts the Algerian border north of Tindouf. Under heavy surveillance, the difficulty of access through this region leads smugglers to make a detour through Algeria, entering Morocco farther north via M'hamid or Errachidia. Although the livestock trade is much older, trafficking in manufactured goods and especially tobacco products, which has grafted itself onto the longer-established commercial network, has today the largest share of the informal "wholesale" market.

Actors of the Informal Economy

Aside from the Derb Raalaf quarter of Casablanca, the "retail" side of Morocco's informal economy does not tend to be centered on particular towns or districts specializing in certain products of the smuggling trade. Distribution networks are on a smaller scale; individual members of contraband networks are known within urban areas and it is to these individual sellers that customers turn. At the other end of the social scale, the circulation of goods in the informal economy depends on "tribal" group connections that persist today across national boundaries. Such links, which may stem from real or fictive kinship affiliation but which might also be religious (through belonging to a shared *zāwiya*) or derived from commonly inherited pastoral practices or economic interdependence in contiguous or shared territory, facilitate the transit of contraband merchandise across the region. No single group specializes in any particular trade; rather, transactions are entered into as opportunities arise. Nor is there any necessary correlation between the importance and influence of an individual within a given family and the role he might play within a contraband network. Although it is, again, impossible to find any firm statistics on the involvement of different groups in the informal economy, interviews in 2007 with *chefs de tribu* (tribal notables) in the region between Assa and Errachidia, via Zag, Tagounite, and M'hamid, discovered that for each of seven major groupings, between twenty-seven and seventy-nine persons were thought to be involved, with most *chefs* suggesting relatively modest numbers between forty-one and fifty-nine, and all concurring that such involvement does exist across the region surveyed.[5] Those working in the informal frontier trade are usually young men drawn from groups of nomadic origin now living in Saharan towns, particularly those with 10,000 inhabitants or more, but also smaller towns such as Assa, Zagora, or Tata, and even smaller centers like M'hamid, Tagounite, and Zac Erfoud, whose populations number no more than 4,000. Three distinct groups can be discerned within the organization of the informal trade: wholesalers, intermediaries, and traffickers.

Wholesalers sit at the top of the pyramid; well versed in the business of contraband and connected to international commercial circuits, they have varied backgrounds and profiles and do not conform to a single type. Wholesalers in contraband may also be engaged in legal import-export or in legitimate livestock trading; they may have retired from such activities; or they may combine "official" business activity with smuggling on the side. In any case they have the means of acquiring the initial capital needed, though this can sometimes be accumulated over time through informal activity. It is also not uncommon to buy merchandise for illicit import and distribution on credit, with personal trust and honor as the guarantees of the economic transaction that is also, in such cases, a personal relationship based on a moral contract.

Intermediaries take delivery of merchandise, especially cigarettes, at points along the Saharan Atlantic coast and store it in the area around Nouakchott; they also operate in the interior, near the Moroccan and Algerian borders, particularly when trading in livestock. Employing a detailed knowledge of the region and its topography, they transport the goods to their points of resale, recruiting drivers, transporters, and guides mainly from within their own social group, although they also employ smugglers from outside their own communities, especially for the hazardous crossing of heavily militarized frontiers. To keep the process under control, the role of cross-border trafficker is mainly taken by young men from within the region, usually those with no other source of income. But, again particularly on the riskier crossings, intermediaries sometimes hire guides from among non-sedentarized nomadic groups, or young men who come to work in the region from elsewhere. The latter tend to be young men from farther north, looking for work in the construction or fishing industries of the western Saharan region, where the economy is stimulated by doubled rates of pay; often, they are also hoping to emigrate via the Atlantic coast to the Canary Islands. For young would-be migrants, who can earn six times their normal income on a cross-border passage with a camel loaded with cigarettes, contraband trafficking is an attractive, lucrative opportunity preparing the way to Europe.

Saharan Towns: The Habitat of an Informal Economy

The parallel economy's lucrative commercial activity animates the urbanization and the inter-urban relations of southern Morocco. Towns provide an attractive investment environment, especially in land and buildings, for contraband entrepreneurs anxious to diversify their activities into legal channels; the legal and informal economies, indeed, coexist and even complement one another. While the level of income generated by contraband trafficking remains unverifiable and impossible to declare openly, acquiring a house or setting up a legitimate business represents the achievement of a certain social promotion for some traffickers; for others, it may simply be a means of laundering money. In either case, the result is a booming speculation in property and construction that has become a feature of almost all the Saharan towns of southern Morocco. This speculation in real estate, coupled with demographic growth and an especially high level of urbanization in the region (71.5 percent in 2004, compared to an average of 55.1 percent for Morocco), has also contributed to the appearance of areas of unregulated, informal, or precarious housing in some towns, such as Laayoune.

Research carried out in the area between Assa (in the lower Draa valley) and Errachidia in 2007 indicated that the profits from contraband trade seem to be primarily invested in buying houses (137 cases). Retail businesses come second (84 cases), and other property, including *téléboutiques* (privately owned public telephone booths), third (53 cases), followed by cafés, transportation services, livestock herds, and travel agencies. Again, the data are indicative only and based on a small number of cases, but they give a useful picture of both the concentration and the diversity of the investments made with the revenues generated through informal activity.

The urban fabric of Saharan towns seems still, even in the twenty-first century, to be influenced by rules of tribal practice. Historically, after all, these settlements have been the centers of sedentarization for an agricultural and pastoral society, characterized by close ties of kinship, where stock raising was the main economic activity and rights to land were held in common. These values have had their effect on Saharan towns, with the members of a group settling in the same quarter, as for example in Guelmim, where in 2009 the occupation of urban space could still be mapped largely according to tribal group (Aït Moussa Ou Ali to the southeast of the center, Aït Oussa to the northeast, Aït Baarmane to the west, and a smaller mixed area on the periphery of the town to the northwest). In defiance of this "rule," however, property investments of the profits of the informal economy seem to be diffused throughout the space of the town. Some patterns of practice, however, can still be discerned: while intermediaries and some traffickers invest in their own local areas, wholesalers choose to place their money in regional centers farther afield, such as Agadir, Ouarzazate, or Marrakesh, so as not to attract envy—or any other kind of attention.

The networks of informal commerce, like those of migration, that can be seen today in the northwestern Saharan between Mauritania and Morocco reflect and reactualize long-standing patterns of exchange. The development of contraband trade between Saharan states indicates, perhaps, nothing more than that the Sahara continues to function as a coherent commercial transit zone despite the existence of borders, whether open or closed. There are, of course, dangers inherent in this "free" movement of goods across borders; the extended range of contraband products, including medicines and an ever-greater variety of manufactured foodstuffs, poses serious threats to health since many of these products are counterfeit and escape any form of medical screening and control. Less fatally, but still with repercussions in the traditional economy and regional development, while much of the revenue generated is reinvested locally, much is not, thus draining even this precarious form of income out of the regional economy.

NOTES

The field research on which this chapter is based was carried out by the author in Guelmim, Tagounite, M'hamid, and the area between Assa and Errachidia, between 2007 and 2009, under the VOLUBILIS Hubert Curien (Morocco) program, grant no. MA/08/201B, code 17251VF.

1. Editors' note: i.e., the southern frontier of the disputed territory of the Western Sahara, currently under Moroccan military control.

2. On this conflict, see Hodges (1983), Lawless and Monahan (1997), and Zunes and Mundy (2010).

3. Editors' note: In November 1975, some 350,000 Moroccans responded to the appeal of the king for a "peaceful reconquest" of the Spanish Sahara, and crossed the frontier into the Spanish-occupied Western Sahara.

4. Interviews, Guelmim, 2007.

5. Interviews, October–December 2007. Results were obtained for the Reguiybat, Oulad Dlim, Aït Oussa, Aït Khabbach, Aït Sfoul, Aït Alouan, and Arib, with twenty-one individuals in total identified from other, smaller groupings. Some of those approached for interviews declined the request.

13

GARAGE OR CARAVANSERAIL

Saharan Connectivity in Al-Khalīl, Northern Mali

Judith Scheele

The considerable investments that are necessary to begin the irrigation of the smallest plot of land, the cost of the development and the maintenance of intensive arboriculture in an extremely dry environment cannot be justified solely by their financial return nor even by general economy. Furthermore, we noticed very often that, for various reasons (political, military, demographic, and so on), oases decline long before they have finished paying back the initial capital outlay. We might thus be surprised by the optimism and the voluntarism of the founders of oases, or in other words by their naivety, if we only consider the economic benefit that they might hope for. Maybe there are rewards other than financial, other benefits, or maybe other obligations of a system within which the agricultural sector is only a necessary, albeit loss-making, part.

—Pascon, *La maison d'Iligh*

Al-Khalīl is a trading town in the northern Malian desert near the Algerian border that, as its inhabitants like to stress, is marked on no map, but is known to all.[1] Its location makes it a haven for smugglers and traders of all kinds, and it has therefore come to represent the rather harsh face of contemporary trans-Saharan exchanges: first and foremost, drug trafficking, but also arms dealing and people smuggling. Al-Khalīl's rise was rapid, carrying within it the promise of an equally rapid decline; its population is stereotypically cosmopolitan; its very survival is dependent on its connections with the outside, as it produces nothing but trades in "everything." It proclaims itself "stateless," but thrives because it is located in the interstices of regional states. It is organized along close-knit networks that stretch far beyond its geographical boundaries, but that nonetheless regulate social interaction and individual status within it. Its fame is legendary throughout northern Mali and southern Algeria, where members of trading families never tire of debating the moral quandaries it brings up, rejecting it while also intimately relying on the revenue it generates. At first sight, then, Al-Khalīl hardly brings to mind the well-known images of historic Saharan trading outposts: dunes, camels, and palm trees, Timbuktu or Ghadamès. However, as a Saharan town in the making, it might help us formulate questions about Saharan settlements more generally, questions that otherwise risk being overlooked due to the sedentary bias of much scholarship, which necessarily sees them as "finished products." Most important, the case of Al-Khalīl draws attention to the intrinsic dependency of settlement on movement and on outside connections, as hinted at by Paul Pascon in the epigraph, and to the effects such dependency might have on the internal organization of settlements.[2]

Ta'rīkh Al-Khalīl wa-sifāthu ("Of the History of Al-Khalīl and the Description Thereof")

Al-Khalīl is a burgeoning center of trade north of Tessalit, fewer than ten kilometers from the border with Algeria and its nearest town, Bordj Badji Mokhtar. Its scattered habitations—several hundred of them, with at times a score of inhabitants each, according to Khalīlī residents—stretch far into the surrounding plain that affords no pasture or shelter, but only constant sandstorms and stony wastes. There is no water, no paved road, no electricity. Its oldest permanent house was built in 1993; at that time, it served as a store for arms for the rebellion of the early 1990s.[3] Fifteen years later, Al-Khalīl has almost developed into a town, with shops, restaurants, and all necessary facilities. Its residents have built two mosques, a primary school is under construction, there is a health center and the remains of a gendarmerie post. Houses, however, are rare. Most people live in what they call *gawārij* (sing. *garāj*, an Arabized term from the French *garage*):[4] large courtyards capable of holding several trucks, enclosed by high concrete walls and protected by solid iron gates, with two or three rooms in a corner serving as a shop, storage place, kitchen, and shelter for the night. In the outskirts of Al-Khalīl, *kaynāt* (from French *coins*), or "corners," of future garages stake claims to further construction sites. Al-Khalīl, in other words, is booming. Yet everything that is consumed here has to be brought across from Algeria. Building materials are all imported, and unsuccessful sub-Saharan migrants provide much of the manual labor. Although, famously, *everything* can be bought or sold in Al-Khalīl, it is often difficult to find milk and bread; even water has to be purchased from an Algerian tank. Most inhabitants agree that the long windy days spent huddled near a wall with an empty stomach, chain-smoking, playing cards, and trying to find some tea to drink are best described—in Spanish-inflected Algerian Arabic—as utter *miseria.*

Most people thus try to cross into Algeria as often as possible, to have a proper meal and a bath—and, of course, to conduct "business." Al-Khalīl exists because of its close connection to Bordj Badji Mokhtar: it is primarily a trans-shipment port for smuggled goods of all kinds. Flour, pasta, and gasoline come down from Algeria; livestock and cigarettes come up from Mali, although for the latter, business has considerably slackened. Narcotics arrive from Mauritania via the western Sahara and travel around the southern tip of Algeria via Niger and Chad to Egypt, and thence to Israel and Europe. Chinese-made arms are unloaded in the large ports in the Gulf of Guinea and are traded throughout the area. Four-wheel-drive vehicles of dubious provenance are supplied with Mauritanian paperwork to avoid the costly customs clearance to which they would otherwise be subject.

Yet there is more to Al-Khalīl's success than mere geography: drivers smuggling gasoline often make considerable detours in order to stop there, for instance taking the long way around from Tamanrasset to Gao, rather than going straight across the border at Tin Zouaten or Timiaouine. They explain this by the better quality of the roads, but some less circumstantial factors might also be at play. Many smuggling networks have their "headquarters" in Al-Khalīl, and family members living in Al-Khalīl or Bordj Badji Mokhtar provide additional security. Al-Khalīl also offers crucial services such as car repairs, spare parts, currency exchange, paperwork, and credit facilities, as well as being a popular meeting point and hub of information exchange for traders.

Al-Khalīl's fortunes can only be understood in conjunction with those of Bordj Badji Mokhtar. Formerly a small military outpost staffed by disgruntled and lonely Algerian soldiers on punitive postings, who more or less successfully controlled (or partook in) the long-standing illegal trade across the border, Bordj Badji Mokhtar started booming with the establishment of refugee camps in the vicinity of the army post during the drought of the 1970s. This not only resulted in much embezzlement of humanitarian aid, fueling illegal trade, but also in the permanent settlement of Malian refugees in the town.[5] Many families who have by now returned to Mali left at least one member behind to look after real estate that they acquired there; all inhabitants of Al-Khalīl have at least some close connections, or even a secondary residence, in Bordj, not least because few women acquiesce to residing in Al-Khalīl. Further, the massive presence of the Algerian army—and, by all accounts, secret police—accounts for much of the business done there, in one way or another. Some branches of trafficking are said to be totally in the hands of the Algerian military, and men in Algerian uniforms shopping for cars, guns, cigarettes, and other things are a familiar sight in Al-Khalīl.

Al-Khalīl is linked in similar ways to Bani w-Iskut, the "Tuareg" (more properly, the Malian and Nigerien) quarter of the Algerian city of Adrar, almost 800 kilometers away and gateway to the Algerian north, and to the "Arab" quarter of the Malian city of Gao on the Niger bend, 700 kilometers in the other direction, on the way to the Malian south and the major ports of the Gulf of Guinea. As people are quick to point out, once you have visited any one of these places, you know them all: they only exist because of each other, they speak the same language and shelter the same people.

Despite the obvious importance of the state for the good functioning of Al-Khalīl—through direct involvement, economic policy, and the provision of infrastructure—the inhabitants of Al-Khalīl like to stress its "statelessness" and total independence. From the "white" Malian point of view, the absence of the state translates into the absence of "Bambara," here used as a shorthand for civil servants from the south. The primary school has no teacher because the person appointed was a Bambara who has been "on his way" for several years; the clinic has no doctor, for exactly the same reason; the gendarmerie is not staffed, "because they were all *sūwādīn* ['black' southerners] who got scared the day they woke up and noticed that we had stolen all their guns." The insistence on the total absence of the state does partly describe a reality, but seems so overdrawn as to warrant attention as a rhetorical device. Further, the state remains central to all assertions of independence: *kull garāj dawla wāhida* (every garage is a state in itself), people like to boast. Algerian soldiers are the stereotypical "other" and are described as "worse than dogs," and people laughingly claim to belong to the "People's Democratic Republic of Al-Khalīl," echoing the official title of Algeria. Past stints in prison are frequently evoked, and Al-Khalīl is described as their antithesis, as the only place "where men can be men." Yet manliness *à la Khalīl* requires guns, friends, and fast four-wheel-drive Toyotas, and thus considerable means. These are best acquired through "properly" illegal traffic: guns and drugs, in particular. This trafficking, everybody agrees, is organized not merely by state officials, but also just like a state, with "ministries," "delegates," "security services," strict discipline, and individual rather than family-based recruitment. Despite constant boasting of their exploits, bravery, and courage, most drivers are painfully aware of their dependency on the *patrons*—few among them own their cars—and the fact that they are risking their lives to make other people rich. But on the face of it, as repeated in many a boast, Al-Khalīl is the only place where men can be free, and Arabs "true Arabs"—through the absence of law and state officials, but also, perhaps, of mothers, wives, and table manners.

This further means that people have to rely on their own networks for protection and fair dealing. Although some collective rules exist in Al-Khalīl—everybody has to pay a nominal fee to the Tuareg "chief" of the area on first settlement, for instance—justice is brought about by appeal to one's friends and, notionally at least, won by those who can muster more guns (these can be hired on a weekly basis, "like a wedding dress") and region-wide support. References to moral standards and conflict resolution thus go beyond Al-Khalīl, and create group boundaries that are much tighter than the town itself, although extending over hundreds of kilometers. These networks are more than mere safety arrangements, but also structure trade: in exchange for free lodgings and security for themselves, their wares, and their means of transportation, and for his services as a local middleman, traders are expected to conclude all business in their host's *garāj* every time they come to Al-Khalīl. There is thus no "free" market in Al-Khalīl: all commercial transactions are conducted behind closed doors. More generally, communal interaction is reduced to a minimum; here, that involves the construction of mosques, representing in a sense the lowest common denominator of identity of its "Saharan" inhabitants. From the outside, though, even this last unifying factor is seen as mere pretense: Al-Khalīl, all my friends in Gao agreed, is a place beyond religion, where no law applies, and people do not even recognize each other as fellow human beings.

The fragmentation and reliance on far-flung networks are also strikingly obvious in the outward appearance of Al-Khalīl. Each *garāj* or cluster of garages constitutes an independent fortification. The town center is composed of a row of restaurants and hostels, or "ghettos," to use the local term, welcoming in turn Nigerians, Ghanaians, Cameroonians, and offering necessary services: phone calls, food, lodging, transportation. "We have people from everywhere here," Khalīlīs say proudly, "from Pakistan, Malaysia, China . . ." However, although many sub-Saharans seem to have more or less settled in Al-Khalīl, either out of desperation or to run services for their compatriots—services that here as elsewhere easily turn into lucrative businesses—they are not seen as part of local society, at least not by my smuggler hosts. The latter stress a very different kind of cosmopolitanism, that of "Saharans," that knits Mauritanians, western Saharans, Malians, and Arabs from Niger and Chad, all equipped with various nationalities and papers, into close networks. As stable as these networks might be at times, they are difficult to pin down: Al-Khalīl never looks the same two days in a row, as people come and go. Most people who live there have at least one secondary residence, preferably in Algeria, in Adrar or Tamanrasset, which are seen as safer and better equipped with the amenities of modern life. These secondary residences are generally maintained by one or several wives, or inhabited by other female members of the family. As much as Al-Khalīl is a place where "men can be men," it is certainly not a place where "women can be (pure) women," and indeed, few live there now, although their numbers are said to be growing. But although women are conspicuously absent from Al-Khalīl, they are indispensable to its functioning. They run the houses at either end of, and at intervals along, the smuggling trail; they hold family networks together; and they forge new alliances. Al-Khalīl thus cannot be understood in isolation, but only as part of a larger whole. This can be seen by tracing one such network and its various ramifications in Algeria and Mali.

Lakhdar and the Awlād Sīdī

During my stay in Al-Khalīl, I was hosted by Lakhdar,[6] who owns two garages in town and knows Al-Khalīl "better than he ought to for his salvation," as I was told in Gao. Lakhdar is in his late thirties; clad in a burnous, a leather jacket, and a dark indigo veil, he appears dodgy, but charming. According to his own friends, he is a "born crook" and a "compulsive liar"; his business is thriving. The first day I spent in his garage brought several well-fed and rosy-cheeked Algerians crossing over from Bordj with "good business" and a pronounced interest in such improbable items as the latest Mauritanian fashion in Moroccan upholstery for the wife back home. There were also a small, skinny Mauritanian, bent with age and moral doubt, who was waiting for the appointed time to truck some camels across the border, and meanwhile trying to find some food and to keep control over his teenage *hartānī* apprentice; a neighbor haggling over a secondhand satellite phone; and a group of rather nervous Arab youths whom I recognized from Gao, waving their AK-47s while looking for a spare tire. Although Lakhdar was rather displeased at my arrival and the questions I had come to ask, he soon—probably after having checked my position with his more powerful "friends"—took great pleasure in bringing a large number of *shifāt l-māfia* (mafia bosses, from the French *chef*) to his garage, telling me gleefully that they were all his friends, and that I should interview them right there and in his presence. These chiefs were all charming and talkative; some wanted to convert me to Islam; and all left me their mobile and satellite phone numbers, saying that I should meet their wives once I arrived in Adrar or Tamanrasset. One cooked us dinner, and then impersonated a hyena as a concluding practical joke—all, in other words, thought that I was absolutely hilarious, and totally at their mercy.

Lakhdar's life story is one of a radical break with his past and home country. He left Mauritania to trade in Mali, and then, on his return, he was imprisoned—"just because I had done a bit of business," he said. After some time in prison during which he was regularly beaten and deprived of sleep, food, and human company, he was set free on condition that he work for "them" (i.e., the Mauritanian secret police). This consummated his break with Mauritanian society at large, and he disappeared as fast as he could to Al-Khalīl, swearing never again to set foot in his own country.[7] He has two wives, one Malian Arab who lives in Adrar, and one Targuiya who lives in Tamanrasset. The latter at first wanted to come and live with him in Al-Khalīl, but there was no way he could have ever accepted this: Al-Khalīl is no place for women, and Lakhdar would never tolerate any meddling in his affairs.

I had been put under Lakhdar's care by our mutual friend and my host in Gao, Lalla. Lalla is now in her early forties, and actively runs her family's affairs in Gao and beyond. Lakhdar hosts her family members when they pass through Al-Khalīl, and he in turn frequently stays at their homes when "in town," either in Algeria or Mali. Accompanied by his two wives, Lalla's father, Sīdī, a scholar of renown, had migrated before independence from his native Mauritania to the Niger bend, where he had been closely linked to a leading *sharīfian* family in Bourem. This family in turn had intermarried with Algerian traders, a connection that proved vital when, in the 1990s, the whole family decided to flee to Algeria. Selling their remaining livestock, they bought a house in Bordj Badji Mokhtar, and started to invest in "business." In 2004, they moved to Gao, leaving a sister behind in Bordj to look after the house and provide beds and dinners to family members traveling through. The family's international connections go back much further, however: Lalla's eldest sister lives in Nouakchott, where she was married to a Mauritanian cousin, and now trades in women's clothes and paraphernalia. Her second-oldest sister has lived in Adrar since the 1970s; she moved there with her husband after having spent several years in the Hijaz. She is well known and widely respected by Malian residents in Adrar, where she deals in women's clothing, and looks after cousins and nephews traveling through from Al-Khalīl. All other sisters, married or not, cluster in the family compounds in Gao, collectively look after a large number of small children, and provide "home" for the family's men on their brief sojourns back in town.

Lalla's eldest brother is chronically ill, and has devoted his life to religious duties and scholarship. The second-oldest brother owns a truck and engages in more or less legal trade—salt from the mines of Tawdeni, pasta, semolina, and flour—or lucrative one-time business opportunities in Burkina Faso, Niger, or Al-Khalīl.[8] His schedule is clearly determined by "deals," and might change from one day to the next; indeed, his truck never seems to be where it is supposed to be, and he spends most of his time hunting it down via his satellite phone. The family also owns a four-by-four that seems to be equally elusive. Various other brothers engage in various other trading ventures of the semi-legal kind, but their exact nature remained obscure to me.

A close friend of the family, Al-Shaykh, who is also from the vicinity of Bourem, from a "good" religious family, and who is married in Adrar but seems to spend more time with Lalla's family than in his own house, owns two trucks that travel between Adrar and Al-Khalīl, and sometimes between Adrar and Gao. These trucks mainly transport common staples—pasta, flour, and semolina—and always travel via Lakhdar's garage. Al-Shaykh also owns a four-by-four in Adrar, and Lalla described him as "wealthy." He is also a member of the *jamā'āt al-tablīgh* and spends his free time preaching at meetings throughout northern Mali and in Bamako.[9] The young men of the family do not trade on their own account, but work as drivers for other traders. One of Lalla's nephews drives Al-Shaykh's truck; another of her nephews, who was brought up in Bani w-Iskut, smuggles gasoline for an unnamed Algerian *patron* based in Al-Khalīl. Lalla's younger brother, who is in his mid-twenties, shuttles smuggled cigarettes between Al-Khalīl and Adrar. His *patron* lives in Bordj Badji Mokhtar, owns several four-by-fours, and employs roughly a dozen young drivers, all Arabs or Tuareg from northern Mali. When he was just sixteen, this brother was arrested for smuggling and spent some time in prison in Adrar. He was released after the family pulled all the strings available to them in Algeria, and presented a fake birth certificate that claimed that he was fourteen and thus could not be tried in a criminal court. He picked up his job as a cigarette smuggler the next day. In 2008, he was arrested again, charged with drug smuggling, and his family is now despairing of ever seeing him again.

Although Lakhdar takes great care to emphasize his independence and his radical break with his family and country, traders in Al-Khalīl can only function by becoming part of larger networks. These tend to be based on family ties alongside an array of other possible connections. Thus, Lalla's family's network includes uncles, nephews, cousins, and good family friends, such as Lakhdar and Al-Shaykh, one of them Mauritanian "just like us" and another from Bourem and of high religious status, "just like us," too. In everyday interaction, these links imply total solidarity and mutual help, unquestioning hospitality, and some grumbling and wrangling, much as family connections usually do, although Lalla criticizes Lakhdar much more freely in public than she would her own younger brothers. Further, despite Lakhdar's insistence on his total independence and disgust with the state, Khalīlīs all aspire to own at least one house in a more "civilized" place, such as Adrar or Tamanrasset, which many see as a precondition for marriage. Although there are no women in Al-Khalīl, and the young men busy boasting around campfires indeed pretend that they could do without them altogether, women are pivotal for the maintenance of these relations, because they provide homes without which hospitality would be meaningless and strengthen ties through mutual obligation and, at times, marriage, in addition to running their own independent businesses. The networks cannot be described as merely commercial; rather, they touch on most aspects of life and are primarily talked about as social networks, although their main purpose might be economic. As such, they can be explained in a whole variety of ways, with little distinction made between historic and putative genealogical connections and more recent ties. The family's Mauritanian origin can be drawn upon as much as their more recent moves, and past connections with Algerian traders, based on clientship and hospitality rather than kinship, are vital for their success.[10] Finally, these larger networks include legal trade and pasta smuggling as much as gasoline and cigarette dealing. Indeed, traders perceive little distinction between these various kinds of business and, if they are free to do so, might switch from one to the other. In everyday conversation, the term *al-frūd* (from the French *fraude*) is used, even by children, to designate indiscriminately all kinds of Saharan trade. If distinctions are drawn, they are not phrased in terms of state law, but rather in terms of Islamic principles, opposing *frūd al-halāl* (licit trafficking) to *frūd al-harām* (illicit trafficking), with the latter term almost uniquely reserved for trade in narcotics.

Lies, Prayer, and Immorality

Distinctions, then, are drawn not in terms of state law, but in terms of Islamic morality. Attempts to morally comprehend and classify Al-Khalīl inform many conversations about it, ultimately, it seems, with the intention to "civilize" or at least "socialize" it and—albeit imperfectly—to integrate it into the moral transnational universe reaching from Gao to Bani w-Iskut. This conceptual socialization of Al-Khalīl seems as central to the making of place as the material aspects so far described. It is, however, far from easy: for most women, any kind of drug smuggling is clearly beyond the pale, to the point where it becomes an almost magical explanatory trope for moral transgression. Bouts of violence and immorality can thus be "explained" by the fact that those responsible are "men corrupted by drug dealing." Living in places like Al-Khalīl makes it impossible to behave like a true Muslim, if only from a practical point of view. It is almost like living outside of Muslim society altogether. Although there are mosques in Al-Khalīl, most people do not go to pray; nobody in Al-Khalīl can lead a proper family life, since there are no families but only women of doubtful virtue. It is a place built on lies, to the point where truth withers on the speaker's tongue before it can pass his lips; not only do Khalīlīs lie to outsiders, but also to their own families, thus clearly not recognizing any social ties at all. Further, drugs (*mukhaddirāt*) are *harām*, and any contact with them is polluting. This means that money made with drugs can never be blessed (*mubārak*), but is barren (*māhil*). Drug traders grow thin with their wealth; any investment made with drug money will necessarily fail; and marriages contracted with it will be barren. Thus, no self-respecting girl should ever marry a drug trader, as she would be knowingly throwing her virginity away for "fake" bride-wealth, like a prostitute.[11] The individual recruitment that is characteristic of the "mafia" is another bone of contention, as it channels unprecedented amounts of wealth along new social networks that people enter without reference to former social ties, and that thereby potentially dismantle preexisting networks and undermine accepted social norms. Tellingly, the rapid accumulation of wealth by people of a formerly lesser status is directly blamed on the drug trade, whether or not there is any evidence to justify such a claim, while also being associated with intracommunal violence, moral failure, and religious transgression—in short, with asocial behavior (see also Scheele 2009).

At the same time, successful *ashāb al-frūd* (smugglers) are keen to legitimize their business and invest in legal or at least morally acceptable trade if they possibly can, even if they have to expend considerable time and resources to do so. Furthermore, debates over the religious implications of drug dealing are vivid, and often less clear-cut than one might think. Folk wisdom easily points to the relevant suras (chapters) of the Qur'an that are known to protect smugglers. Amulets are readily provided for them, for prices that acknowledge their special status, by known specialists in Bani w-Iskut who seem to have fewer qualms about the barrenness of drug money. One intense debate was prompted by my astonishment and mirth as I saw Lakhdar trundle off to the mosque in Adrar in the company of Al-Shaykh, with a pious face, although I had never seen him pray in Al-Khalīl. Al-Shaykh is a relatively wealthy man and conducts much trade with Al-Khalīl, so Lakhdar's evident desire to accommodate him could easily be attributed to this, as well as showing his own truly "cosmopolitan" ability to adapt to circumstances. Yet although Lalla initially agreed with me that Lakhdar was probably beyond saving, and that it might be an outrage to God to pray while in the polluted state of living as a notorious drug dealer, Al-Shaykh later rejected this, adopting a different logic: drugs are not polluting as such, he said, but are criminal because they are destructive to other people. Drug smuggling is thus a crime against humanity, whereas not praying is a crime against God, and thus infinitely worse: "You open two different accounts, and beware never to mix human concerns with godly ones, or else think they are equal in value." Al-Shaykh, known for his piety, generosity, and intense activity as an Islamic preacher, was clearly familiar with this argument—indeed, his own business and acquaintances might at times throw some suspicion on the provenance of his charitable funds. Meanwhile, Lakhdar just sat and smirked: as a wealthy businessman, he finds that people tend to insist on trying to "civilize" him and to include him in "proper," law-bound society, as long as he acknowledges its norms when he is in town. Lakhdar represents the inherent paradox of Al-Khalīl: although, especially for women of good society in Gao, it has come to be seen as a place of immorality, it is central to their own economic survival, independence, morality, and indeed their ability to live up to locally perceived "Arab" standards of relative female reclusion and inactivity. In much the same way, it allows young men to realize at least partially their own chivalrous ideal of true Arabness, despite their painful awareness that even with their loudly proclaimed freedom and autonomy, they are but pawns in a larger game.

Al-Khalīl and Saharan Connectivity

Al-Khalīl obviously represents a special case, less because of its apparent modernity than because those who live there or pass through do not describe it as a civilized place, but rather as an outpost in the *bādiya* (the desert, or "wilderness") that is not fit for complete human life, but that only lends itself to immoral dealings and asocial activity. However, this is strangely reminiscent of memories of the newly established trading posts in the Sahel as recalled by elderly southern Algerian traders.[12] Their stories are also couched in terms of a civilizing mission to the *bilād al-sūdān,* the stereotypical "country of blacks," where they "built the first house" or "introduced tea" or "religion and Arabic."[13] Life there was "sweet," they recall, as women were "cheap and accessible," wealth was to be had for the asking, and pasture abundant. Even today, the fear of losing husbands or fathers to the tempting immorality of the Sudan pervades all female accounts of past trading greatness. We might thus be dealing here with a variation on a familiar trope, encompassing notions of the inherent moral danger of traveling, and legends of the civilizing missions of first settlers, turning *bādiya* into *qariya,* wilderness into village. Moreover, most people seem to think that Al-Khalīl's inherent immorality is only transient; they point to the growing number of women who have been moving there, who might eventually—despite their own "loose morals"—succeed in civilizing it.

Although that idea is in the realm of speculation, other aspects of Al-Khalīl might be more directly relevant to the study of other Saharan settlements: for instance, its rapid growth that seems to carry the promise of an equally rapid decline. The history of the Sahara indeed reads like an endless succession of the rise and decline of certain trading centers; early travel accounts never quite match up in their appreciation of the importance of various markets (Mauny 1961),[14] and French archival records are littered with ruins and misery. At times, we can guess at shifts in trade routes that took place within living memory, sometimes more than once, which point to their inherent flexibility and dependence on sociopolitical as well as geographical factors.[15] Al-Khalīl has nothing to warrant settlement except its situation with respect to roads and, most important, areas of political and economic influence. Much of its current success is due to its location at the meeting point of two different economic and legal regimes—one relatively wealthy, one poor—and its consequent ability to act as a trans-shipment point. This has allowed it to develop the necessary infrastructure to facilitate unofficial trading, and, as noted above, traders now undertake considerable detours in order to go through Al-Khalīl. This was also the case with successful historic Saharan trading posts: writing on nineteenth-century Ghadamès, Haarmann (1998: 28) notes that traders from Lake Chad and Bornu to Timbuktu transited at times vie Ghadamès and the Touat in order to benefit from the commercial services and facilities offered there, thus crossing the Sahara twice for no obvious geographic reason.[16] Mobility and movement were prior to place, making the latter inherently fragile. While Pascon (in the epigraph above) notes the need for outside investment in the initial establishment of Saharan irrigation systems, the investment in Al-Khalīl—made possible by modern technology—is total and constant, as Al-Khalīl could not survive a single day without outside input. This insight might enable us to better understand established Saharan markets and their contemporary socioeconomic quandaries (see, e.g., Pliez 2003; Bisson 2003; Bensaād 2005a).

This intrinsic dependency on the outside seems to determine Al-Khalīl's internal organization and its physical appearance. It is tempting to describe the omnipresent *gawārij* as a modern-day *fanādiq* (pl. of *funduq*: inn, *caravanserail*), fulfilling similar functions: storage, lodging, trade, organization of transportation, communication, protection, and, at times, keeping strangers under lock and key.[17] Much as in accounts of historic Saharan trans-shipment posts,[18] there is no open market in Al-Khalīl: all deals are conducted behind closed doors, as part of larger preexisting networks. The layout of the "town center," occupied by international restaurants and "ghettos" for sub-Saharan nationals, points toward travel, movement, and far-reaching connections; the same can be said for the garages, each of which, to the well-informed eye, represents a certain trading and family network, and stands for particular neighborhoods or even houses in Gao, Timbuktu, Bordj Badji Mokhtar, Tamanrasset, and Adrar. One might be reminded of historic French descriptions of Akabli in the Algerian Tidikelt:

> Akabli is composed of small villages, constructed at different times by natives from the most diverse backgrounds, settled there by the hazards of Saharan life. This is why next to the Foulanes from Sudan we find some Oulad Zenani; next to the Kunta from the Azawad some Oulad Sidi Mohammed who say they are descendants of the Ansar [companions of the Prophet] of Medina. All these families live next to each other without mixing too much and keeping their traditions and religious attachments. They each have their own little *qsar* [fortified residence].[19]

Although the clear "ethnic" distinctions set out here are certainly not valid for Al-Khalīl, and might indeed never have been of much heuristic value for Akabli either, this image of a set of small groups that coexist alongside each other, but whose closest connections are not to be found locally but hundreds of kilometers away, in turn determining their local status, position, and alliances, sounds familiar.

Other apparent parallels might be more misleading. I have already mentioned the ambivalent but close relationship of Al-Khalīl with the idea and fact of the state. Financial arrangements provide a similar conundrum: although in Al-Khalīl everybody constantly talks about money, there is little of it around. Values are described in euros or, more frequently, dollars, but the only money that I ever saw changing hands—this might of course be due to secrecy and care, or blindness on my part—was Algerian dinars in small-denomination banknotes, to buy food and other daily essentials. As perhaps in the past, most transactions seem to be based on trust, exchanges for goods to be delivered later or elsewhere, with family connections serving as an ultimate (if not always totally effective) guarantee: "we all know where everybody else's family lives, so there is no cheating."[20] Indeed, it seems doubtful that there is enough cash in the area to account for the value of the goods going through it, and regional currencies are totally disregarded. Albeit on a smaller scale, a similar paradox long puzzled French colonial observers in the "markets" of the Algerian south, which, despite strong local preoccupations with cash and currencies, suffered from a constant shortage of coin, and whatever did circulate was of foreign mint.[21] Yet these apparent parallels might point toward change rather than continuity. Although scholars are now correcting an erroneous emphasis on *trans*-Saharan rather than (intra-)Saharan trade in historical research (E. A. McDougall 2005a), the growing importance of narcotics does indeed mean that much initiative and freedom of action have been taken out of the hands of Saharan traders, adding to the perceived asociality of such enterprises and to the local absence of "real" money. Nonetheless, one should note that Khalīlīs themselves like to stress continuity over change and seek out historic parallels, avoiding a rhetoric of total rupture partly, it seems, as an aspect of attempts to socialize Al-Khalīl within known frameworks of moral propriety or masculinist heroism. This is perhaps why I saw so much boasting and long debates about Islam with notorious *ashāb al-frūd* who, while sitting on boxes of smuggled cigarettes, were keen to prove their religious ancestry and their families' centuries-long involvement in the "civilization" and "Islamization" of the *bilād al-sūdān*.

Al-Khalīl is a cosmopolitan place where solidarities are transregional rather than local, and where identity, power, and movement are closely interlinked. Place here exists as the result of permanent movement: the constant arrival and departure of trucks full of flour and pasta; four-by-fours loaded with gasoline, cigarettes, or narcotics; small cars shuffling across the border; illegal shepherds driving illegal sheep to Algerian markets; old men with loaded donkeys coming back from Bordj Badji Mokhtar; and gossip and satellite phone signals traveling both north and south. It is a place that produces nothing, but where everything can be procured, if you have the necessary connections. It is a place where without such connections, you simply cannot survive; a place that only makes sense through its relationship to other places, while also helping to maintain them; a place that scorns "the state," but only survives through its proximity to it. It is a legend and a moral outrage as well as a rather unpleasant reality. All these characteristics are closely connected to the peculiar historical, political, economic, and geographical context that gave rise to Al-Khalīl, yet they might also help us to think more insightfully about Saharan settlement more generally. Important points in this respect are the extreme flexibility of Saharan exchange and its changeability over time, which are so clearly reflected in Al-Khalīl's rapid rise to fame and its reliance on outside connections. Settlements, in such cases, might be rather "nomadic"; connections and movement might be logically and even chronologically prior to place, to the point where they seem to provide the key to understanding apparently unrelated features such as spatial layout, architecture, and internal social organization and hierarchy. While this is obvious for Al-Khalīl, it remains to be seen how far it might also apply to other Saharan places, beyond the rapid survey of superficial parallels suggested above. In any case, if we trust the judgment of Al-Khalīl's inhabitants, Al-Khalīl is "but the child" of Gao, Timbuktu, and Kidal. We should look out, then, for family resemblances tempered by generational differences—or, indeed, for generational differences tempered by family resemblances.

NOTES

1. Even the name of Al-Khalīl is open to some debate: local Tamasheq-speakers insist that it is rightly called In Khalīl (the place of Khalīl, in Tamasheq); Arabic-speakers refer to it either as Ayn Khalīl (the spring of Khalīl, in Arabic) or simply as Al-Khalīl or Khalīl. Such debates indirectly refer to conflicts over who had first access to the site and, implicitly, ultimate sovereignty. I will use Al-Khalīl throughout this chapter.

2. Research for this chapter was carried out during a Fellowship by Examination at Magdalen College, Oxford; additional funding for fieldwork undertaken in 2007 and 2008 was provided by the British Academy (grant no. SG-47632). I would like to thank Morgan Clarke and all participants at the September 2008 conference for their very helpful comments and criticisms. Even more is owed to my Malian, Algerian, and Khalīlī hosts.

3. Since national independence in 1960, northern Mali has been shaken by a series of droughts and rebellions, mainly turning on questions of regional and local sovereignty, and

the role of and access to the state. On the 1990s, see Maiga (1997), Klute (2001), Grémont et al. (2004), and Lecocq (2010).

4. Most of my fieldwork was conducted among Arabic-speakers, and Arabic has become the lingua franca for most traders in the region; there might therefore be a linguistic bias toward Arabic expression in this chapter.

5. On the drought and some of its immediate economic, social, and political consequences, see Comité d'Information du Sahel (1975), Ag Foni (1979), Ould Sidi (1979), and Boilley (1999).

6. All names have been changed.

7. This, of course, does not necessarily mean that he refused to work for the Mauritanian secret police, as many smugglers probably do. By all accounts, Al-Khalīl is "infested," especially with Algerian secret police. Whether these are cases of officers pretending to be traders in order to obtain information or to trade, or traders pretending to be spies in order to trade more easily, is difficult to tell, and indeed matters little. With the political changes in Mauritania since 2008, Lakhdar has sold his *garāj* to Lalla's brother and is now by all accounts working for the government.

8. Tawdeni is situated several hundred kilometers north of Timbuktu and has played a crucial part in trade in and through that city (see, e.g., Clauzel 1960a; Saad 1983; and the large number of commercial documents kept at the Centre Ahmed Baba in Timbuktu). Its salt is still preferred by many people in the north, and trade, albeit on a much smaller scale and mostly by truck rather than camel, continues, especially at times when other kinds of business are slack.

9. The *jamā'āt al-tablīgh* is an association of Muslim preachers, originally founded in South Asia in the 1920s. It is very popular throughout Mali, and Pakistani delegates from the movement have been a frequent sight in Kidal and its surroundings, where they have close connections with several leading local families (see also Lecocq and Schrijver 2007). On the *jamā'āt al-tablīgh* more generally, see Masud (2000); for a case study in the Gambia, see Janson (2005).

10. Indeed, where many Tuareg blame their own inborn "lack of commercial instinct" for the Arabs' relatively greater success in trade, connections with large and influential Algerian families, more frequently established by Arabic-speakers, seem to provide a more plausible explanation.

11. Of course some women do marry drug smugglers, but such notions further their social isolation and "incompleteness."

12. This paragraph is based on interviews conducted with southern Algerian trading families in Adrar, Aoulef, and Tit in 2007 and 2008.

13. The "introduction of tea to the Sudan" is a familiar trope with which merchant families throughout the Sahara indicate their prominence; see Lydon (2009: 24) and Leriche (1953). "Arabic" and "Islam" had of course been introduced to the area centuries before then; see Norris (1986, 1990).

14. The various early Arabic accounts compiled and translated in Levtzion and Hopkins (1981) abound in descriptions of abandoned towns. Thus, for instance, al-Idrīsī, writes in the twelfth century: "Eight stages north of the location of the Saghwa tribe is a ruined town called Nabranta. In the past it was one of the famous cities, but according to what is related, sand overwhelmed its dwellings until these fell into ruins, and covered its waters until these dried up. Its population diminished and at the present time only their

remnants live there, clinging on to the remaining ruined homes out of affection for their native place. . . . South of it [Santariyya] is a town called Shabrû, now in ruins, but which was in the past most populous. Its buildings have crumbled, the waters dried up, the animals fled and its landmarks have become unrecognizable. Other than a sterile remnant of palm-groves, only decaying ruins and blurred traces remain" (Levtzion and Hopkins 1981: 120, 125).

15. See, for example, Dinaux's 1905 report on southern Algeria, the Adagh, and the Aïr in the Centre des Archives d'Outre Mer, Aix-en-Provence, France: Archives du gouvernement général de l'Algérie (hereafter, FR/CAOM/AGGA), 22H68; and the large documentation on shifts in trade routes and French attempts to influence them (FR/CAOM/AGGA, 22H26, 22H45, and 24H53); and compare to Carette (1844, 1848).

16. In the very different context of Indian Ocean trade, Chaudhuri (1985) similarly observes that the preference for certain trading outposts cannot merely be explained by their location, but rather by the various services they offer to traders.

17. For a detailed account of the history of *fanādiq* and related institutions, see Constable (2003).

18. See, e.g., French descriptions of In Salah (Annual reports, Annexe du Tidikelt, 1908 and 1911, FR/CAOM/AGGA, 23H10; Note on the Tidikelt by Simon, 20 June 1900, 22H50), Timimoun (Report on Saharan trade by Colonieu, n.d., 22H26), and Aoulef ("Aoulef" by Chardenet, n.d. [early 1900s], 22H50); and most famously, Caillié's (1830) disappointment at first sight of the apparent poverty of the Timbuktu market.

19. Akabli by the head of the annex of In Salah, Captain Chardenet, n.d. (early 1900s), FR/CAOM/AGGA, 22H50.

20. The reliance on such guarantees and the frustration to which this might lead are familiar to anyone who has perused Saharan commercial correspondence, such as the letters held at the Centre Ahmed Baba in Timbuktu. For a summary of the various methods of conducting business without money in nineteenth-century Mauritania and Morocco, see Lydon (2008).

21. On the chronic shortage of cash, see the Annual Reports of the Tidikelt, FR/CAOM/AGGA, 23H10; for the abundance of currencies used, see Chentouf (1984) and the French colonial records in FR/CAOM/AGGA, 22H50. That cash values were nonetheless used for reference is proven by the frequency with which local legal documents mention currencies; see Scheele (2010).

MOVEMENTS OF PEOPLE AND GOODS

Local Impacts and Dynamics of Migration to and through the Central Sahara

Julien Brachet

The central Sahara, an area long characterized by mobility, has experienced large-scale migration since the beginning of the 1990s. Despite the many obstacles to movement in this region—effects of the malfunctioning government of Niger, general insecurity, and the tightening of North African migration policies—several thousand sub-Saharan African migrants travel each year to North Africa via Agadez in northern Niger. Although these migrations have, since the late 1990s, become an important issue in relations between sub-Saharan, North African, and European countries, they are anything but a new phenomenon: citizens of what are now the countries of the Sahel have been in the habit of taking up seasonal employment in Algeria since the 1950s. Yet in the early 2000s, the focus of the media and of European and African governments on migrants traveling to Europe has meant that virtually all journeys undertaken by sub-Saharans in the Sahara are misinterpreted as intercontinental economic migrations. This particular emphasis on transit migration to Europe, endorsed by much academic writing, feeds an unfounded fear of invasion in the countries north of the Mediterranean, while obscuring the diversity and flexibility of contemporary Saharan mobilities and their local impacts. In order to better understand the roles of and relations between the different actors, we need to analyze the history and the broad organizational features of this migration system, with particular attention paid to the ways in which the transporting of people toward and through the central Sahara is linked to the movement of goods, especially in northern Niger, hence illuminating the local impacts and dynamics of regional and transnational migrations.[1]

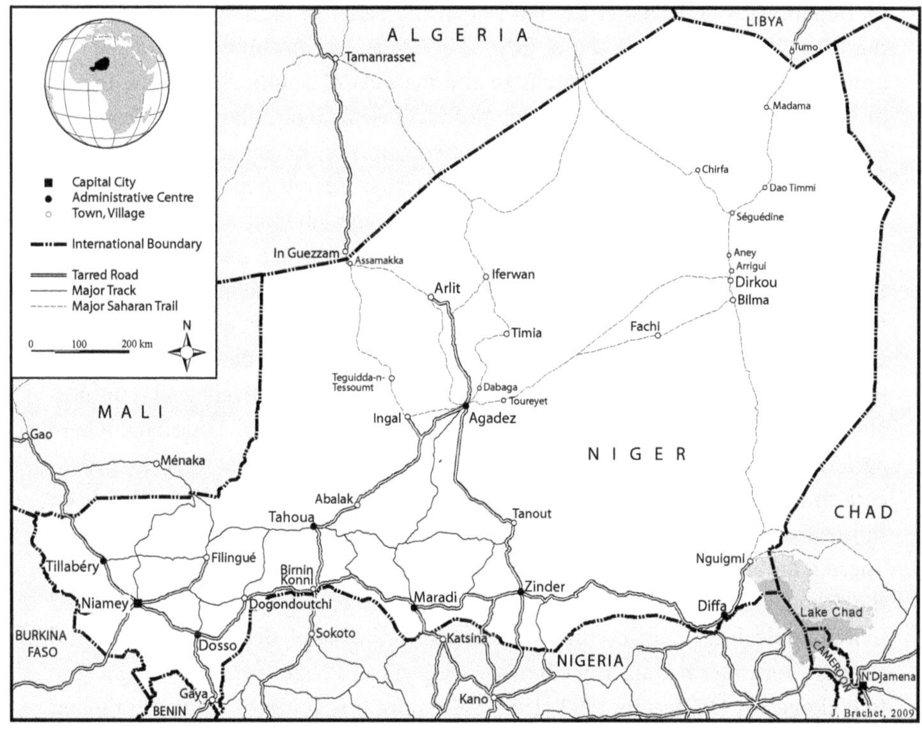

Map 14.1. Main roads in Niger. J. Brachet 2009

The Development of Migration in the Central Sahara: Tuareg and Other Travelers

With Algerian independence in 1962 and the sudden prosperity of Libya due to the discovery and subsequent exploitation of its oil reserves beginning in 1961, the governments of both countries were keen to develop the Saharan regions of their national territories. The resulting large-scale construction and development projects required a large, unskilled labor force that could not be supplied locally, in Algeria because of the migration of Saharan population groups to the north and to Tunisia, and in Libya because of the already small and scattered population.

Until the end of the 1960s, camel caravans linked the Tuareg populations of southern Algeria to those of northern and central Niger (Bourgeot 1994a; Hama 1967).[2] Moving southward, the Kel Ahaggar and Kel Ajjer from the regions of Tamanrasset and Djanet carried salt to the Sahel in exchange for millet; in the other direction, the Kel Aïr from the Agadez region moved from the Aïr mountains and surrounding areas to the markets of southern Algeria, to sell or to exchange livestock for various products (tea, sugar, blankets). From the early 1960s on, however, the gradual monetization of the Saharan economy led to a growing need for cash, and young Nigerien Tuareg began to accompany northbound caravans in search of temporary wage labor in southern Algeria. The Algerian government's agrarian reform program, which had various phases from 1963 through the early 1970s, created a considerable demand for labor in the agricultural and pastoral sectors. Many Nigerien Tuareg, especially the Kel Owey, horticultural experts of the Aïr, responded to this demand, taking up employment in a trade that they knew well and that was relatively well remunerated in Algeria. Some made it as far as In Salah, Ouargla, or Ghardaïa, where agricultural labor was equally well paid; others aimed for the various hydrocarbon installations, or Reggane and In Ekker where unskilled labor had been in great demand since the opening of French nuclear bases in the late 1950s.[3] These temporary migrations involved relatively few people before the onset of the drought of 1969–1973, a period of climatic and ecological crisis that resulted in a rapid decline of agricultural production in the Sahel, decimating herds and severely limiting caravan traffic between Algeria and Niger before putting a stop to it altogether (E. Bernus 1993 [1981]; Grémont this volume). The pastoral and agricultural economy of the entire Sahelian region was severely hit, and many Tuareg pastoralists, deprived of the most basic means of subsistence, went to Algeria looking for work. Various factors facilitated this movement: established practices of mobility, long-standing connections across the central Sahara dating from the era of caravan trade, and the widespread intelligibility of regional dialects of their shared language (Tamasheq).

With the seizure of power by Muammar Qaddafi in 1969, Libya also became a popular destination for young Tuareg susceptible to the appeal of the revolutionary leader's rhetoric of Saharan regional unity. This ideological attraction, which became particularly salient during the political crises and rebellions of the 1980s and 1990s in Niger, was backed by the economic pull factor of Libya's oil-generated prosperity. From the early 1970s, "a strong Libyan demand for labour, as well as for meat on the hoof, can be perceived. . . . In many cases, the drovers of livestock [found] employment in the oasis and administrative centre of Sebha, and only return[ed] to Niger several months later" (E. Bernus 1993 [1981]: 248). Those who left their home communities to spend time in the Maghreb or in large West African cities became known as *ishumar.*[4] This term was initially positive, implying access to the modern consumer goods with which these emigrant laborers returned home. But it quickly took on a negative meaning, connoting the low esteem in which *ishumar* were held by the receiving society (E. Bernus 1999), which treated them as poor refugees, forced to leave their home countries by drought and political crises.[5] This public image of Tuareg migrants in the Maghreb was perpetuated and reinforced by the drought of the early 1980s and the consequently greater spread of migratory movements.

In 1985, the government of Niger opened a consulate in Tamanrasset to facilitate the administrative regularization of its nationals in Algeria and "for obvious political reasons (the surveillance of Nigerien Tuareg resident in Algeria)" (Grégoire 1999: 216). Later, the rebellion of the early 1990s forced many Tuareg to seek refuge in the Algerian and Libyan Sahara, "where most of them settled in camps near the border, or on the outskirts of the main cities" (Pliez 2004b: 151). These migrations are still experienced and perceived by some as forced and marginalizing, and are sometimes linked to political exile.[6] Yet at the same time, many Tuareg less concerned with the rebellion quite simply went north to find work, like Aboussaghid, an *ashamor* from the oasis of Timia in the Aïr mountains, who traveled first to Algeria and then to Libya in the 1990s. Aboussaghid was nineteen years old when, in 1993, in the middle of the rebellion that troubled northern Niger, he decided to go to Algeria to work: "I paid for [a ride on] the truck of the [Timia] cooperative as far as Arlit. In Arlit, there were thirty-five of us. We each paid 20,000 CFA francs to go to Djanet [on top of goods loaded in the back of a pickup truck]." He spent a year working as a gardener. When he returned to Timia, he had 250,000 CFA francs,[7] but after six months, he had spent all his money. He set out again, this time to Libya:

> I worked in Sebha for a year and a half. When you get to Sebha, if you don't know the town, there are friends there, friends from Timia who are already there. . . . you go with them, this is how you find work. . . . But Libya isn't easy. There are policemen who come sometimes, there are many problems . . . but if you speak Arabic you're fine. I speak Arabic. The police sell Libyan identity cards for 50,000 CFA francs. If you speak their language, you're OK, you can chat with them. But if you only speak Tamasheq, they'll make you suffer. . . . After eighteen months in Sebha I went to Tripoli.

Travel on Libyan roads is subject to frequent police checks. In order to avoid being arrested and imprisoned, Aboussaghid explains, it is necessary to speak Libyan Arabic and to have a Libyan identity card. But that is not all: migrants also need Nigerien paperwork if they want to succeed:

> I spent two years in Tripoli, two years without going back to Timia. . . . I was working in gardens. . . . Then, the money you've earned, you change it to get CFA francs . . . you can change it at our embassy . . . but to do so you need an

> identity card from Niger. If you show your card from Niger, they'll say: OK, it's for Niger. You have to be very clever to come and work like this. If you leave Niger to come looking for money you have to be smart. . . . Before, in Niger, there were many gardens, but today there's nothing . . . and the rebellion hasn't changed anything, nothing at all . . . except for those who've been taken into the army.[8] If I can get work in Timia, I'll stay for good, there are no problems in the village. But if I can't find work, I'll leave again. If you stay here, if you don't work, that's bad. . . . If I can't get work I'll go back to Libya. . . . You have to work, it doesn't matter where, you have to look for work. If I leave again, my wife will go back to her family. . . . I'll send her money until I can come back. The *ishumar* will go back into exile, to Djanet, to Ghat. . . . You can't just stay like this and do nothing. You have to work.[9]

In a few decades, temporary labor migration to Algeria and Libya has become an integral part of life for many Tuareg in Niger, both urban and rural. Emmanuel Grégoire (1999: 227) estimates that, in the 1990s, half of all migrants from Niger to Libya were Tuareg, while Nigeriens accounted for half of all sub-Saharans who entered Libya from Niger. Aboussaghid's account equally illustrates the various ways in which state officials are involved in the Saharan migration system. The Libyan police control, tax, arrest, and sometimes deport migrants, more or less at random; at the same time, individual officers sell identity papers to the migrants. Nigerien diplomats exchange Libyan dinars (nonconvertible outside the country) for West African currency. State officials thereby publicly blur the boundaries between the legal and the illegal, and they help to maintain extralegal practices of migration.

Like the Tuareg, since the 1960s young Tubu and Kanuri from the Kawar and Djado regions of northeastern Niger have traveled to the Fezzan in southwest Libya, where they settled in easily, helped by the Libyan Tubu community and long-standing commercial links between the two areas (Biarnes 1982; Clanet 1981; Kollo 1989). In the 1960s, only a few other Nigerien nationals, especially members of the Hausa and Beri-Beri communities from southern Niger, went to Algeria and Libya on a regular basis, mainly during the dry season, a slack period in the agricultural calendar of the Sahel. Although travel to Algeria was easier at that time, many migrants preferred to go to Libya, where work was better paid and where, until 1971, no entry restrictions applied to holders of Nigerien identity cards. Since October 1971, all migrants traveling to Libya have been nominally obliged to present various documents (residency and work permits, vaccination booklet, passport, proof of nationality) in an attempt by the Libyan authorities to control the flow of immigration from Niger. This policy is difficult to apply, however, and has had little effect on the ground. Well-organized private transportation networks take people across the border illegally; meanwhile, in Agadez, "the acquisition of official documents [has] translated into a market in bribery" (Adamou 1979: 173).

During the period of drought that devastated the Sahel between 1969 and 1973, migrants from various West African countries made their first appearance in Agadez, on their way to North Africa, where they hoped to find work or, less frequently, intended to pursue their studies. Although their numbers remained relatively small until the late 1980s, providing these migrants with trans-Saharan transportation quickly became a lucrative and attractive opportunity, and certain Tuareg from the Aïr became occasional people smugglers. In 1975, a camel driver was stopped in the north of Iferwan while guiding 150 people toward Algeria; another was arrested at the Libyan border accompanied by 90 migrants (Adamou 1979). Many such migrants, crossing the desert on foot, died along the way.

At the same time, the motorized transport of migrants was developing.[10] Truckers, first Libyan and then Nigerien, started to carry passengers between Agadez, Bilma, and Sebha on top of their loads for a fee that then varied between 10,000 and 20,000 CFA francs.[11] This was highly profitable and allowed many truckers to grow rich very quickly, but in the early 1980s, strained diplomatic relations between Niger and Libya put an end to such activities.[12] In addition, falling oil prices made Libya painfully aware of its dependency on immigrant labor—mainly from neighboring Arab countries rather than from sub-Saharan Africa—and contributed to a change in migration policy (Pliez 2004b). From then on, the government attempted to reduce immigration, but without much success. Irregular migrants were now running a considerable risk of deportation, in Algeria as well as in Libya; in Libya, those who were caught were taken to the military camp of Al-Qatrun and then escorted to the border with Niger, where they were dropped off near a well. Aware of this, Nigerien soldiers began frequent patrols in the border area, picking up expelled migrants and taking them to the military camp of Madama and then on to Dirkou, where they were questioned about their stay in Libya (work, political activities, military training) before being released.

From the mid-1980s on, as relations between the governments of Muammar Qaddafi and Seyni Kountché improved, raising hopes for an official reopening of the land traffic between the two countries, trade picked up more quickly than transborder migrations, which remained illegal though tolerated.[13] "In 1988, Libyan trucks started to come to Niger," explains the warrant officer of the gendarmerie at Bilma, "Libyan trucks that went all the way to Agadez. Trucks from Niger only started to travel toward Libya in 1994. But they only ever go as far as Dirkou, they never go all the way to Libya."[14] Eventually, as Libyan traders obtained from the Nigerien government official approval for carrying passengers on their way back to Libya, an overarching organization of migrant transport emerged.

Niger between Emigration and Transit: The Watershed of the 1990s

The final decade of the twentieth century marked a turning point in the history of trans-Saharan migrations, due to the greater numbers and the growing diversity of migrants; it also saw the development of an integrated migration system in the central Sahara. Until the 1990s, Saharan migrations remained relatively small-scale. However, migrants returned from North Africa with considerable gains (mostly in kind), spreading the image of a Libyan and Algerian "El Dorado" even beyond areas directly touched by migration. In the 1990s, the slow development of Saharan migration gave way to a series of rapid changes, largely because of the reorientation of Libya's African policy, and new regions throughout West and Central Africa began to be involved in what would become a continental-wide migration system.

Following the bombings of Pan Am flight 103 above the small Scottish town of Lockerbie in December 1988 and of UTA flight 772 over Niger in September 1989, attacks for which Libyan agents, protected by their government, were suspected of responsibility, the UN Security Council on 15 April 1992 declared an air and military embargo against Libya.[15] In order to limit Libya's isolation on the international stage following the UN sanctions and similar measures taken at the same time by the United States and the European Union, Muammar Qaddafi sought to attract support from African states by speaking publicly in favor of African immigration to Libya. This change of direction in Libya's African policy, already begun in July 1990 with a treaty establishing the free movement of people between Libya and Sudan, inspired much enthusiasm among young Africans, who saw in it a variety of opportunities.[16] The result was a significant revival of trans-Saharan migration to Libya, to a lesser degree to Algeria, and sometimes even to Europe. Other factors also influenced this expansion of migration: the tightening of European migration policies, for instance, which meant that visas became mandatory and increasingly difficult to obtain,[17] or the devaluation of the CFA franc in January 1994, which led to the impoverishment of a whole sector of the African middle classes in the countries concerned.[18]

Yet, although these economic and political factors certainly encouraged the extension and diversification of trans-Saharan migration to a certain degree, considered separately and especially when one examines the cases of individual migrants, their explanatory power remains limited. On the ground, migration has always been difficult: in the early 1990s, Algeria, for instance, "intensified the fight against illegal immigration begun in 1986" (Bredeloup 1995: 120) by expelling large numbers of sub-Saharan migrants. Despite a rhetoric of open borders, the Libyan government has similarly continued to deport foreigners; and the intensification of migratory flows preceded the devaluation of the CFA franc. I will thus set aside the search for common causative factors of these central Saharan migrations, and focus rather on the ways in which they are organized and the strategies adopted by the different actors involved.

The closure of the border between Chad and Libya due to the conflict in the Aouzou strip,[19] the risks involved in traveling the routes that link northern Mali to Tamanrasset in Algeria (e.g., the harsh environment and local banditry),[20] and the layout of the northwest African road network have meant that since the early 1990s, the majority of migrants have chosen to travel through Niger, following routes that give access to Algeria and to Libya. As news of the easiest passage circulates rapidly in the region, any itinerary that "works" becomes quickly popular.[21] Although it had previously been primarily a sender country, Niger in the 1990s became a transit country despite the lack of security in its northern areas.

When the Tuareg and Tubu rebellion broke out in 1991,[22] rebels and bandits began holding up vehicles in the north of the country, on paved roads and on desert tracks. Confronted with this general insecurity, which continued for several years after the conclusion of a peace agreement in 1995, the government of Niger began to organize military convoys to supply the northern towns. All vehicles (personal, passenger, or freight) traveling between Tahoua and Agadez, and on to Dirkou and Arlit, were asked to do so only in convoy and under army protection. Once this system was in place, only a few drivers (apart from smugglers) still traveled on their own, and only because they could not, or did not want to, wait for the convoys, which would sometimes leave only once or twice a month toward the Kawar oases. This organization of overland transportation by the army made it possible to control migrants more thoroughly, since they were necessarily traveling together. The major result was that migrants were arbitrarily taxed by the gendarmes and military officers in charge of these convoys and of their inspection in the towns through which they passed.

In the following account, Babaye, a migrant from Agadez, describes how the Libyan and Nigerien authorities controlled migrants during the rebellion. His story shows not only how Libya's alleged open-border policies have to be taken with a pinch of salt (on both the Nigerien and the Libyan sides), but also how, from the mid-1990s on, private and public actors have succeeded in making a profit from migrants in transit.

> I left for Libya in 1995 on a big truck, a Mercedes 19/4. . . . That kind of truck takes about a hundred people from Agadez. . . . You get to the first village after eighty kilometers, that's Toureyet. . . . The trucks were traveling with military

> escort, because this was during the rebellion. The trucks congregate on the way out of town, up to one hundred, even up to one hundred and fifty of them, all with passengers and their luggage. . . . When the soldiers are ready, they come to escort the trucks all the way to Dirkou. At that time, Dirkou was a small town . . . there was just one military company. . . . The others who were traveling, they weren't just from Niger, there were others from Ghana, from Mali, from Nigeria, they came to Agadez to go to Libya. . . . The escort stops in Dirkou. Now to get from Dirkou to Libya, you don't go the normal way. Everybody who was traveling at that time had to go by *fraude* [clandestinely]. Once you get to the border, you go through military camps, there are no villages . . . the last military post is Madama. . . . once you're in Tumo, there are Libyan soldiers. . . . I didn't see anything after Madama, and the trucks go fast . . . the truck drivers are Tubu. They have triple nationality: from Niger, Chad, and Libya. They know the area extremely well. When you leave Agadez, the owners of the trucks are Libyans who come to buy livestock and others, there are also some from Niger. . . . After the border, you have to be careful. . . . In 1995, people couldn't move around freely in Libya . . . and if the police caught you, they threw you in prison straightaway.[23]

The rebellion of 1990–1995, far from putting a stop to Saharan travel, on the contrary marked the establishment of transportation networks and an "institutionalization from below" of the role of Nigerien state agents in the Saharan migration system. In a time of great instability for the state, members of the various security agencies routinely engaged in practices that were not part of their official duties and that were at times illegal, without encountering any opposition from the ruling circles or from their direct superiors.

Although motorized transportation has been common in the central Sahara since the 1940s, until the late 1980s passenger transport was exclusively provided by traders on trucks as an adjunct to the transport of goods. In the late 1990s, the large number of migrants traveling via Agadez created a significant demand for transportation to the cities of southern Algeria and Libya, a demand to which freight carriers were the first to respond. Owners of four-wheel-drive pickups, especially Tuareg from Agadez, followed suit, and started to profit from their knowledge of the area and its many smuggling routes (knowledge that they had acquired as migrants and tour guides, or during the rebellion, rather than from older pastoral and nomadic traditions), offering their services as drivers, guides, and escorts for migrant workers. They also opened the first official local Saharan travel agencies, with the consent of local politicians. After the peace agreement of April 1995, many former rebels returned to Agadez and joined the large group of people with no formal occupation but access to cars who, from time to time, took migrants across the desert. Their knowledge of the area and connections in local political circles allowed them rapidly to develop new companies, or "brokerage

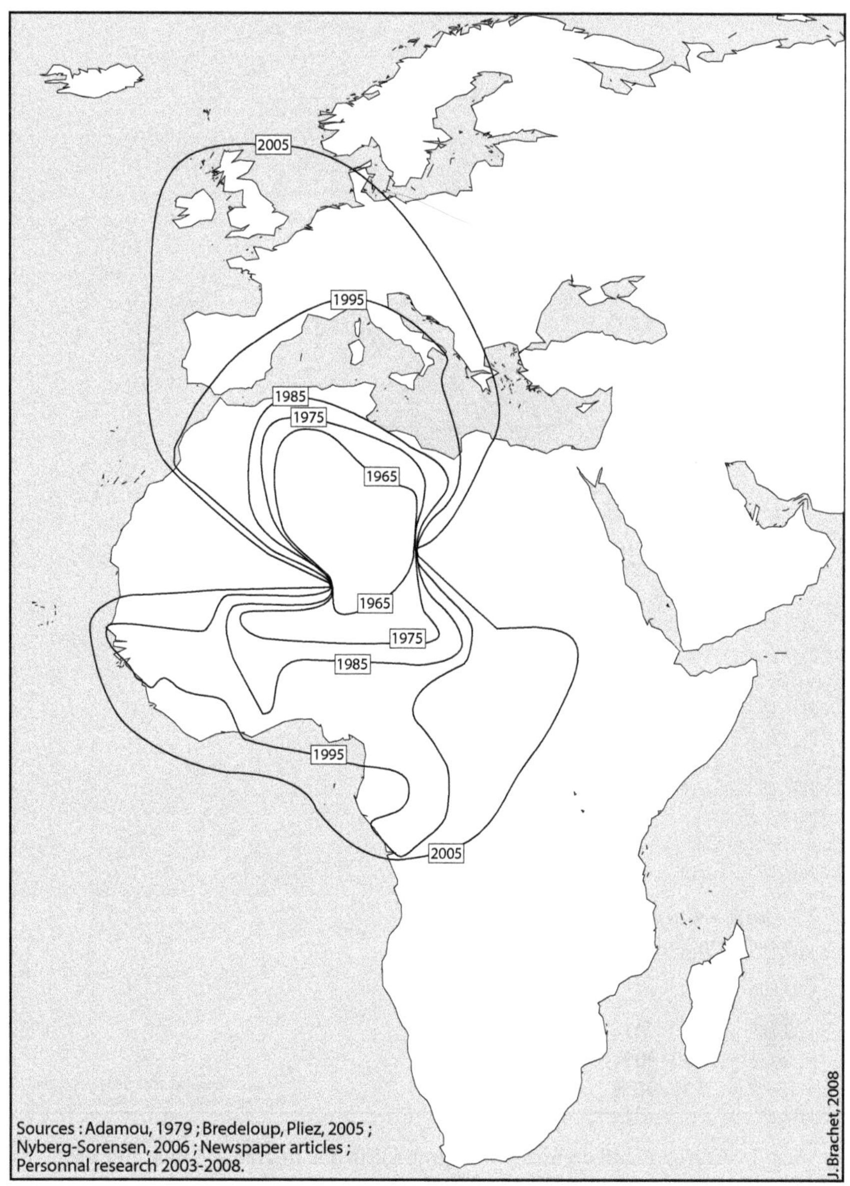

Map 14.2. Progressive extension of the range of migration from and through Niger (1965–2005). J. Brachet 2008

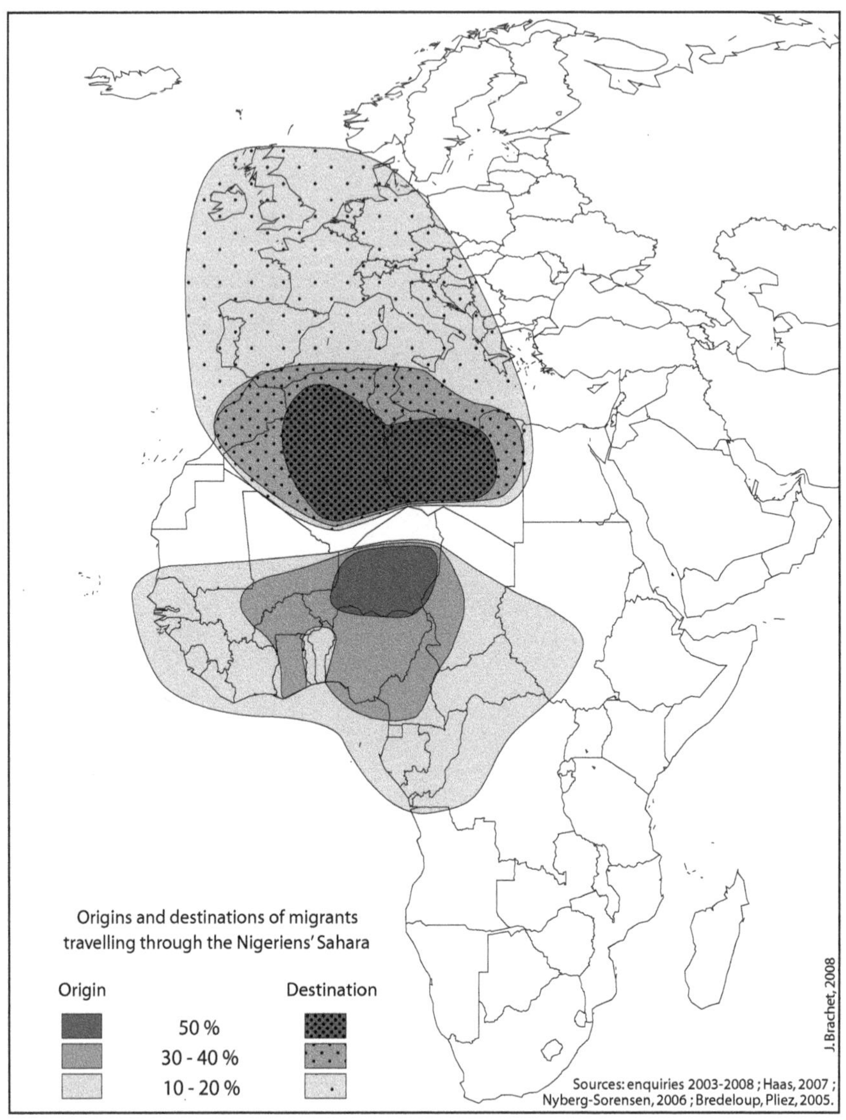

Map 14.3. Origins and destinations of (trans-)Saharan migrants. J. BRACHET 2008

agencies,"[24] specializing in the transport of migrants between Niger, Algeria, and Libya, resulting in the reprofessionalization of local transportation.

Freight Haulage and Migrant Transport across Northern Niger Today

The bustle of trans-Saharan migration routes that has been the focus of much public and academic debate should not obscure the fact that these routes are also—and sometimes primarily—circuits of intraregional trade. The international interest in the Sahara as a migration hotspot does not mean that local and long-distance commercial exchanges have ceased in the area. Rather, commercial exchange has been revitalized by migration, and continues to structure regional relations on all levels. From Tuareg camel drivers, to the members of various agricultural cooperatives in northern Niger, to large-scale Hausa and Arab traders, the number of people coming to Agadez to buy, sell, or barter their goods is large, turning the city into a genuine center of supply and commerce. Situated at the northern limit of the paved road connecting Niger and Libya, Agadez is also an obligatory trans-shipment point for goods. And despite the development of travel agencies, several traders continue to combine freight and passenger transport, either by carrying them together or by alternating between goods and people according to the route traveled.

On the way to Algeria, the three official tracks that lead to the border post of Assamakka start in Tchin Tabaraden, In Gal, and Arlit. As these tracks are relatively free of sand, semi-trailer trucks (with carrying capacities of up to twenty or thirty tons) can use them easily, avoiding the additional costs of trans-shipment between tracks and paved roads. From Agadez via Arlit, relatively few goods are legally exported to Algeria. These are mainly livestock and agricultural produce (garlic, onions, peanuts), whose value annually amounts to less than 250 million CFA francs. This is only a small percentage of the trade traveling in this direction, the vast majority consisting of re-exported, mostly manufactured goods: cloth, green tea, spare parts for cars, and especially cigarettes, which account for 90 percent of all goods traded. Since 2000, a part of these cigarette exports has been redirected toward Libya, causing the overall value of re-exports to Algeria to fall. Imports to Niger consist of second-rate dates and salt for the Arlit mines, to which is added a small amount of various foodstuffs and manufactured goods (which enter Niger legally, despite being illegally exported from Algeria).[25] Trucks engaged in such semi-official trade only rarely carry migrants to Algeria. Drivers refuse to cross the border with illegal migrants because they know that Algerian customs officials will not let them pass and that they will have to pay a fine. In this direction, mixed transport (of freight and passengers) is thus limited to the stretch between Arlit and Assamakka. However, on the way back to Niger from Tamanrasset, drivers have no qualms about carrying migrants. Although they might still be held up, this is much less likely to happen on the way south.[26]

In addition to official trade, which is duly registered and taxed, much if not most commercial exchange between Niger and Algeria is part of the "parallel," "underground," or "informal" economy (Ellis and MacGaffey 1997). These exchanges, of which the authorities are neither directly nor officially apprised and which do not therefore figure in official statistics, are too important to be considered merely as an annex to the cross-border economy. As a spokesman for one transportation company admitted to me, "There are many trucks that trade with Algeria, that cross the border in the desert, there are very many. . . . Usually, they have to clear customs here or in Agadez . . . but more than half go through undeclared."[27] Different kinds of unofficial exchanges need to be distinguished here: first, according to whether they concern licit or illicit goods (the latter composed of mainly arms and drugs; see Scheele this volume); and second, within the trade in licit goods, whether they occasion illegal deals with state officials who are in charge of controlling trade, or whether they are carried on in secret, beyond the control of state agents. Livestock from Niger, for example, is carried illegally into Algeria. At the same time, large quantities of staple foodstuffs that are subsidized by the Algerian government,[28] as well as certain manufactured goods, are taken secretly into Niger. The markets of northern Niger are mostly supplied through such smuggling. Because of their low cost when retailed, these goods are considered by many to be indispensable to the survival of the people of the Agadez region, or at least to the maintenance of their standard of living.

Livestock accounts for more than 90 percent of official exports from Niger to Libya.[29] Illegal exports are so numerous, however, that it is difficult to evaluate the volume of overall trade. Most of these animals, bred in the pastoral zones of Niger, belong to Nigerien Arabs. They are taken directly to Libya from rural Niger, either in large caravans or loaded on trucks. Such caravans can be made up of several hundred animals accompanied by two trucks carrying fodder for the trip, which can take up to a month. The trucks, usually belonging to the owner of the livestock, are generally driven by Arabs, while Tuareg or Tubu camel herders take care of the animals. Such camel caravans travel all the way to the urban centers of southern Libya, where every animal can be sold for two to four times the price it would fetch in Niger, and the owners make considerable profits.[30] If livestock is carried on trucks, they can travel the 1,700 kilometers that separate Agadez from Sebha in a week, but the cost of transportation per head is much higher. With the help of drivers or guides, migrants sometimes take advantage of these convoys to travel to Libya more cheaply and with fewer risks. At the border crossings, they pretend to be camel herders traveling with their animals. Libyan officials, who actively support the import of livestock, tend to turn a blind eye to their (lack of) papers.

Here, as with Algeria, the direct exports are much less important than the re-exports. For example, in 2004, direct exports were valued at 220 million CFA francs (of which 211 million was in livestock), and Niger re-exported goods worth almost 24 billion CFA francs (cigarettes accounted for almost all of it, 23.5 billion CFA francs).[31] Apart from livestock, all goods exported or re-exported from Niger to Libya transit via Agadez, where they are loaded on off-road trucks especially equipped for Saharan crossings. Nigerien truckers then take them to Dirkou or Madama, where they are loaded onto Libyan trucks, with drivers from Libya, Chad, or Sudan, that take them the rest of the way. This trans-shipment provides an opportunity for additional regional exchanges of goods, as Nigerien drivers on their return trip carry dates or salt produced in the oases of the Kawar.

The principal goods imported from Libya are staple foodstuffs (oil, flour, rice, pasta, tomato puree) and hydrocarbons (diesel, kerosene). The prices of these products are subsidized in Libya and their export is illegal. Nonetheless, various channels of illegal exports to neighboring countries have been set up through the *sūq libya* (state-run markets) through which such goods are distributed throughout the country. A small part of these illegal exports from Libya become legal imports upon their arrival in Niger, where they are subject to a high-rate wholesale value tax,[32] to which have to be added the various unofficial taxes levied by army, gendarmerie, police, or customs officers. Thus, between Sebha and Agadez, a Libyan truck can pay up to a million CFA francs in unofficial taxes. This is why, as the warrant officer of the Bilma gendarmerie explains, some "Libyan trucks have two [registration] plates. As soon as they get to Niger, they put on their Nigerien plates to avoid problems."[33] Others, who might otherwise take their goods all the way to Agadez, now sell them to one of their local correspondents in the Kawar to avoid traveling in Niger, thus limiting the additional expenditure of unofficial taxation.

Until the early 2000s, mixed transport was very common on this route. Up until then, the Libyan authorities tolerated the entry of illegal migrants, thus allowing truck drivers to increase their incomes substantially (since the traders who actually owned the trucks or the goods being transported were not always made aware of this additional activity). But the tightening of Libyan migration policy, mainly in response to pressure from the European Union, especially from Italy (Perrin 2008), has virtually put an end to this complementary movement of goods and persons. For some years now, it has become almost impossible for migrants to enter Libya illegally at the border post of Tumo. To avoid the risks of "taxation" or imprisonment, drivers only accept passengers on their way north between Agadez and the Kawar oases or the border. Only those few legal migrants whose documents are checked before departure are still taken all the way to Libya. To get across the border, most migrants now rely on specialized networks of people smugglers, whose drivers have detailed knowledge of the area and its smuggling routes (Brachet 2009b). In the other direction, on the way back from Libya, mixed transport is still authorized by the Libyan authorities and remains common. Frequently, all of the goods on a truck are owned by the migrants traveling with them.

As with trade across the Algerian border, official trade between Niger and Libya only represents a small part of the real exchange. Traders frequently avoid the strictures of import-export laws and the high official taxes for clearing customs. They travel between the two countries either through legal border posts, where they pay off state officials, or secretly, in order to avoid paying such unofficial taxes. In either case, the goods they carry do not appear in official export statistics. Further, many informal exchanges are part of a kind of "suitcase peddling," carried out by migrants who bring back from Libya various goods for sale. These different types of exchange, though obviously difficult to quantify, undoubtedly contribute to the basic supply and to the commercial dynamism of Niger's Saharan regions, and they make regional mobility an integral part of local economies.

From the International to the Local: Toward an Alternative View of (Trans-)Saharan Movement

While the establishment of colonial borders initially interrupted trans-Saharan exchanges and then led to the development of smuggling, the national borders that developed after independence quickly became a driving force for cross-border trade (Guitart 1992). Major traders, mainly Arabs but also Hausa and Jerma-Songhay, have been successful in establishing connections with national administrations and with various state institutions, while maintaining religious or family networks on both sides of the Sahara, and in elaborating commercial strategies based on corruption or other types of *fraude* that allow them to avoid paying customs duties and to sidestep import and export regulations. While thus escaping or at least limiting the main constraints imposed by the existence of borders (taxes, controls, prohibitions, nonconvertible currencies), they have been able to take advantage of the various economic opportunities that borders also create. Differences in the availability and price of goods on the two sides of the Sahara, mainly due to Libyan and Algerian state subsidies, allow them to engage in a dynamic and lucrative cross-border trade that is increasingly part of internationalized or even globalized commercial networks. And for some of them, trading has become inseparable from transporting migrants.

Within this system, global and regional dynamics are intimately related. On the one hand, major circuits of intercontinental commodity distribution, such as the trade in cigarettes, are not themselves influenced by migratory flows, but can underpin them. The opportunities for transport that they create in the Sahara are often extensive and contribute significantly to the movement of migrants through the desert. On the other hand, regional and cross-border traffic that helps to supply a large part of the market in northern Niger can be revitalized by migrations and the need for transportation that they create.

In addition to this complementary relation between freight and passenger transport, migration toward and across the central Sahara has had an important economic impact on relay towns in northern Niger by encouraging the development of specialized transportation companies; stimulating the local infrastructure of hostels, restaurants, and telecommunication centers; transforming local job markets through the availability of cheap labor; or injecting a considerable amount of hard currency into the local economy (Brachet 2009a). (Trans)-Saharan migrations are thus an important factor in the contemporary developmental dynamism of the central Sahara. But in the same way that the impact of small cross-border traffic in foodstuffs and daily consumer goods is often hidden—from the eyes of political decision makers—by large-scale illicit trafficking, the local stakes and effects of Saharan migration are often concealed by the habit of treating them as a "migration problem" on an international level (Brachet 2011).

Indeed, for some years now, official meetings between European and African states dealing with irregular migration have become regular occurrences. Several European countries have publicly stated their determination to stop the "wave of illegal migrants" as far back along their itineraries as possible, even if this entails active participation in the surveillance of African borders. Their attention is increasingly turned toward the Sahara, which, alongside the Mediterranean and Atlantic coasts, is considered a priority zone in the fight against illegal immigration from countries south of the Sahara. Yet, although it is true that some migrants who travel illegally to Europe first had to cross the Sahara, only a minority of those who travel in the central Sahara intend to continue to Europe. The habit of classifying all trans-Saharan movement, or circular movement *within* Saharan Africa, as potential trans-Mediterranean migration is based on a completely mistaken view of the realities on the ground. Through diplomatic pressure or economic and military "cooperation," European countries are hoping to encourage North African governments to fight against irregular trans-Saharan migrations, thereby putting pressure on a historic migration system that underpins much economic dynamism and development in the Sahara, which should be of little concern to European governments.

NOTES

1. This chapter is based on two years of fieldwork carried out in Niger between 2003 and 2008, as part of doctoral (Brachet 2009a) and postdoctoral research on contemporary (trans-)Saharan migrations.

2. From the 1930s on, after the "pacification" of the Aïr and its surrounding areas by the French colonial army, large-scale Algerian traders settled in the north of what is now Niger, where they joined some of their co-nationals who had long resided there, conducting trans-Saharan trade. After the end of World War II, using equipment left by the French and Italian armies, they developed an active freight transportation system between Algeria and French West Africa, thereby giving rise to a flourishing black market (Guitart 1989).

3. Both bases were handed over to the Algerian government in 1967.

4. Sing. *ashamor*: a Tamasheq word derived from the French *chômeur,* "unemployed" (see also Grémont this volume).

5. This perception of foreign Tuareg as exiles derives partly from the movement of Tuareg refugees to Algeria in the wake of the rebellion led by the Malian Kel Adagh in 1963–1964 (Lecocq 2010).

6. In such cases, the term *teshumara,* which can be translated as the "community of *ishumar,*" indicates a state of rebellion as well as one of marginality.

7. After the devaluation of 12 January 1994, 10,000 CFA francs were worth 100 French francs (approx. £10, $18). Since 1 January 2002, the exchange rate has been fixed at 10,000 CFA francs for €15.24 (approx. £9.50, $13).

8. The 1995 peace agreement that ended the first phase of the northern Nigerien Tuareg revolt stipulated that a certain number of former rebels be incorporated into the regular army.

9. Interview, Timia, Niger, 23 August 2003.

10. Regular flights also operated between Agadez and Sebha (for 32,000 CFA francs one way), without ever really competing with overland routes.

11. Libyans were exporting cheap staples (pasta, oil, wheat flour) and manufactured goods (carpets, blankets, teapots). In Bilma, they sold some of their load and took on salt and dates that they carried to Agadez, Tahoua, and Zinder, where they sold their cargo to buy livestock and sometimes also some millet and henna.

12. This crisis eventually led to the closure of the Libyan embassy in Niamey on 13 January 1981 (see Robinson 1984).

13. In 1989, two years after Seyni Kountché's death, this formal rapprochement was made official by President Ali Saibou's state visit to Libya.

14. Interview, Bilma, 8 December 2004.

15. The UN embargo was lifted in April 1999, after an agreement was reached to bring two Libyan nationals implicated in the Lockerbie bombing to trial in the Netherlands. Also in 1999, six Libyans accused of involvement in the bombing of UTA 772 were convicted in

absentia by a court in Paris. Between 2004 and 2008, Libya paid compensation to victims of terror attacks of which the Qaddafi regime had been accused, including the UTA and Pan Am bombings, but without accepting responsibility.

16. Qaddafi's pan-African policies were developed after the failure of his attempts to foster pan-Arab unity (in turn meant to continue Gamal Abd al-Nasser's projects) and the failure of Libya's military intervention in Chad (1972–1987).

17. Beginning in 1985, visas were introduced through bilateral agreements; since 1995, procedures have been standardized in accordance with the Schengen Agreements on the free movement of persons within the EU.

18. These are the eight countries of the West African Economic and Monetary Union (Benin, Burkina Faso, Côte d'Ivoire, Guinea-Bissau, Mali, Niger, Senegal, and Togo) and the six member states of the Central African Monetary and Economic Community (Cameroon, Central African Republic, Chad, Republic of the Congo, Equatorial Guinea, and Gabon). On the devaluation of the CFA franc, see Conte (1994) and Dupraz (1994).

19. Libya's claim to the Aouzou strip (a desert territory parallel to the border in northern Chad) dates back to 1954. Occupied by Libyan troops in 1972, the strip was evacuated by Libya in 1987 after Chadian forces supported by the French defeated the Libyan incursion. The International Court of Justice in The Hague ruled in favor of Chad on the status of the territory in 1994, a decision accepted by Libya.

20. Because of these risks, the tracks that link southern Algeria to the cities of northern Mali (Timbuktu, Gao, and Kidal) were little used until 2000, with the exception of the road between Gao and Reggane, which was used by Malian migrants. More recently, migrants from various countries have started to cross the Tanezrouft (a particularly unforgiving and roadless region of the west-central Sahara, along the Algerian-Malian border) toward Adrar and Tamanrasset (Pellicani and Spiga 2007).

21. The road from Sudan to Libya (via Khartoum or Atbara to El Jawf and Kufra) was then also very popular. The route through Mauritania only became important in the 2000s, with the growth of traffic seeking to avoid part of the Saharan crossing by aiming for the Canary Islands (Choplin this volume).

22. In 1989, the regime of Colonel Ali Saibou (president of Niger, 1987–1993) repeatedly encouraged Nigerien migrants living in Libya (among whom were many Tuareg) to return, offering inducements that promised their social and economic reintegration. But the government did not keep its promises, and those who returned were settled in makeshift camps. The Nigerien army, suspecting young Tuareg of having enlisted in the Libyan army, arrested many of them, creating a tense political climate. On the night of 6–7 May 1990, young Tuareg attempted to occupy the gendarmerie of Tchin Tabaraden in protest against the army's arbitrary arrests of people from their community. They then attacked the subprefecture's administrative offices and the civil prison. Army units sent into the area responded with violent repression, destroying several nomad camps and committing abuses that resulted in several deaths. These events, often considered the proximate cause of the rebellion, were at least a foretaste of the revolt before it truly got off the ground in November 1991, with an attack on the army post of In Gall. For more detail, see Bourgeot (1994b, 1996) and Djibo (2002).

23. Interview with Babaye (Nigerien), Agadez, 17 November 2004.

24. *Agences de courtage* is the official name given to agencies specializing in carrying migrants to neighboring Arab countries (i.e., Algeria and Libya).

25. Apart from dates, salt, and handicrafts, only blankets and plastic and metal wares can be legally exported from Algeria to its southern neighbors (Republic of Algeria, Direction Générale des Douanes algériennes: Arrêté interministeriel fixant les modalités d'exercice du commerce de troc frontalier avec le Niger et le Mali, 14 December 1995).

26. In any case, it seems much easier to get into Niger from Algeria than vice versa, as the director of overland transport in Agadez observed, barely hiding his annoyance: "If a truck from Niger wants to get into Algeria, this causes all the problems in the world . . . it's not easy to get in. On the other hand, they, when they come, they can do as they please. When we go to Algeria, we really have to put up with a lot of administrative problems and hassle from the police" (interview, Agadez, 29 November 2004).

27. Interview, Arlit, April 2003.

28. Since the end of official government subsidies on basic goods in the mid-1990s, staples have been indirectly subsidized through their production by state-owned factories.

29. In 2002, 4,000 camels and 1,000 sheep were officially taken to Libya, with a value of 360 million CFA francs (Republic of Niger, Direction Générale des Douanes: Service départemental des Ressources animales de Bilma: Rapport annuel d'activité [2002], in author's possession).

30. In Libya, a camel can be sold for up to the equivalent of 500,000 CFA francs.

31. This sharp rise in re-exports from 1999 on is due both to the change of direction of parts of the Algerian cigarette trade to Libya, and to the overall rise in official cigarette exports from Niger to North Africa.

32. These taxes amount to 30 percent for wheat flour, 34 percent for dates, 40.1 percent for semolina, 47.7 percent for cooking oil and for powdered milk, and 52.5 percent for luxury items (tomato puree, videos, etc.).

33. Interview, Bilma, 8 December 2004.

GLOSSARY

Ar.	**Arabic**	**Gk.**	**Greek**
Bam.	**Bamana**	**Lat.**	**Latin**
Fr.	**French**	**Tam.**	**Tamasheq/Berber**
Ful.	**Fula/Fulfulde (Pulaar)**		

ʿabd, pl. ʿabīd (Ar.): slave

ashamor, pl. ishumar (Tam.): young Tuareg migrant in North Africa; from *chômeur* (Fr., unemployed person)

ʿashīra (Ar.): extended family group in the Mzab (Algeria)

ʿazzāba (Ar.): Ibadi Muslim clerics in the Mzab

bīdān (Ar.): lit., whites; Arabic-speaking Mauritanians

bilād al-sūdān (Ar.): lit., country of the blacks; the countries of the Sahel belt as seen from the Sahara or the Mediterranean Arab world

bourgoutière (Fr.): type of water meadow, used as pasture in the Niger bend

cabotage; caboteur (Fr.): short-distance coastal trade; a trader who engages in this

dāʾira (Ar.): Sufi circle, *or* administrative district

faggāra, pl. fagāgīr (Ar.): underground irrigation canals

faqīh, pl. fuqahāʾ (Ar.): religious scholar

fātiha (Ar.): opening chapter of the Qurʾan, often recited as a prayer

fuwra (Ar.): millet porridge

garāj, pl. gawārij (Ar.): trading entrepôt, from *garage* (Fr.)

garum (Lat.): ancient Roman fish sauce

gendarmerie (Fr.): paramilitary state security force, especially in rural areas

hartānī, fem. hartāniyya, pl. harātīn (Ar.): descendants of former slaves or of original Saharan populations, mostly of lower status

hassān (Ar.): high-status Mauritanian tribes, traditionally identified with a military rather than a religious vocation

imajeghen (Tam.): high-status Tuareg

ittifāq, pl. ittifāqāt (Ar.): lit., agreement; here, decisions taken by Mzabi assemblies jamā'a (Ar.): assembly

jatigi (Bam.): landlord, patron; *or* host, guarantor

jinn, pl. jnūn (Ar.): spirit

leydi (Ful.): territory

majlis, pl. majālis (Ar.): lit., sitting; assembly, court

mawlid (Ar.): celebration in honor of the Prophet Muhammad's birthday

mrābit, pl. mrabtīn (Ar.): descendant of Muslim saints

nāzila, pl. nawāzil (Ar.): legal case brought before a qādi and quoted as exemplary

Nigerian: citizen of Nigeria

Nigerien: citizen of Niger

ostracon, pl. ostraca (Gk.): inscribed pottery fragment

qādi, pl. qudāh (Ar.): Islamic judge

qā'id, pl. quwwād (Ar.): government administrative officer

qsar, pl. qsūr (Ar.): fortified settlement, oasis town, *or* fortified granary or storehouse

qubba (Ar.): cupola built over a saint's tomb

sharī'a (Ar.): Islamic law

sharīf, fem. sharīfa, pl. shurafā' (Ar.): recognized descendant of the Prophet Muhammad

shaykh (Ar.): honorific for an older man or an Islamic scholar

sūdānī, pl. suwādīn *or* sūdān (Ar.): lit., blacks; inhabitants of West Africa who do not speak Arabic

sūq (Ar.): market

tālib, pl. tullāb *or* talaba (var. tolbā) (Ar.): student, especially of Islamic law and religious learning

tarīqa, pl. turuq (Ar.): lit. path; Sufi order

trabendo (Algerian vernacular): informal trade; from *contrebande* (Fr., contraband, smuggling)

wādi (Ar.): valley, (dry) riverbed

walī, pl. awliyā' (Ar.): Muslim saint

wilāya (Ar.): administrative district (Algeria)

zāwiya, pl. zawāyā (Ar.): religious stronghold, center of learning (often of a Sufi tarīqa), *or* scholarly group; the plural form zwāya indicates high-status Mauritanians traditionally associated with a religious vocation

BIBLIOGRAPHY

Abitbol, M. 1979. *Tombouctou et les Arma.* Paris: Maisonneuve et Larose.

Abulafia, D. 2005. Mediterraneans. In *Rethinking the Mediterranean,* ed. W. V. Harris, 64–93. Oxford: Oxford University Press.

Abulafia, D., ed. 2003. *The Mediterranean in History.* London: Thames and Hudson.

Adamou, A. 1979. *Agadez et sa région: Contribution à l'étude du Sahel et du Sahara nigériens.* Niamey: Institut de recherche en sciences humaines.

Adams, J. N. 1994. Latin and Punic in Contact? The Case of the Bu Njem Ostraca. *Journal of Roman Studies* 84, 87–112.

Adelkhah, F., and J.-F. Bayart. 2007. *Voyages de développement: Émigration, commerce, exil.* Paris: Karthala.

Adelman, J., and S. Aron. 1999. From Borderlands to Borders: Empires, Nation-States, and the Peoples in Between in North American History. *American Historical Review* 104/3, 814–841.

Ag Ahar, E. 1990. L'initiation d'un ashamur. *Revue des mondes musulmans et de la Méditerranée* 57, 141–152.

Ag Baye, Ch., and R. Bellil. 1986. Une société touarègue en crise: Les Kel Adrar du Mali. *Awal* 2, 49–84.

Ag Foni, E. 1979. L'impact socio-économique de la sécheresse dans le cercle de Kidal. Final diss., ENSUP, Bamako.

Agier, M. 2006. Protéger les sans-états ou contrôler les indésirables: Où en est le HCR? *Politique africaine* 103, 101–105.

Ag Youssouf, I. 1999. Inzamman: Voix 1. In *Le pouvoir du savoir de l'Arctique aux Tropiques,* ed. J. Boutrais, S. Gerrard, L. Holtedahl, and M. Z. Njeuma, 307–326. Paris: Karthala.

Albarella, U., K. Dobney, and P. Rowley-Conwy. 2006. The Domestication of the Pig (*Sus scrofa*): New Challenges and Approaches. In *Documenting Domestication: New Genetic and Archaeological Paradigms,* ed. M. A. Zeder, D. G. Bradley, E. Emshwiller, and B. Smith, 209–227. Berkeley: University of California Press.

Almàsy, L. 1939. *Unbekannte Sahara: Mit Flugzeug und Auto in der Libyschen Wüste.* Leipzig: Brockhaus.

Amat, C. 1885. *L'esclavage au M'zab, étude anthropologique des nègres.* Paris: A. Hennuyer.

Amnesty International. 2008. Personne ne veut de nous. http://www.amnesty.org/fr/library/info/AFR38/001/2008/fr (accessed July 2010).

Andezian, S. 2001. *Expériences du divin dans l'Algérie contemporaine: Adeptes des saints de la région de Tlemcen.* Paris: CNRS.

Antil, A., and A. Choplin. 2003. Le chaînon manquant: La route Nouakchott-Nouadhibou, dernier tronçon de la transsaharienne Tanger-Dakar. *Afrique contemporaine* 208, 115–126.

Appadurai, A. 1996. *Modernity at Large: Cultural Dimensions of Globalization.* Minneapolis: University of Minnesota Press.

Asiwaju, A. I. 1996. Borderlands in Africa: A Comparative Research Perspective with Particular Reference to Western Europe. In *African Boundaries: Barriers, Conduits, and Opportunities,* ed. P. Nugent and A. I. Asiwaju, ch. 13. London: Pinter.

Aucapitaine, H. 1861. *Étude sur la caravane de la Mecque et le commerce de l'intérieur de l'Afrique.* Paris: J. Claye.

Austen, R. A. 1987. *African Economic History: Internal Development and External Dependency.* London: James Currey/Portsmouth, N.H.: Heinemann.

———. 1990. Marginalization, Stagnation and Growth: Trans-Saharan Caravan Trade, 1500–1900. In *The Rise of Merchant Empires: Long-Distance Trade in the Early Modern World,* ed. J. Tracy, 311–350. Cambridge: Cambridge University Press.

———. 2010. *Trans-Saharan Africa in World History.* Oxford: Oxford University Press.

Ba, C. O., and A. Choplin. 2005. "Tenter l'aventure" par la Mauritanie: Migrations trans-sahariennes et recompositions urbaines. *Autrepart* 36, 21–42.

Badi, D. 2004. *Les régions de l'Ahaggar et du Tassili n'Azjer: Réalité d'un mythe.* Algiers: ANEP.

———. 2007. Le rôle des communautés sahéliennes dans l'économie locale d'une ville saharienne: Tamanrasset (Sahara algérien). In *Les nouveaux urbains dans l'espace Sahara-Sahel: Un cosmopolitisme par le bas,* ed. E. Boesen and L. Marfaing, 259–278. Paris: Karthala.

Baier, S. 1980. *An Economic History of Central Niger.* Oxford: Clarendon Press.

Baier, S., and P. Lovejoy. 1975. The Desert-Side Economy of the Central Sudan. *International Journal of African Historical Studies* 8/4, 551–581.

Baistrocchi, M. 1989. Reperti romani rinvenuti nella tomba di Tin Hinan ad Abalessa. *L'Africa Romana* 7/1, 89–99.

Baratta, G. 2008. La produzione delle pelle nell'Occidente e nelle province africane. *L'Africa Romana* 17/1, 203–221.

Barendse, R. J. 2002. *The Arabian Seas: The Indian Ocean World of the Seventeenth Century.* London: Sharpe.

Barker, G., D. Gilbertson, B. Jones, and D. Mattingly. 1996. *Farming the Desert: The UNESCO Libyan Valleys Archaeological Survey.* London: Society for Libyan Studies.

Barth, F. 1969. *Ethnic Groups and Boundaries: The Social Organization of Culture Difference.* London: Allen and Unwin.

Barth, H. 1857–1858. *Travels and Discoveries in North and Central Africa.* 5 vols. London: Longman et al.

Batran, A. 2001. *The Qadiriyya Brotherhood in West Africa and the Western Sahara: The Life and Times of Shaykh Mukhtar al-Kunti, 1729–1811.* Rabat: Institut des études africaines.

Baud, M., and W. van Schendel. 1997. Toward a Comparative History of Borderlands. *Journal of World History* 8/2, 211–242.

Bayart, J.-F. 2004. Le crime transnational et la formation de l'État. *Politique africaine* 93, 93–104.

Bayart, J.-F., P. Geschiere, and F. Nyamnjoh. 2001. Autochtonie, démocratie et citoyenneté en Afrique. *Critique internationale* 10, 177–194.

Becker, C. J. 2002. "We Are Real Slaves, Real Ismkhan": Memories of the Trans-Saharan Slave Trade in the Tafilalet of South-Eastern Morocco. *Journal of North African Studies* 7/4, 97–121.

Bédoucha, G. 1987. *L'eau, l'amie du puissant: Une communauté oasienne du sud tunisien.* Paris: Éditions des archives contemporaines.

Bellil, R. 1999–2000. *Les oasis du Gourara, Sahara algérien.* Louvain: Peeters.

Bellil, R., and D. Badi. 1993. Évolution de la relation entre Kel Ahaggar et Kel Adagh. In *Le politique dans l'histoire touarègue,* ed. H. Claudot-Hawad, 95–110. Aix-en-Provence: IREMAM.

———. 1995. Les migrations actuelles des Touaregs du Mali vers le Sud de l'Algérie. *Études et documents berbères* 13, 79–98.

Ben Arrous, M. 2004. La translocalité, pour quoi faire? In *Les relations transsahariennes à l'époque contemporaine: Un espace en constante mutation,* ed. L. Marfaing and S. Wippel, 415–442. Paris: Karthala.

Bensaâd, A. 2002. La grande migration africaine à travers le Sahara. *Méditerranée* 99/3–4, 41–50.

———. 2005a. Eau, urbanisation et mutations sociales dans le Bas-Sahara. In *La ville et le désert, le bas Sahara algérien,* ed. M. Côte, 95–122. Paris: Karthala.

———. 2005b. Les migrations transsahariennes, une mondialisation par la marge. *Maghreb—Machrek* 185, 13–36.

———. 2009. L'immigration en Algérie: Une réalité prégnante et son occultation officielle. In *Le Maghreb à l'épreuve des migrations subsahariennes,* ed. A. Bensaâd, 15–42. Paris: Karthala.

Benyoucef, B. 1986. *Le M'zab, les pratiques de l'espace.* Algiers: ENAL.

Bernus, E. 1993 [1981]. *Touaregs nigériens: Unité culturelle et diversité régionale d'un peuple pasteur.* Paris: L'Harmattan.

———. 1999. Exodes tous azimuts en zone sahélo-saharienne. In *Déplacés et réfugiés: La mobilité sous contrainte,* ed. V. Lassailly-Jacob, J.-Y. Marchal, and A. Quesnel, 195–208. Paris: IRD.

Bernus, S. 1981. Relations entre nomades et sédentaires des confins sahariens méridionaux: Essai d'interprétation dynamique. *Revue de l'Occident musulman et de la Méditerranée* 32, 23–35.

Biarnes, A. 1982. Systèmes de production et de commercialisation des oasis du Kaouar. Final diss., Institut national agronomique Paris-Grignon, Paris.

Bierschenk, T. 1988. Religion and Political Structure: Remarks on Ibadism in Oman and the Mzab (Algeria). *Studia Islamica* 68, 107–128.

Birks, J. S. 1978. *Across the Savannas to Mecca: The Overland Pilgrimage Route to West Africa.* London: Hurst.

Bisson, J. 2003. *Mythes et réalités d'un désert convoité: Le Sahara.* Paris: L'Harmattan.

Boesen, E., and L. Marfaing, eds. 2007. *Les nouveaux urbains dans l'espace Sahara-Sahel: Un cosmopolitisme par le bas.* Paris: Karthala.

Boilley, P. 1996. Aux origines des conflits dans les zones touarègues et maures. *Relations internationales et stratégiques* 23, 100–107.

———. 1999. *Les Touaregs Kel Adagh: Dépendances et révoltes du Soudan français au Mali contemporain.* Paris: Karthala.

Boivin, N., and D. Fuller. 2009. Shell Middens, Ships and Seeds: Exploring Coastal Subsistence, Maritime Trade and the Dispersal of Domesticates in and around the Ancient Arabian Peninsula. *Journal of World Prehistory* 22, 113–180.

Bonète, Y. 1962. Contribution à l'étude des pasteurs nomades Arbā'a. Doctorat de 3e cycle, Paris.

Bonte, P. 1987. L'herbe ou le sol: L'évolution du système foncier pastoral en Mauritanie du sud-ouest. In *Hériter en pays musulman: Habus, lait vivant, manyahuli,* ed. M. Gast, 193–214. Paris: CNRS.

———. 1998. Fortunes commerciales à Shingîti (Adrar mauritanien) au XIXe siècle. *Journal of African History* 39, 1–13.

———. 2000. Faire fortune au Sahara: Permanences et ruptures. *Autrepart* 16, 49–65.

———. 2001a. Droit musulman et pratiques foncières dans l'Adrār mauritanien. *Études rurales* 155–156, 93–106.

———. 2001b. *La montagne de fer: La SNIM.* Paris: Karthala.

Bordes, P., and A. Labrousse. 2004. Économie de la drogue et réseaux de corruption au Maroc. *Politique africaine* 93, 63–82.

Bose, S. 2006. *A Hundred Horizons: The Indian Ocean in the Age of Global Empire.* Cambridge, Mass.: Harvard University Press.

Boubekri, H. 2000. Échanges transfrontaliers et commerce parallèle aux frontiers tuniso-libyennes. *Maghreb—Machrek* 120, 39–51.

Bouche, D. 1968. *Les villages de liberté en Afrique Noire Française 1887–1910.* Paris: Mouton.

Bouguetaia, B. 1981. *Les frontières méridionales de l'Algérie: De l'hinterland à l'uti-possidetis.* Algiers: SNED.

Boukhobza, M. 1976. *Nomadisme et colonisation: Analyse des mécanismes de déstructuration et de disparition de la société pastorale en Algérie.* Paris: EHESS.

Bourdieu, P. 1958. *Sociologie de l'Algérie.* Paris: Presses universitaires de France.

Bourgeot, A. 1991. Territoire. In *Dictionnaire de l'ethnologie et de l'anthropologie,* ed. P. Bonte and M. Izard, 704. Paris: Presses universitaires de France.

———. 1994a. L'agro-pastoralisme des Touaregs Kel Owey (Aïr). In *Au contact Sahara-Sahel: Milieux et sociétés du Niger,* ed. L. Bridel, A. Morel, and I. Ousseini, 137–155. Grenoble: Institut de Géographie Alpine.

———. 1994b. Révoltes et rébellions en pays touareg. *Afrique contemporaine* 170, 3–19.

———. 1995. *Les sociétés touarègues: Nomadisme, identité, resistances.* Paris: Karthala.

———. 1996. Les rébellions touarègues: Une cause perdue? *Afrique contemporaine* 177, 99–115.

Bousquet, C. 1986. Les nouveaux citadins de Beni Isguen, M'Zab. In *Petites villes et villes moyennens dans le monde arabe 2, Fascicule de recherché URBAMA* 17, 435–450.

Bouterfa, S. 2005. *Les manuscrits du Touat: Le Sud algérien.* Algiers: Barzakh.

Bovill, E. W. 1968. *The Golden Trade of the Moors.* Oxford: Oxford University Press.

Bowles, P. 1949. *The Sheltering Sky.* London: Lehmann.

Boyer, F. 2005. Le projet migratoire des migrants touaregs de la zone de Bankilaré: La pauvreté désavouée. *Stichproben: Wiener Zeitschrift für kritische Afrikastudien* 8, 47–67.

Brachet, J. 2005. Migrants, transporteurs et agents d'état: Rencontre sur l'axe Agadez-Sebha. *Autrepart* 36, 43–62.

———. 2009a. *Migrations transsahariennes: Vers un désert cosmopolite et morcelé (Niger).* Bellecombe-en-Bauges: Croquant.

———. 2009b. Irrégularité et clandestinité de l'immigration au Maghreb: Cas de l'Algérie et de la Libye. In *Le Maghreb à l'épreuve des migrations subsahariennes: Immigration sur emigration,* ed. A. Bensaâd, 109–135. Paris: Karthala.

———. 2011. The Blind Spot of Repression: Migration Policies and Human Survival in the Central Sahara. In *Transnational Migration and Human Security: The Migration-Development-Security Nexus,* ed. T.-D. Truong and D. Gasper, 57–66. New York: Springer.

Braudel, F. 1972 [1966]. *The Mediterranean and the Mediterranean World in the Age of Philip II.* London: Collins.

Bredeloup, S. 1995. Expulsion des ressortissants ouest-africains au sein du continent africain (1954–1995). *Mondes en développement* 23/91, 117–121.

———. 2007. *La diams'pora du fleuve Sénégal: Sociologie des migrations africaines.* Toulouse: Presses universitaires du Mirail, IRD.

———. 2008. L'aventurier, une figure de la migration africaine. *Cahiers internationaux de sociologie* 125, 281–306.

Bredeloup, S., and O. Pliez, eds. 2005. Migrations entre les deux rives du Sahara. *Autrepart* 36 (special issue).

Brett, M. 1983. Islam and Trade in the Bilād al-Sūdān, Tenth to Eleventh Century AD. *Journal of African History* 24, 431–440.

Broodbank, C. 2008. The Mediterranean and Its Hinterland. In *The Oxford Handbook of Archaeology,* ed. B. Cunliffe, C. Gosden, and R. Joyce, 677–722. Oxford: Oxford University Press.

———. Forthcoming. *The Making of the Middle Sea.* London: Thames and Hudson.

Brooks, G. E. 1993. *Landlords and Strangers: Ecology, Society and Trade in Western Africa 1000–1630.* Boulder, Colo.: Westview.

Brower, B. C. 2009. *A Desert Named Peace: The Violence of France's Empire in the Algerian Sahara, 1844–1902.* New York: Columbia University Press.

Burke, E. 2000. Theorizing the Histories of Colonialism and Nationalism in the Arab Maghrib. In *Beyond Colonialism and Nationalism in the Maghrib: History, Culture, and Politics,* ed. A. Ahmida, 17–36. New York: Palgrave.

Caillié, R. 1830. *Journal d'un voyage à Tombouctou et a Jenné, dans l'Afrique centrale.* Paris: Imprimerie Royale.

Carette, E. 1844. *Étude sur les routes suivies par les Arabes dans la partie méridionale de l'Algérie et de la Régence de Tunis pour servir à l'établissement du réseau géographique de ces contrées.* Paris: Imprimerie Royale.

———. 1848. *Recherches sur la géographie et le commerce de l'Algérie méridionale.* Paris: Imprimerie Royale.

Certeau, M. de. 1987. *La faiblesse de croire.* Paris: Seuil.

Chaudhuri, K. N. 1985. *Trade and Civilisation in the Indian Ocean: An Economic History from the Rise of Islam to 1750.* Cambridge: Cambridge University Press.

———. 1990. *Asia before Europe: Economy and Civilisation in the Indian Ocean from the Rise of Islam to 1750.* Cambridge: Cambridge University Press.

Chentouf, T. 1984. Les monnaies dans le Gourara, le Touat et le Tidikelt dans la seconde moitié du 19e siècle. In *Enjeux sahariens,* ed. P.-R. Baduel, 79–94. Paris: CNRS.

Choplin, A. 2008. L'immigré, le migrant et l'allochtone: Circulations migratoires et figures de l'étranger en Mauritanie. *Politique africaine* 109, 73–90.

———. 2009. *Nouakchott: Au carrefour de la Mauritanie et du monde.* Paris: Karthala.

Choplin, A., and J. Lombard. 2007. Destination Nouadhibou pour les migrants africains. *Revue mappemonde* 88. http://mappemonde.mgm.fr/num16/lieux/lieux07401.html.

———. 2008. Migrations et recompositions spatiales en Mauritanie: "Nouadhibou du monde:" Ville de transit—et après? *Afrique contemporaine* 228, 151–170.

Ciavolella, R. 2010. *Les Peuls et l'État en Mauritanie—Une anthropologie des marges.* Paris: Karthala.

Clancy-Smith, J. A. 1994. *Rebel and Saint: Muslim Notables, Populist Protest, Colonial Encounters: Algeria and Tunisia, 1800–1904.* Berkeley: University of California Press.

Clancy-Smith, J. A., S. G. Miller, A. A. Ahmida, M. El-Mansour, J. McDougall, and K. J. Perkins. forthcoming. *A History of the Maghrib.* Cambridge: Cambridge University Press.

Clanet, J.-C. 1981. L'émigration temporaire des Toubou du Kanem vers la Libye. *Cahiers géographiques de Rouen* 15, 17–33.

Claudot-Hawad, H. 1990. Honneur et politique: Les choix stratégiques des Touaregs pendant la colonisation française. *Revue des mondes musulmans et de la Méditerranée* 57, 11–47.

———. 1996. Identité et alterité d'un point de vue touareg: Eléments pour un débat. *Les cahiers de l'IREMAM* 7–8, 132–140.

Clauzel, J. 1960a. *L'exploitation des salines de Taoudeni.* Algiers: Institut des Recherches Sahariennes.

———. 1960b. Transports, automobiles, et caravanes dans le Sahara soudanais. *Travaux de l'institut des recherches sahariennes* 19, 161–168.

Cleaveland, T. 1998. Islam and the Construction of Social Identity in the Nineteenth-Century Sahara. *Journal of African History* 39, 365–388.

———. 2002. *Becoming Walata: A History of Saharan Social Formation and Transformation.* Portsmouth, N.H.: Heinemann.

CNUCED/ICC. 2004. Guide de l'investissement en Mauritanie (March). www.unctad.org/fr/docs/iteiia20044_fr.pdf.

Cohen, A. 1971. Cultural Strategies and the Organisation of Trading Diasporas. In *The Development of Indigenous Trade and Markets in West Africa,* ed. C. Meillassoux, 266–281. Oxford: Oxford University Press.

Collins, R. O., ed. 1968. *Problems in African History.* Englewood Cliffs, N.J.: Prentice Hall.

Comaroff, J., and J. Comaroff. 2005. Naturing the Nation: Aliens, Apocalypse and the Postcolonial State. In *Sovereign Bodies: Citizens, Migrants and States in the Postcolonial World,* ed. T. Blom Hansen and F. Stepputat, 120–147. Princeton, N.J.: Princeton University Press.

Comité d'Information du Sahel. 1975. *Qui se nourrit de la famine en Afrique?* Paris: Maspéro.

Constable, R. O. 2003. *Housing the Stranger in the Mediterranean World: Lodging, Trade, and Travel in Late Antiquity and the Middle Ages.* Cambridge: Cambridge University Press.

Conte, B. 1994. L'après-dévaluation: Hypotheses et hypothèques. *Politique africaine* 54, 32–46.

Cooper, F. 2002. *Africa since 1940: The Past of the Present.* Cambridge: Cambridge University Press.

Coquery-Vidrovitch, C. 2004. De la périodisation en histoire africaine: Peut-on l'envisager? A quoi sert-elle? *Afrique & Histoire* 2, 31–65.

Corbin, H. 1983. *Face de dieu, face de l'homme: Herméneutique et soufisme.* Paris: Flammarion.

Cordell, D. 1985. The Awlad Sulayman of Libya and Chad: Power and Adaptation in the Sahara and Sahel. *Canadian Journal of African Studies* 19/2, 319–343.

———. 1999. No Liberty, Not Much Equality, and Very Little Fraternity: The Mirage of Manumission in the Algerian Sahara in the Second Half of the Nineteenth Century. In *Slavery and Colonial Rule in Africa,* ed. S. Miers and M. A. Klein, 38–56. London: Cass.

Cordell, D., J. W. Gregory, and V. Piché. 1996. *Hoe and Wage: A Social History of a Circular Migration System in West Africa.* Boulder, Colo.: Westview.

Cornell, V. J. 1998. *Realm of the Saint: Power and Authority in Moroccan Sufism.* Austin: University of Texas Press.

Côte, M., ed. 2005. *La ville et le désert, le bas Sahara algérien.* Paris: Karthala.

Crawley Quinn, J. C. 2009. North Africa. In *The Blackwell Companion to Ancient History,* ed. A. Erskine, 260–272. Oxford: Blackwell.

Cremaschi, M., M. Pelfini, and M. Santili. 2006. Cupressus dupreziana: A Dendroclimatic Record for the Middle-Late Holocene in the Central Sahara. *Holocene* 16/2, 293–303.

Cressey, G. B. 1958. Qanats, Karez and Foggaras. *Geographical Review* 48, 27–44.

Crombé, X., and J. H. Jézéquel, eds. 2008. *Niger 2005: A Natural Catastrophe?* London: Hurst.

Crone, G. R. 1937. *The Voyages of Cadamosto and Other Documents on Western Africa in the Second Half of the Fifteenth Century.* London: Hakluyt Society.

Curtin, P. 1975. *Economic Change in Pre-Colonial Africa: Senegambia in the Era of the Slave Trade.* Madison: University of Wisconsin Press.

Dalton, G. 1976. Review: *An Economic History of West Africa. African Economic History* 1, 51–101.

Davis, E. A. 1999. Metamorphosis in the Culture Market of Niger. *American Anthropologist,* n.s., 101/3, 485–501.

Davoine, R. 2003. *Tombouctou: Fascination et malédiction d'une ville mythique.* Paris: L'Harmattan.

Delheure, J. 1986. *Timegga d-Yiwalen n At-Mzab: Faits et Dires du Mzab.* Paris: SELAF.

Denham, D., H. Clapperton, and W. Oudney. 1826. *Narrative of Travels and Discoveries in Northern and Central Africa in the Years 1822, 1823 and 1824.* London: John Murray.

Derrécagaix, V.-B. 1882. *Exploration du Sahara: Les deux missions Flatters.* Paris: Société de Géographie.

Derrien, I. 1879. *Le Chemin de fer transsaharien d'Oran au Touat.* Oran: A. Perrier.

Desanges, J. 1999a. Aperçus sur les contacts transsahariens d'après les sources classiques. In *Toujours Afrique apporte fait nouveau: Scripta minora,* ed. M. Reddé, 239–247. Paris: Boccard.

———. 1999b. Libyens noirs ou libyens noircis? In *Toujours Afrique apporte fait nouveau: Scripta minora,* ed. M. Reddé, 229–238. Paris: Boccard.

Deutsch, J.-G., and B. Reinwald, eds. 2002. *Space on the Move: Transformations of the Indian Ocean Seascape in the Nineteenth and Twentieth Century.* Berlin: Klaus Schwarz.

Diop, H., and I. Thiam. 1990. Quelques aspects des migrations de pêcheurs du secteur artisanal maritime en Mauritanie. *Bulletin scientifique du CNROP* 20, 63–72.

Diouf, M. 2000. The Senegalese Murid Trade Diaspora and the Making of a Vernacular Cosmopolitanism. *Public Culture* 12/3, 679–702.

Djibo, M. 2002. Rébellion touarègue et question saharienne au Niger. *Autrepart* 23, 135–156.

Dore, J., A. Leone, and J. Hawthorne. 2007. Pottery and Other Finds. In *The Archaeology of Fazzān*, vol. 2: *Site Gazetteer, Pottery and Other Survey Finds*, ed. D. Mattingly, 305–431. London: Society for Libyan Studies.

Dozon, J. P. 2000. La Côte d'Ivoire entre démocratie, nationalisme et ethnonationalisme. *Politique africaine* 78, 45–62.

Dupraz, P. 1994. Paroles de "dévalués." *Politique africaine* 54, 117–126.

Dupront, A. 1987. *Du sacré: Croisades et pèlerinages, images et langages.* Paris: Gallimard.

Duveyrier, H. 1860. Coup d'œil sur le pays des Beni M'zab et sur celui des Chaanba occidentaux. *Revue algérienne et coloniale* 2, 125–141.

Echallier, J. C. 1973. Forteresses berbères du Gourara: Problèmes et résultats des fouilles. *Libyca* 21, 293–302.

Eickelman, D. 1976. *Moroccan Islam: Tradition and Change in a Pilgrimage Center.* Austin: University of Texas Press.

———. 1985. New Directions in Interpreting North African Society. In *Contemporary North Africa: Issues of Development and Integration*, ed. H. Barakat, 164–177. London: Croom Helm.

Eldblom, L. 1968. *Structure foncière, organisation et structure sociale: Une étude sur la vie socio-économique dans les trois oasis libyennes de Ghat, Mourzouk et particulièrement Ghadamès.* Lund, Sweden: Uniskol.

Ellis, S., and J. MacGaffey. 1997. Le commerce international informel en Afrique subsaharienne. *Cahiers d'études africaines* 37, 11–37.

Evers Rosander, E. 2005. Cosmopolites et locales: Femmes sénégalaises en voyage. *Afrique & Histoire* 4, 103–121.

Faget, J., ed. 2005. *Médiation et action publique: La dynamique du fluide.* Pessac: Presses universitaires de Bordeaux.

Faidherbe, L. C. 1889. *Le Sénégal.* Paris: Hachette.

Faragher, J. M. 1998. *Rereading Frederick Jackson Turner: "The Significance of the Frontier in American History" and Other Essays.* New Haven, Conn.: Yale University Press.

Farb, P., and G. Armelagos. 1980. *Consuming Passions: The Anthropology of Eating.* Boston: Houghton Mifflin.

Fentress, E. 2007. Where Were North African Nundinae Held? In *Communities and Connections: Essays in Honour of Barry Cunliffe*, ed. C. Gosden, H. Hamerow, P. de Jersey, and G. Lock, 125–141. Oxford: Oxford University Press.

———. 2009. Slavers on Chariots: The Garamantes between Siwa and the Niger Bend. Paper presented at the British Museum Conference "Saharan networks," Institute of Archaeology, University College, London, 6 March.

———. 2011. Slavers on Chariots. In *Money, Trade and Routes in Pre-Islamic North Africa*, ed. A. Dowler and E. Galvin, 65–71. London: British Museum.

Fentress, E., A. Drine, and R. Holod, eds. 2009. *An Island through Time: Jerba Studies*, vol. 1: *The Punic and Roman Periods.* Portsmouth, N.H.: Journal of Roman Archaeology.

Földessy, E. 1994. Entraide et solidarité chez les Mozabites ibadites. Master's diss. in ethnography, University of Paris X-Nanterre.

Fontana, S. 1995. I Manufatti romani nei corredi funerari del Fezzan: Testimonianze dei commerci e della cultura dei Garamanti (I–III, sec. d. C.). In *Productions et exportations africaines: Actualités archéologiques,* ed. P. Trousset, 405–420. Paris: Comité des travaux historiques et scientifiques.

Foucault, M. 1979. *History of Sexuality,* vol. 3: *The Care of the Self,* trans. Robert Hurley. London: Allen Lane.

Frachetti, M. D. 2009. Geography. In *An Island through Time: Jerba Studies,* vol. 1: *The Punic and Roman Periods,* ed. E. Fentress, A. Drine, and R. Holod, 55–71. Portsmouth, N.H.: Journal of Roman Archaeology.

Freitag, U., and W. G. Clarence-Smith, eds. 1997. *Hadrami Scholars, Traders, and Statesmen in the Indian Ocean, 1750s–1960s.* Leiden: Brill.

Fresia, M. 2009. *Les Mauritaniens réfugiés au Sénégal: Une anthropologie critique de l'asile et de l'aide humanitaire.* Paris: L'Harmattan.

Friedman, T. 2005. *The World Is Flat: A Brief History of the Globalized World in the Twenty-First Century.* London: Allen Lane.

Garrard, T. 1982. Myth and Metrology: The Early Trans-Saharan Gold Trade. *Journal of African History* 23, 443–461.

Gast, M. 1989. Échanges transsahariens et survie des populations locales. *Bulletin d'écologie humaine* 7/2, 3–24.

Gaudio, A., ed. 2002. *Les bibliothèques du désert: Recherches et études sur un millénaire d'écrits.* Paris: L'Harmattan.

Gellner, E. 1969. *Saints of the Atlas.* Chicago: University of Chicago Press.

———. 1995. *Anthropology and Politics: Revolutions in the Sacred Grove.* Oxford: Blackwell.

Geoffroy, A. 1887. Arabes pasteurs nomades de la tribu des Larbas. *Les Ouvriers des deux mondes* 1/8, 409–464.

Ghazal, A. N. 2010a. The Other Frontiers of Arab Nationalism: Ibadis, Berbers, and the Arabist-Salafi Press in the Interwar Period. *International Journal of Middle East Studies* 42/1, 105–122.

———. 2010b. *Islamic Reform and Arab Nationalism: Expanding the Crescent from the Mediterranean to the Indian Ocean (1880s–1930s).* London: Routledge.

Gide, A. 1902. *L'immoraliste.* Paris: Mercure de France.

Gilbertson, D. D. 1996. Explanations: Environment as Agency. In *Farming the Desert: The UNESCO Libyan Valleys Archaeological Survey,* vol. 1: *Synthesis,* ed. G. Barker, D. D. Gilbertson, G. D. B. Jones, and D. J. Mattingly, 291–317. London: UNESCO and the Society for Libyan Studies.

Gilbertson, D., C. O. Hunt, and G. Gilmore. 2000. Success, Longevity, and Failure of Arid-Land Agriculture: Romano-Libyan Floodwater Farming in the Tripolitanian Pre-Desert. In *The Archaeology of Drylands: Living at the Margin,* ed. G. W. W. Barker and D. Gilbertson, 137–159. London: Routledge.

Giuffrida, A. 2005. Clerics, Rebels and Refugees: Mobility Strategies and Networks among the Kel Antessar. *Journal of North African Studies* 10/3–4, 529–543.

Glantz, M., ed. 1976. *The Politics of Natural Disaster: The Case of the Sahel Drought.* New York: Praeger.

Glick Schiller, N., L. Basch, and C. Szanton Blanc. 1995. From Immigrant to Transmigrant: Theorizing Transnational Migration. *Anthropological Quarterly* 68/1, 48–63.

Grandguillaume, G. 1973. Régime économique et structure du Pouvoir: Le système des foggara du Touat. *Revue de l'Occident musulman et de la Méditerranée* 13–14, 437–457.

———. 1978. De la coutume à la loi: Droit de l'eau et statut des communautés locales dans le Touat précolonial. *Peuples méditerranéens* 2, 119–133.

Grant, A. 2006. Animal Bones from the Sahara: Diet, Economy and Social Practices. In *The Libyan Desert: Natural Resources and Cultural Heritage*, ed. D. Mattingly et al., 179–185. London: Society for Libyan Studies.

Grégoire, E. 1999. *Touaregs du Niger, le destin d'un mythe.* Paris: Karthala.

Grégoire, E., and J. Schmitz, eds. 2000. Afrique noire et monde arabe: Continuité et ruptures. *Autrepart* 16 (special issue).

Grémont, C. 2005. Comment les Touaregs ont perdu le fleuve: Eclairage sur les pratiques et les représentations foncières dans le cercle de Gao (Mali), XIXe–XXe siècles. In *Patrimoines naturels au Sud: Territoires, identités et stratégies locales,* ed. M. C. Cormier-Salem et al., 237–290. Paris: IRD.

———. 2009. Des Touaregs à l'épreuve de la frontière: Cohabitation et confrontations dans la zone de Tedjarert (nord-est du Mali). *L'Ouest saharien* 9/2, 27–66.

———. 2010. *Les Touaregs Iwellemedan (1647–1896): Un ensemble politique de la Boucle du Niger.* Paris: Karthala.

Grémont, C., A. Marty, R. Ag Moussa, and Y. Hamara Touré. 2004. *Les liens sociaux au Nord-Mali: Entre fleuve et dunes.* Paris: Karthala.

Grévoz, D. 1989. *Sahara 1830–1881: Les mirages français et la tragédie Flatters.* Paris: L'Harmattan.

Gsell, S. 1926. *Promenades archéologiques aux environs d'Alger (Cherchel, Tipaza, le tombeau de la chrétienne).* Paris: Belles Lettres.

Guitart, F. 1989. Le rôle des frontières coloniales sur le commerce transsaharien central (région d'Agadez 1900–1970). *Cahiers géographiques de Rouen* 32, 155–162.

———. 1992. Commerce et transport à Agadez au début des années 1970. In *Les transports en Afrique (XIXe–XXe),* ed. H. D'Almeida-Topor, C. Chanson-Jabeur, and M. Lakroum, 247–258. Paris: L'Harmattan.

Gutelius, D. 2001. Between God and Men: The Nasiriyya and Economic Life in Morocco, 1640–1830. Ph.D. diss., Johns Hopkins University.

———. 2002. The Path Is Easy and the Benefits Large: The Nasiriyya, Social Networks and Economic Change in Morocco, 1640–1830. *Journal of African History* 43, 27–49.

Haarmann, U. 1998. The Dead Ostrich: Life and Trade in Ghadamès (Libya) in the Nineteenth Century. *Die Welt des Islams* 38/1, 9–94.

Haas, H. de. 2007. The Myth of Invasion: Irregular Migration from West Africa to the Maghreb and the European Union. Research report, International Migration Institute, University of Oxford.

Haefeli, E. 1999. A Note on the Use of North American Borderlands. *American Historical Review* 104/4, 1222–1225.

Haggett, P., A. D. Cliff, and A. Frey. 1977. *Locational Analysis in Human Geography,* 2nd ed. London: Edward Arnold.

Hahn, H. P., and G. Klute, eds. 2007. *Cultures of Migration: African Perspectives.* Münster: Lit Verlag.

Hall, B. 2011. *A History of Race in Muslim West Africa, 1600–1960*. Cambridge: Cambridge University Press.

Hall, L. 1927. *Timbuctoo*. New York: Hemper.

Hama, B. 1967. *Recherches sur l'histoire des Touaregs sahariens et soudanais*. Paris: Présence africaine.

Hamdun, S., and N. King, eds. and trans. 1975. *Ibn Battuta in Black Africa*. London: Collings.

Hannerz, U. 1992. *Cultural Complexity: Studies in the Global Organization of Meaning*. New York: Columbia University Press.

Harris, W. V., ed. 2005. *Rethinking the Mediterranean*. Oxford: Oxford University Press.

Hawad. 1990. La teshumara, antidote de l'état. *Revue des mondes musulmans et de la Méditerranée* 57, 123–140.

Hayot, A. 2002. Pour une anthropologie de la ville dans la ville: Questions de méthodes. *Revue Européenne des Migrations Internationales* 18/3, 93–105.

Heffernan, M. 2001. "A Dream as Frail as Those of Ancient Time": The Incredible Geography of Timbuctoo. *Environment and Planning D: Society and Space* 19/2, 203–225.

Herman, E. 2006. Migration as a Family Business: The Role of Personal Networks in the Mobility Phase of Migration. *International Migration* 44/4, 191–230.

Hily, M.-A., and C. Rinaudo. 2003. Cosmopolitisme et altérité: Les nouveaux migrants dans l'économie informelle. *Tsantsa* 8, 48–57.

Ho, E. 2002. Names beyond Nations: The Making of Local Cosmopolitans. *Études rurales* 163–164, 215–232.

———. 2006. *The Graves of Tarim: Genealogy and Mobility across the Indian Ocean*. Berkeley: University of California Press.

Hobsbawm, E. 1983. Introduction: Inventing Traditions. In *The Invention of Tradition*, ed. E. Hobsbawm and T. Ranger, 1–14. Cambridge: Cambridge University Press.

Hodges, T. 1983. *Western Sahara: The Roots of a Desert War*. Beckenham, England: Croom Helm.

Holl, A. F. C. 2004. *Holocene Saharans: An Anthropological Perspective*. London: Continuum.

Holsinger, D. 1980. Migration, Commerce and Community: The Mizabis in Eighteenth- and Nineteenth-Century Algeria. *Journal of African History* 21/1, 61–71.

Hopkins, A. G. 1973. *An Economic History of West Africa*. London: Longman.

———. 1976. *An Economic History of West Africa*: A Comment. *African Economic History* 2, 81–83.

Horden, P. 2005. Mediterranean Excuses: Historical Writing on the Mediterranean since Braudel. *History and Anthropology* 16/1, 1–6.

Horden, P., and N. Purcell. 2000. *The Corrupting Sea*. Oxford: Blackwell.

———. 2006. The Mediterranean and the New Thalassology. *American Historical Review* 111/3, 722–740.

Houafani, Z. 1986. *Les Pirates du desert*. Algiers: ENAL.

Houdas, O., ed. and trans. 1898, 1900. *Documents arabes relatifs à l'histoire du Soudan: Ta'rīkh es-Soudan*. 2 vols. Paris: Publications de l'École des langues orientales vivantes.

Houdas, O., and M. Delafosse, eds. and trans. 1964 [1913]. *Documents arabes relatifs à l'histoire du Soudan: Ta'rīkh el-fettach*. Paris: UNESCO.

Hunwick, J. O. 1985. *Sharī'a in Songhay: The Replies of al-Maghīlī to the Questions of Askia al-Ḥājj Muhammad*. Oxford: Oxford University Press.

———. 1994. The Religious Practices of Black Slaves in the Mediterranean Islamic World. In *Slavery on the Frontiers of Islam*, ed. P. E. Lovejoy, ch. 8. Princeton, N.J.: Markus Wiener.

———. 1999. *Timbuktu and the Songhay Empire: Al-Sa'di's Ta'rīkh al-Sūdān Down to 1613 and Other Contemporary Documents.* Leiden: Brill.

Iliffe, J. 1995. *Africans: The History of a Continent.* Cambridge: Cambridge University Press.

Jah, A. U. 1986. Paysannerie et évolution foncière dans la province Halaybe (région de Bogué). Master's thesis in history, Ecole Normale Supérieure de Nouakchott.

Janson, M. 2005. Roaming about for God's Sake: The Upsurge of the Tabligh *Jamā 'at* in the Gambia. *Journal of Religion in Africa* 35/4, 450–481.

Jolles, A. 1972. *Formes simples,* trans. Antoine Marie Buguet. Paris: Seuil.

Kaba, L. 1981. Archers, Musketeers and Mosquitoes: The Moroccan Invasion of the Sudan and the Songhay Resistance (1591–1612). *Journal of African History* 22/4, 457–475.

Kamara, M. 1998. *Florilège au jardin de l'histoire des noirs: Zuhūr al Basātīn,* ed. J. Schmitz. Paris: CNRS.

Kané, O. 1974. Les Maures et le Futa-Toro au XVIIIe siècle. *Cahiers d'études africaines* 54, 237–255.

Kané, S. 2005. Histoire de l'esclavage et des luttes anti-esclavagistes en Mauritanie. http://aircrigeweb.free.fr/parutions/SoudMaurit/SD_bibliokane.html (accessed summer 2009).

Kateb, K. 2001. *Européens, indigènes et juifs en Algérie, 1830–1962: Réalités et représentations des populations.* Paris: INED.

Kea, R. A. 2004. Expansion and Contractions: World-Historical Change and the Western Sudan World-System. *Journal of World-Systems Research* 10, 723–816.

Keenan, J. 2005. Waging War on Terror: The Implications of America's "New Imperialism" for Saharan Peoples. *Journal of North African Studies* 10/3–4, 619–647.

———. 2009. *The Dark Sahara: America's War on Terror in Africa.* London: Pluto.

Keïta, Y. 1998. De l'essai d'un bilan des législations foncières en Afrique francophone de 1960 à 1990. In *Quelles politiques foncières pour l'Afrique rurale? Réconcilier pratiques, légitimité et légalité,* ed. P. Lavigne Delville, 374–382. Paris: Karthala.

Khaled, N., D. Aiteur, M. Daouda, S. Tadjine, M. Soumer, D. Haddad, and R. Redjam. 2007. *Profils des migrants subsahariens en situation irrégulière en Algérie.* Preliminary research report. Algiers: CISP/SARP/UNHCR. www.afvic.info/documents/SyntheseurleprofildesmigrantssubsahariensenAlgerie.pdf.

Klein, M. A. 1998. *Slavery and Colonial Rule in French West Africa.* Cambridge: Cambridge University Press.

Klute, G. 1995. Hostilités et alliances: Archéologie de la dissidence des Touaregs au Mali. *Cahiers d'études africaines* 137, 55–71.

———. 2001. Die Rebellionen des Tuareg in Mali und Niger: Habilitationschrift. Universität zu Siegen.

Kollo, A. 1989. Contribution à la connaissance du Nord-Est nigérien: Les aspects sociaux et politiques de l'histoire du Kawar, du Jado et de l'Agram au XIXe siècle. Master's thesis, Department of History, University of Niamey.

Kopytoff, I., ed. 1987. *The African Frontier: The Reproduction of Traditional African Societies.* Bloomington: Indiana University Press.

Krätli, G., and G. Lydon, eds. 2010. *The Trans-Saharan Book Trade: Arabic Literacy, Manuscript Culture, and Intellectual History in Islamic Africa.* Leiden: Brill.

Labat, J. B. 1728. *Nouvelle relation de l'Afrique occidentale.* Paris: Chez Guillaume Cavelier.

Lamar, H., and L. Thompson, eds. 1981. *The Frontier in History: North America and Southern Africa Compared.* New Haven, Conn.: Yale University Press.

Laperche, B., ed. 2008. *L'innovation pour le développement.* Paris: Karthala.

Lattimore, O. 1940. *Inner Asian Frontiers of China.* New York: American Geographical Society.

Law, R. C. C. 1967. The Garamantes and Trans-Saharan Enterprise in Classical Times. *Journal of African History* 8, 181–200.

Lawless, R., and L. Monahan, eds. 1997. *War and Refugees: The Western Sahara Conflict.* London: Pinter.

Layish, A. 2005. *Sharīʿa and Custom in Libyan Tribal Society: An Annotated Translation of Decisions from the Sharīʿa Courts of Ajdābiya and Kufra.* Leiden: Brill.

Lecocq, B. 2004. Unemployed Intellectuals in the Sahara: The Teshumara Nationalist Movement and the Revolutions in Tuareg Society. *International Review of Social History* 49, 87–109.

———. 2010. *Disputed Desert: Decolonisation, Competing Nationalisms and Tuareg Rebellions in Mali.* Leiden: Brill.

Lecocq, B., and P. Schrijver. 2007. The War on Terror in a Haze of Dust: Potholes and Pitfalls on the Saharan Front. *Journal of Contemporary African Studies* 25/1, 141–166.

Lemarchand, R., ed. 1998. *The Green and the Black: Qadhafi's Policies in Africa.* Bloomington: Indiana University Press.

Leriche, A. 1953. De l'origine du thé au Maroc et au Sahara. *Bulletin de l'IFAN* 15, 731–736.

Leroy, E. 1998. De l'appropriation à la patrimonialité, une brève introduction à la terminologie foncière. In *Quelles politiques foncières pour l'Afrique rurale? Réconcilier pratiques, légitimité et légalité,* ed. P. Lavigne Delville, 23–27. Paris: Karthala.

Leroy-Beaulieu, P. 1904. *Le Sahara, le Soudan, et les chemins de fer transsahariens.* Paris: Guillaumin.

Leservoisier, O. 1994. *La question foncière en Mauritanie: Terres et pouvoirs dans la région du Gorgol.* Paris: L'Harmattan.

———. 2009. Contemporary Trajectories of Slavery in Haalpulaar Society (Mauritania). In *Reconfiguring Slavery: West African Trajectories,* ed. B. Rossi, 140–151. Liverpool: Liverpool University Press.

Levtzion, N. 1973. *Ancient Ghana and Mali.* London: Methuen.

———. 1975. North-West Africa: From the Maghrib to the Fringes of the Forest. In *The Cambridge History of Africa,* vol. 4: *1600–1790,* ed. R. Gray, ch. 3. Cambridge: Cambridge University Press.

———. 2000. Islam in the Bilad al-Sudan to 1800. In *The History of Islam in Africa,* ed. N. Levtzion and R. Pouwels, ch. 3. Oxford: James Currey.

Levtzion, N., and J. F. P. Hopkins, eds. 1981. *Corpus of Early Arabic Sources for West African History.* Cambridge: Cambridge University Press.

Lewicki, T. 1955. *Études ibadites nord-africaines.* Warsaw: Panstwowe Wydam.

———. 1960. Quelques extraits inédits relatifs aux voyages des commerçants et des missionaires ibadites nord-africains au pays du soudan occidental et central au moyen âge. *Folia Orientalia* 2, 1–27.

———. 1976. *Études maghrébines et soudanaises.* Warsaw: Editions scientifiques de Pologne.

Liverani, M. 2000a. The Libyan Caravan Road in Herodotus IV.181–185. *Journal of the Economic and Social History of the Orient* 43, 496–520.

———. 2000b. The Garamantes: A Fresh Approach. *Libyan Studies* 31, 17–28.

———. 2003. Aghram Nadharif and the Southern Border of the Garamantian Kingdom. In *Arid Lands in Roman Times: Papers from the International Conference, Rome, July 9th–10th 2001,* ed. M. Liverani, 23–36. Florence: All'insegna del giglio.

Liverani, M., ed. 2005. *Aghram Nadharif: The Barkat Oasis (Sha'abiya of Ghat, Libyan Sahara) in Garamantian Times.* Florence: All'insegna del giglio.

Loualich, F. 2003. Les esclaves noirs à Alger (fin du XVIIIème–début du XIXème siècle): De l'esclave à l'affranchi, vers une relation d'allégéance. *Mélanges de l'école française de Rome* 115/1, 513–522.

Lovejoy, P. E. 1980. *Caravans of Kola: The Hausa Kola Trade 1500–1900.* Oxford: Oxford University Press.

———. 1986. *Salt of the Desert Sun: A History of Salt Production and Trade in Central Sūdān.* Cambridge: Cambridge University Press.

———. 2000 [1983]. *Transformations in Slavery: A History of Slavery in Africa,* 2nd ed. Cambridge: Cambridge University Press.

Lovejoy, P. E., ed. 2004. *Slavery on the Frontiers of Islam.* Princeton, N.J.: Markus Wiener.

Lydon, G. 2005. Writing Trans-Saharan History: Methods, Sources and Interpretations across the African Divide. *Journal of North African Studies* 10/3–4, 293–324.

———. 2008. Contracting Caravans: Partnership and Profit in Nineteenth-Century Trans-Saharan Trade. *Journal of Global History* 3/1, 89–113.

———. 2009. *On Trans-Saharan Trails: Islamic Law, Trade Networks, and Cross-Cultural Exchange in Nineteenth-Century Western Africa.* Cambridge: Cambridge University Press.

MacDonald, K. C., and D. N. Edwards. 1993. Chickens in Africa: The Importance of Qasr Ibrim. *Antiquity* 67, 584–590.

MacDonald, K. C., R. Vernet, M. Martinon-Tórres, and D. Q. Fuller. 2009. Dhar Néma: From Early Agriculture to Metallurgy in Southeastern Mauritania. *Azania* 44/1, 3–48.

Maiga, M. 1997. *Le Mali: De la sécheresse à la rebellion nomade.* Paris: L'Harmattan.

Malkin, I., C. Constantakopoulou, and K. Panagopoulou, eds. 2009. *Greek and Roman Networks in the Mediterranean.* London: Routledge.

Mammeri, M. 1984. *L'ahellil du Gourara.* Paris: MSH.

Manchuelle, F. 1997. *Willing Migrants: Soninke Labor Diasporas, 1848–1960.* Athens: Ohio University Press.

Mangeot P., and P. Marty. 1918. Les Touareg de la boucle du Niger. *Bulletin du comité d'études historiques et scientifiques de l'AOF* 3, 87–136, 257–288, 422–475.

Manning, P. 1990. *Slavery and African Life: Occidental, Oriental, and African Slave Trades.* Cambridge: Cambridge University Press.

Marfaing, L. 2005. Du savoir-faire sénégalais en matière de pêche sur les côtes mauritaniennes: Une approche historique. *Stichproben: Wiener Zeitschrift für kritische Afrikastudien* 8, 69–98.

———. 2007. Constructions spatiales et relationnelles dans un espace urbain: Commercantes sénégalaises à Casablanca. In *Les nouveaux urbains dans l'espace Sahara-Sahel: Un cosmopolitisme par le bas,* ed. E. Boesen and L. Marfaing, 159–185. Paris: Karthala.

———. 2008. Migration saisonnière, va-et-vient, migration internationale? L'exemple des Sénégalais à Nouakchott. *Asylon* 3. www.terra.rezo.net.

———. 2009a. Vom Transitraum zum Ankunftsland: Migranten im Sahara-Sahel-Raum als Entwicklungspotential: Der Fall Mauretanien. *Sociologus* 59/1, 67–88.

———. 2009b. "Profession? Commis!": Les employés de l'administration coloniale en Mauritanie et leurs rapports avec les populations. In *La question du pouvoir en Afrique du Nord et de l'Ouest*, vol. 1: *Du rapport colonial au rapport de développement*, ed. S. Caratini, 12–58. Paris: L'Harmattan.

Marfaing, L., and W. Hein. 2008. Das EU-Einwanderungsabkommen—kein Ende der illegalen Migration aus Afrika. *GIGA Focus Global* 8.

Marfaing, L., and S. Wippel, eds. 2004. *Les relations transsahariennes à l'époque contemporaine*. Paris: Karthala.

Marichal, R. 1992. *Les ostraca de Bu Njem*. Tripoli: Département des Antiquités.

Markovits, C. 2000. *The Global World of Indian Merchants, 1750–1947*. Cambridge: Cambridge University Press.

Martin, A.-G.-P. 1908. *À la frontière du Maroc: Les oasis sahariennes (Gourara, Touat, Tidikelt)*. Algiers: Imprimerie algérienne.

Marty, P. 1921. *Étude sur l'Islam et les tribus Maures: Les Brakna 1850–1903*. Paris: Leroux.

Masud, M. K., ed. 2000. *Travellers in Faith: Studies of the Tablīghī Jamā'at as a Transnational Islamic Movement for Faith Renewal*. Leiden: Brill.

Mattingly, D. J. 1995. *Tripolitania*. London: Batsford.

———. 2000. Twelve Thousand Years of Human Adaptation in Fezzan (Libyan Sahara). In *The Archaeology of Drylands: Living at the Margin*, ed. G. W. W. Barker and D. Gilbertson, 160–179. London: Routledge.

Mattingly, D. J., ed. 2003. *The Archaeology of Fazzān*, vol. 1: *Synthesis*. London: Society for Libyan Studies.

———. 2007. *The Archaeology of Fazzān*, vol. 2: *Site Gazetteer, Pottery and Other Survey Finds*. London: Society for Libyan Studies.

———. 2010. *The Archaeology of Fazzān*, vol. 3: *Excavation of C. M. Daniels*. London: Society for Libyan Studies.

Mattingly, D., S. al-Aghab, M. Ahmed, F. Moussa, M. Sterry, and A. Wilson (with contributions by F. Cole, V. Leitch, A. Radini, T. Savage, K. Schörle, and D. Veldhuis). 2010. DMP X: Survey and Landscape Conservation Issues around the Taqallit Headland. *Libyan Studies* 41, 105–132.

Mattingly, D., and D. Edwards. 2003. Religious and Funerary Structures. In *The Archaeology of Fazzān*, vol. 1: *Synthesis*, ed. D. Mattingly, 177–234. London: Society for Libyan Studies.

Mattingly, D., M. Lahr, and A. Wilson. 2009. DMP V: Investigations in 2009 of Cemeteries and Related Sites on the West Side of the Taqallit Promontory. *Libyan Studies* 40, 95–132.

Mattingly, D., and A. Wilson. 2003. Farming the Sahara: The Garamantian Contribution in Southern Libya. In *Arid Lands in Roman Times: Papers from the International Conference, Rome, July 9th–10th 2001*, ed. M. Liverani, 37–50. Florence: All'insegna del giglio.

———. 2010. Concluding Thoughts: Made in Fazzān. In *The Archaeology of Fazzān*, vol. 3: *Excavation of C. M. Daniels*, ed. D. Mattingly, 523–530. London: Society for Libyan Studies.

Matvejević, P. 1999. *Mediterranean: A Cultural Landscape.* Berkeley: University of California Press.

Mauny, R. 1956. Monnaies antiques trouvées en Afrique au sud du limes romain. *Libyca* 4/2, 249–261.

———. 1961. *Tableau géographique de l'ouest africain au moyen âge.* Dakar: IFAN.

Mbida, C., H. Doutrelepont, L. Vrydaghs, R. Swennen, H. Beeckman, E. De Langhe, and P. de Maret. 2005. The Initial History of Bananas in Africa: A Reply to Jan Vansina, *Azania* 2003. *Azania* 40/1, 128–135.

McDougall, E. A. 1976. The Role of Salts in the Economic History of West Africa. M.A. thesis, University of Toronto.

———. 1980. The Ijil Salt Industry: Its Role in the Pre-Colonial Economy of the Western Sudan. Ph.D. thesis, University of Birmingham.

———. 1985. Camel Caravans of the Saharan Salt Trade: Traders and Transporters in the Nineteenth Century. In *The Workers of African Trade,* ed. P. E. Lovejoy and C. Coquery-Vidrovitch, 99–122. Beverly Hills, Calif.: Sage.

———. 1986. The Economies of Islam in the Southern Sahara: The Rise of the Kunta Clan. *Asian and African Studies* 20, 45–60.

———. 1989. A Topsy-Turvy World: Slaves and Freed Slaves in Colonial Mauritania. In *The End of Slavery in Africa,* ed. S. Miers and R. Roberts, 362–388. Madison: University of Wisconsin Press.

———. 1990. Salts of the Western Sahara: Myths, Mysteries and Historical Significance. *International Journal of African Historical Studies* 23/2, 231–257.

———. 1994–1995. The Question of Tegaza and the Conquest of Songhay: Some Saharan Considerations. In *Le Maroc et l'Afrique subsaharienne aux débuts des temps modernes: Les Sa'adiens et l'empire Songhay,* 251–282. Rabat: Institut des Études Africaines.

———. 1998. Research in Saharan History. *Journal of African History* 39/3, 467–480.

———. 2002a. Perfecting the "Fertile Seed": The *Compagnie du Sel Aggloméré* and Colonial Capitalism, c. 1890–1905. *African Economic History* 30, 53–80.

———. 2002b. Discourse and Distortion: Critical Reflections on Studying the Saharan Slave Trade. *Revue française d'outre-mer,* special issue (December), 55–87.

———. 2004. From Prosperity to Poverty: A History of Tichit c. 1900–1945. In *La Mauritanie: Cent ans d'histoire 1899–1999.* Nouakchott: Université de Nouakchott.

———. 2005a. Conceptualising the Sahara: The World of Nineteenth-Century Beyrouk Commerce. *Journal of North African Studies* 10/3–4, 369–386.

———. 2005b. Living the Legacy of Slavery: Between Discourse and Reality. *Cahiers d'études africaines* 179–180, 957–986.

———. 2006a. Dilemmas in the Practice of *Rachat* in French West Africa. In *The Ethics and Economics of Slave Redemption,* ed. K. A. Appiah and M. Bunzl, 158–178. Princeton, N.J.: Princeton University Press.

———. 2006b. Snapshots from the Sahara: Salt the Essence of Being. In *The Libyan Desert: Natural Resources and Cultural Heritage,* ed. D. Mattingly et al., 295–303. London: Society for Libyan Studies.

———. 2007a. The Caravel and the Caravan: Reconsidering Received Wisdom in the Sixteenth-Century Sahara. In *The Atlantic World and Virgina: 1550–1624,* ed. P. Mancell, 155–180. Chapel Hill: University of North Carolina Press.

———. 2007b. "Si un homme travaille, il doit être libre": Les serviteurs *hrātīn* et le discours colonial sur le travail en Mauritanie. In *Colonisations et héritages actuels au Sahara et au Sahel: Problèmes conceptuels, état des lieux et nouvelles perspectives de recherche (XVIIIe–XXe siècle),* ed. M. Villasante Cervello, 2:229–264. Paris: L'Harmattan.

———. 2010a. The Politics of Slavery in Mauritania: Rhetoric, Reality and Democratic Discourse. *Maghreb Review* 35/3, 259–286.

———. 2010b. "To Marry One's Slave Is as Easy as Eating a Meal": The Dynamics of Carnal Relations within Saharan Slavery. In *Sex, Power and Slavery: The Dynamics of Carnal Relations under Enslavement,* ed. G. Campbell and E. Elbourne. Athens: Ohio University Press.

———. 2010c. The Sahara in *An Economic History of West Africa:* A Critical Reflection on Historiographical Impact and Legacy. In *Africa, Empire and Globalization: Essays in Honor of A. G. Hopkins,* ed. T. Falola. Durham, N.C.: Carolina Academic Press.

McDougall, E. A., ed. 2007. *The War on Terror in the Sahara. Journal of Contemporary African Studies* (special issue) 21/5.

McDougall, E. A., and M. Nouhi. 1996. ". . . You Have Known Power": Zwaya Development and the Evolution of Saharan Politics, Seventeenth and Eighteenth Centuries. Paper presented at the conference "L'ordre politique tribal au Maroc saharien et en Mauritanie," Goulimime, Morocco, November 1996.

McDougall, J. 2011. Dream of Exile, Promise of Home: Language, Education, and Arabism in Algeria. *International Journal of Middle East Studies* 43/2, 251–270.

McGovern, M. 2005. Islamist Terror in the Sahel: Fact or Fiction? International Crisis Group Africa report no. 92, 31 March. http://www.crisisgroup.org/en/regions/africa/west-africa/092-islamist-terrorism-in-the-sahel-fact-or-fiction.aspx.

McLaughlin, G. 1997. Sufi, Saint, Sharif: Muhammad Fadil wuld Mamin: His Spiritual Legacy and the Political Economy of the Sacred in Nineteenth-Century Mauritania. Ph.D. diss., Northwestern University.

McPherson, K. 1993. *The Indian Ocean: A History of People and the Sea.* Oxford: Oxford University Press.

Meillassoux, C., ed. 1971. *The Development of Indigenous Trade and Markets in West Africa: L'évolution du commerce africain depuis le XIXème siècle en Afrique de l'Ouest.* Oxford: Oxford University Press.

———. 1975. *L'esclavage en Afrique pré-coloniale.* Paris: Maspéro.

Merghoub, B. 1972. *Le développement politique en Algérie: Étude des populations de la région du Mzab.* Paris: Armand Colin.

Miège, J.-L. 1981. Le commerce transsaharien au 19e siècle: Essai de quantification. *Revue de l'occident musulman et de la Méditerranée* 32, 93–119.

Miers, S., and I. Kopytoff, eds. 1977. *Slavery in Africa.* Madison: University of Wisconsin Press.

Mikesell, M. 1955. Notes on the Dispersal of the Dromedary. *Southwestern Journal of Anthropology* 11/3, 231–245.

———.1960. Comparative Studies in Frontier History. *Annals of the Association of American Geographers* 50/1, 62–74.

Mitchell, P. 2005. *African Connections: An Archaeological Perspective on Africa and the Wider World.* Walnut Creek, Calif.: AltaMira.

Mollat de Jourdin, M. 1984. *Les explorateurs du XIIIe au XVIe siècle: Premiers regards sur des mondes nouveaux.* Paris: Lattès.

Morand, P. 1928. *Paris—Tombouctou: Documentaire.* Paris: Flammarion.

Moraes Farias, P. F. de. 2003. *Arabic Medieval Inscriptions from the Republic of Mali: Epigraphy, Chronicles, and Songhay-Tuāreg History.* Oxford: Oxford University Press.

Museur, M. 1977. Un exemple spécifique d'économie caravanière: L'échange sel-mil. *Journal des africanistes* 47, 49–80.

Nachtigal, G. 1879–1889. *Saharâ und Sûdân: Ergebnisse sechsjähriger Reisen in Afrika.* Berlin: Weidmannsche Buchhandlung.

Nadi, D. 2007. Installation dans une ville de transit migratoire: Le cas de la ville de Tamanrasset en Algérie. In *Les nouveaux urbains dans l'espace Sahara-Sahel: Un cosmopolitisme par le bas,* ed. E. Boesen and L. Marfaing, 279–294. Paris: Karthala.

Newbury, C. W. 1966. North African and Western Sudan Trade in the Nineteenth Century: A Reevaluation. *Journal of African History* 7/2, 233–246.

Niane, D. T. 1965. *Soundiata: An Epic of Old Mali.* London: Longman.

Nicolaisen, J. 1963. *Ecology and Culture of the Pastoral Tuareg.* Copenhagen: National Museum.

Nijenhuis, K. 2003. Does Decentralization Serve Everyone? The Struggle for Power in a Malian Village. *European Journal of Development Research* 15/2, 67–92.

Nixon, S. 2009. Excavating Essouk-Tadmekka (Mali): New Archaeological Investigation of Early Islamic Trans-Saharan Trade. *Azania* 44/2, 217–255.

Norris, H. T. 1968. *Šhinqiti Folk Literature and Song.* Oxford: Clarendon Press.

———. 1972. *Saharan Myth and Saga.* Oxford: Oxford University Press.

———. 1975. *The Tuaregs: Their Islamic Legacy and Its Diffusion in the Sahel.* Warminster, England: Aris and Phillips.

———. 1986. *The Arab Conquest of the Western Sahara: Studies of the Historical Events, Religious Beliefs and Social Customs Which Made the Remotest Sahara a Part of the Arab World.* London: Longman.

———. 1990. *Sūfī Mystics of the Niger Desert.* Oxford: Clarendon Press.

Nouhi, M. L. 2009. Religion and Society in a Saharan Tribal Setting: Authority and Power in the Zwaya Religious Culture. Ph.D. diss., University of Alberta.

Nugent, P. 1996. Arbitrary Lines and the People's Minds: A Dissenting View on Colonial Boundaries in West Africa. In *African Boundaries: Barriers, Conduits, and Opportunities,* ed. P. Nugent and A. I. Asiwaju, ch. 2. London: Pinter.

Nugent, P., and A. I Asiwaju. 1996. The Paradox of African Boundaries. In *African Boundaries: Barriers, Conduits, and Opportunities,* ed. P. Nugent and A. I. Asiwaju. London: Pinter.

Nyamnjoh, F. 2006. *Insiders and Outsiders: Citizenship and Xenophobia in Contemporary Southern Africa.* Dakar: CODESRIA.

Ondaatje, M. 1992. *The English Patient.* London: Bloomsbury.

Osborne, A. H., et al. 2008. A Humid Corridor across the Sahara for the Migration of Early Modern Humans Out of Africa 120,000 Years Ago. *Proceedings of the National Academy of Sciences* 105/43, 16444–16447.

Osswald, R. 1986. *Die Handelsstädte der Westsahara: Die Entwicklung der arabisch-maurischen Kultur von Sinqīt, Wādān, Tīsīt und Walāta.* Berlin: Reimer.

———. 1993. *Schichtengesellschaft und islamisches Recht: Die Zawāyā und Krieger der Westsahara im Spiegel von Rechtsgutachten des 16.–19. Jahrhunderts.* Wiesbaden: Harrassowitz.

Ould Ahmed Salem, Z. 2005. *Les trajectoires d'un Etat-frontière: Espaces, évolution politique et transformations sociales en Mauritanie.* Dakar: CODESRIA.

Ould Ramdane, H. 2007. Droit des étrangers et protection des réfugiés en Mauritanie. In *Memorandum: Revue juridique de droit mauritanien.* Nouakchott: Pilote.

Ould Sidi, A. 1979. L'impact de la sécheresse sur la vie des nomades de Tombouctou et sa région. Final diss., ENSUP Bamako.

Oussedik, F. 2007. *Relire les itiffaqat: Essai d'interprétation sociologique.* Algiers: ENAG.

Parker, A. J. 1992. *Ancient Shipwrecks of the Mediterranean and the Roman Provinces.* Oxford: Tempus Reparatum.

Parkin, D., and R. Barnes, eds. 2002. *Ships and the Development of Maritime Technology in the Indian Ocean.* London: Routledge.

Pascon, P. 1984. *La maison d'Iligh.* Rabat: Pascon.

Patterson, O. 1982. *Slavery and Social Death: A Comparative Study.* Cambridge, Mass.: Harvard University Press.

Pélissier, P. 1966. *Les paysans du Sénégal: Les civilisations agraires du Cayor à la Casamance.* Saint-Yrieix: Fabrègue.

Pellicani, M., and S. Spiga. 2007. Analyse comparée des espaces charnières de la mobilité migratoire entre "Nord" et "Sud": Le cas de Pouilles (Italie) et du Touat (Algérie). In *Les migrations internationales: Observation, analyse et perspectives,* 277–296. Paris: Presses universitaires de France.

Pelling, R. 2008. Garamantian Agriculture: The Plant Remains from Jarma, Fezzan. *Libyan Studies* 39, 41–72.

Perrin, D. 2008. L'étranger rendu visible au Maghreb: La voie ouverte à la transposition des politiques juridiques migratoires européennes. *Asylon* 4. www.terra.rezo.net.

Pliez, O. 2003. *Villes du Sahara: Urbanisation et urbanité dans le Fezzan libyen.* Paris: CNRS.

———. 2004a. Proche Libye. In *La nouvelle Libye: Sociétés, espaces et géopolitique au lendemain de l'embargo,* ed. O. Pliez, 7–18. Paris: Karthala.

———. 2004b. De l'immigration au transit? La Libye dans l'espace migratoire euro-africain. In *La nouvelle Libye: Sociétés, espaces et géopolitique au lendemain de l'embargo,* ed. O. Pliez, 139–157. Paris: Karthala.

———. 2006. Nomades d'hier, nomades d'aujourd'hui: Les migrants africains réactivent-ils les territoires nomades au Sahara? *Annales de Géographie* 652, 688–707.

Polanyi, K. 1944. *The Great Transformation.* Boston: Beacon.

Popenoe, R. 2004. *Feeding Desire: Fatness, Beauty, and Sexuality among a Saharan People.* London: Routledge.

Portes, A. 1999. La mondialisation par le bas: L'émergence des communautés transnationales. *Actes de la recherche en sciences sociales* 129, 15–25.

Poutignat, P., and J. Streiff-Fénart. 1995. *Théories de l'ethnicité.* Paris: Presses universitaires de France.

Raffenel, A. 1846. *Voyage dans l'Afrique occidentale exécuté en 1843 et 1844.* Paris: Arthur Bertrand.

Rebbo, A. M. 1990. Le Sahara dans l'imaginaire marocain. *Autrement* 48, 182–183.

Rebuffat, R. 2004. Les Romains et les routes caravanières africaines. In *Le Sahara: Lien entre les peuples et les cultures,* ed. M. H. Fantar, 221–260. Tunis: Alif.

Reichmuth, S. 2000. Islamic Education and Scholarship in Sub-Saharan Africa. In *The History of Islam in Africa,* ed. N. Levtzion and R. Pouwels, ch. 19. Oxford: James Currey.

Retaillé, D. 1993. Afrique: Le besoin de parler autrement qu'en surface. *Espaces Temps* 51–52, 52–62.

Richer, A. 1924. *Les Touaregs du Niger (région de Tombouctou-Gao): Les Oulliminden.* Paris: Larose.

République Islamique de Mauritanie, Ministère de l'emploi, de l'insertion et de la formation professionnelle. 2007. Étude sur la situation de la main d'œuvre étrangère en Mauritanie: Projet de stratégie de gestion de la main d'œuvre étrangère (May).

Robinson, P. 1984. Playing the Arab Card: Niger and Chad's Ambivalent Relations with Libya. In *African Security Issues: Sovereignty, Stability and Solidarity,* ed. B. Arlinghaus, 171–184. Boulder, Colo.: Westview.

Rossi, B. 2009. Slavery and Migration: Social and Physical Mobility in Ader (Niger). In *Reconfiguring Slavery,* ed. B. Rossi, 182–206. Liverpool: Liverpool University Press.

Saad, E. 1983. *Social History of Timbuktu: The Role of Muslim Scholars and Notables 1400–1900.* Cambridge: Cambridge University Press.

Saint-Exupéry, A. de. 1943. *Le petit prince.* New York: Reynal and Hitchcock.

Sal, I. 1978. Les relations entre les Haalpulaar'en et les Brakna 1850–1903. Master's thesis in history, University of Dakar.

Salifou, A. 1973. *Kaoussan ou la révolte sénoussiste.* Niamey: Centre Nigérien des recherches en sciences humaines.

Sanders, G. D. R., and Whitbread, I. K. 1990. Central Places and Major Roads in the Peloponnese. *Annual of the British School at Athens* 85, 333–361.

Sanneh, L. O. 1979. *The Jakhanke: The History of an Islamic Clerical People in Senegambia.* London: International African Institute.

Sautter, G. 1982. Quelques réflexions sur les frontières africaines. *Pluriel* 30, 47–48.

Sautter, G., and P. Pélissier. 1964. Pour un atlas des terroirs africains, structure-type d'une étude de terroir. *L'Homme* 4/1, 56–72.

Savage, E., ed. 1992a. *The Human Commodity: Perspectives on the Trans-Saharan Slave Trade.* London: Cass.

Savage, E. 1992b. Berbers and Blacks: Ibadi Slave Traffic in Eighth-Century North Africa. *Journal of African History* 33/3, 351–368.

Schacht, J. 1954. Sur la diffusion des formes d'architecture religieuse musulmane à travers le Sahara. *Travaux de l'Institut des Recherches Sahariennes* 11, 11–27.

Scheele, J. 2009. Tribus, États et fraude: La region frontalière algéro-malienne. *Études rurales* 184, 79–94.

———. 2010a. Traders, Saints and Irrigation: Reflections on Saharan Connectivity. *Journal of African History* 52/1, 1–20.

———. 2010b. Councils without Customs, Qadis without States: Property and Community in the Algerian Touat. *Islamic Law and Society* 17/3, 350–374.

Schimmel, A. 1985. *And Muhammad Is His Messenger: The Veneration of the Prophet in Islamic Piety.* Chapel Hill: University of North Carolina Press.

Schmitz, J. 1986. L'État géomètre: Les leydi des Peuls du Fuuta Tooro (Sénégal) et du Maasina (Mali). *Cahiers d'études africaines* 103, 349–394.

Schoenbrun, D. L. 1998. *A Green Place, a Good Place: Agrarian Change, Gender, and Social Identity in the Great Lakes Region to the 15th Century.* Portsmouth, N.H.: Heinemann.

Schrüfer-Kolb, I. E. 2007. Metallurgical and Non-Metallurgical Industrial Activities. In *The Archaeology of Fazzān,* vol. 2: *Site Gazetteer, Pottery and Other Survey Finds,* ed. D. Mattingly, 448–462. London: Society for Libyan Studies.

Searing, J. F. 2002. *"God Alone Is King": Islam and Emancipation in Senegal: The Wolof Kingdoms of Kajoor and Bawol, 1859–1914.* Portsmouth, N.H.: Heinemann.

Shaw, B. 2006. *At the Edge of the Corrupting Sea: A Lecture Delivered at New College, Oxford, on 9th May 2005.* Oxford: Oxford University Press.

Silver, P. R. 2008. *Our Savage Neighbors: How Indian War Transformed Early America.* New York: Norton.

Simmel, G. 1999. *Sociologies: Études sur les formes de la socialisation.* Paris: Presses universitaires de France.

Simpson, E., and K. Kresse, eds. 2007. *Struggling with History: Islam and Cosmopolitanism in the Western Indian Ocean.* London: Hurst.

Spiga, S. 2002. Tamanrasset, capitale du Hoggar: Mythes et réalités. *Méditerranée* 99, 83–90.

Spittler, G. 1993. *Les Touareg face aux sécheresses et aux famines: Les Kel Ewey de l'Aïr.* Paris: Karthala.

Squatriti, P. 2002. Review Article: Mohammed, the Early Medieval Mediterranean, and Charlemagne. *Early Medieval Europe* 11, 263–279.

Stewart, C. 1973. *Islam and Social Order in Mauritania.* Oxford: Clarendon Press.

Stoller, P. 1995. *Embodying Colonial Memories: Spirit Possession, Power and the Hauka in West Africa.* London: Routledge.

Strasser, T. F., et al. 2010. Stone Age Seafaring in the Mediterranean: Evidence from the Plakias Region for Lower Palaeolithic and Mesolithic Habitation of Crete. *Hesperia* 79/2, 145–190.

Streiff-Fénart, J., and P. Poutignat. 2006. De l'aventurier au commerçant transnational, trajectoires croisées et lieux intermédiaires à Nouadhibou (Mauritanie). *Cahiers de la Méditerranée* 73, 129–149.

Swanson, J. T. 1975. The Myth of Trans-Saharan Trade during the Roman Era. *International Journal of African Historical Studies* 8, 582–600.

Tabak, F. 2008. *The Waning of the Mediterranean 1550–1870: A Geohistorical Approach.* Baltimore: Johns Hopkins University Press.

Tall, S. M. 2002. L'émigration sénégalaise d'hier à demain. In *La société sénégalaise entre le global et le local,* ed. M.-C. Diop, 549–578. Paris: Karthala.

Tarrius, A. 2000. *Les nouveaux cosmopolitismes: Mobilités, identités, territoires.* La Tour d'Aigues: L'Aube.

———. 2002. *La Mondialisation par le bas: Les nouveaux nomades de l'économie souterraine.* Paris: Balland.

———. 2007. *La remontée des Sud: Afghans et Marocains en Europe méridionale.* La Tour d'Aigues: L'Aube.

Taylor, R. 1995. Warriors, Tributaries, Blood Money and Political Transformation in Nineteenth-Century Mauritania. *Journal of African History* 36, 419–441.

———. 1996. Of Disciples and Sultans: Power, Authority and Society in the Nineteenth-Century Mauritanian Gebla. Ph.D. diss., University of Illinois.

———. 2000. Statut, médiations et ambiguïté ethnique en Mauritanie précoloniale (XIXe siècle): Le cas des Ahl al-Gibla et des Ahl Ganaār du Trarza. In *Groupes serviles au Sahara: Approche comparative à partir du cas des arabophones de Mauritanie,* ed. M. Villasante-de Beauvais, 83–95. Paris: CNRS.

Tennyson, A. 1829. *Timbuctoo: A Poem, Which Obtained the Chancellor's Medal at the Cambridge Commencement, M.DCCC.XXIX.* Cambridge: Cambridge University.

Terray, E. 1995. *Une histoire du royaume abron du Gyaman: Des origines à la conquête coloniale.* Paris: Karthala.

Thanheiser, U. 2002. Roman Agriculture and Gardening in Egypt as Seen from Kellis. In *Dakleh Oasis Project: Preliminary Reports on the 1994–1995 to 1998–1999 Field Seasons,* ed. C. A. Hope and G. Bowen, 299–310. Oxford: Oxbow.

Triaud, J.-L. 1995. *La légende noire de la Sanûsiyya: Une confrérie musulmane saharienne sous le regard français (1840–1930).* Paris: MSH.

Triaud, J.-L., and D. Robinson, eds. 2000. *La Tijaniyya: Une confrérie musulmane à la conquête de l'Afrique.* Paris: Karthala.

Tripier, M. 2008. Circulations entre catégories du sens commun, catégories administratives, catégories statistiques: À propose du débat sur les statistiques ethniques. *Asylon* 4. www.terra.rezo.net.

Trousset, P. 1984. L'idée de la frontière au Sahara et les données archéologiques. In *Enjeux sahariens,* ed. P.-R. Baduel, 47–78. Paris: CNRS.

———. 2005. Le tarif de Zaraï: Essai sur les circuits commerciaux dans la zone présaharienne. *Antiquités Africaines* 38–39, 355–374.

Turner, F. J. 2008 [1894]. *The Significance of the Frontier in American History.* London: Penguin.

UNFPA. 2006. State of World Population. http://www.unfpa.org/swp/2006/english/introduction.html (accessed July 2010).

Van Berchem, M. 1953. *Sédrata, une ville du moyen âge ensevelie dans les sables du Sahara algérien.* Algiers: Service d'information du cabinet du gouverneur général de l'Algérie.

———. 1954. Sedrata, un chapitre nouveau de l'histoire de l'art musulman, campagne de 1951–52. *Ars Orientalis* 1, 157–172.

———. 1960. Sedrata et les anciennes villes berbères du Sahara dans les écrits des explorateurs du 19ème siècle. *Bulletin de l'Institut Français d'Archéologie Orientale* 59, 289–308.

Van der Veen, M. 2006. Food and Farming in the Libyan Sahara. In *The Libyan Desert: Natural Resources and Cultural Heritage,* ed. D. Mattingly et al., 171–178. London: Society for Libyan Studies.

———. 2011. *Consumption, Trade and Innovation: Exploring the Botanical Remains from the Roman and Islamic Ports at Quseir al-Qadim, Egypt.* Frankfurt: Africa Magna.

Vidal, M. 1924. *Rapport sur la tenure des terres indigènes au Fouta dans la vallée du Sénégal.* Saint-Louis, report MAS, no. 72.

Vikør, K. 1982. The Desert-Side Salt Trade of Kawar. *African Economic History* 11, 115–144.

———. 1999. *The Oasis of Salt: The History of Kawār, a Saharan Centre of Salt Production.* Bergen, Norway: Centre for Middle Eastern and Islamic Studies.

Viollier, B. 2003. Les conditions d'exercice du metier. In *La France d'outre-mer (1930–1960): Témoignages d'administrateurs et de magistrats*, ed. J. Clauzel, 73–149. Paris: Karthala.

Viti, F. 2000. La construction de l'espace politique baulé (Côte d'Ivoire). In *Lignages et territoire en Afrique aux XVIIIe et XIXe siècles: Stratégies, compétition, intégration*, ed. C.-H. Perrot, 113–152. Paris: Karthala.

Wallerstein, I. 1974–1989. *The Modern World-System*. New York: Academic.

Webb, J. L. A. 1995. *Desert Frontier: Ecological and Economic Change along the Western Sahel, 1600–1850*. Madison: University of Wisconsin Press.

Webb, W. P. 1952. *The Great Frontier*. Boston: Houghton Mifflin.

Weber, D. J., and J. M. Rausch. 1994. *Where Cultures Meet: Frontiers in Latin American History*. Wilmington, Del.: SR Books.

Werbner, P. 2006. Vernacular Cosmopolitanism. *Culture and Society* 23/2–3, 496–498.

White, O. 1991. *The Middle Ground: Indians, Empires, and Republics in the Great Lakes Region, 1650–1815*. Cambridge: Cambridge University Press.

Wilkinson, J. C. 1987. *The Imamate Tradition of Oman*. Cambridge: Cambridge University Press.

Wilks, O. 2000. The Juula and the Expansion of Islam into the Forest. In *The History of Islam in Africa*, ed. N. Levtzion and R. Pouwels, ch. 4. Oxford: James Currey.

Williams, T. 1949. An Allegory of Man and His Sahara. *New York Times*, 4 December.

Willis, J. R. 1974. The Western Sudan from the Moroccan Invasion (1591) to the Death of Mukhtar al-Kunti (1811). In *History of West Africa*, ed. J. A. Ajayi and M. Crowder, vol. 1, ch. 12. London: Longman.

Wilson, A. 2006. The Spread of Foggara-Based Irrigation in the Ancient Sahara. In *The Libyan Desert: Natural Resources and Cultural Heritage*, ed. D. Mattingly et al., 205–216. London: Society for Libyan Studies.

———. 2009. Saharan Trade: Short-, Medium-, Long-Distance Networks in the Roman Period. Paper presented at the British Museum conference "Saharan Networks." Institute of Archaeology, University College, London, 6 March.

Wilson, A., and D. Mattingly. 2003. Irrigation Technologies: Foggaras, Wells and Field Systems. In *The Archaeology of Fazzān*, vol. 1: *Synthesis*, ed. D. Mattingly, 235–278. London: Society for Libyan Studies.

Wingate, O. 1934. In Search of Zerzura. *Geographical Journal* 83/4, 281–308.

Wright, J. 2007. *The Trans-Saharan Slave Trade*. New York: Routledge.

Zartman, W., ed. 1963. *Sahara: Bridge or Barrier*. New York: International Conciliation, Carnegie Endowment for International Peace.

Zunes, S., and J. Mundy. 2010. *Western Sahara: War, Nationalism and Conflict Irresolution*. Syracuse, N.Y.: Syracuse University Press.

CONTRIBUTORS

Dida Badi holds a research position in anthropology at the National Centre for Research in Prehistory, Anthropology, and History (CNRPAH) in Algiers, and is completing his doctoral dissertation at Bayreuth University, Germany. His publications include *Les régions de l'Ahaggar et du Tassili n'Azjer: Réalité d'un mythe.*

Julien Brachet is a geographer at the Development Research Institute (IRD) in Paris and a member of the CNRS research group on environment and development at the Université Paris-I (Panthéon-Sorbonne). He is the author of *Migrations transsahariennes: Vers un désert cosmopolite et morcelé.*

Armelle Choplin is a lecturer in geography at the Université Paris-Est, Marne-la-Vallée. She is the author of *Nouakchott: Au carrefour de la Mauritanie et du monde.*

Charles Grémont, a historian, is a research associate of the CEMAf (Center for the Study of African Worlds) in Paris and Marseille. He is author of *Les Touaregs Iwillemmedan, 1647–1896: Un ensemble politique de la boucle du Niger.*

Peregrine Horden is Professor of medieval history at Royal Holloway, University of London, and an Extraordinary Research Fellow of All Souls College, Oxford. He is author (with Nicholas Purcell) of *The Corrupting Sea,* and author of *Hospitals and Healing from Antiquity to the Later Middle Ages.*

Olivier Leservoisier teaches anthropology at the Université de Lyon II-Lumière, where he is a member of the Centre for Research in Anthropology (CREA) and a member of the research group Languages, Music, and Society (CNRS/Université de Paris-V). He has studied land ownership in the Gorgol region of Mauritania and slavery among the Haalpulaaren. He is author of *La question foncière en Mauritanie* and editor of *Terrains ethnographiques et hiérarchies sociales: Retour réflexif sur la situation d'enquête.*

Laurence Marfaing trained as a historian of Europe and Africa and is a researcher at the German Institute of Global and Area Studies in Hamburg. Her numerous publications include *Les relations transsahariennes à l'époque contemporaine: Un espace en constante mutation* (edited with S. Wippel) and *Les nouveaux urbains dans l'espace Sahara-Sahel: Un cosmopolitisme par le bas* (edited with E. Boesen).

E. Ann McDougall is Professor of history and classics and director of the Middle Eastern and African Studies program at the University of Alberta, Canada. Her research has focused on Saharan political economy, regimes of unfree labor, cultural models of power, the evolution of clerical groups, and methodological questions pertaining to the use of oral history, on all of which she has published widely. She was guest editor of a special issue of the *Journal of Contemporary African Studies* providing critical perspectives on the "war on terror" in the Sahara.

James McDougall is Fellow and Tutor in modern history and University Lecturer in twentieth-century history at Trinity College, Oxford. He previously taught at Princeton and at the School of Oriental and African Studies, London, and his research interests include modern and contemporary North African history and politics, Arabic historiography, and the history of the French colonial empire in Africa. He is editor of *Nation, Society and Culture in North Africa* and author of *History and the Culture of Nationalism in Algeria.*

Abderrahmane Moussaoui is an anthropologist whose field research has focused on the northern Algerian Sahara. He teaches at the Maison Méditerranéenne des Sciences de l'Homme (CNRS/Université de Provence) in Aix-en-Provence, France, and the Université Mohamed Boudiaf, Oran, Algeria. His publications include *De la violence en Algérie: Les lois du chaos.*

Mohamed Oudada is a lecturer in geography at the Interdisciplinary Faculty of the University of Ouarzazate, Morocco. He has written on regional integration and development in southern Morocco and on water resources and urbanization in southern Morocco and the western Sahara.

Fatma Oussedik is a researcher in sociology at the Centre for Applied Research in Development (CREAD), Algiers. She has worked extensively on issues pertaining to women in urban Algerian society and on the legal and social systems of the Ibadi community in the Mzab region of the northern Algerian Sahara. She is author of *Relire les ittifaqat: Essai d'interprétation sociologique.*

Judith Scheele, a social anthropologist, is a Research Fellow at All Souls College, Oxford. She has conducted extensive fieldwork on southern Algeria and northern Mali. Her publications include *Village Matters: Knowledge, Politics and Community in Kabylia.*

Katia Schörle is a doctoral candidate in classical archaeology at the Institute of Archaeology and St. Cross College, Oxford.

INDEX

Page numbers in italics refer to maps.

PUBLIC CULTURES OF THE MIDDLE EAST AND NORTH AFRICA

Paul A. Silverstein, Susan Slyomovics,
and Ted Swedenburg
EDITORS

Berbers and Others: Beyond Tribe and Nation in the Maghrib
EDITED BY Katherine E. Hoffman and Susan Gilson Miller

Memorials and Martyrs in Modern Lebanon
Lucia Volk

Connected in Cairo:
Growing up Cosmopolitan in the Modern Middle East
Mark Allen Peterson

Lightning Source UK Ltd.
Milton Keynes UK
UKHW01f0925200818
327335UK00021BA/1230/P

9 780253 001269